War, Government an
in Late Medieval France

War, Government and Power in Late Medieval France

edited by
CHRISTOPHER ALLMAND

LIVERPOOL UNIVERSITY PRESS

First published 2000 by
Liverpool University Press
Liverpool
L69 7ZU

British Library Cataloguing-in-Publication Data
A British Library CIP record is available

ISBN 0–85323–695-x (hardback)
0–85323–705-0 (paperback)

Design and production: Janet Allan

Typeset in 10/13 Stempel Garamond by
Koinonia, Bury
Printed and bound in Great Britain by
Alden Press, Oxford

Contents

Acknowledgements viii

Abbreviations ix

Introduction xi

1 From the Court of Hainault to the Court of England: The Example of Jean Froissart JEAN DEVAUX 1

2 Froissart and his Second Book PETER AINSWORTH 21

3 Alain Chartier and the Arts of Crisis Management, 1417–1429 JAMES LAIDLAW 37

4 Intellectual Patterns and Affective Reactions in Defence of the Dauphin Charles, 1419–1422 NICOLE PONS 54

5 War, Propaganda and Diplomacy in Fifteenth-Century France and England CRAIG TAYLOR 70

6 History and the Literature of War: The *Boke of Noblesse* of William Worcester CHRISTOPHER ALLMAND and MAURICE KEEN 92

7 Commynes on Kingship JOËL BLANCHARD 106

8 'Centre', 'Power' and 'Periphery' in Late Medieval French Historiography: Some Reflections KATHLEEN DALY 124

9 Centre and Periphery in Late Medieval France: Tournai, 1384–1477 GRAEME SMALL 145

10 'Decayed Feudalism' and 'Royal Clienteles': Royal Office and Magnate Service in the Fifteenth Century GARETH PROSSER 175

11 Justification and Theory of the Death Penalty at the *Parlement* of Paris in the Late Middle Ages CLAUDE GAUVARD 190

12 *Membra disjecta* of the Breton *Chambre des Comptes* in the Late Middle Ages: Treasures Revisited and Rediscovered MICHAEL JONES 209

Glossary 221

Index 223

For
Peter Lewis,
with thanks

Acknowledgements

Many of the chapters contained in this book were presented as papers at a small colloquium of scholars held at Liverpool in September 1998, to mark the retirement of Peter Lewis from his Fellowship of All Souls College, Oxford. At least two others first saw the light, in one form or other, at meetings of the Seminar on Later Medieval France which, organised and chaired by Peter Lewis, met weekly every Hilary term in All Souls College for a period of more than twenty years. Those which fall into neither category are contributed by scholars who none the less have a lively awareness of the great contribution which the dedicatee has made to the study of French history, and so wish to be associated with this tribute.

I would like to thank contributors for their patience and forebearance while the volume was being prepared for publication. I also wish to thank Madame Marie Doublier, of the Délégation Culturelle Française at Manchester, for her help and advice, and the Director of the Institut Français du Royaume-Uni for generously agreeing to subsidise the costs of travel incurred by delegates coming to Liverpool from France. Peter Ainsworth, as Director of the Humanities Graduate School of the University of Liverpool, also helped by authorising a grant to cover other expenses, while he and Dr Godfried Croenen gave practical assistance with the preparation of the texts.

I also wish to thank Robin Bloxsidge, Secretary of the Liverpool University Press, for having accepted responsibility for the publication of this book. Colin Rogers took enormous care over the copy-editing of the contributions, which have all benefited from his sympathetic but critical eye. The delicate task of organising and overseeing the final stages of production was completed with great efficiency by Janet Allan. I am grateful to them all.

C. T.A.

Abbreviations

Add. Ms.	Additional Manuscript
AN	Archives Nationales
Annales ESC	*Annales, Economies, Sociétés, Civilisations*
APAE	*Anciens Pays et Assemblées d'États*
Arch. Comm.	Archives Communales
Arch. Dép.	Archives Départementales
Arch. Mun.	Archives Municipales
ASRHAT	*Annales de la Société Royale d'Histoire et d'Archéologie de Tournai*
BCRH	*Bulletin de la Commission royale d'Histoire*
BEC	*Bibliothèque de l'École des Chartes*
BIHR	*Bulletin of the Institute of Historical Research*
BJRL	*Bulletin of the John Rylands Library*
BL	British Library
BNF	Bibliothèque Nationale de France
CNRS	Centre National de la Recherche Scientifique
EETS	Early English Text Society
EHR	*English Historical Review*
l.t.	*livre(s) tournois*
MA	*Le Moyen Age*
ms. fr.	manuscrit français
ms. lat.	manuscrit latin

ms. nouv. acq. fr.	manuscrit nouvelle acquisition française
MSHLT	*Mémoires de la Société historique et littéraire de Tournai*
MSRHAT	*Mémoires de la Société royale d'Histoire et d'Archéologie de Tournai*
Ordonnances	*Ordonnances des roys de France de la troisième race* (22 vols, Paris, 1723–1849)
PCEEB	*Publications du Centre européen d'études bourguignonnes*
RBAHA	*Revue belge d'Archéologie et d'Histoire de l'Art*
RH	*Revue Historique*
RHistS	Royal Historical Society
RN	*Revue du Nord*
RS	Rolls Series
RT	*Revue Tournaisienne*
SATF	Société des Anciens Textes Français
SHF	Société de l'Histoire de France
SHN	Société de l'Histoire de Normandie
TRHistS	*Transactions of the Royal Historical Society*

Introduction

The study of French history of the late Middle Ages has advanced on many fronts in the past generation. It has benefited from a growing under-standing of the variety of sources which contribute to a fuller appreciation of any country's history, how such sources may be used to best advantage, and from a growing discourse between specialisms which has led to a broadening of scholarly horizons. Some two-thirds of the chapters in the present collection have an important factor in common: they are concerned with contemporary works or writings which reflect the authors' observations of, and usually their preoccupations with, the public life of late medieval France.

In recent years, the study of the historical work of Jean Froissart has been boosted by the publication of monographs and, significantly, by new editions of his chronicles. The chapter by Jean Devaux is mainly concerned to show how a chivalric culture common to the courts of both Hainault and England underlay the young Froissart's attempts to secure royal patronage, and then greatly influenced the nature of his historical writing. Froissart has long been regarded with some suspicion by historians of the fourteenth century as a writer with a great sense of occasion, whose skills of evocation were such that they cannot but impress the reader. Justifiably or not, Froissart's emphasis on the part played by the nobility, and on noble values and practices in war, together with his apparent lack of sympathy for those of lesser estate, has not made of him, in today's world, the most appreciated of writers on the fourteenth-century scene. In recent years, however, a move towards a better understanding of his work has led scholars to take an increasingly sympathetic view of Froissart's chronicles, which has meant trying to understand the man within the wider context of his poetic skills as well. The problems of editing his huge historical oeuvre are considerable: some of these are described in the chapter presented by Peter Ainsworth, in which he sets out the difficulties standing in the way of a modern critic who, asked to prepare an edition, has to decide what 'Book II' really is (or was), as well as other related problems of how to present the writings, many of them reworked long after they were originally composed, which Froissart left behind him at the end of an active working life.

A number of chapters describe the contribution of writers to win the minds of men at crucial moments of the Hundred Years War. Alain Chartier, priest, royal secretary, ambassador, was one of the foremost writers in both verse and prose of the early fifteenth century, best remembered, perhaps, for his *Quadrilogue Invectif*, written in 1422, in which the ills of France are discussed and analysed by four characters. Important as his work is, we should not lose sight of the broader significance of his career and, in particular, of his correspondence written as a royal secretary. In this, we see Chartier taking the part of legitimacy against the usurping English, using the formal royal letter (for whose writing he was responsible) as a means of securing support for his royal master, and travelling abroad to further the cause in which he believed so strongly. In a famous line, cited in James Laidlaw's chapter, Chartier set out his belief that the written word had an important part to play in securing and maintaining loyalties; in effect, that it had now become an instrument to be used in time of war, echoing the words found in the *Voeux du Héron*, written in the fourteenth century: 'je le guerreray et en fais et en dis' ('I shall make war on him with both deeds and words').

These were critical years for France, a country divided in its loyalties for which the Valois monarchy, the dukes of Burgundy, as well as the kings of England, were in contention. Central to the conflict would be the Treaty of Troyes, sealed in May 1420, whose terms, which favoured the English to the extent that it recognised their conquest of part of the country and disinherited the dauphin, the last surviving son of Charles VI, in favour of Henry V and his heirs, would prove to be more capable of causing division than of creating unity and peace. Chartier was not alone in condemning it. As Nicole Pons shows, others did so in no uncertain terms, launching vicious, heated attacks upon the dukes of Burgundy, regarded as the persons responsible for the present ills of France and the uncertainties which she faced in the future. At the centre of all discussion lay the matter of the legitimate succession. Some saw it primarily as a legal issue, capable of being discussed with feeling, certainly, but in an analytical and objective manner. Others felt very differently, condemning the treaty and all involved in its making in virulent, emotional terms. Works of polemic were composed, mostly written in Latin, sometimes translated into even more strident vernacular, demonstrating the affective, visceral reaction of some writers to what was being done to their country in this 'time of divisions'. The historian's difficult task is to judge how far such writings influenced the creation and development of public opinion hostile to the enemy and supportive of the war against them.

The literature of war came in different forms. Another was the largely historically-based work, often written by members of the royal entourage or administration (as Chartier had been), which set out to justify the legitimacy of the Valois monarchy to rule in France. In this group, arguments from law and history were to predominate; their tone was altogether calmer, more intellectual than many of the works referred to above. The problem of their circulation and possible influence remains a constant one. On the first of these matters, we may be reasonably sure that they were not read by many. Who, then, were they intended to influence? Or does the word 'inform' get us nearer the truth? With the findings of Craig Taylor we are now presented with the argument, convincingly marshalled, that these writings were put together mainly to help the king's diplomats (such as Alain Chartier) understand the legal and historical background of the arguments which they would voice at meetings with the ambassadors of England and other countries. Historians have often noted the very legal and historical nature of diplomatic positions expressed at such meetings; we are now in a better position to appreciate more fully the relationship between these writings, the work of royal secretaries (as Chartier had been) and other 'civil servants' at court, and the persons for whom they were primarily composed. To the question 'Why do we not find the English creating such dossiers or files?', Dr Taylor answers that these works are part of a cultural development particular to France. Can one also argue that their existence suggests the fragility of the Valois hold upon the throne of France and upon the loyalty of its people, a fragility which had to be built up in times of defeat and uncertainty regarding the future and what it might bring? It is in moments of doubt (the product of defeat) that the human being needs reassurance that what he is doing is right. More than anybody, those who lived at court around the king or the dauphin needed to be reassured that the future lay with them.

It may not be without significance that William Worcester and John Fortescue, the two Englishmen whose works came closest to emulating certain characteristics of the polemic composed by their French contemporaries, both had practical experience of life in France. Worcester, whose *Boke of Noblesse* is the subject of a further chapter, had read Chartier's *Quadrilogue Invectif*; both may be classed as belonging to the 'literature of defeat', both look to a revival of fortune of their respective futures. In Worcester's call for a renewal of interest in the war against France, a war which had recently turned against England, are themes which could have been found in French works; the need for the king (of England) to reassert his position, as well as that of his demoralised country (now divided on dynastic issues), by going to war and winning victories so as to regain lands lost to the enemy; and the paramount need for that effort to be made by the entire (English) people, united behind its king, whose position could thus be restored to that enjoyed (as history showed it had been) by his predecessors.

Power, and the exercise of power, is a thread running through most of the chapters in this collection. The chapter by Joël Blanchard gives an unusual perspective on the power and exercise of kingship; but, then, Philippe de Commynes, whose ideas are considered, was no ordinary man, and his views fell into no known category. Instead of according almost divine powers to his king (in this case, Louis XI) as most of his contemporaries (the main exceptions being the Italians, who may have influenced Commynes) did to theirs, Commynes presented Louis as a very ordinary man, 'a man like us', with his faults and foibles and fears. Why did he do this? The answer, says the author, lies in the very close, everyday relationship which Commynes had with the king over the years, during which time he was able to observe him and get to know him as a human being. Louis was no lover of the pomp and ceremony associated with court life; in his case, power was used in a very different way, and was in no respect dependent upon the outward trappings of the office which he exercised.

Two chapters are concerned to see how the 'centre' (not simply a geographical expression, rather a way of describing where the king was), and the 'periphery' got on in the fifteenth century. What was the working relationship between the king and those parts which made up his kingdom? How far did France dance to the tune played by the court? Certainly the king represented national unity and identity: 'rex est imperator in regno suo', as the legal dictum had it ('the king is supreme in his own kingdom'). But as Kathleen Daly shows, there were those parts of France (and she is not discussing those areas, such as Burgundy or Brittany, which could act almost as independent states) which showed a healthy sense of independence of the centre. They did this not by challenging the royal authority directly; they used more discreet ways of asserting themselves, one of which was to take a leaf out of the royal book and to write their own histories, thereby increasing their own sense of self-awareness and local identity. So while Noël de Fribois (at the centre) wrote history to underline the royal claim that all should obey the king, in the Dauphiné (for example) Mathieu Thomassin could try to show that, historically, the dauphin enjoyed a measure of freedom from the crown of France, while at the same time admitting that it was an honour to form part of the wider kingdom. Yet the problem of who had the last word, the dauphin or the king, remained to trouble Thomassin. In the case of the county of Foix, Michel du Bernis wrote a chronicle of its comital house in the mid-fifteenth century. Geography was kind to Foix-Béarn; it was a long way from the kingdom's institutional centre, far from being wholly dependent upon France, and it did not pay homage to the French king until the expulsion of the English from neighbouring Gascony in 1453. So du Bernis could help when the king challenged his master's right to rule 'by the grace of God', and he could establish a comital genealogy to underline the true, independent succession to power within the county. Such actions were interesting at different levels. The use of history and genealogies to justify a particular house was taking a major leaf out of the king's own book. At another level, while demonstrating a sense of independence, the works of du Bernis are in no way an attempt to encourage or justify a break from France. These men were loyal, and would help the king in time of war. But they did not want to be too dependent on the crown, or subject to too many orders coming from the French court.

At the geographically opposite side of the kingdom, the 'frontier' city of Tournai was working out its own relationship with the 'centre'. In this case, and by using both chronicles and archive materials (the destruction of the originals in war fully justifying the decision to print the main town records taken many years ago), Graeme Small shows how this important city, whose well-being depended on maintaining an active relationship with a large and economically prosperous area around it, and much of the time within the Burgundian sphere of influence, chose to associate its fortunes with those of France, at the same time preferring to keep the influence of the 'centre' where it was said to be, 'a long way away', or at least at a reasonable distance. It is of interest to see how the relationship was maintained, one way mainly through the royal *bailli*, the other through full-time agents who lived in Paris, as well as through the occasional use made of a special representative to further contacts with the king as and when it was deemed necessary. Crises were few in number, and in the case of Tournai, the relationship between 'centre' and 'periphery' was generally a good one.

In an important chapter, Gareth Prosser discusses how power was distributed and exercised in Normandy in the generation or so following the expulsion of the English from the duchy in 1450. Unlike in England, clientage and patronage in fourteenth- and fifteenth-century France have not received the attention they deserve, other than at the hands of Peter Lewis. Created as part of the *ordonnance*, or royal army system which emerged in the 1440s, the system of patronage changed considerably as time passed and circumstances themselves developed. The new opportunities which emerged allowed the political energies of many of the nobility of different ranks to be put to good use. We are shown how this influenced the exercise of power by both the king and his leading officers, many of them holders of high positions, who built up authority and influence both through the exercise of their offices (some of these being military, others not) and through the networks of clientage thus created. The patronage system brought into being helped both the crown and those in its service to influence local affairs: it also enabled the locality (the 'periphery') to have some say in the formulation of royal policy at the 'centre'.

Did the crown of France use the courts to extend its authority? The traditional answer would probably be affirmative. In her chapter on the application of the death penalty by the *Parlement* of Paris, Claude Gauvard casts doubts on this judgement. The sentencing policy (if 'policy' is the correct word to use) of the Court was not to impose virtually mandatory sentences of death and thereby to create martyrs, but rather to use the judicial process as a means of reconciling and healing a society affected by public crime. This was never going to be easy. For crimes of violence, in particular, both the victim's kin and the wider community demanded some kind of retribution, or vengeance; some say, too, in the sentence imposed. Yet an execution, automatically imposed, might do more harm than good to an already damaged social fabric. Judges, therefore, were obliged to tread carefully, and we are shown how they reacted to public opinion or revulsion over particular crimes. It is clear that, by the fifteenth century, the sentencing of criminals in the highest court in the kingdom was conditioned more by the ability of justice to heal rifts in society caused by crime than by any 'book-led' determination to impose the power of the state upon those who contravened social regulations. Are we here in the presence of a form of justice exercised more in keeping with the principles of the Italian post-glossators or of the English system of equity, systems which moved away from too literal an interpretation of the law and its system of set penalties in favour of a view which, allowing for change, was less condemnatory of the accused and readier to understand the wider circumstances in which a crime had been committed?

The last chapter, by Michael Jones, stands for a form of historical material which features but little in this collection, the *pièce d'archive*, or record. The tale which is told contains a number of important lessons for the historian. It may make him reflect upon the work which has gone into the creation of public records over the years. It may make him think, too, about the element of good fortune required for documents, their original role (in the *Chambre des Comptes*, for instance) now ended by war or revolution, to evade the fate of those taken away as 'scrap' by unsympathetic waste-paper merchants of the day. All searchers in archives, rather than complain that documents have got lost over the years, should be grateful for those which have survived. The story is also an optimistic one: important documents still have an uncanny habit of turning up, and the more educated the public is, the greater is their chance of survival and ultimate preservation for purposes of historical research.

I

From the Court of Hainault to the Court of England: The Example of Jean Froissart

JEAN DEVAUX

From the court of Hainault to that of England. Such was the path followed by the young Jean Froissart when, a mere novice, he left his native land in search of patronage to enable him to pursue a career as a writer. One of the characteristics of the poet-chronicler lay in his inclination to describe himself in a manner which, from time to time, would allow the reader to join him, albeit furtively, in some of the major moments of his life. Among the many memories recorded in his work, the one which clearly touched him most was his long sojourn at the English court between 1362 and 1369. Fascinated from his earliest days by the world of chivalry, Froissart calls to mind the ostentatious living of that glittering society. Here, he moved among the followers of the highest in the land, glorying with them in the prestige of their recent victories. Constituting, as they did, the determining period of his career, these seven years allowed Froissart to establish his reputation. His first successes, so he felt, were made possible by the sovereign lady who, generously, accorded him her protection:

Phelippe eut nom la noble dame;
Propisces li soit Diex a l'ame!
J'en sui bien tenus de priier
Et ses largeces escriier,
Car elle me fist et crea …

Philippa was the noble lady's name,
May God take her into His care
I am bound to pray for her
And all her kind acts to describe,
For it was she who created me …[1]

Nothing could be clearer: 'it was she who created me'. It was Queen Philippa of England who, alone, through her *largeces* gave him the chance to assume his role as a writer. Notwithstanding Philippa's contribution, we should not fail to

1] Jean Froissart, *Le Joli Buisson de Jonece*, ed. A. Fourrier, Geneva, 1975, p. 55, ll. 233–37.

recognise the profound influence of the courtly circle which oversaw Froissart's origins. In addition to the young poet's personal experience, it is above all to the components of that literary circle that attention should be drawn here. This cultural environment drew its strength and influence from contacts established, over a period of some forty years, between two centres of French culture, the royal court of England and the comital court of Hainault, a milieu all the more remarkable for having encouraged the talent, in the 1360s, of another great figure of European literature, Geoffrey Chaucer.

French Literature at the Court of Hainault

The radiance of the culture of Hainault and the prestige which it enjoyed at the court of England stem, above all, from the remarkable literary flowering which characterised the reign of Count William I. Historians have long praised the political skills shown by this man who ruled over Hainault from 1303 to 1337. While his father, Count John II, had been exposed to the exhausting dispute involving the families of Avesne and Dampierre,[2] William ensured for his lands a long period of peace and prosperity which won him the epithet 'le bons comtes Guillaume' from contemporary chroniclers.[3] Having inherited widely dispersed lands, including Hainault, Holland and Zeeland, he administered them very effectively, aware of the specific needs of each. In addition, his policy of neutrality, along with the alliances which he made with Guelders, Brabant and Flanders, made William into one of the most powerful princes of the Low Countries, conferring on him truly international status. Finally, links achieved through matrimonial alliances brought him connections with three of the sovereign houses which dominated western European society. Husband of Jeanne de Valois, sister of Philip VI, King of France, he married his daughter, Margaret, to the emperor, Louis of Bavaria, while he also became father-in-law of Edward III, King of England. Such were the rather exceptional unions contracted by William which, when added to his personal reputation for political skill and wisdom, gradually made him one of the arbiters of the broad European political scene.[4]

Over a period of time, Count William's favourite residence, Valenciennes,

2] See J.-M. Cauchies, 'Jean d'Avesnes (1280–1304) et le Hainaut: les traits forts d'un principat houleux', in *700 ans de franchises à Mons: les privilèges de Jean d'Avesnes (1295). Actes du colloque du 14 octobre 1995*, ed. J.-M. Cauchies, Mons, 1996, pp. 11–15.
3] *Récits d'un Bourgeois de Valenciennes (XIVe siècle)*, ed. J. Kervyn de Lettenhove, Louvain, 1877, p. 160; Jean Froissart, *Chroniques. Livre I. Le manuscrit d'Amiens. Bibliothèque municipale n°. 486*, ed. G. T. Diller, 5 vols, Geneva, 1991–98, Vol. I, p. 205.
4] See F. de Reiffenberg, *Histoire du comté de Hainaut*, 3 vols, Brussels, 1849–50, Vol. III, pp. 35–62; H. Pirenne, *Histoire de Belgique des origines à nos jours*, 4 vols, Brussels, 1900, repr. 1948–52, Vol. I, pp. 270–71, 313; H. S. Lucas, *The Low Countries and the Hundred Years' War, 1326–1347*, Ann Arbor, 1929, pp. 79–101, 167–75, 204–09; G. Bohy, *Hainaut ou l'épopée d'un peuple*, 2 vols, Charleroi, 1971, Vol. I, pp. 111–27.

became the seat of a glittering court to which messengers from all over Europe were drawn. The stimulus provided by the count and his entourage created a setting very favourable to the flowering of literature. From this cultured society arose the highly talented poet, Jean de Condé, the count's titular minstrel, whose career coincided almost exactly with the rule of his master and patron. This prolific writer has left to us some 20 000 lines of verse, reflecting the forms most commonly encountered at the time, from the moral tale to the fabliau to the narrative lay.[5] Remarkable as it was, this poetry was not an isolated phenomenon; rather it was clear proof of the intense literary activity characteristic of the court of Hainault at the time.

It is difficult to identify each and every trace of such work, since what we now have is the output of anonymous poets seldom anxious to reveal the identity of their protectors. However, clear indications do exist which associate the *Roman de Perceforest* with this milieu. In addition to the many topographic clues which betray the author's links with Hainault, the prologue refers implicitly to the rich patronage of Count William I, reputed to have discovered the romance before seeking the help of the monks of Saint-Landelin in translating it from Latin into French. This abbey, not far from Valenciennes, enjoyed close links with the court of Hainault. In the same way the narrator pays discreet homage to this friend of literature while recommending to the public the remarkable contents of a hybrid text in which the author mixes the Alexander cycle with Arthurian matter.[6] Likewise, this country was the home of several writers of epic poems. *Tristan de Nanteuil*, *Lion de Bourges*, *Dieudonné de Hongrie*, *La belle Hélène de Constantinople* – such are examples of works which, on linguistic evidence, may be associated with the court circle.[7] If these epics incorporate romantic adventures, it would none the less be wrong to regard them with disdain, for

5] *Dits et contes de Baudouin de Condé et de son fils Jean de Condé*, ed. A. Scheler, 3 vols, Brussels, 1866–67; and, above all, Jean de Condé, *Opera. I: I manoscritti d'Italia*, ed. S. Mazonni Peruzzi, 2 vols, Florence, 1990. See also J. Ribard, *Un ménestrel du XIVᵉ siècle. Jean de Condé*, Geneva, 1969.

6] *Le Roman de Perceforest. Première partie*, ed. J. H. M. Taylor, Geneva, 1979; *Quatrième partie du Roman de Perceforest*, ed. G. Roussineau, Geneva, 1987; *Troisième partie du Roman de Perceforest*, ed. G. Roussineau, 3 vols, Geneva. 1988–93. See also W. Van Hoecke, 'La Littérature française d'inspiration arthurienne dans les anciens Pays-Bas', in *Arturus Rex. Volumen I: Catalogus. Koning Artur en de Nederlanden. La matière de Bretagne et les anciens Pays-Bas*, ed. W. Verbeke, J. Janssens and M. Smeyers, Louvain, 1987, pp. 195–96, 221–23.

7] *Tristan de Nanteuil*, ed. K. V. Sinclair, Assen, 1971, p. 58; *Lion de Bourges, poème épique du XIVᵉ siècle*, ed. W. W. Kibler, J.-L. G. Picherit and T. S. Fenster, 2 vols, Geneva, 1980, Vol. I, pp. cxvii–cxxi; *La Belle Hélène de Constantinople, chanson de geste du XIVᵉ siècle*, ed. C. Roussel, Geneva, 1995, p. 96. On the song of *Dieudonné de Hongrie*, sometimes known as the *Roman de Charles le Chauve*, see L.-F. Flutre, 'Dieudonné de Hongrie, chanson de geste du XIVᵉ siècle (*alias* Roman de Charles le Chauve)', *Zeitschrift für Romanische Philologie*, Vol. LXVIII, 1952, pp. 396–400; R. Bossuat, '"Charles le Chauve". Etude sur le déclin de l'épopée française', *Les Lettres Romanes*, Vol. VII, 1953, pp. 107–32, 187–99.

they constitute evidence of a desire to achieve something new by associating the old heroic tradition with the fantastic and with the charm of romance.[8]

This was certainly true of the *chansons de geste* normally grouped together as the *Deuxième cycle de la croisade*. This epic collection, most recently dated to the mid-fourteenth century, was almost certainly produced in the immediate entourage of the court of Hainault. Most of its heroes, starting with Baudouin de Sebourc, come from the region around Valenciennes. Likewise, the song of the *Bâtard de Bouillon* and the 30 000 lines of the *Chevalier au Cygne* appear to have come from the same versifiers who, it seems, constituted a kind of workshop which manipulated legends and techniques under the inspiration of contemporary court culture.[9] Indeed, this renewal of interest in voyages to the East comes, in all probability, from the chivalric atmosphere found at the court of William I. There can be no doubt about the enthusiasm which this prince and his entourage showed for the crusading projects of the King of France around 1330. Froissart himself bears witness to the warlike sentiments found all over Europe during this period.[10] In the light of such texts, one can better appreciate the famous lines by Jean de Condé deploring the loss of his master, whom he called the father (*leur pere*) of all minstrels.[11]

Another great lord, Jean de Beaumont, Count William's younger brother, also used his patronage to encourage literary activity at court; he is known in

8] See in particular F. Suard, 'L'Épopée française tardive', *Etudes de philologie romane et d'histoire offertes à Jules Horrent à l'occasion de son soixantième anniversaire*, ed. J.-M. D'Heur and N. Cherubini, Liège, 1980, pp. 449–60; C. Roussel, *Conter de Geste au XIVe siècle. Inspiration folklorique et écriture épique dans 'La Belle Hélène de Constantinople'*, Geneva, 1998.

9] *Li romans de Bauduin de Sebourc, IIIe roy de Jhérusalem, Poème du XIVe siècle publié pour la première fois d'après les manuscrits de la Bibliothèque Royale*, ed. L. N. Boca, 2 vols, Valenciennes, 1841; *Le Batard de Bouillon, chanson de geste*, ed. R. F. Cook, Geneva, 1972, pp. lvi–lxii; 'Le Chevalier au Cygne et Godefroid de Bouillon, poème historique', in *Monuments pour servir à l'histoire des provinces de Namur, de Hainaut et de Luxembourg (Deuxième division, légendes historico-poétiques)*, ed. F. de Reiffenberg and A. Borgnet, Vols 4–6, Brussels, 1846–54 (*Collection de chroniques belges*). See E.-R. Labande, *Etude sur Baudouin de Sebourc, chanson de geste. Légende poétique de Baudouin II du Bourg, roi de Jérusalem*, Paris, 1940, pp. 63–76; S. Duparc-Quioc, *Le Cycle de la Croisade*, Paris, 1955, pp. 118–43; R. F. Cook and L. S. Crist, *Le Deuxième Cycle de la Croisade. Deux études sur son développement. Les textes en vers. Saladin*, Geneva, 1972; S. Duparc-Quioc, 'Les Poèmes du 2e cycle de la croisade: problèmes de composition et de chronologie', *Revue d'histoire des textes*, Vol. IX, 1979, pp. 141–81. The links of *Baudouin de Sebourc* with Bruges, a point well brought out by J. F. Van der Meulen, do not necessarily imply that the work was a product of that region. See J. F. Van der Meulen, 'Bruges, Brendan and Baudouin de Sebourc', *Queeste. Tijdschrift over middeleeuwse letterkunde in de Nederlanden*, Vol. III, 1996, pp. 1–17.

10] Jean Froissart, *Chroniques*, ed. S. Luce, SHF, Paris, 1869, Vol. I, p. 118, as well as pp. clxxxi–clxxxiii, 115–18; Froissart, *Chroniques,...Amiens*, ed. Diller, Vol. I, p. 165; E. Perroy, *La Guerre de Cent Ans*, Paris, 1945, pp. 65–69; N. Housley, *The Later Crusades, 1274–1580. From Lyons to Alcazar*, Oxford, 1992, pp. 34–36.

11] Jean de Condé, *Opera*, ed. Mazonni Peruzzi, p. 368, ll. 54–56.

particular for the support that he gave to the writing of Jean le Bel's chronicle. Although born a member of the patriciate of Liège, of whose cathedral chapter he later became a member, le Bel was no less a genuine chronicler from Hainault, companion in arms to and member of the household of the Lord of Beaumont, who urged him to record the most glorious deeds of the county's nobility.[12] In doing this, Beaumont was acting in a historiographical tradition familiar in Hainault since the twelfth century.[13]

However, the encouragement given by this lord did not neglect the claims of poetry, and in particular those verses composed to record the great actions of the time. The *Voeux du Héron*, which can be attributed to a member of his household, includes the famous scene in which Robert d'Artois urges Edward III and his followers to commit themselves on oath to conquer the kingdom of France. The fictional elements of this poem have long fascinated critics.[14] Far from reproducing a historical event, the poem is pure imagination, freely based on the political tensions which were emerging at the beginning of the Hundred Years War. It is a biting satire of English knighthood, the best role being given to the Lord of Beaumont who denounces the evils of war, reflecting pacifist ideas encountered throughout the Low Countries at that time.[15] A poem in praise of Beaumont appears a few years later in a contemporary work describing the Battle of Stavoren (September 1345). The piece certainly originated in Hainault, in so far, that is, as it recalled the tragic death of Count William II. Besides being shown as a man of courage in battle, Beaumont is also revealed as a model of good sense, advising his nephew to retreat rather than confront an enemy superior in numbers.[16]

12] Jean le Bel, *Chronique*, ed. J. Viard and E. Déprez, 2 vols, SHF, Paris, 1904–05. See N. Chareyron, *Jean le Bel. Le maître de Froissart, grand imagier de la Guerre de Cent Ans*, Brussels, 1996, pp. 51–53.

13] For a recent synthesis, see G. Small, 'Chroniqueurs et culture historique au bas Moyen Age', in *Valenciennes aux XIVe et XVe siècles. Art et Histoire*, ed. L. Nys and A. Salamagne, Valenciennes, 1996, pp. 271–96.

14] J.-B. de la Curne de Sainte-Palaye, *Mémoires sur l'ancienne chevalerie*, 3 vols, Paris, 1781, Vol. III, pp. 1–137; F.-R. de Chateaubriand, *Analyse raisonnée de l'histoire de France et fragments depuis Philippe VI jusqu'à la bataille de Poitiers suivis de l'analyse raisonnée de l'histoire de France depuis Jean II jusqu'à Louis XVI*, Paris, 1826; repr. 1998, pp. 189–92.

15] G. Bertoni, 'I "Voeux du hairon" (ms. di Berna, n°. 323)', *Archivum Romanicum*, Vol. V, 1921, pp. 426–36. See B. J. Whiting, 'The Vows of the Heron', *Speculum*, Vol. XX, 1945, pp. 261–78; A. Coville, 'Poèmes historiques de l'avènement de Philippe de Valois au traité de Calais (1328–1360)', *Histoire littéraire de la France*, Vol. XXXVIII, Paris, 1949, pp. 268–82; J. L. Grigsby, 'L'Intertextualité interrompue par l'histoire: le cas des *Voeux du Héron*', *Courtly Literature, Culture and Context*, ed. K. Busby and E. Kooper, Amsterdam and Philadelphia, 1990, pp. 239–48.

16] *Panégyriques des comtes de Hainaut et de Hollande Guillaume I et Guillaume II*, ed. C. Potvin, Mons, 1863, pp. 11–20, 41–57 ('La mort du conte de Henau'). On the obligation of every captain to exercise *sagesse*, see J. Devaux, 'L'Image du chef de guerre dans les sources littéraires', *Publication du centre européen d'études bourguignonnes (XIVe–XVIe s.)*, Vol. XXXVII, 1997, pp. 121–25.

It is also to one of Beaumont's poets that we owe one of the surviving historical poems on the Battle of Crécy (August 1346). The author deplores the losses experienced by the French cavalry, announcing his intention to do all he can to guarantee the immortality of these noble warriors. The poet presents himself as a minstrel called Colins, a native of Hainault, while from the rubric to the manuscript we learn that he was a member of Beaumont's entourage.[17] According to evidence supplied by Jacques de Hemricourt, it seems that Jean le Bel himself derived pleasure from writing verse. We imagine that the *chanchons et vierlais* (songs and poems) written by le Bel also contributed to the literary radiance of the court of Hainault.[18] Nor should we forget to mention here the practical patronage offered by other lords of the region, such as Gui de Châtillon, Count of Blois who, as Lord of Avesnes, gave his protection to Watriquet de Couvin, who almost certainly came from the village of the same name situated only a few miles from the lands of Jean de Beaumont.[19]

Nor can we ignore the influence exercised in this domain by the local bourgeoisie. The remarkable economic development reflected in the country's great towns was closely linked, at least among urban elites, with a cultural flowering. The rich historiographical tradition associated with the court of Hainault encouraged the bourgeoisie to seek in such work an affirmation of its own identity. This is underlined by two texts from Valenciennes which, acting at one and the same time as general histories and local chronicles, provide much detail on urban life as well as providing original testimony to the causes of the Hundred Years War.[20] Above all, we find in Valenciennes many of those fraternities, partly cultural, partly religious, known locally as *puys*. These societies, which reached their apogee in the first half of the fourteenth century, were in close contact with court circles, and played their part in the powerful intellectual ferment which characterised Hainault at this period.[21]

17] A. Dinaux, *Les Trouvères brabançons, hainuyers, liégeois et namurois*, Brussels, 1863, pp. 166–84 (edn of the poem). See also Coville, 'Poèmes historiques', pp. 282–88.

18] Jacques de Hemricourt, *Le Miroir des Nobles de Hesbaye (1353–1398)*, ed. C. de Borman, A. Bayot and E. Poncelet, 3 vols, Brussels, 1910–31, Vol. I, p. 227.

19] *Dits de Watriquet de Couvin*, ed. A. Scheler, Brussels, 1868. See C.-V. Langlois, 'Watriquet, ménestrel et poète français', *Histoire littéraire de la France*, Vol. XXXV, Paris, 1921, pp. 394–421; J. Ribard, 'Littérature et société au XIVe siècle, le ménestrel Watriquet de Couvin', in *Court and Poet. Selected Proceedings of the Third Congress of the International Courtly Literature Society (Liverpool, 1980)*, ed. G. S. Burgess, Liverpool, 1981, pp. 277–86. Let us also note that J. F. Van der Meulen considers that the *Dit de la panthère*, hitherto attributed to Nicole de Margival, can be linked to the court of Hainault. This seductive hypothesis still needs further proof. See J. F. Van der Meulen, 'De panter en de aalmoezenier. Dichtkunst rond het Hollands-Henegouwse hof', in *Een zoet akkoord. Middeleeuwse lyriek in de Lage Landen*, ed. J. B. Oosterman, Amsterdam, 1992, pp. 93–108, 343–48.

20] *Récits d'un bourgeois de Valenciennes*; E. Delcambre, 'Une chronique valenciennoise inédite', *Bulletin de la Commission Royale d'Histoire*, Vol. XCIV, 1930, pp. 1–102. See Small, 'Chroniqueurs et culture historique', pp. 279–81.

21] G. A. J. Hécart, *Serventois et sottes chansons couronnés à Valenciennes, tirés des*

Cultural Relations between Hainault and England

This literary melting-pot would become a kind of cultural model for England, with which a privileged relationship was to be established. This influence, which increased over the years, depended above all upon the close political links gradually established between the two states. It began with the important military aid given by Hainault to King Edward II's wife, Isabella, and to her son, the future Edward III, as they sought political support for their attempts to redress the situation then prevailing in their country. A force of 700 men-at-arms, mostly nobles from Hainault, secured their return to England and helped crush Edward II and his favourites (1326).[22] A year later, the leaders of Hainault's knighthood played an active role in a raid into Scotland provoked by a challenge issued to the young Edward III by the Scottish king, Robert Bruce.[23] These two military campaigns did more than was immediately apparent; they set in motion cultural exchanges, for the leader of the force from Hainault was none other than Jean de Beaumont, now at the peak of his reputation, and closely linked to both King Edward and his mother, Queen Isabella.

The marriage of Edward III and Philippa in 1328 furthered links between the two countries, since a considerable number of the count's subjects soon established themselves at the English court. Meanwhile, Philippa surrounded herself with *damoiseles* from her native Hainault, while Edward III materially rewarded many knights and esquires from this region, notably Michel de Ligne, Robert de Fiennes, Nicolas d'Aubrecicourt and Guillaume de Saint-Omer, the last-mentioned being appointed seneschal of the future Black Prince's household.[24] Far from isolating England from the rest of Europe, the period leading to the Hundred Years War effectively multiplied cultural contacts with the court of Hainault. In addition to the presence of English armies on the continent, diplomatic contacts were on the increase, to the extent that in December 1336, Edward III appointed Count William I as his delegate in the Low

---

manuscrits de la Bibliothèque du Roi, Paris, 1834; G. Gros, *Le Poète, la Vierge et le Prince du Puy. Etude sur les Puys marials de la France du Nord du XIVe siècle à la Renaissance*, Paris, 1992, pp. 40–44; idem, *Le Poème du Puy marial. Etude sur le serventois et le chant royal du XIVe siècle à la Renaissance*, Paris, 1996, pp. 34–40, 84–97.

22] S. A. Waller Zeper, *Jan van Henegouwen, heer van Beaumont. Bijdrage tot de geschiedenis der Nederlanden in de eerste helft der veertiende eeuw*, The Hague, 1914, pp. 83–95; Lucas, *The Low Countries*, pp. 52–56; N. Fryde, *The Tyranny and Fall of Edward II, 1321–1326*, Cambridge, 1979, pp. 176–206; C. Valente, 'The Deposition and Abdication of Edward II', *EHR*, Vol. CXIII, 1998, pp. 852–81.

23] Waller Zeper, *Jan van Henegouwen*, pp. 97–112; R. Nicholson, *Edward III and the Scots. The Formative Years of a Military Career, 1327–1335*, Oxford, 1965, pp. 15–41.

24] For more details, see Froissart, *Chroniques*, ed. J. Kervyn de Lettenhove, 25 vols, Brussels, 1870–77, Vol. II, pp. 513–14 (notes). On Guillaume and Elizabeth de Saint-Omer, see R. Barber, *Edward, Prince of Wales and Aquitaine. A Biography of the Black Prince*, Woodbridge, 1978, p. 19.

Countries.[25] Nor should we forget Jean le Bel's description of the magnificent English embassy which the Bishop of Lincoln led to Valenciennes, still less the sumptuous reception accorded to it by the count and nobility of Hainault, to which the burgesses of the town made a notable contribution.[26]

Moreover, a number of cultural influences predisposed the English court to be receptive to models provided by Hainault. We need hardly be reminded of the strong francophone tradition developed among the cultivated elite of England during the previous two-and-a-half centuries. None the less it was also true that, from the early fourteenth century onwards, Anglo-Norman had been in retreat before the advance of English as the spoken language, an advance encouraged by a growing sense of patriotism. In 1362, Edward III had ordered court cases to be heard in English, since French was 'trop desconue en ledit realme' ('not sufficiently known in the said kingdom'). None the less, research has shown the tenacity of Anglo-Norman, in aristocratic circles at least; it had the further advantage of transcending local English dialects, and was valuable in international exchanges, whether written or spoken. For many, Anglo-Norman remained the language of prestige, as well as the language of literature. So it was that Henry of Grosmont, first Duke of Lancaster, wrote his *Livre de Seyntz Medicines* in French, although he confessed to have had but little practice in the use of that language. As for the *Enseignements*, verses composed for the future Black Prince at the request of Edward III, they, too, were written in French.[27]

Most literary works composed up to this moment in England, whether fictional narratives, chronicles or lives of saints, were written in Anglo-Norman. Furthermore, England in the fourteenth century witnessed a steady increase in the influence of continental models, whether that of romance with its train of heroic or courtly motifs, or that of a more recent form of writing now in full expansion, allegory, dominated in France by the *Roman de la Rose* of Guillaume de Lorris and Jean de Meun.[28] This constant French influence, which was to provide the inspiration for many works in Middle English, is underlined by library inventories which reflect contemporary tastes. Of the 21 volumes in the

25] *Foedera, conventiones, literae, et cujuscunque generis acta publica*, ed. T. Rymer, 10 vols, The Hague, 1737–45, Vol. II, pt 3, p. 157. See Pirenne, *Histoire de Belgique*, Vol. I, p. 313.
26] Le Bel, *Chronique*, Vol. I, pp. 124–25; Froissart, *Chroniques*, ed. Luce, Vol. I. pp. 124–25; E. Déprez, *Les Préliminaires de la Guerre de Cent Ans. La Papauté, la France et l'Angleterre (1328–1342)*, Paris, 1902; repr. Geneva, 1975, pp. 152–53; Lucas, *The Low Countries*, pp. 204–09.
27] Henry de Lancastre, *Le Livre de Seyntz Medicines*, ed. E. J. Arnould, Oxford, 1940; Froissart, *Chroniques*, ed. K. de Lettenhove, Vol. I, pp. 541–53 ('Les enseignements d'Edouard III'). See K. R. Lambley, *The Teaching and Cultivation of the French Language in England during Tudor and Stuart Times; with an Introductory Chapter on the Preceding Period*, Manchester and London, 1920, pp. 3–25; and, for a recent synthesis, see W. Calin, *The French Tradition and the Literature of Medieval England*, Toronto, 1994, pp. 3–16.
28] See especially Calin, *The French Tradition*, passim.

library of Simon Burley, knight of the royal household, no less than eight were French romances, mostly in the Arthurian tradition.[29]

Furthermore, the courts of both England and Hainault were also committed to the encouragement of chivalric display.[30] Over a period of some thirty years, Count William proved to be one of the greatest organisers of jousts and *pas d'armes* in northern Europe. All the important events which distinguished his rule were crowned with sumptuous entertainments, not least the feast organised at Mons in 1310 to celebrate the peace concluded with Robert of Flanders; this is one of the best-documented tournaments of the fourteenth century, its imposing list of participants having come to us through several manuscripts.[31] In addition to the Lord of Beaumont, known as a model of chivalric gallantry, William I and William II of Hainault both enjoyed the support of the prosperous bourgeoisie who often played a leading role in these entertainments, since they themselves enjoyed jousting alongside the nobility.[32] It was not simply chance which made King John of Bohemia, the very personification of the princely knight, choose the town of Condé-sur-l'Escaut in 1327 for a magnificent tournament where up to 260 jousters came together (an appreciable number of them from England).[33] Over the years, such occasions would allow the chivalry of both lands to meet in each other's country. According to legend, it was in England that Count William II would one day lose his reason, as the result of a wound sustained at a tournament.[34]

Literary works created under the aegis of the court of Hainault translated perfectly the chivalric ideal which these entertainments aimed to create. In the work of Jean de Condé, as in that of the anonymous author of the *Roman de Perceforest*, is to be found a strong desire to act as defender of the traditional virtues which make a knight such an exceptional being.[35] To this end, Condé

29] V. J. Scattergood, 'Two Medieval Book Lists', *The Library*, 5th series, Vol. XXIII, 1968, pp. 236–39.

30] See J. Vale, *Edward III and Chivalry: Chivalric Society and its Context, 1270–1350*, Woodbridge, 1982.

31] A. Behault de Dornon, 'Un tournoi à Mons au XIVe siècle', *Annales du Cercle Archéologique de Mons*, Vol. XIX, 1886, pp. 383–411; idem, 'Le Tournoi de Mons de 1310', ibid., Vol. XXXVIII, 1908–09, pp. 103–256.

32] See E. Van den Neste, *Tournois, joutes, pas d'armes dans les villes de Flandre à la fin du Moyen Age (1300–1486)*, Paris, 1996, pp. 123–34, 189–90, 211–332 ('Chronologie des tournois').

33] Froissart, *Chroniques*, ed. Luce, Vol. I, pp. 39–40; Jean Froissart, *Chroniques. Dernière rédaction du premier livre. Edition du manuscrit de Rome Reg. lat. 869*, ed. G. T. Diller, Geneva and Paris, 1972, pp. 104–06; Froissart, *Chroniques. Livre I. Le manuscrit d'Amiens*, ed. Diller, Vol. I, p. 40. See R. Cazelles, *Jean l'Aveugle, comte de Luxembourg, roi de Bohême*, Bourges, 1947, p. 165; *Un itinéraire européen. Jean l'Aveugle, comte de Luxembourg et roi de Bohême (1296–1346)*, ed. M. Margue and J. Schroeder, Brussels, 1996, p. 176; Van den Neste, *Tournois*, pp. 126, 218.

34] See Reiffenberg, *Histoire du comté de Hainaut*, Vol. III, p. 89; Van den Neste, *Tournois*, pp. 125–26.

35] J. Lods, *Le Roman de Perceforest. Origines, composition, caractères, valeur et influence*, Geneva and Lille, 1951, pp. 201–17; Ribard, *Un ménestrel du XIVe siècle*, pp. 140–45.

exploited two main literary genres which he favoured: the didactic poem and the narrative lay. To the lessons set out in the *Dit des .III. mestiers d'armes* or the *Castois dou jouene gentil homme* were added the long digressions which the poet added to his romantic fiction which, quite often, assumed the character of a chivalric handbook. The narrative thread of each work was closely concerned with this preoccupation, giving pride of place to the warlike achievements demanded of the hero by the lady to whom he had lost his heart. This subtle intertwining of love and feats of arms would reappear on a much larger scale in the monumental romance, *Perceforest*, whose narrative contained countless descriptions of jousts and tournaments in which the author described the many chivalric practices followed at the time at the court of Hainault.[36] Indeed, *Perceforest* makes it possible for a close relationship between literature and the life of the 'real' world to be adduced. The originality of the work lies in the way it connects two great romance cycles of the Middle Ages: the Romance of Alexander and the Quest for the Grail. One of the scenes represented on the occasion of the Feast of the Peacock celebrated at Valenciennes on 16 July 1330 reproduced very precisely the 22 household knights of King Alexander.[37] Similar evidence confirms recent hypotheses that the *Roman de Perceforest* should be dated to the closing years of Count William I's rule.[38]

There is a further reason why we should be interested in this classic chivalrous romance: it presents us with clear evidence of the cultural ties woven at the time between the courts of Hainault and England. The author seeks to justify his ambitious project by presenting this complex romance as a free adaptation of a work in Latin previously discovered by the count, a literary fiction concerning a manuscript lost, only to be found again, a theme which has seduced writers of fiction from Rabelais to Umberto Eco.[39] It was reputedly while on a visit to England to attend the marriage of Edward II and Isabella of France that Count William was said to have made this discovery. While on a visit to the imaginary abbey of Wortimer, the count was given a precious volume, hidden for centuries under a tower, by the abbot.[40] In addition, the author of *Perceforest* showed that he had a good deal of knowledge regarding Scotland and its people. Not only did he describe with a degree of realism the country's extensive areas of wilderness; he also provided picturesque details of the primitive customs of its people, such as their methods of cooking venison.[41] This should hardly surprise us, for the

36] Lods, *Roman de Perceforest*, pp. 218–33; Ribard, *Un ménestrel du XIVe siècle*, pp. 262–66.
37] *Récits d'un bourgeois de Valenciennes*, pp. 48–49.
38] J. Barchilon and E. Zago, 'Renaissance du *Roman de Perceforest*', *Les Lettres Romanes*, Vol. XLVI, 1992, pp. 283–84.
39] François Rabelais, *Gargantua. Première édition critique faite sur l'Editio princeps*, ed. R. Calder and M. Screech, Geneva, 1970; U. Eco, *Il nome della rosa*, Milan, 1980.
40] *Roman de Perceforest. Première partie*, ed. Taylor, pp. 120–24, and also p. 33; Lods, *Roman de Perceforest*, pp. 275–76.
41] Ibid., pp. 137–38.

author would have learned much from soldiers who had taken part in Beaumont's campaign in Scotland in 1327.[42] One cannot but compare such an account to that written from first-hand experience by Jean le Bel, who was also impressed by the roughness of the countryside, whose forbidding characteristics he described while admiring certain dietary practices which enabled the Scots to overcome hunger while on campaign.[43]

It is rare for firm evidence of such contacts between the two cultures to have survived. The archives of Valenciennes occasionally reveal traces of minstrels attached to the English court being rewarded on visits to Hainault.[44] Cultural exchanges sometimes take on artistic or literary characteristics. Bibliothèque Nationale de France, ms. fr. 571 was given to Edward III by his young wife, Philippa, about 1326 or 1327, probably as a wedding present. This composite volume appears to have been put together over a period of time at the instigation of the court of Hainault. Its first item, Brunetto Latini's *Livre du Trésor*, was highly regarded in northern Europe,[45] and was here transcribed in a Picard dialect by a copyist called Michaus Ariespeil who, in the work's colophon, describes himself as a canon of Saint-Géry, one of Valenciennes' main parishes, situated near the comital palace. Several indications suggest that the volume was finished in England; not only are the other French texts which it contains produced in Anglo-Norman *scripta*, but the decoration is that of an English, perhaps East-Anglian, workshop.[46] However, the influence of Hainault is to be found in the last text included in the collection, the *Dit de Fauvain* of Raoul le Petit, a work clearly composed within the sphere of influence of Count William, since it refers to the town of Ath, in Hainault.[47]

A further figure of importance to emerge from this same cultural background is that of Jean de le Mote who, years earlier, had followed a path later to be trodden by Froissart himself. In the 1320s this minstrel, who also came from

42] See above, n. 23.

43] Le Bel, *Chronique*, pp. 51–52, 63–73. See J. Devaux, 'L'Alimentation en temps de guerre: l'apport des sources littéraires', in *La Vie matérielle au Moyen Age. L'apport des sources littéraires, normatives et de la pratique. Actes du colloque international de Louvain-la-Neuve (3–5 octobre 1996)*, ed. J.-P. Sosson and C. Thiry, Louvain-la-Neuve, 1997, pp. 98–99.

44] J.-C. Herbin, 'Activité poétique et ménestrels à Valenciennes aux XIVe et XVe siècles', *Valenciennes aux XIVe et XVe siècles*, pp. 306–07.

45] Brunetto Latini, *Li Livres dou Tresor*, ed. F. J. Carmody, Berkeley, 1948, p. xli.

46] M. A. Michael, 'A Manuscript Wedding Gift from Philippa of Hainault to Edward III', *Burlington Magazine*, Vol. CXXVII, 1985, pp. 582–99. Some critics have been inclined to attribute the work to English artists living in Valenciennes. See F. Avril and P. D. Stirnemann, *Manuscrits enluminés d'origine insulaire. VIIe–XXe siècle*, Paris, 1987, pp. 149–52 and plates 75–78; D. Vanwynsberghe, 'La Miniature à Valenciennes: état des sources et aperçu chronologique de la production (fin XIVe–1480)', *Valenciennes aux XIVe et XVe siècles*, pp. 190, 370.

47] Raoul le Petit, *L'Histoire de Fauvain*, ed. A. Långfors, Paris, 1914. See G. Paris, 'Le Roman de Fauvel', *Histoire littéraire de la France*, Vol. XXXII, Paris, 1898, pp. 113–14.

Hainault, was serving as a copyist attached to the count's chancellery. On arrival at the court of England, however, his reputation was to grow apace. Between the years 1330 and 1350 he lived regularly in the entourage of Edward III whom he served as a court poet. Besides writing the *Regret Guillaume*, composed at the request of Queen Philippa in 1339, he is recorded as having been a member of the royal household in 1338 and 1343, receiving rewards in particular for his musical skills.[48] Around 1350, Le Mote's relations with the English court were strengthened by the literary joust in which he was involved with the French writer, Philippe de Vitri, friend of Petrarch. There still exists a series of six ballads in which Le Mote finds himself at odds with two writers who criticise him for stuffing his poetical works with a mythological medley which is difficult to understand. It is clear that Vitri's complaints have a political dimension, for he accuses Le Mote of having fled France to sell his muse 'en Albion de Dieu maudite' ('in Albion accursed by God') and, in so doing, becoming a 'renoyé trayte' ('renegade traitor'). Le Mote's reply to the accusation merits attention. He does not regard himself as guilty of treason, not in the least because he sees himself as a foreigner on French soil while the court of England, in contrast, has granted him fulfilment as a writer: never had he received such help elsewhere, he asserts.[49] Such a statement is at least symptomatic of a clear line to be drawn between writers whom one can regard as French and those belonging to the literary circle of Hainault who, along with their English counterparts, formed a distinct cultural group of their own.

Although scarcely known today, Le Mote was held in high esteem by contemporaries, as is witnessed by one of the major writers of the day, the chronicler and poet from Tournai, Gilles li Muisis.[50] Le Mote's originality is shown in the brief allegorical poem which he wrote in 1339 in memory of Count William I, which he used as a kind of poetical manifesto intended to establish himself as a leader of a school.[51] It is not surprising that this daring and original work,

48] Isabelle de la Motte, lady of the queen's chamber, features in a charter of 24 July 1337. See Froissart, *Chroniques*, ed. K. de Lettenhove, Vol. I, *Introduction (Première Partie)*, p. 76; A. Thomas. 'Jean de le Mote, trouvère', *Histoire littéraire de la France*, Vol. XXXVI, Paris, 1927, pp. 66–86; N. Wilkins, 'Music and Poetry at Court: England and France in the Late Middle Ages', *English Court Culture in the Later Middle Ages*, ed. V. J. Scattergood and J. W. Sherborne, London, 1983, p. 192.

49] '... oncques n'eus ailleurs vent ne volee' (E. Pognon, 'Ballades mythologiques de Jean de le Mote, Philipe de Vitri, Jean Campion', *Humanisme et Renaissance*, Vol. V, 1938, pp. 409–10).

50] *Poésies de Gilles li Muisis*, ed. J. Kervyn de Lettenhove, 2 vols, Louvain, 1882, Vol. I, p. 89.

51] Jean de le Mote, *Li Regret Guillaume, comte de Hainaut. Poème inédit du XIVe siècle*, ed. A. Scheler, Louvain, 1882. See E. Hoepffner, 'Die Balladen des Dichters Jehan de le Mote', *Zeitschrift für Romanische Philologie*, Vol. XXXV, 1911, pp. 153–66; J. I. Wimsatt, *Chaucer and his French Contemporaries. Natural Music in the Fourteenth Century*, Toronto, 1991, pp. 48–76; Van der Meulen, 'De panter en de aalmoezenier', pp. 103–08.

destined to be imitated by both Guillaume de Machaut and Geoffrey Chaucer, should have been written at the English court in honour of Hainault's greatest prince.

So it may be seen that Froissart's career, much of it spent in England, is characteristic of the progressive ascendancy enjoyed by the literary circle close to Queen Philippa at the very point when the court of Hainault, in contrast, was about to suffer a period of decline. The death of William I was to be followed by that of his son, William II, killed by a Frisian archer at the Battle of Stavoren (1345). In the wake of these events, Hainault experienced long years of troubles brought on by the conflict which pitted the Countess Margaret against her son, William of Bavaria, and then by the madness which struck the Wittelsbach family, leading in turn to the difficulties which Albrecht of Bavaria experienced establishing himself as regent.[52] By contrast, the same years witnessed the English royal house in full flower. The peace sealed with France in May 1360 marked the start of a period of peace which would enable Edward III to develop the splendour of his court. Instead of campaigning, the king spent long periods in favourite residences such as Eltham. The presence at his court of the French king, Jean II, taken prisoner at the Battle of Poitiers (1356), acted as a stimulant for Edward. What better way for the English king to reveal his artistic and literary tastes than to show himself to be, like his prisoner, a promoter of French culture? When the hostages, surrendered under the terms of the Treaty of Brétigny, arrived in England, the feasts of Edward III were to be attended by some of the elite members of the nobility of France.[53]

Jean Froissart at the Court of Queen Philippa

Such was the milieu to which Froissart was to be introduced at the start of his career. Contrary to the current view,[54] it was not in 1361 but in the following year that the young poet discovered the English court. He reports having been present, in the year of his arrival, at an entertainment given at Berkhamsted, one of the Black Prince's favourite manors. According to Froissart, the occasion was linked to an event of significance, the raising to the rank of Prince of Aquitaine of the Black Prince, who was preparing to visit his new possessions. The queen

52] Reiffenberg, *Histoire du comté de Hainaut*, Vol. III, pp. 77–91. Waller Zeper, *Jan van Henegouwen*, pp. 263–369; Lucas, *The Low Countries*, pp. 508–09, 535–43, 556–59; F. Quicke, *Les Pays-Bas à la veille de la période bourguignonne (1356–1384). Contribution à l'histoire politique et diplomatique de l'Europe occidentale dans la seconde moitié du XIVe siècle*, Brussels, 1947, pp. 54–62; Bohy, *Hainaut ou l'épopée d'un peuple*, Vol. I, pp. 129–34.

53] See in particular M. Packe, *King Edward III*, London, 1983, pp. 251 ff; J. Deviosse, *Jean le Bon*, Paris, 1985, pp. 378 ff.

54] M. Darmesteter, *Froissart*, Paris, 1894, p. 13; F. S. Shears, *Froissart, Chronicler and Poet*, London, 1930, p. 14; J. Bastin, *Froissart. Chroniqueur, romancier et poète*, Brussels, 1942, p. 6; *Dictionnaire des lettres françaises. Le Moyen Age*, Paris, 1992, p. 771.

herself came to Berkhamsted to greet her son before his departure. Although Froissart describes the scene as occurring in 1361, it must have taken place after the Prince's investiture on 19 July 1362. This date coincides very well with the indication provided by manuscript A regarding Froissart's earliest poetic activity.[55] Such chronological indications lend strong support to the hypothesis that 1338 (rather than 1337) was the year of the writer's birth. Froissart says that he was 24 years old at the time of the Berkhamsted meeting, information confirmed by his *Joli Buisson de Jonece*, known to have been composed in 1373, in which he revealed that he was at that time 35 years old.[56]

The year 1362, then, marked the time when, leaving Valenciennes, Froissart joined the court of the Queen of England, who immediately retained him. He did not arrive empty-handed. As he wrote many years later, he presented Philippa with a 'livre tout compilé' ('book all ready prepared') which would enable her to judge the talents of her new protégé.[57] Such was the nature of the work, now lost, which has always whetted the appetite of scholars. As Peter Ainsworth has rightly pointed out, the work must consist of poetry. Was this an initial verse draft of the *Chroniques* or, rather, as Michel Zink has suggested, a small offering in verse on a subject of lesser significance intended, in the eyes of the poet, to provide an 'introduction' into the presence of the queen?[58]

Whichever it was, it is unlikely that this offering was, in itself, sufficient to accredit at the English court a man who, so far, enjoyed no perceptible reputation. Who, from his past, could have presented him to the queen? Tradition favours Jean de Beaumont, usually regarded as Froissart's first protector.[59] In spite of his qualifications, we may be sceptical. For one reason, Beaumont had died in 1356, when Froissart was only eighteen. For another, he does not feature on the list of benefactors which Froissart was to include in one of his poems, the *Joli Buisson*

55] Froissart, *Chroniques*, ed. K. de Lettenhove, Vol. XVI, pp. 142–43, 235; Froissart, *Chroniques...Amiens*, ed. Diller, Vol. III, p. 276; Jean Froissart, *Dits et débats*, ed. A. Fourrier, Geneva, 1979, pp. 7–9. See Barber, *Edward, Prince of Wales*, p. 175; P. F. Ainsworth, *Jean Froissart and the Fabric of History. Truth, Myth and Fiction in the 'Chroniques'*, Oxford, 1990, p. 44.

56] Froissart, *Chroniques*, ed. K. de Lettenhove, Vol. XVI, p. 143; Froissart, *Joli Buisson de Jonece*, p. 74, ll. 793–94, and p. 76, l. 860. In 1390 Froissart declared himself to be 57 years old. The number LVII can, however, be read as a badly formed LII. In the same passage he says that he has worked on his history for thirty-seven years. This figure may possibly have caused the copyist to make the error referred to above. G. Paris and A. Jeanroy, *Extraits des chroniqueurs français. Villehardouin, Joinville, Froissart, Commines*, 6th edn, Paris, 1905, p. 165, n. 1.

57] Froissart, *Chroniques*, ed. Luce, Vol I. p. 210.

58] N. R. Cartier, 'The Lost Chronicle', *Speculum*, Vol. XXXVI, 1961, pp. 424–34; Ainsworth, *Jean Froissart*, pp. 32–50; M. Zink, *Froissart et le temps*, Paris, 1998, pp. 19–36.

59] Froissart, *Chroniques*, ed. K. de Lettenhove, Vol. I, *Introduction (Première Partie)*, pp. 35–36; M. Wilmotte, *Froissart*, Brussels, 1948, p. 16; P. F. Dembowski, *Jean Froissart and his Meliador. Context, Craft and Sense*, Lexington, 1983, p. 41; J. Trotin, 'Vie et oeuvre de Jean Froissart', *Valentiana*, No. 4, December 1989, pp. 11–12.

de Jonece.[60] How can one explain the omission of such a supporter whose prestige would have reflected advantageously upon Froissart himself?

Are we to suppose, then, that on landing in England, Froissart had no one to support him? In an attempt to resolve this problem, attention should be drawn to one of the author's pastoral poems probably written before his departure for the English court. Generally speaking, the manuscript of Froissart's poems is characterised by the fact that the texts are written down, in most cases, in their order of composition. Furthermore, several of these pastoral poems are carefully contextualised by the poet, the opening lines usually indicating the place where he was at the time of writing.[61] We can therefore say that the first poem in this manuscript was certainly composed in Hainault, before Froissart's departure in 1362. Indeed, the writer places the action near Valenciennes, 'entre Aubrecicourt et Mauni', two villages situated to this day on the road running from Bouchain to Douai. The second of these villages deserves close attention, for the Lord of Mauny was one of the leaders of the nobility of Hainault: Walter de Mauny, hero of the Hundred Years War, would be mentioned on many occasions in Froissart's *Chroniques*. We know, too, from the *Joli Buisson de Jonece* that Mauny acted as one of the poet's first protectors:

> Des dons monsigneur de Mauni
> Me lo, ne pas ne les reni.

> I have nothing but praise for the gifts of the lord of Mauny,
> And I do not repudiate them.[62]

Everything suggests that Froissart wrote his first pastoral poem on a visit to the castle at Mauny. Indeed, the poem is a skilfully worded appeal for help. Froissart praises the many advantages of the generous garment called a *houppelande*; its only drawback is that he cannot afford one![63] It is likely that the protector did more than satisfy Froissart's broad hint. Mauny was well known in English court circles. Originally an esquire in the service of the queen, he had been knighted by the king in person, and had played a leading role in most of his campaigns. He was a perfect example of the knight from Hainault fully integrated into the nobility of England. He was thus in the best possible position to recommend Froissart to the queen.[64]

60] Froissart, *Joli Buisson de Jonece*, pp. 55–60.
61] E. Hoepffner, 'La Chronologie des pastourelles de Froissart', *Mélanges offerts à Emile Picot par ses amis et ses élèves*, 2 vols, Paris, 1913, Vol. II, pp. 27–42.
62] Froissart, *Joli Buisson de Jonece*, p. 56, ll. 265–66.
63] Jean Froissart, *The Lyric Poems. A Critical Edition*, ed. R. R. McGregor, Chapel Hill, NC, 1975, pp. 151–53.
64] On this personage, see La Curne de Sainte-Palaye, *Mémoires*, Vol. III, pp. 21–72; Froissart, *Chroniques*, ed. K. de Lettenhove, Vol. XXII, *Table analytique des noms historiques (J–Q)*, pp. 176–84; H. Pirenne, 'Gautier de Mauny', *Biographie Nationale de Belgique*, Vol. XIV, 1897, cols 100–02. It is possible that Mauny may have arranged for

Once a clerk of the queen's chamber, Froissart soon became her personal poet, and was referred to as such in certain books of accounts.[65] It is important at this stage to stress the part played by tradition in Hainault in the granting of this semi-official role. In this respect, the first half of the fourteenth century constituted a period of change during which the *jongleur* and the minstrel, hitherto court entertainers, slowly graduated to the position of men of letters.[66] Count William I of Hainault was one of the first to encourage such a development. Whereas Baudouin de Condé, also a poet, had certainly occupied a subordinate position at court, that of his son, Jean, reflected the change now taking place. So Jean could proclaim himself openly a member of Count William's household (*familia*), which gave him plenty of time to exercise his talents:

> Jehans de Condet, qui estoit
> De son maisnage et qui viestoit
> Des robes de ses esquiiers ...
>
> Jean de Condé who was
> Of his household and who wore
> The robes of his esquires ...[67]

Was it not natural, then, that Queen Philippa should have encouraged this development in England by welcoming to the court of England two of her compatriots, Jean de le Mote and Jean Froissart?[68] To follow yet again the evidence of the *Chroniques*, Froissart would very soon become one of the queen's courtiers: witness the intimate scene in which the queen confides in the poet, recalling memories of her youth, and even telling him of her meeting with her future husband, the king. Froissart concludes with understandable pride:

> Ainsi l'ay je oy depuis recorder de la bonne damme qui fu royne d'Engleterre et dallés qui je demouray et fui ... Si me fist elle tant de biens que j'en suis tenus de priier à tous jours més ...

Froissart to visit Valenciennes in the summer of 1364 (Froissart, *Chroniques*, ed. K. de Lettenhove, Vol. I, *Introduction [Première Partie]*, pp. 123–27).

65] A. Pinchart, 'Etudes sur l'histoire des arts au moyen âge. La cour de Jeanne et de Wenceslas et les arts en Brabant, pendant la seconde moitié du XIVe siècle. Musiciens et poètes', *Revue trimestrielle*, Vol. XIII, 1857, pp. 37, 59.

66] R. F. Green, *Poets and Princepleasers. Literature and the English Court in the Late Middle Ages*, Toronto, 1980, pp. 103–05; J. Cerquiglini-Toulet, *La Couleur de la mélancolie. La fréquentation des livres au XIVe siècle (1300–1415)*, Paris, 1993, pp. 38–47.

67] Jean de Condé, *Opera*, ed. Mazonni Peruzzi, p. 371, ll. 165–67. On his high notion of the poet's role, see Ribard, *Un ménestrel du XIVe siècle*, pp. 86–95; Jean de Condé, *La Messe des Oiseaux et le Dit des Jacobins et des Fremeneurs*, ed. J. Ribard, Geneva, 1970.

68] On the status accorded to Jean de le Mote, see Wimsatt, *Chaucer and his French Contemporaries*, p. 52.

> Such are the memories confided to me by the good lady who was Queen of England, when I was living continually in her company ... She did so much for me that I must always thank God for it ...[69]

The admission of Froissart into the heart of the court circle, a reflection of the status accorded him, was to exercise an increasingly determining influence on his development as a writer. Not content with granting him her protection, Philippa introduced him into a literary circle which would help him sharpen his creative genius. It is difficult to penetrate the activities of this cultivated group which met around the queen and which was inspired, as we have seen, by the court of Hainault. It is likely that it consisted of a small group who enjoyed reciting or singing poems, or debating questions of love among themselves. While we cannot yet talk of a proper 'cour d'amour', as the term would be understood by the end of the century and, in particular, at the court of the French king, Charles VI,[70] it none the less seems that the *familia regis* enjoyed this kind of refined recreation in a more informal gathering where poetry and *jeux d'amour* were brought together. Froissart himself appears to refer to activity of this kind when he recalls the feasts given by the queen to celebrate the English naval victory off Winchelsea in August 1350: 'Si passèrent celle nuit li seigneur et les dames en grant reveil, en parlent d'armes et d'amours' ('the lords and ladies spent the night in celebration, talking of arms and love').[71] One cannot fail to compare this episode with the entertainments organised at the court of Orthez by the Pyrenean prince, Gaston Fébus, who would one day welcome Froissart to his court where, every night, the poet would be asked to declaim his *Meliador* before an audience of lords and ladies assembled in the gallery of the castle at Moncade.[72]

On the evidence, it is likely that Chaucer, too, made his literary debuts within the queen's circle. Already an esquire of the royal house, Chaucer married, no later than 1366, a maid of honour of the queen's household, Philippa Paon de Roet, daughter of a knight from Hainault.[73] From then on the young poet was to

69] Froissart, *Chroniques. Livre I. Le manuscrit d'Amiens*, ed. Diller, Vol. I, p. 23.
70] A. Piaget, 'La Cour amoureuse, dite de Charles VI', *Romania*, Vol. XX, 1891, pp. 417–54; C. Bozzolo and H. Loyau, *La Cour Amoureuse dite de Charles VI*, 2 vols, Paris, 1982–1992; Cerquiglini-Toulet, *Couleur de la mélancolie*, pp. 49–56.
71] Froissart, *Chroniques*, ed. Luce, Vol. IV, pp. 97–98. See G. Paris, 'Les Cours d'amour au Moyen Age', *Journal des Savants*, 1888, pp. 664–75, 727–36; Green, *Poets and Princepleasers*, pp. 122–25; R. F. Green, 'The *Familia Regis* and the *Familia Cupidinis*', in *English Court Culture in the Later Middle Ages*, ed. Scattergood and Sherborne, pp. 87–108; D. Pearsall, *The Life of Geoffrey Chaucer: A Critical Biography*, Cambridge, Mass., 1992, pp. 58–61.
72] P. Tucoo-Chala, 'Froissart dans le Midi pyrénéen', in *Froissart: Historian*, ed. J. J. N. Palmer, Woodbridge and Totowa, NJ , 1981, pp. 118–31; idem, *Gaston Fébus, prince des Pyrénées (1331–1391)*, Pau, 1993, pp. 275–308. The phrase '*d'armes et d'amours volontiers se devisoit*' ('which gave itself equally to arms and to love') is used by Froissart to describe both the person of Gaston and the court of Edward III (Froissart, *Chroniques*, ed. L. Mirot, SHF, Paris, 1931, Vol. XII, p. 77).
73] Pearsall, *Life of Geoffrey Chaucer*, pp. 35, 47–51.

be a regular member of that group from Hainault, and he must have met Froissart on many occasions. Indeed, the influence of Froissart on Chaucer's early poetry is well recognised.[74] It is even possible that the *Canterbury Tales* may include personalities from Hainault. The figure of the prioress could have been based on the queen's sister, Elizabeth, who ended her days in the English convent of Stratford at Bow, the very house to which Chaucer's prioress belonged. For more than one reason, too, the portrait of the monk included in the 'Prologue' reminds one of Jean le Bel, another prestigious figure from Hainault.[75]

Right through her life Queen Philippa continued to welcome those who came from her native country to her court in England. Froissart tells us so in the poignant epitaph in which he deplores the loss of his patron. Never, he says, did she cease to bestow acts of kindness, in particular upon those who came from Hainault, for it was these whom she appreciated above all.[76]

Such was the case, it appears, of André Beauneveu, sculptor from Valenciennes, whose visit to England, attested by Froissart, occurred between 1364 and 1370.[77] With such a circle one might also be tempted to associate the name of Chandos Herald, author of the *Life of the Black Prince*, upon whom Froissart drew freely – or was it the other way round?[78] This writer referred to since 1363 as herald to Sir John Chandos certainly came from Hainault, as we learn from Picard characteristics of his *Life*.[79] It is equally certain that it was in the household of Queen Philippa that Froissart met Gui de Blois, one of the three sons of Louis I of Blois and Jeanne, only daughter and heiress of Jean de Beaumont. Gui de Blois was one of the hostages surrendered to Edward III in fulfilment of the Treaty of Brétigny, and he was to remain in England from 1360 to 1367.[80] Grandson of Jean de Beaumont, and consequently cousin to the

74] Wimsatt, *Chaucer and his French Contemporaries*, pp. 174–209; Pearsall, *Life of Geoffrey Chaucer*, pp. 68–70.

75] J. M. Manly, *Some New Light on Chaucer*, Gloucester, Mass., 1959, pp. 201–20; P. Mertens-Fonck, 'Un chroniqueur liégeois sur la route de Canterbury', *Bulletin de la Société Royale Le Vieux-Liège*, Vol. CCLXXIX, 1997, pp. 707–18.

76] Froissart, *The Lyric Poems*, p. 108, ll. 92–96.

77] Froissart, *Chroniques*, ed. K. de Lettenhove, Vol. XIV, p. 197; P. Pradel, 'Les Tombeaux de Charles V', *Bulletin Monumental*, Vol. CIX, 1951, pp. 280–81. On the career of André Beauneveu, see F. Baron and L. Nys, 'La Sculpture valenciennoise aux XIVe et XVe siècles', *Valenciennes aux XIVe et XVe siècles*, pp. 127–28, 138–39, 372–75.

78] J. J. N. Palmer, 'Froissart et le Héraut Chandos', *MA*, Vol. LXXXVIII, 1982, pp. 271–92; P. F. Ainsworth, 'Collationnement, montage et *jeu parti*: le début de la campagne espagnole du Prince Noir (1366–1367) dans les *Chroniques* de Jean Froissart', *MA*, Vol. C, 1994, pp. 369–411.

79] *'Life of the Black Prince' by the Herald of Sir John Chandos*, ed. M. K. Pope and E. C. Lodge, Oxford, 1910, pp. xxix–xxxiii; *'La Vie du Prince Noir' by Chandos Herald*, ed. D. B. Tyson, Tübingen, 1975, pp. 11–18.

80] Froissart, *Chroniques*, ed. Luce, Vol. VI, p. 55; Froissart, *Chroniques…Amiens*, ed. Diller, Vol. III, p. 251.

queen, he must have been welcomed into her circle where he would have met Froissart. The fact is all the more significant since, upon his return to Hainault, Blois would act as the prime sponsor of the *Chroniques*. When later, Froissart was to occupy the benefice of Estinnes, Gui de Blois invited him frequently to the castle at Beaumont and was eventually to retain him in his household as a chaplain.[81]

Such is the scattered evidence which gives us some idea of the milieu, based upon the courts of Hainault and England, in which there grew up the young writer whose works seem to represent the purest emanation of a cultural relationship, created over many years, between the two courts, one which, naturally enough, Froissart would emphasise in his *Chroniques*. In this respect, the first section of Book I, in which, following Jean le Bel, Froissart describes the origins of the alliance between England and Hainault, bears closer examination. One revealing example, found in the Amiens manuscript, acts as a prelude to the visit made by Queen Isabella to the court of Count William I. In this section, Froissart makes much use of direct speech, putting into the mouth of Robert d'Artois praise of William and his brother, Beaumont, who, he states, would not fail to provide the queen with all the support she might need.[82] This passage is all the more symptomatic of the chronicler's sympathies as the words attributed to Robert d'Artois are totally fictional, since that prince had no reason whatever to act against the policies of the French king, Charles IV.[83]

The same sense of nostalgia was to pervade the text of the Rome manuscript in which, in the last years of his life, Froissart was to re-write a good portion of the first book of the *Chroniques*. This sentiment was doubtless cruelly revived by the last visit which he made to England in 1395, and the disappointment which he experienced on this occasion when he found no signs of the cultivated elite whom he had known 30 years earlier.[84] As Peter Ainsworth has shown, more so than the earlier texts the Rome manuscript would tend to glorify what constituted, in Froissart's eyes, the most memorable period of all, the reign of Edward III.[85] This, the chronicler's final text, leaves patently obvious his

81] See particularly Froissart, *Chroniques*, ed. K. de Lettenhove, Vol. I, *Introduction (Première Partie)*, pp. 280–82, 291–301; Darmesteter, *Froissart*, pp. 46–51, 57–63; Shears, *Froissart, Chronicler and Poet*, pp. 37, 41–43.

82] Froissart, *Chroniques...Amiens*, ed. Diller, Vol. I, p. 18. On this kind of procedure, see P. F. Ainsworth, 'Style direct et peinture des personnages chez Froissart', *Romania*, Vol. XCIII, 1972, pp. 498–522.

83] See Lucas, *The Low Countries*, p. 53. This speech is not included in most versions of the *Chroniques* (see Froissart, *Chroniques*, ed. Luce, Vol. I, p. 20). In the Rome manuscript it is uttered by the Earl of Kent (*Chroniques...Rome*, ed. Diller, p. 56).

84] Froissart, *Chroniques*, ed. K. de Lettenhove, Vol. I, *Introduction (Première Partie)*, pp. 374–91; Darmesteter, *Froissart*, pp. 133–39; Shears, *Froissart, Chronicler and Poet*, pp. 60–71; M.-T. de Medeiros, 'Voyage et lieux de mémoire. Le retour de Froissart en Angleterre', *MA*, Vol. XCVIII, 1992, pp. 419–28; Zink, *Froissart et le temps*, pp. 21–22, 84–87.

85] Ainsworth, *Jean Froissart*, pp. 254–302.

enduring fascination with earlier years when the court of England had been so greatly influenced by Hainault. One may take as an example of this the eulogy of Queen Philippa included in the account of the siege of Calais (1346-47), in which the chronicler acts as the mouthpiece of enthusiastic statements made by soldiers encamped before the town:

> Vive la bonne Phelippe de Hainnau, la roine d'Engleterre, nostre chiere et redoubtee dame, car elle amena et aporta entre nous et en Engleterre, honnour, pourfit, grace et tranqillité; et tant conme elle vivra, biens, honnours, largueces et pourfis nous habonderont. Et elle [est] de un si bon pais, si douls, si courtois, et si amiable et raempli de bonnes gens, et qui dou tout s'enclinent a nous amer et honnourer; et fu fille de si bon signeur et si sage et si vaillant, que elle ne poroit que tous biens faire.
>
> Long live the good Philippa of Hainault, Queen of England, our dear and redoubted lady, who brought to us in England honour, advantage, grace and peace; and as long as she lives we shall have good fortune, honours, largesse and advantages in plenty. She comes from such a fine country, so benevolent, courteous and friendly and filled with good people who are well disposed to love and honour us; and as the daughter of so fine, wise and valiant a lord, she herself could only do good.[86]

The good works of this tutelary queen, guarantor of the well-being experienced by her subjects, are closely associated, in Froissart's view, with her origins in Hainault. If Philippa appeared to him as another Guenevere, this was not simply because of her many qualities but, above all, because she was Philippa 'de Hainnau' and had, for the chronicler, become the emblem of that providential union between Hainault and England which had given him his best years.[87] The history of the kingdom is thus inextricably linked to the personal experience of the chronicler himself, obsessed by the memory of an age now passed, not unlike Marcel Proust, on the promenade at Cabourg, seeking, through the magic exercised by the written word, to breathe in the scent of his youthful years.

86] Froissart, *Chroniques...Rome*, ed. Diller, p. 788.
87] On the image of the queen in the *Chroniques*, see M.-T. de Medeiros, 'Le Pacte encomiastique: Froissart, ses *Chroniques* et ses mécènes', *MA*, Vol. XCIV, 1988, pp. 251–55, from which, however, the 'Hainault dimension' is omitted.

2

Froissart and his Second Book

PETER AINSWORTH

Without being a 'poor relation', Froissart's Second Book has to date received relatively less attention from critics, editors and translators than either the First, Third or Fourth Books. Anthologies usually include a few extracts from chapters recounting the Flemish Revolt and its suppression; this is partly because they are so dramatically written, but also because they still constitute an acknowledged source of information about the events of 1378–85. A partial translation into Modern French was published some ten years ago under the title *Chroniques de Flandre, de Hainaut et d'Artois au temps de la Guerre de Cent Ans.*[1] This offers no more than sixty pages' coverage of events in Flanders between 1380 and 1382, but the editors are to be commended for pointing out that, however partial Froissart's depiction of events in the Low Countries may be, he contrives to adopt such a wide range of viewpoints that essential aspects of the conflict are constantly placed before the reader. They also remind us that Froissart evinces considerable sympathy here for the rebels of Ghent. Worried that modern Flemish readers might take umbrage at the amount of space allotted in this edition to the tragedy of Roosebeke, the author of the *Avant-Propos* (F. Suard) proffers the following reassurance:

> ... que nos amis Flamands veuillent bien nous excuser: l'importance que nous donnons ici au récit de Froissart ne résulte pas d'une délectation suspecte, que l'attitude de l'historien n'autoriserait guère: si Froissart se révèle partisan des Français, c'est parce qu'il redoute la 'contagion communale', mais il montre de l'estime pour les Flamands.

> We crave our Flemish readers' indulgence: the amount of space allotted to Froissart's account does not proceed from a questionable enjoyment on our part, which the chronicler's attitude would not in any case warrant: if Froissart shows himself favourable to the French, it is because he is afraid

1] *Chroniques de Flandre, de Hainaut et d'Artois au temps de la Guerre de Cent Ans (1328–1390) de Jean Froissart*, trans. D. Poulet, with an introduction by M. Sommé, Troesnes, 1986.

> that political unrest in the Communes may prove contagious; he does, however, evince respect for the Flemings.[2]

It is refreshing to read Monique Sommé's reminder that Froissart 'ne put exercer ses activités d'écrivain que grâce à l'appui de protecteurs qui, tous, avaient des liens étroits avec la puissante maison comtale du Hainaut' ('was only able to exercise his skills as a writer thanks to the support afforded by patrons who all enjoyed close links with the powerful comital house of Hainault').[3] This reference to Froissart's debt to patrons from Hainault and the Low Countries calls to mind what is surely one of the best short essays of recent years on Froissart, *as historian*.[4] The author acknowledges the important role played in the chronicler's life by his Hainaulter patrons, and by Gui de Blois; but goes on to observe that, 'though Froissart had compelling reasons for wishing to include much of the history of the Low Countries, he rarely allowed his personal predilections or the interests of his patrons to dictate the overall shape of his work'.[5] That said, 'anything which did not directly relate to this epic struggle [that between Plantagenet and Valois for hegemony in western Europe], he ruthlessly discarded ... Froissart jettisoned whole blocks of le Bel's chapters devoted to the internal history of the Low Countries (le Bel, I, 220–44).'[6] Even so, J. van Herwaarden argues here, with some justification, that Froissart's account in Book II of the years 1379–85 'is the work of a mature and independent historian', adding that the chronicler's narrative, 'vivid and dramatic' though it may be, does none the less afford some 'shrewd insights' into the mainsprings of the conflict and its development:

> For although he recorded his opinion that the persistent state of war in these years was the work of the devil, he did not allow this pious conclusion to prevent him from observing the faults and responsibilities of the parties involved.[7]

A proponent of good government and of the rule of law, and palpably fearful that the overthrow of the established order throughout northern Europe was not an unlikely prospect in view of what was going on in the early 1380s in England, Normandy and the French capital, let alone on his own doorstep, Froissart, if he espoused any cause, was above all the advocate of *mesure*. Although the word *tyrandise* ('tyranny') rarely occurs in the *Chroniques*, Froissart seems to have understood what it meant: he 'believed that princes had a duty to take into account the interests of their urban subjects, who in their turn had to respect

2] Ibid., p. 9.
3] Ibid., p. 11.
4] J. van Herwaarden, 'The War in the Low Countries', in *Froissart: Historian*, ed. J. J. N. Palmer, Woodbridge and Totowa, NJ, 1981, pp. 101–17.
5] Ibid., p. 101.
6] Ibid.
7] Ibid., p. 105.

the existing order'. In the same breath as he extolled acts of prowess in war between hereditary enemies, therefore, the chronicler acknowledged the need for *civil* peace, 'whereby the prosperity of his subjects would allow the prince and his knights to carry out their function in just wars'.[8]

One further point made by Van Herwaarden deserves consideration; this relates to Froissart's evident awareness of at least some of the complexities involved in the urban politics of Bruges and Ghent. His depiction of demagoguery and political rivalries, and of the pragmatic exploitation of the credulous; his portrayal of factions and their often colourful if shortlived leaders; his masterly evocation of the use of intimidation and cajolery to stir up the populace – all this may well be dramatic and literary in inspiration, but it is none the less shrewdly observed. Moreover, such material actually encourages the reader to ask pertinent questions, and in this wise establish a critical distance between narrator and events recounted. Froissart's narratives certainly betray an informed awareness of the respective roles played in the urban politics of the late 1370s by the demagogues of Ghent and their notorious White Hoods, but he also allows us to glimpse the privations and sufferings of the rank and file weavers, dyers and shippers. More importantly, the chronicler overtly censures the dereliction of duty whereby those pillars of the community, the *poorters*, allowed this tyranny by demagoguery to arise in the first place. This was a part of the world that Froissart knew well, and it was uncomfortably close to home. His depiction of events is all the more sharply observed for that reason.

Some forty years before the appearance of Van Herwaarden's essay, the Belgian scholar, F.-L. Ganshof, had published an invaluable article featuring several of the hitherto less well-known manuscripts of the *Chroniques* held in Belgian research libraries.[9] His essay includes one of the most percipient critical evaluations we have of the chronicler's prose in his Second Book, and remains to this day a reliable starting-point for anyone wishing to explore a part of the *Chroniques* which is exceptionally rich in its coverage of popular and urban revolt.

The aim of the present chapter is neither to revisit in close detail the chronicler's account of politics in the Low Countries, nor yet to provide a broader analysis of the other theatres addressed in this part of the *Chroniques*.[10] It is, rather, to *defamiliarise* the very notion of a clearly-delineated, unproblematic 'Book II', and thus to establish the basis for a fresh critique. A secondary aim is to provide an account of how and why the production of a modern edition of Book II raises

8] Ibid., p. 116.
9] F.-L. Ganshof, 'Jean Froissart', *Annales de la Société Archéologique de Bruxelles*, Vol. XLII, 1938, pp. 256–72.
10] Some of these issues were dealt with by P. Ainsworth, 'Du berceau à la bière: Louis de Male dans le Deuxième Livre des *Chroniques* de Froissart', in *Dies Illa. Death in the Middle Ages*, ed. Jane H. M. Taylor, Liverpool, 1984, pp. 125–52.

so many questions, and to suggest a few tentative answers.[11] This is a section of the *Chroniques* which has all too often been taken for granted; yet it still poses fascinating problems for critic and editor alike.

* * * * *

In a recently-published study of Froissart's poetry and prose, Michel Zink has advanced the argument that the most fruitful way to address the *Chroniques* – as a historian or as a literary scholar – is by revisiting the volumes as they normally appear on the library shelf.[12] For Book II, we are advised, is in fact continuous and co-extensive with Book I, at least in terms of its approach to the events recorded. There are indeed several entirely respectable reasons for endorsing this suggestion and 'doing away with Book II', as we shall see below. Zink's second point is that a radical distinction needs to be made between this earlier work ('Book I plus II'), and the 'Memoirs' found in Books III and IV. Maintaining that it is of no small significance that Froissart should have written virtually no verse after 1389, the year in which he returned to his *forge* to write up the notes collected in the course of his journey southward to Orthez and during his subsequent sojourn at the court of Gaston Fébus in Béarn, Zink argues that, from this point onwards, all the writer's sensibility and intellectual and creative energies were to be invested in his *prose*. This in turn was to have a major impact upon the handling of time in Book III: 'On voit alors les *Chroniques* combiner au temps de l'histoire un temps proprement poétique, le temps du récit et le temps de la mémoire' ('from this point onwards, the *Chroniques* combine chronological sequence with a specifically poetic temporality; the time of narration and the time of remembering').[13] It is in the early narratives of that section of Book III known, since the late Armel Diverres' edition of 1953, as the *Voyage en Béarn*,[14] that we encounter what Zink terms an 'imbrication du temps de la vie et du temps de l'écriture' ('interpenetration of the time of lived experience and of that of writing about it').[15] Before that, argues Zink, we are dealing with a different kind of work altogether:

> ... les *Chroniques* nous induisent en erreur par leur apparente continuité. Il y a deux ouvrages différents, les deux premiers livres d'une part, les deux derniers de l'autre. L'ultime et tardive rédaction du livre I porte la marque de cet autre ouvrage que sont les deux derniers livres. Un autre ouvrage qui mériterait davantage le titre de mémoires. Un autre ouvrage, parce qu'en

11] See the introduction to *Les 'Chroniques' de Jean Froissart*, Vol. I, ed. G. Diller (Book I) and P. Ainsworth (Book II), Coll. 'Lettres Gothiques', Paris, forthcoming.
12] M. Zink, *Froissart et le temps*, Paris, 1998, pp. 17–18; see also pp. 65, 78.
13] Ibid., p. 17.
14] Jean Froissart, *Voyage en Béarn*, ed. A. H. Diverres, Manchester, 1953.
15] Zink, *Froissart et le temps*, p. 16.

> rattrapant le temps de l'événement, en racontant au jour le jour – et pourtant ce ne peut être au jour le jour – Froissart modifie le temps de l'écriture. Un autre ouvrage parce que le temps d'une vie, il a découvert une autre nature du temps littéraire.

> We are led astray by the *Chroniques*' ostensible continuity. There are two distinct works: the first two Books on the one hand, and the two later Books on the other. The final, late redaction of Book I bears the same stamp as that other work constituted by the two last Books, a work that has a greater claim than the first two to the title of Memoirs. The distinctiveness of this later work may be attributed to the manner in which – in his attempts to 'catch up with' the time of the events he is narrating, and by recounting these events from one day to the next (and yet this cannot be the case) – Froissart modifies the time of writing itself. This is another kind of work because, within the space of a lifetime, the chronicler has discovered that literary time can be something different again.[16]

Zink's demonstration of this thesis is convincing. Some of the best pages in his book deal with Froissart's subtle orchestration of the account provided of Richard II's downfall, in Book IV. Here, the comments of the people of London, reported as indirect or direct speech interventions, and resembling a Greek chorus, are just one aspect of the chronicler's creation of a discourse that is both tragic and tragedic, as well as historically penetrating. For with this new manner, suggests Zink, expressed in the memoir-like prose of Books III and IV, the latter of which in particular displays a growing *désenchantement* with English chivalry and the francophile, pleasure-seeking Ricardian regime of the late 1390s, Froissart performs the subtle, insistent task of lifting what Zink calls, in a brilliant phrase, 'les masques de l'indicible' ('the masks of the ineffable').[17] The passage in which this image occurs is worth quoting in its entirety; it considers why and how the chronicler's detailed portrayal of Richard's funeral is in effect a blind (*leurre*) which serves, by its sheer thoroughness, to evoke what has in fact been suppressed: the (patently missing) account of the circumstances in which the king died or was put to death:

> Au récit escamoté de la mort de Richard, Froissart substitue celui, détaillé, de ses obsèques. C'est la conclusion la plus radicale qui soit – 'on jette un peu de terre sur la tombe et en voilà pour jamais', mais c'est une conclusion décevante, au sens ancien comme au sens moderne du mot, une information qui est de toutes les façons un leurre: les funérailles de Richard II sont celles du roi qu'il n'était plus et tous les détails fournis sur elles n'apprennent rien de plus sur sa mort. C'est un nuage de fumée pour gazer mais aussi pour mettre en évidence

16] Ibid., pp. 17–18.
17] Ibid., p. 104.

> ce blanc, ce silence sur les conditions de la mort du roi. La gratuité même du récit des funérailles montre que Froissart n'est plus ébloui par les fastes des cours et qu'il sait très bien signifier que leur éclat comme la description qu'il en fait sont les masques de l'indicible.

> Froissart replaces the evasive narrative of Richard's death with a detailed account of the king's funeral. One could scarcely be more final – 'a few shovelfuls of earth, and that's an end of it for all eternity' – yet this is at once a disappointing and deceptive conclusion, providing information that only serves in any case as a blind: Richard's funeral is that of a king who has become a king in name only, and the myriad details supplied tell us nothing fresh about his death. What we are offered is a smoke-screen, there to conceal but also to point up an absence, the silence surrounding the circumstances of the king's demise. The sheer gratuitousness of the funeral narrative shows how Froissart is no longer dazzled by the pomp of aristocratic society and that he knows only too well how to encode his awareness that its splendour and brilliance, as well as the descriptions he provides of it are, as it were, so many masks to conceal that which dare not be uttered in the open.[18]

Book IV, it is suggested here, is Froissart's crowning glory – high praise indeed for a writer so often castigated for being a mediocre historian[19] but who, at his best, displays a sense of the tragic that is worthy of Shakespeare himself:

> Froissart, cet homme aisément réputé superficiel, finit ainsi par manifester un sens profond de la dramatisation et de l'éloquence de l'histoire. Un sens du suspens et de l'euphémisme terrifiants. Un sens des situations shakespeariennes. Non pas la simplicité du noeud tragique racinien, mais le foisonnement de l'histoire, indéfiniment poursuivie de roi en roi et de succession en succession – *de rei en rei e d'eir en eir* – , comme le disait ce *Roman de Brut* dont il invoque deux fois le témoignage, et aussi le foisonnement trompeur du destin, qui laisse croire que les chemins et les issues sont multiples, alors qu'il n'est qu'étouffement et resserrement vers l'inévitable.

> In this wise, Froissart, a man so readily taxed with being superficial, contrives to display a deep understanding of the dramatic and eloquent properties of history; a terrifying awareness of suspense and of the power of understatement. A knowledge of Shakespearean situation. Not the pared-down simplicity of the tragic dilemma so belovèd of Racine, so much as the profuse growth of history, pursued indefinitely from king to king and from succession to succession – *de rei en rei e d'eir en eir* – as the *Roman de Brut* [Wace's *Brut*] had expressed it, whose testimony he invokes on two occasions, but also the deceptive proliferation of destiny, which bids one believe its paths and exits

18] Ibid.
19] The charge is vigorously rebutted by Zink (ibid., pp. 52–56).

to be manifold, whilst offering nothing but a progressive stifling and inexorable restriction as the inevitable beckons.[20]

Zink goes on to argue cogently that only in Froissart's later work, which includes the Rome manuscript redaction of Book I, does one encounter the chronicler's subtler literary effects, allied, paradoxically, to his most penetrating critique of contemporary chivalry and royal tyranny. This thesis can certainly be sustained, and accords with much that has been written in previous years by critics such as George Diller or the author of the present chapter.[21]

Yet it would be premature, in our view, to dismiss Book II so promptly, or to align it in every respect with the relatively less sophisticated prose of the earliest versions of Book I. For signs of the very unease on Froissart's part which Zink describes are already present, in fact, in several of the most consummately written narratives to be found in Book II. This is certainly true of his account of Louis de Male's funeral, which can – like that of Richard II's in Book IV – be read as an ironic if elegiac commentary on the last years of Louis' rule, and indeed of his life as a prince. But perhaps the most intriguing textual development in Book II, for present purposes, is the account provided of a battle which took place on 3 May 1382: the *Beverhoutsveld*, or field of the beaver hats. In the *Chroniques*, this battle serves as the instrument whereby Louis de Male's hubris begins to suffer condign punishment, as he and his allies from Bruges are roundly defeated by a ragtail army of no more than 5000 men of Ghent led by Philip van Artevelde. The sequel is well known: it involves the Count of Flanders hurrying from door to door through the streets of Bruges in search of somewhere to hide. That Froissart should have penned at least two quite distinct versions of the story is of no small account.[22]

Having counselled the people of Ghent not to surrender to Count Louis, who is hardly going to spare them after all, Philip rouses them to fight, on the grounds that they will in this wise at least retain their honour. Even if they are to die, they will have the satisfaction of knowing that the memory of their courage will live on after them. The Ghentish militia will be as it were a second Judith, bringing down the might of this new Nebuchadnezzar, Louis of Flanders. Froissart informs us at this point that 5000 men were duly selected to fight. He chooses this juncture in the narrative to impart the information that the people of Ghent had only seven waggonloads of provisions left to sustain them for the coming fray, comprising five laden with baked bread, and two with wine. Before their

20] Ibid., p. 110.
21] G. T. Diller, *Attitudes chevaleresques et réalités politiques chez Froissart*, Geneva, 1984; P. Ainsworth, *Jean Froissart and the Fabric of History*, Oxford, 1990; idem, 'Configurations of Transience in Jean Froissart's *Chroniques*: Intimations of *(Old) Mortality*', in *Froissart across the Genres*, ed. D. Maddox and S. Sturm-Maddox, Gainesville, 1998, pp. 15–39.
22] For more detailed analysis of this episode, see the essay referred to in n. 10, above.

departure, the 5000 warriors receive the blessings of their friends and families, who pray for their safe return. As they muster before the conflict, they hear a sermon delivered by friars attached to the host, on the theme of the Exodus:

> Et là leur fu remonstré par ces clers, Frères Menours et autres, comment il se figuroient au peuple d'Israël que li rois Faraon d'Egipte tint lonc tamps en servitude, et comment depuis, par la grace de Dieu, il en furent delivret et menet en tère de promision par Moïse et Aaron, et li rois Pharaon et li Egiptiien mort et peri. 'Enssi, bonnes gens, dissoient chil Frère Preceur en leurs sermons, estes vous tenu en servitude par vostre signeur le conte et vos voisins de Bruges'.[23]

> There it was explained to them by these men of religion, friars minor and others, how they might be compared to the people of Israel whom king Pharaoh of Egypt kept so long in servitude, and who by the grace of God were subsequently delivered and led into the Promised Land by Moses and Aaron, whilst Pharaoh and the Egyptians died and perished. 'In like manner, good people', said these preaching friars in their sermons, 'have you been held in servitude by your lord the Count and by your neighbours in Bruges.'

After hearing mass, the soldiers of Philip's urban militia prepare to consume their *earthly* bread and wine, but they have first to listen to yet another sermon, this time delivered by Philip van Artevelde himself. He serves here as the chronicler's chosen mouthpiece for words recalling those of St Paul in I Corinthians 11, about the proper manner in which to partake of the Lord's Supper. The harangue also reminds the attentive reader of Jesus' words in Luke IX ('No one who puts his hand to the plough and looks back is fit for the kingdom of God'), a chapter which coincidentally includes the evangelist's account of the Feeding of the Five Thousand with five loaves and two fish. We have here, it would seem, a typological superimposition of Exodus and Salvation, with the miracle of the Feeding in turn overlaid with the Last Supper. Froissart's account of the ensuing *déjeuner sur l'herbe* steers just this side of blasphemy, lending as it does a tragic pathos to the scene and its eventual outcome, a victory for the new Israelites from Ghent:

> A ces paroles se ordonnèrent il mout humblement, et furent les chars deschargiés et les sachiées de pain données et departies par connestablies et li tonnel de vin tourné sus le fons. Là desjeunèrent il de pain et de vin raisonnablement et en heurent pour l'eure chascuns assés, et se trouvèrent après le desjunner fors et en bon point et plus aidables et mieux aidant de leurs membres que se il eussent plus mengié.[24]

23] J. Froissart, *Chroniques*, ed. S. Luce, G. Raynaud, L. and A. Mirot, 15 vols, Paris, 1869–. See Vol. X (ed. Raynaud), pp. 221–22.
24] Ibid., Vol. X, p. 223.

> Upon hearing these words they came together in an orderly and humble fashion; the waggons were unloaded, and portions of bread distributed to each according to their divisions, whilst the wine tuns were up-ended on the spot. There they partook of bread and wine in a fitting and proper manner, and each had enough according to his needs; and after they had eaten they found themselves strong and alert, and as nimble as though they had eaten a great deal more.

The outcome – Louis' defeat and subsequent humbling at the hands of an army of townsmen – is equally interesting, yet the richly-layered, typological narrative of the preliminaries to the conflict deserves our close attention because of the subtle manner in which it invites the reader to re-read the circumstances, and to query the moral probity of the parties involved, as well as the outcome. Other, equally subversive devices employed in Book II (found elsewhere only in Books III and IV) include the use of synecdoche and symbol to convey the workings of Nemesis.[25] In short, one does not have to wait until Book III, let alone Book IV, to find symptoms of growing disillusion on Froissart's part, or to find him using rhetorical devices which foreground spatial and poetic relations within a chronological narrative, and which have the direct effect of conveying to the reader the chronicler's potential for at least adumbrating moral and political dilemmas, or judgements.[26] In sum, whilst most of Book II as we know it is in many respects avowedly a 'continuation' of the *earlier* versions of Book I, it does not unfailingly espouse their more palpable enthusiasm for chivalric ideology.

Clearly, then, Book II has every entitlement to independent existence and critical recognition; yet there is at least one other respect in which its existence might with some justification be called into question. The problem this time is material and codicological, rather than thematic or ideological. We know at least something of Froissart's movements in the 1380s. Zink reminds us that the chronicler was to lose his patron, Wenceslas of Brabant, in 1383, and that it was at about the same time that he became more closely associated with a French patron, Gui de Châtillon, who, until he sold his birthright (the county of Blois) to Louis of Touraine in 1391, was to remain the writer's prime patron and source of patronage.[27] We know that Froissart had already accompanied Gui de Châtillon on the punitive military campaign of 1382 led by Charles VI and his uncles against the Flemish rebels. That campaign was to issue in the victory of

25] See P. Ainsworth, 'Knife, Key, Bear and Book: Poisoned Metonymies and the Problem of *translatio* in Froissart's later *Chroniques*', *Medium Aevum*, Vol. LIX, 1990, pp. 91–113.

26] See our discussion of the notion of 'redress', in Ainsworth, 'Configurations of Transience', pp. 16–20. Cf. Zink (*Froissart et le temps*, p. 52): 'Ne sait-il pas admirablement – et de mieux en mieux à mesure que sa carrière avance et qu'il acquiert plus d'expérience – montrer les réticences, les violences, les trahisons enrobées dans le discours féodal de la fidélité?'.

27] *Froissart et le temps*, pp. 10–13.

Roosebeke, and in the subsequent death of Philip van Artevelde. We have no certain knowledge of what the chronicler was doing between 1383 and 1384, but in 1385 we find him present at a double marriage in Cambrai which united the son and daughter of another patron, Albrecht of Bavaria, to the daughter and son of Philip, Duke of Burgundy. Instrumental in the arranging of this double wedding had been the widow of Wenceslas of Brabant, the Duchess Jeanne. The ceremony, we are told, took place in the presence of Charles VI. We know that Froissart attended another wedding in 1386, because he commemorates the event in one of his *pastourelles*.[28] This time it was Gui de Châtillon's own son, Louis, who was marrying Marie, daughter of John, Duke of Berry. Later that year, Froissart made his way to the Flemish port of Sluys, where he waited in vain with many others for the departure of the ultimate invasion force, portable towns and all, which was destined for England but never set sail. The *Chroniques* are unusually forthright in their criticism of the fiasco, and in particular of the waiting-game played by the Duke of Berry (though J. W. Sherborne has pointed out that Charles VI was getting cold feet, too).[29]

This brings us to 1387, when Froissart is at Blois completing the second book of his *Chroniques*.[30] Book II covers events that had taken place between 1378 and 1385, yet the processes and phases involved in the composition of Book II are far from straightforward. To be fair to Michel Zink, he does use the verb 'achever' ('to complete'), and is at least as aware as the present writer of the issues explored in the remainder of this chapter. But the image suggested ('En 1387 il est à Blois chez le comte et il achève le livre II des *Chroniques*' ['In 1387 he was at Blois, staying with the count, and there he completed Book II of the *Chroniques*']), though useful as a rough chronological guide, is above all convenient for present purposes in that it provides an ironic *antitype* to what must actually have occurred, as what modern critics refer to as 'Book II' gradually came into existence. Two points need underscoring. First, we cannot be absolutely certain that it was Froissart who 'finished' Book II of the *Chroniques* as we have it, even though there can be no doubt that the chronicler was working on what we may call a 'Book II *text*' in the course of 1387. Every self-respecting Froissart scholar is entirely convinced that this work was to all intents and purposes complete by the time he set out the following year on his journey to Béarn (which was to issue in the compilation of what we now call Book III). Yet whatever he wrote during those months may not, in the final analysis, be precisely coterminous with what we may read in the earliest extant manuscript that we possess for 'Book II': the Leiden codex.[31]

28] Ibid., p. 11.
29] J. W. Sherborne, 'Charles VI and Richard II', in *Froissart: Historian*, ed. J. J. N. Palmer, Woodbridge and Totowa, NJ, 1981, pp. 58–59.
30] *Froissart et le temps*, p. 11.
31] The Leiden codex is described thus: 'Jean Froissart, *Chroniques*, Book II. Added at the end (in another hand): letters from Henry of England to Louis of Orléans, 1402–1403 (fol. 224–229v). Early 15th century. Parchment, 229 fols' (J. P. Gumbert, 'Medieval

Even the latter was to undergo a complex process of rewriting and 'cut-and-paste' before it surfaced in what Gaston Raynaud refers to as the first family of the 'primitive' redaction of Book II.[32] The second point to be made is more straightforward. It is, quite simply, that as far as Froissart himself was concerned, there may never have been any such entity as a Book II or *Deuxième Livre*.

The argument is, of course, partly rhetorical. A number of incipits to what may be termed 'complete sets' of the *Chroniques* inform us that they are 'devisées en quatre parties' (divided into four parts). But these sets are, virtually without exception, from the very latest period of Froissart manuscript production (1450–70), compiled in workshops employed by the Valois dukes of Burgundy. Earlier manuscripts can be not a little disconcerting to the unwary: BNF, ms. fr. 2650, for example, copied early in the fifteenth century, concludes with the words, 'Cy fine le second livre des Croniques Froissart, contenant des aventures de France et d'Angleterre' ('Here ends the second book of Froissart's *Chroniques*, containing events in both France and England'); yet this 'second livre' is in fact the text used by the Société de l'Histoire de France for its edition of *Book III*. The explanation is a simple one: an earlier tome, now lost, almost certainly contained a text for what we know as Books I and II. For the copyist at least, the codex containing his text of Book III was, in consequence, the '*second* livre des Croniques Froissart'. Several manuscripts of Book I, including BNF, ms. fr. 2641, subdivide the text into eight 'livres',[33] and an even more interesting case is provided by Mons, Bibliothèque centrale de l'Université, ms. 240/359: here, no distinction is made between Books III and IV, either in the text or the Table (which lists the chapters from 1 to 196).[34]

In most 'sets', in fact, the second volume generally contains the text of what

---

Manuscripts in French in the Leiden University Library: A Handlist', in *Medieval Codicology, Iconography, Literature, and Translation. Studies for Keith Val Sinclair*, ed. P. R. Monks and D. D. R. Owen, Leiden, New York and Cologne, 1994, p. 38). See also *Oeuvres de Froissart*, ed. J. Kervyn de Lettenhove, 25 vols, Brussels, 1870–77, Vol. I$^{2-3}$, pp. 365–66, 415.

32] Froissart, *Chroniques*, SHF edn, Vol. IX (ed. Raynaud), Introduction, p. vi. In this edition, the text of the Leiden manuscript occupies Vol. IX, § 83 (p. 119) to the end of Vol. XI inclusive.

33] See *Oeuvres de Froissart*, ed. J. Kervyn de Lettenhove, Vol. I$^{2-3}$, pp. 201–02.

34] Ibid., pp. 250–51, 330. Incipit du Troisième Livre (fol. 394): 'Cy commenche l'autre partye principale des Croniques messire Jehan Froissart qui contient les guerres ...' ('Here begins the other main part of the *Chroniques* of messire Jean Froissart which contains the wars ...'). The Table announces the beginning of Book III as follows: 'Cy commenche la tierce partye principalle des croniques ...' ('Here begins the third main part of the *Chroniques* ...'). Brussels, Bibliothèque Royale, ms. II 88 (Jean Froissart, *Chroniques*, Books I, II, and III, fragments) has the following incipit for Book III (fol. 16): 'Ci commence l'autre partie principale des Croniques sire Jehan Froissart qui contient les nouvelles guerres ...' ('Here begins the other main part of the *Chroniques* of Sir Jean Froissart which contains the recent wars ...') (transcriptions by Godfried Croenen). See *Chroniques*, ed. J. Kervyn de Lettenhove, Vol. I$^{2-3}$, pp. 248–50.

we call Book II; but it was not always so. As Kervyn de Lettenhove himself explains, 'The division according to books has not been retained, there being no basis for it in any of the oldest manuscripts. Notwithstanding, there can be no doubt that the division itself originated with Froissart; we shall therefore use this division in our Introduction, as it is so familar to the chronicler's readers.'[35] The task of establishing exactly where the 'Deuxième Livre' proper begins and ends may well constitute the last frontier of Froissart studies, at least as far as the *Chroniques* are concerned. The surest guide, in this respect, may be the Amiens redaction of Book I, publication of which is now complete.[36] Its text ends with the death of the Black Prince in 1376 and the subsequent accession of the eleven-year-old Richard II – but also with the piecemeal loss of virtually all of the remaining Anglo-Gascon possessions in Poitou and Aquitaine. On almost the final folio of the Amiens manuscript, Froissart announces a forthcoming section on the Duke of Burgundy, before breaking off rather abruptly at the end of Diller's § 944 with a promise to deal with the Duke of Anjou's campaign against the remaining Anglo-Gascon fortresses, 'quant j'en seray mieus enfourmés' ('when I shall be better informed').[37] There is no announcement, at this juncture, of any Second Book.

Book I is of epic proportions. In some of the extant manuscripts it overlaps with the beginning of what modern editors have *published* as 'Book II' (the common ground is constituted by §§ 1–82 of Volume IX of the Société de l'Histoire de France edition, which ends on page 119), usually derived from the second *tome* of two-, three- or four-volume manuscript 'sets'. This factor, taken together with the writer's avowed need, expressed at the very end of the Amiens manuscript version, to procure further information, may, as Diller has suggested,[38] account for the decision taken by Froissart or a scribe, or even a patron, to make the cut between *tomes* I and II at this juncture. But there may have been at least one other factor at work. It is in the Amiens manuscript that Froissart refers to his work as 'nostre histoire des rois' ('our history of kings').[39] In a redaction increasingly marked by the need not to offend pro-French sentiment, but written by Edward III's greatest admirer, news in 1376 of the recent death of the Black Prince must have caused the chronicler to draw breath. He may have had no thoughts at all of a 'Book II' as such, at this moment. What is clear is that the material end of the Amiens MS redaction (and of several other manuscripts for

35] Ibid., p. 183.
36] Jean Froissart, *Chroniques. Livre I. Le manuscrit d'Amiens. Bibliothèque municipale no. 486*, ed. G. T. Diller, 5 vols, Geneva, 1991–1998. The text occupies Vols I–IV.
37] Jean Froissart, *Chroniques. Livre I. Le manuscrit d'Amiens. Bibliothèque municipale no. 486. Tome I: depuis le règne d'Edouard II jusqu'à l'ouverture des hostilités entre le roi de France et le roi d'Angleterre (1307–1340)*, ed. G. T. Diller, Geneva, 1991, p. 382. See the review by the present author in *French Studies*, Vol. XLVII, 1993, pp. 60–61.
38] Ibid., Vol. I, p. xxii.
39] Ibid., Vol. IV, pp. 165–66.

Book I) leads logically into the opening of the text provided by most manuscript 'sets' as the start of *tome* II: for instance, § 933 of Amiens announces the Schism, which is picked up again early in *tome* II at §§ 36–39 in the edition published by the Société de l'Histoire de France.[40] However, what editors of the *Chroniques* generally designate as 'Book II' does not appear to commence *thematically* – a modern preoccupation, of course – until Froissart begins his account of the wars in Flanders (announced at the end of SHF, Vol. IX, § 100, and begun at § 101 – though without a full-scale prologue).[41] Yet the opening folios of the earliest manuscripts of Book II[42] offer us a text which in Raynaud's tome IX begins even earlier, at his § 83 ('Vous avés bien chi dessus oï recorder comment li sire de Moucident se tourna françois...' ['You have had it recorded above how the lord of Moucident "turned" French']).[43] For this text, Raynaud published the Leiden manuscript, Vossius fol. gall. 9 II: it offers a 'freestanding' text of what he terms the primitive redaction of Book II. This version is not preceded by any extant, related codex containing a version of Book I. A *revised* version commences at Raynaud's § 1.[44] Of this (moderately) revised version, Raynaud published only the section covered by his §§ 1–82 inclusive, using for the purpose BNF, ms. fr. 5006, from fol. 78v.

Clearly, much more work needs to be done on the origins, status and material identity of 'Book II' and its different manuscript families. Any scholar willing to grasp this particular nettle will have to address other problems that can only be sketched here. These include the still uncertain status of the version of the Flemish Wars section of 'Book II' which we now call the 'Chronique de Flandre' and which is contained in BNF, ms. fr. 5004 (two manuscript fragments of this version are held at the Bibliothèque Municipale, Cambrai).[45] Did it precede or follow the composition of 'Book II', whatever that is? And what are we to make of the Middle Dutch translation, which contains some material ostensibly not based on its supposed Middle French model, and which may therefore derive, ultimately, from a version of 'Book II' now almost certainly lost to scholars?[46] Questions such as these are waiting to be addressed, whilst new editions of both

40] SHF edn, Vol. IX, pp. 48–54.
41] Ibid., Vol. IX, p. 158 (start of § 101).
42] Raynaud's *rédaction primitive, première famille*.
43] SHF edn, Vol. IX, p. 119.
44] Yet another manuscript family follows this pattern, but with an initial interpolation of the closing section of tome I, as found at the end of the preceding codex which usually accompanies it, i.e., Book I, § 788 in the SHF edition.
45] Cambrai, Bibliothèque Municipale, ms. 677, Molinier catalogue no. 746 (incomplete at the beginning) and ms. 700, Molinier catalogue no. 792 (has no rubrics and is incomplete at the end). See also *Oeuvres de Froissart*, ed. J. Kervyn de Lettenhove, Vol. I$^{2-3}$, pp. 99–104.
46] *Jehan Froissart's Cronyke van Vlaenderen getranslateert uuten Franssoye in Duytscher tale bij Gerijt Potter van der Loo in de XVe eeuw*, ed. N. de Pauw, 2 vols, Ghent, 1898–1909.

the Middle French *Chronique de Flandre* and its Middle Dutch avatar are currently in preparation.[47] One thing at least is certain: any solutions that may, in time, be found to the conundrums outlined in this chapter, however tentative they may be, can only enrich our understanding of the complex manuscript tradition of the *Chroniques*, and renew our respect for the sheer complexity underlying their author's methods of composition.

* * * * *

The reader may now grasp more easily why identifying the ideal, publishable text for 'Book II' is not an altogether straightforward business. Neither Kervyn de Lettenhove nor Gaston Raynaud suffered any pangs of conscience when preparing their editions of Leiden Vossius fol. gall. 9 II. Faced with the challenge of preparing an edition of 'Book II' for the 'Lettres Gothiques' series, the author of the present chapter found himself rejecting the Leiden codex, even though it almost certainly contains the earliest extant text (finished *c.* 1403–4). For a start, the printed version of the Leiden manuscript occupies no less than three volumes of about three hundred pages each, in the Société de l'Histoire de France edition. Written in a Middle French strongly flavoured with Picard forms and spellings, it offers a coherent text, but one that is nine hundred pages long and extremely diffuse and repetitive, as well as likely to prove rebarbative to the modern, non-specialist reader. Given that the 'Lettres Gothiques' edition – to comprise, in theory, as much as possible from Books I and II – is to occupy no more than a single volume, the editors were in any case obliged to look elsewhere for a solution. The manuscript finally chosen contains a complete text for a version of Book II which almost certainly derives directly from the Leiden codex text. It can safely be described as genuine Froissart, but is the fruit of a consummate copy-editing operation on the part of either Froissart himself or a shrewd copyist. Pleonasms, redundant formulae and patronising *rappels* are all systematically expunged. Yet virtually nothing essential is lost, and the narrative flows smoothly and intelligibly from start to finish. A further advantage is that the manuscript selected is written in relatively unmarked Middle French. There are just enough tell-tale picardisms to prove that it was copied from a Picard original, whilst a scattering of Burgundian traits sets it within the south Champagne area. According to Raynaud, it belongs to the same redaction as Leiden Vossius fol. gall. 9 II, but given that it is only a third of its length, thanks to the ingenious copy-editing technique referred to above, the difference between the two *families* emerges as much greater than one might have expected. This in itself would lead one to conclude that the remaining families and their manuscripts may yet have surprises in store for editors of the *Chroniques*.

47] By Dr Godfried Croenen, Research Fellow, Dept of French, University of Liverpool.

The manuscript chosen for the 'Lettres Gothiques' edition is now kept at the Morgan Library in New York, shelfmarked M.804.[48] It was copied between 1404 and 1410, though part of its decoration may have been completed no earlier than 1418–20. Folios 1–260 contain an excellent text for the 'première rédaction proprement dite' (first redaction) of Book I (possibly the earliest version in prose). The last third of the codex (folios 265–363, plus a Table of chapters for Book II at folios 261–264v) offers the text known to Kervyn de Lettenhove as the 'second series of the first redaction of Book II'. Gaston Raynaud, in contrast, believed that there was only one *rédaction* of Book II, divisible into several different 'branches', each characterised by minor differences of detail: incipits, explicits or transposed, omitted or additional chapters, etc.

The text for Book II provided by the Morgan Library manuscript derives immediately, it would appear, from the oldest extant version, of which only three manuscripts survive (MSS *A* 1, *A* 2 and *A* 3 respectively), belonging to what Raynaud called the 'first family of the primitive redaction'. They are: Universiteitsbibliotheek, Leiden Vossius fol. gall. 9 II;[49] Bibliothèque Royale Albert 1er, Brussels, ms. IV 1102; and the former ms. 148 of Lord Ashburnham's library, now BNF, nouv. acq. fr. 9606. Unlike the other two manuscripts, the Leiden codex is almost entirely without decoration or ornament, save for some rubrication.

According to Raynaud, Morgan Library ms. M.804 (which he designated *A* 5) belonged to the second family of this primitive redaction. Only one other witness to this family survives, BL, Arundel ms. 67.II (Raynaud's *A* 4) – used by the 'Lettres Gothiques' editor whenever faced with a defective lesson or lacuna in the New York manuscript. If we return for a moment to the text of Book I, Léon Mirot posited a strong connection between the *Book I* text of the Morgan Library manuscript and manuscripts BNF, mss. fr. 2640 (copied by Raoul Tainguy du Chastel), 2657 (paper), 2662 and 2675 (all of which have a Book I text with identical or similar incipit and explicit, and all of which have miniatures of a similar style). This further compounds and complicates our understanding of how Morgan Library ms. M.804 may have been copied, collated, decorated and disseminated. It is worth noting, in this respect, that Kervyn de Lettenhove identified BNF, mss. fr. 2664 and 2658 (as well as Bibliothèque Municipale, Besançon, ms. 864, and a manuscript from Sir Thomas Phillipps' collection at Cheltenham) as belonging to a *première rédaction* of Book II, characterised by the incipit: 'Vous avés bien cy-dessus oy recorder comment li sires de Mucident, etc' ('You have heard it recorded above how the lords of Mucident, etc.').[50]

48] See my essay, 'A Parisian in New York: Pierpont Morgan Library MS. M.804 Revisited', in *Text and Image: Studies in the French Illustrated Book from the Middle Ages to the Present Day*, ed. D. J. Adams and A. Armstrong, special issue of the *Bulletin of the John Rylands University Library of Manchester*, Vol. 81, 1999, pp. 127–51.
49] Used by Raynaud in SHF edn from § 83, and by Kervyn de Lettenhove in Vol. IX ff.
50] *Oeuvres de Froissart*, ed. J. Kervyn de Lettenhove, Vol. I$^{2-3}$, pp. 242–44.

Clearly, we are far from done with Book II. Froissart may have finished with it by the end of 1387, but critics do not know for certain when he actually started it (*c.* 1376?), and it is certainly not clear that he ever quite decided where it began as a narrative in its own right – if, indeed, it ever did – or whether he conceived it at any point in its genesis as an independent work with fixed beginning and conclusion. Much more research remains to be done on subsequent redactions and families, identified but not described in any detail by Raynaud. Perhaps the most fitting conclusion to this chapter is furnished by the explicit of the Morgan Library manuscript. At the bottom of folio 363 the scribe has written:

> Cy fine le second livre
> maistre Jehan Frossart
> *Iste liber pertinet* … (No name supplied)
>
> Here ends the Second Book
> Of Master Jean Froissart
> This book belongs to …

3
Alain Chartier and the Arts of Crisis Management, 1417–1429

JAMES LAIDLAW

In the Tradition of the *Orateurs*

In the summer of 1422 Alain Chartier addressed an open letter to the princes, nobility, clergy and common people of France:

> A la treshaulte et excellente majesté des princes, a la treshonnouree magnificence des nobles, circumspection des clers et bonne industrie du peuple françoys, Alain Charretier, humble secretaire du roy nostre sire et de mon tresredoubté seigneur, monseigneur le regent, loingtain imitateur des orateurs, salut en crainte de Dieu, humiliacion soubz sa justice, cognoissance de ses jugemens et retourner a sa misericorde soubs la pointure de sa punicion.[1]

> To the most high and excellent majesty of the princes, to the most honoured magnificence of the nobles, the circumspection of the clergy and the good industry of the people of France, Alain Chartier, humble secretary of our lord the King and of my most revered lord, my lord the Regent, and distant imitator of the Orators, greetings and prayers for salvation in the fear of God, humiliation under His justice, awareness of His judgements and a return to His mercy under the pricks of His punishment.

The opening salutation of the *Quadrilogue Invectif* takes a traditional form, but is greatly expanded to allow Chartier to present his credentials. He is secretary to Charles VI, *le roy nostre sire*, and to the regent, the dauphin, who was shortly to succeed to the throne as Charles VII. Chartier is both secretary and man of letters, schooled in the works of the *orateurs* whom he will imitate, however distantly. He is schooled also in religion, as his conclusion makes clear. The salutation used by the royal chancellery usually ended with *salut* or *salut et dilection*,[2]

1] Toulouse, Bibliothèque municipale MS 826, fol. 1r. See also *Alain Chartier: Le Quadrilogue Invectif*, ed. E. Droz, rev. edn, Paris, 1950, p. 1.

2] For examples see C. J. H. Walravens, *Alain Chartier: études biographiques, suivies de pièces justificatives, d'une description des éditions et d'une édition des ouvrages inédits*, Amsterdam, 1971, pp. 152, 158–61. *Salut*, 'salutations, greetings' and 'salvation'; the word conveys both those meanings. *Dilection*, 'affection, love'.

three words at most, but here it is developed to enjoin repentance and amendment of life. Chartier, secretary and man of letters, is also a man of God, who had been appointed a canon of Notre-Dame de Paris two years earlier.[3]

Letters of the period traditionally ended with information about when and where they were written, but this one does not, for it is interrupted. Weariness causes the author to fall asleep and to dream the dream which forms the framework of the *Quadrilogue Invectif* proper, a dialogue between Dame France and the three estates of the realm, Nobility, Clergy and Common People. A passage in which Chartier represents Henry V of England glorying in the defeats inflicted on the French shows that the work was composed in the summer of 1422:

> Comme doncques, en l'an mil cccc vint et deux, je veysse le roy angloys, ancien adversaire de ceste seigneurie, soy glorifier en nostre ignominieux reprouche, enrichir de noz despoilles et desprisier noz faiz et noz courages, et des nostres qu'il a vers soy actraiz fortiffier les volentés en son aliance, et avec ce noz vices croistre avec le temps et noz avuglees affections adjouster tousjours quelque chose a nostre confusion, j'ay conclud en ma pensee que la main de Dieu est sur nous et que sa fureur a mis en euvre ce flaiel de persecucion. Si ay curieusement encerchié par les discours des Saintes Escriptures les faultes et les punicions de noz perez et des premerains et en grant crainte debatu en ma pensee se ceste doloreuse affliction est en verge de pere pour nostre chasti ou en rigueur de juge pour nostre exterminacion.[4]

> Since therefore in the year 1422 I saw the English king, the ancient enemy of this dominion, glory in our ignominy and shame, grow rich on our spoils, hold our deeds and our courage in contempt, and strengthen the wills of those of our party whom he has attracted to ally themselves with him, and since I also saw our vices grow greater with time and the blindness of our passions continually add to our confusion, my reflections have led me to conclude that the hand of God is upon us and that His fury has unleashed this plague and persecution. I have therefore carefully searched in the passages of Holy Scripture for the errors and punishments which affected our fathers and the earliest generations of men, and have in great fear debated in my thoughts whether these painful afflictions are to be seen as a father's rod applied for our chastisement or the severity of a judge, intended to cause our extermination.

A royal secretary would naturally begin the year at Easter, following the practice of the French chancellery, and so the *Quadrilogue* can be dated after 12 April 1422 and before the death of Henry V on 31 August of that same year.

The *Quadrilogue* was inspired by the threat of further English offensives

3] *The Poetical Works of Alain Chartier*, ed. J. C. Laidlaw, Cambridge, 1974, p. 26.
4] Toulouse MS 826, fol. 2v; *Quadrilogue Invectif*, pp. 4–5.

which, if successful, might well lead to the fall of France. Chartier's purpose is to unite the nation against the English, France's old enemy, and to rally support to the dauphin and regent. The work was written south of the Loire, somewhere in the territories which had been ruled by the dauphin since his escape from Paris on 29 May 1418 after the city was seized by the Burgundians. Alain Chartier was one of a very small number of royal secretaries who followed the dauphin into 'exile'.[5]

We can trace Chartier's career in detail over only twenty years, from some time after February 1409 until his death in March 1430 at Avignon. During those twenty years France was in a state of permanent crisis. The immediate cause was the murder of Louis, Duke of Orléans by followers of John the Fearless, Duke of Burgundy on 23 November 1407. Following Louis' death, the long-standing rivalry between the houses of Orléans and Burgundy was transformed into almost permanent civil war. It was not long before the English saw and seized the opportunities for conquest; Henry V's first campaign was marked by his dramatic victory achieved at Agincourt on 25 October 1415.[6] Chartier lived through the ups and downs of those twenty years – many more downs than ups. His role, assigned to him by Dame France in the *Quadrilogue Invectif*, is to fight with his pen and his tongue:

> Et puis que Dieu ne t'a donné force de corps ne usage d'armes, sers la chose publique de ce que tu puis, car autant exaulsa la gloire des Romains et renforça leurs courages a vertu la plume et langage des orateurs comme les glaives des combatans.[7]

> And since God has not given you strength of body or skill in arms, serve the public good in the ways that you can, for the pens and words of the Orators exalted the reputation of the Romans and strengthened their resolve just as much as did the swords of those who fought.

Chartier comments on contemporary events in very varied ways, for he is by turns secretary, ambassador, propagandist, poet, author, philosopher and theologian. Whatever form they take, his writings and orations are marked by his belief in God, his loyalty to the Crown, his love of France, and his awareness of human frailties. His God is the God of the Old as well as the New Testament, who works his purpose out in history and controls the fortunes of men and of nations.

5] 'Mon dolent exil' ('My unhappy exile') is the phrase used by Chartier himself. See *Alain Chartier: Le Livre de l'Espérance*, ed. F. Rouy, Paris, 1989, p. 1.
6] On the *Livre des Quatre Dames*, a long narrative poem inspired by the defeat of Agincourt, see *Poèmes d'Alain Chartier*, ed. J. Laidlaw, Paris, 1988, pp. 14–20, 43–138; J. Laidlaw, 'Les Belles Dames sans mercy d'Alain Chartier', *Autour de Marguerite d'Ecosse: reines, princesses et dames du XVe siècle*, ed. G. et P. Contamine, Paris, 1999, pp. 33–44.
7] Toulouse MS 826, fol. 32r; *Quadrilogue Invectif*, p. 65.

Secretary and Propagandist

The first known reference to Alain Chartier is in the household accounts of Yolande of Anjou, Queen of Jerusalem and Sicily, which run from 19 February 1409 to 19 September 1414. His name is included among the 'gens et officiers de l'ostel de ladicte dame [Yolande] et ses enfans' ('the members and officers of the household of the said lady [Yolande]') to whom money is owed, but the accounts do not tell us when he joined the household or what office he filled.[8] In the early stages of the conflict between the Burgundians and the Orléanists, the sympathies of the court of Anjou inclined towards Burgundy: King Louis II and Queen Yolande hoped that John the Fearless would provide them with the material support they needed to make a further attempt to conquer the kingdom of Sicily. Steps towards an alliance between the two houses were taken in 1410 when Catherine of Burgundy was betrothed to the young Louis of Anjou and came to live at the Angevin court, in accordance with the custom of the time. It was not long, however, before events in Paris, particularly the Cabochian revolt in the spring and summer of 1413, led the house of Anjou to change sides.

Following the Peace of Pontoise, negotiated in August 1413, the Burgundians lost control of the capital to the Orléanists or Armagnacs, as they came to be called. Realising that their interests would be best served by severing their ties with Burgundy, Louis and Yolande cancelled the marriage agreement, and Catherine of Burgundy was ceremonially returned to her parents in November 1413. The insult was public, the break complete, and years would pass before those two princely houses could be reconciled.[9] A month later, on 18 December 1413, the process of realignment was taken further by the betrothal of Marie of Anjou to Charles, Count of Ponthieu and third surviving son of Charles VI. In the closing months of 1413, therefore, the court of Anjou lost Catherine of Burgundy and gained Charles of France, who came to live in the house of his future bride. That news must have caused John the Fearless more irritation than alarm, for who could have predicted that less than four years later Charles would find himself dauphin after the death of his two older brothers?

From early in 1414, then, the queen's 'children', to use the term employed in her accounts, were to include Charles, who was brought up from the age of ten under the tutelage of Queen Yolande and her servants, at a court which had small love for Burgundy and increasingly supported the cause of the Armagnacs. The circumstances in which Charles was brought up were important, as Malcolm Vale has pointed out:

> Between [Charles'] betrothal, as a child of ten, in 1413, and his accession, as a youth of nineteen, in 1422, a governing group had formed round Charles. It

8] *Poetical Works*, pp. 2–3.
9] *La Chronique d'Enguerran de Monstrelet*, ed. L. Douet-d'Arcq, 6 vols, SHF, Paris, 1857–62, Vol. II, p. 414.

> was to be the source of many of his most able and most trusted servants. With the future wife of the dauphin came her formidable mother and her servants.[10]

Those servants included Alain Chartier, whose appointment as a royal secretary seems to date from the time when an independent household was formed to serve the new dauphin. The two earliest known royal letters signed by Chartier were written in September 1417, on behalf of Charles who had become dauphin five months earlier, on 4 April. The first letter, sent from Paris to the people of Tournai on 16 September, was prompted by the siege of Caen by the English; it requests and requires the despatch of troops, suitably equipped, to reinforce the royal army.[11] The letter is admirably succinct and persuasive: in less than 300 words it recalls the long-standing enmity between France and England, stresses how reasonably the French have always responded to English demands, and emphasises that the French have God and right on their side, before outlining the present emergency and indicating the measures to be taken. The second letter, written on 27 September 1417, confirms an exemption granted to the town of Villeneuve-Saint-Georges, and is of purely administrative interest.[12]

The absence of a complete catalogue of the letters of Charles VI and Charles VII means that our knowledge of Chartier's work in the royal Chancellery is fragmentary.[13] Analysis of the documents known to bear his signature shows that these two letters are broadly representative of the duties which he undertook between 1417 and 1428.[14] There was much routine administration, of which the letter to Villeneuve-Saint-Georges is a good example. The letter to Tournai, on the other hand, was written under pressure at a time of crisis. It was the first of many such documents: in the years which followed, Chartier was frequently given the task of composing letters or instructions of especial significance, difficulty or delicacy.

A letter written to Lyon on 31 January 1418 cautions the inhabitants that the Duke of Burgundy plans to seize the town, informs them that Queen Isabeau has been kidnapped by the duke, and warns them that he may make use of her to give his plans a veneer of legitimacy; on no account are they to open their gates

10] M. G. A. Vale, *Charles VII*, London, 1974, pp. 22–23.

11] G. du Fresne de Beaucourt, *Histoire de Charles VII*, 6 vols, Paris, 1881–91, Vol. I, pp. 437–38. See also Walravens, *Alain Chartier*, p. 149, where Beaucourt's text is reprinted, the original letter having been destroyed in 1940.

12] Arch. Nat., Y 10, fols 14v–15 (copy).

13] The catalogue of the letters of Charles VII to which Beaucourt refers in his *Histoire de Charles VII*, (Vol. I, pp. lxxxii–lxxxiv) was never published. Although no letter of Charles VI bearing Chartier's signature has been discovered, it is important to remember that he describes himself as one of the king's secretaries in the opening lines of the *Quadrilogue Invectif*.

14] For a list of these documents, see *Poetical Works*, pp. 18–21. Documents in French are signed 'Alain', those in Latin are signed 'Alani'. The fact that Chartier does not use his surname means that Alain, the secretary, has not always been identified with Alain Chartier, the writer.

either to the duke or the queen. The letter has been drafted as carefully as the missive sent to Tournai four months earlier. Burgundy's designs are described in language which is firm and direct: John the Fearless aims 'to sow dissension' ('mectre turbacion'), to pursue the same evil business ('malvaises entreprises') as he has elsewhere; he will have recourse to acts of sedition and other disloyal and senseless means ('sedicions et autres manieres desloyales et desraisonnables') to achieve his ends.[15]

In three further letters sent to Lyon four-and-a-half months later, Chartier's tone is very different.[16] The earlier threats from John the Fearless must have seemed relatively unimportant when compared with the crisis which followed the capture of Paris by the Burgundians on 29 May 1418. Two of the letters were written at Bourges on 13 June, a fortnight after the dauphin's escape, and the third followed some two weeks later. The letters mark the start of a propaganda campaign which aimed to win hearts and minds, to rally public opinion to the dauphin's cause, and to canvass the material support necessary to recapture Paris and to wage war on Burgundy and England.

The first two letters, both dated 13 June 1418, focus on the treachery of the Burgundians who had seized the capital at the very time when peace negotiations were being concluded. The city had been lightly defended, as Chartier is forced to acknowledge. The reasons he gives – the mood of optimism created by the expectation of peace, and the need to divert troops to engage the English – are less than convincing; one can sense his discomfort as he is forced to present lame excuses. The references to the slaughter, pillage and disorder which followed on the invasion are general, for detailed information must still have been scarce. Certain facts were already known, however: the rebels had captured the king, the queen and the dauphine; furthermore, the great seal had also fallen into enemy hands. Hence the need to warn Lyon (and no doubt other loyal towns) to place credence only in documents sealed with the privy seal and bearing the dauphin's signature.[17] Chartier takes care to state what is the basis of the dauphin's authority. As the king's only son, it falls to him to safeguard and preserve his father's kingdom; his authority derives both from natural law and from his father's commission, naming him lieutenant general of the kingdom.

The third letter, sent from Aubigny, just north of Bourges, on 29 June 1418, exactly a month after Paris had been occupied, shows that further information had reached the dauphin, who now realised the magnitude of the slaughter and destruction which had taken place in the capital. Between two and three thousand people have been killed, writes Chartier in a chilling account:

15] Walravens, *Alain Chartier*, p. 150.
16] Ibid., pp. 151–56.
17] The warning is repeated in the letter of 29 June 1418.

> Et depuis ces choses [*sc.* la fuite du Dauphin], et que nous les vous eusmes escriptes et fait savoir, les diz rebelles et desobeissans, non contens d'avoir fait et perpetré les maulx, crimes, desobeissances et cruaultez dessus diz, furieusement et desordonneement, comme gens sans congnoissance de Dieu et tout hors de la pitié humaine, se sont transportez en toutes les prisons qui estoient en la dicte ville et la ont inhumainement et crueusement meurdry et detrenchié les connetable et chancellier de mon dit seigneur, plusieurs prelas, evesques, chevaliers, escuiers, officiers de mon dit seigneur, et autres gens d'eglise, notables bourgeois et marchans, jusques au nombre de deux a trois mil personnes qui la estoient prisonniers, lesquelx, tailliez en pieces comme bestes, ilz ont tous mis, gectez et detraynez sur les quarreaux de la dicte ville, sans avoir aucune compassion de l'effusion du sang humain, et mesmes les femmes et enfans des dessus diz ont ilz occis, nayez et mis a mort, et mis ladicte ville, qui est chief de ce royaulme et a la quelle chascun doit avoir recours en justice, ainsi que a gast, perdicion et desolacion.[18]

> And since those events [leading to the flight of the dauphin] and since we wrote to tell you of them, the said rebels, disobedient [to our commands], not content with having committed and perpetrated the evils, crimes and acts of disobedience and cruelty above mentioned in a furious and disorderly manner, like people who do not know God and lack human pity, have betaken themselves to all the prisons in the said town and there have inhumanly and cruelly killed and cut to pieces the Constable and the Chancellor of my said lord, many prelates, bishops, knights, esquires and officers of my said lord, and other churchmen, prominent townspeople and merchants to a total of two to three thousand people who were prisoners there; and they have butchered them like beasts, and then taken, thrown and dragged them on to the streets of the said town, taking no pity for the shedding of human blood, and they have even killed, drowned and put to death the wives and children of those above mentioned, and in that way they have sacked, destroyed and laid waste the said town which is the capital of this realm, to which everyone should have recourse for justice.

The language of that long sentence is angry and high-coloured; nouns and verbs are combined in twos, threes or even fours to press the message home. Chartier's purpose is to shock and horrify the Lyonnais, and to persuade them to hold fast in their support for the cause of the king and the dauphin. In communicating the dauphin's outrage, Chartier is also expressing his own horror and shock. The royal officers who had been killed included friends and colleagues: royal secretaries such as Gontier Col and Jean de Montreuil, both of them Latinists of distinction, and professional men of letters such as the translator, Laurent de Premierfait, or

18] Walravens, *Alain Chartier*, pp. 154–55.

Ambrogio dei Migli, the Italian humanist.

Three months later we find Chartier involved in a more complicated exercise in public relations. All through the summer of 1418, efforts had been made to bring about a reconciliation between the dauphin and the Duke of Burgundy. Charles had reluctantly agreed to take part in peace negotiations and to send ambassadors to Corbeil for that purpose. The Duke of Brittany had volunteered to act as mediator and had been altogether too successful in that role, for he had taken it upon himself to reach an agreement with John the Fearless in the absence of the dauphin's envoys. The resulting 'peace' had been announced to the people of Paris amid general rejoicing.

The task of dissociating the dauphin from the Peace of Saint-Maur, as it is generally known today, fell to Alain Chartier, a task made all the more delicate because of the need not to alienate the Duke of Brittany, despite all the problems he had caused. The strategy adopted is simple, but effective: to lay all the blame at the door of the Duke of Burgundy, and to present the dauphin as the injured party who, despite all the wrongs done to him, has been prepared to turn the other cheek. Chartier rehearses the events of the previous five months, making reference to the earlier peace negotiations aborted by the capture of Paris, and to the outrageous crimes committed after the capital had fallen. Nonetheless, at the insistence of Queen Yolande and others, the dauphin has 'condescended' to resume peace negotiations with John the Fearless. The reference to the dauphin's condescension indicates that he occupies the moral and the feudal high ground. Chartier goes on to name the four ambassadors sent to Corbeil, and demonstrates his master's good faith by attaching to the letter a copy of the powers issued to the envoys. The proclamation of the 'peace' is represented as a *cautelle*, a 'cunning ruse' devised by Burgundy to mislead the common people. No credence is to be given to any missive purporting to announce a peace treaty unless it is sealed with the dauphin's own great seal and signed by his own hand. Any messages, written or oral, from the Duke of Burgundy or from the king's court – the phrase is a reminder that the king is not his own master – are to be disbelieved.

To parade the crimes and bad faith of John the Fearless and to blacken his name was relatively straightforward, an altogether easier task than to explain and excuse the conduct of the Duke of Brittany. The solution Chartier adopts is to present possibilities without adopting any of them:

> … nous avons entendu que, apres ce que nostre dit frere [*sc.* le duc de Bretagne] a esté vers Paris et que aux lieux de Charenton et de Saint Mor il a convenu avec le dit de Bourgogne, a laquelle convention nos ambaxeurs n'ont esté, ils ont, comme l'en dit, fait certain traitié entr'eulx sans nos dits ambaxadeurs, parce peut estre nostre dit frere n'estoit pas le plus fort et que, pour la cruauté qui regne par dela, il n'a pas osé debattre ainsi que la matiere le requiert ou autrement, ne sçavons comment et a été accordé le dit traictié,

jasoit ce que nos dits ambaxeurs eussent puissance de traictier, accorder et de conclure pour nous et non autre, et que nostre dit frere fust seulement mediateur sans avoir voulu prendre autre charge de nostre part, et toutesvoyes nos dits ambaxeurs n'y ont esté oys ni appellez, comme il promist par les lettres qu'ils ont escriptes sur ce.[19]

... we have heard that after our said brother [the Duke of Brittany] had been near Paris and had met with the said [Duke of] Burgundy at Charenton and Saint Maur, at which meeting our ambassadors were not present, they agreed between themselves, it is said, a certain treaty in the absence of our ambassadors, because our said brother was perhaps not the stronger of the two and because, by reason of the cruelty which is prevalent in that part of the world, he did not dare to provoke a discussion, as the matter requires, or for some other reason, we know not how, and so the said treaty was agreed, even though our said ambassadors, and only they, had powers to treat, agree and conclude on our behalf, and although our said brother was only a mediator, having been unwilling to undertake any other responsibility for us, and yet our ambassadors were neither heard nor summoned, as he promised by the letters which they have concerning that matter.

Perhaps the Duke of Brittany had not been the stronger of the two parties, perhaps he had not dared to provoke a discussion because of the cruelty which is prevalent in that part of the world. Those deliberately enigmatic words suggest that Brittany may have been bullied or browbeaten and serve to offer some excuse for his actions.

The letter just discussed is known only from an imperfect copy which was apparently addressed to the governor and people of Dauphiné on 29 September.[20] It was followed by others of similar tenor sent to Lyon on 14 and 31 October.[21] These three letters are all that seems to survive from what was almost certainly an energetic letter campaign which saw multiple copies being sent to towns and to royal officers throughout France, and not just to those parts of the country which remained loyal to the dauphin.

A third and much more important letter campaign followed the killing of John the Fearless at Montereau-fault-Yonne on 10 September 1419, and continued until February 1420. That campaign has been studied by Bernard Guenée, who gives an excellent account of the vigour with which the prolonged war of written words was conducted, particularly on the Burgundian side. His article is very informative about the mechanics of such operations in an age before

19] Walravens, *Alain Chartier*, p. 157.
20] BNF Coll., Anjou et Touraine, 9, no. 3827 (copy). The letter is published in *Pierre de Fenin: Mémoires*, ed. Mlle Dupont, SHF, Paris, 1837, pp. 272–73, and in Walravens, *Alain Chartier*, pp. 156–57.
21] Beaucourt, *Histoire de Charles VII*, Vol. I, pp. 472–73. The letter of 14 October was signed by Villebresme. Beaucourt does not say who signed the letter of 31 October.

photocopiers, computers, fax machines and electronic mail; it also reminds us that the sources available to us today are much more fragmentary than we had perhaps realised.[22] The dauphin's chancellery engaged in that war of written words with equal vigour. The survival of an unusually rich set of documents composed between 11 September and 15 October 1419 shows that Alain Chartier was once again entrusted with the preparation of particularly sensitive correspondence and instructions. The documents comprise letters to Paris and Carcassonne, to Duke Philip of Burgundy and his wife, Michelle, the dauphin's sister, together with instructions and an *aide-mémoire* for envoys sent to the Burgundian court.[23]

Chartier and the other officials who accompanied the dauphin to Montereau can have slept little on the night of 10 September, after John the Fearless was killed, for there was an urgent need to prepare the dauphin's version of how the duke had met his death. Then, as now, it was vital to be first with the news. The day after the murder, letters signed by the dauphin and by Alain Chartier were despatched to the city and to the University of Paris. Their two signatures appear also on a longer, more detailed letter sent to Carcassonne sixteen days later, on 27 September. Bernard Guenée has pointed out that one of the reasons why it took so long for the dauphin's letters to be dispatched was a shortage of manpower: he seems to have had only three secretaries available to him. Priority had to be given to informing Paris; it was no doubt hoped that no great harm would result if a dispatch to a faithful southern town like Carcassonne was sent over a fortnight after the Duke of Burgundy had been killed. Nonetheless, there was the risk that the first news to reach distant towns would be in letters from the king or from John the Fearless's widow or his heir. The king and queen were at Troyes when they learned what had happened at Montereau, whereupon the royal chancellery was put on an emergency footing. We are told that five clerks, working for four days and nights, produced 106 'pairs' of letters which were sent to different towns.[24] Further letters – but we do not know how many – were sent to the king's vassals and officers.

The letter to the city of Paris is an admirable piece of propaganda, all the more remarkable since it was composed under the pressure of events. Moreover, it serves as the template for documents prepared later. Chartier begins by stressing the dauphin's good faith, his statesmanship and his patience. The meeting at Montereau is presented as the continuation of an earlier encounter at Pouilly-le-Fort during which Charles had shown himself generous, conceding all the duke's demands in order to achieve his primary aim, a lasting peace. Before they

22] Guenée, 'Les Campagnes de lettres qui ont suivi le meurtre de Jean sans Peur, duc de Bourgogne (septembre 1419–février 1420)', *Annuaire-Bulletin de la Société de l'Histoire de France*, 1993, pp. 45–65.
23] Walravens, *Alain Chartier*, pp. 164–84.
24] Guenée, 'Campagnes de lettres', p. 51.

agreed to adjourn their talks, the duke had made certain promises which he failed to keep, in particular his promise to wage war on the English within a month of leaving Pouilly. The dauphin had come to Montereau at the time agreed for their second meeting, but had been kept waiting for eighteen days until the duke appeared. On his arrival, Charles had even vacated his quarters in the castle, making them available to the duke.

The interview itself began with the dauphin reproaching the duke for not keeping his word, especially for failing to attack the English and to withdraw his garrisons from certain towns. All this was done 'amiablement' ('in a friendly fashion'), writes Chartier. In response, the duke uttered 'plusieurs outrageuses paroles' ('many intemperate and presumptuous remarks'), and drew his sword with the intention of attacking the dauphin and taking him captive, as it later became clear. Thereupon Charles' followers came to his rescue, leaving the duke dead 'par son outrage' ('because of his temerity and presumption'). The dauphin is sure that the Parisians will rejoice at hearing of his fortunate escape; there is some irony in this observation made more in hope than in expectation. The letter concludes by urging the city to maintain the peace agreed with Burgundy and to concentrate attention on the war against the English.

The letter to Paris is relatively brief: the priority is to be first with the news. When he writes separate letters to the Duke and Duchess of Burgundy four days later and prepares accompanying instructions for the dauphin's envoy, the Count of Aumale, Chartier has time to pen a more circumstantial account. He is able to make use of the intelligence gathered in the interim, partly from interrogation of the members of the duke's entourage who had been taken prisoner. He includes a much more detailed account of John the Fearless's activities in the two months which had separated the meetings at Pouilly and Montereau. During that time, the duke is said to have opened fresh negotiations with the English, to have surrendered the town of Pontoise to them, and to have entered into an alliance against the dauphin with 'aucuns seditieux de Paris' ('some seditious inhabitants of Paris'). The account of the duke's death is materially different from that given earlier. The Sire de Navailles,[25] not John the Fearless himself, is said to have been the first to draw his sword. However, the duke had also made a hostile move: '[il] s'efforça de attempter a nostre personne' ('he endeavoured to attack our person'), is how Chartier puts it. As a result, the dauphin's followers, mindful of the duke's past actions and remembering above all the fate of Louis, Duke of Orléans, had rushed to defend their master.

It was hardly surprising that the Count of Aumale failed in his mission, for the court of Burgundy had by then heard the very different account of events at Montereau given by two servants of the Sire de Navailles who swore that John

25] 'Nouailles' is the form given by Walravens (*Alain Chartier*, pp. 166, 168, 172). On Archambaud de Foix, Sire de Navailles see R. Vaughan, *John the Fearless: The Growth of Burgundian Power*, London, 1966, pp. 276–77, 279.

the Fearless had been attacked by the dauphin's men, with Tanguy du Chastel as ringleader. In any case, no ambassador who arrived from the dauphin's court less than a fortnight after the duke's death could have expected to be received with anything but suspicion and hostility, however carefully his letters of credence and his instructions had been prepared. A month later, Regnier Pot, the dauphin's second envoy, fared no better. The *aide-mémoire* which he was charged to present to Duke Philip covers the same ground as Aumale's instructions, but at greater length. In fine, the dauphin's letter campaign was a failure. By letters patent of 17 January 1420, Charles VI adjudged the dauphin guilty of parricide and stripped him of his right to succeed to the throne. Four months later there followed the Treaty of Troyes which acknowledged Henry V of England as heir to the French throne following his marriage to Katherine of France.

Propaganda and Diplomacy 1419–27

The documents considered so far were written under pressure, as Chartier and the other officers of the chancellery reacted to one emergency after another. But the continuing crisis also demanded measures which, it was hoped, would have effect over the longer term. It was essential to keep up the morale of the dauphin's supporters and to win wider support for his cause both in France and abroad. Chartier plays an important role in these campaigns, as propagandist and as royal envoy.

His letter *Ad universitatem parisiensem*, written before the murder of the Duke of Burgundy in September 1419, is the first of a series of works in which Chartier sought to rally support for his master.[26] Having described the miseries of life in war-torn France, he entreats the university to embrace the cause of peace, and to urge the parties to the civil war to repent and to seek divine forgiveness. Unless they do so, the kingdom risks even harsher punishment at God's hands and faces annihilation. Almost three years later, Chartier returns to these themes in the *Quadrilogue Invectif*. As he surveys the calamitous state of France and asks himself whether the kingdom's destruction may not be part of the divine plan, the author falls asleep. In his dream he witnesses a dialogue between France and her three children, the estates of the realm. The three estates are depicted in different poses of inactivity in front of the house of France, which is tottering, on the point of collapse. As Chartier watches, France stretches out her arm just in time to prevent a section of wall collapsing:

> Lors que ceste dame regarda cellui seigneurieux edifice et maison royal presque cheoir, elle, qui leans avoit esté nourrie en habondance de biens et d'onneurs, descouvri de dessoubz son mantel l'un de ses braz couvert et paré de fleurs de

26] *Les Œuvres latines d'Alain Chartier*, ed. P. Bourgain-Hemeryck, Paris, 1977, pp. 221–24.

lis et de daulphins en quartiers, et estayoit le costé qui plus lui penchoit et par pesante s'enclinoit et tiroit grant partie du surplus a tendre en ruine, et contretenoit de cellui bras le plus principal pan de mur et qui portoit le branle du surplus, et neantmoins se dementoit et decrevoit en pluseurs lieux et les [*ms*: des] principaulx pilliers s'enclinoient aux fes des aucuns. Or fu moult fort grevee de si long [*ms*: loing] travail, sy se retourna, le visage couvert de lermes, a l'entour / [fol. 5r] de soy, comme desireuse de secours et contrainte par besoing.[27]

When this lady looked at that seigneurial edifice and royal house which was on the point of collapse, she, who had been brought up there, surrounded by abundant wealth and honours, reached out from beneath her cloak one of her arms covered and adorned with a coat of arms (quarterly, fleurs-de-lis and dolphins), and she held up the side which was leaning out most towards her and was causing much of the superstructure to fall into ruins, and with that arm she supported the main stretch of wall which was withstanding the movement in the superstructure, and nonetheless many parts of it were collapsing and falling apart and the main pillars were leaning out because of the weight of the others. She was greatly wearied by such long travail and, with her face bathed in tears, she looked around her, seeking help and compelled to do so in her necessity.

The armorial bearings which adorn the arm with which France supports the collapsing wall are those of the dauphin whom Chartier depicts as the kingdom's literal mainstay.

France speaks first, followed by the Knight and the People who speak twice each, exercising their right of reply. The tone is harsh, critical, and largely negative. The Knight and the People blame each other roundly for the decline in the nation's fortunes, and are reluctant to accept their full share of responsibility for the disaster which threatens. There is no sense of national unity, no hint that either estate is prepared to subordinate its interests to those of the nation as a whole. It is left to the Clergy, the estate to which Chartier himself belonged, to put forward a plan to ensure France's survival and recovery. The plan has three elements: *savance*, a sober appreciation of the current state of affairs; *chevance*, the recognition that resources are required and a readiness to provide them; and *obeissance*, willingness to subordinate self-interest and class interest to *la chose publique* (the common good), and to give unquestioning obedience.

The *Quadrilogue* is an eloquent and subtle piece of propaganda on behalf of the dauphin. The analysis of France's problems is perceptive, more general than detailed.[28] Rather than engage in a polemic about recent history, about the rights

27] Toulouse MS 826, ff. 4v–5r; *Quadrilogue Invectif*, pp. 9–10.
28] The *Quadrilogue Invectif* came to be seen as a political treatise of wider applicability, and was translated into both Castilian and English in the fifteenth century; it would also

and wrongs of the quarrel between the Armagnacs and the Burgundians, about the injustice of the Treaty of Troyes, Chartier focuses on France, highlighting the shameful straits in which a once proud and prosperous nation now finds herself. He appeals to national pride and patriotic sentiment, presenting the English as the main danger and urging the nation as a whole to recover its pride and unite against 'le roy angloys, ancien adversaire de ceste seigneurie' ('the King of England, the old enemy of this realm').[29] The message is eloquent; the images and examples are memorable, chosen from the Bible and from Roman and French history. Equally important, the text is short, and thus the more likely to be read.

Some months later, probably in January 1423, Chartier wrote the *Ad detestacionem belli gallici et suasionem pacis*.[30] Its contents recall the *Quadrilogue*, but the tone is more positive. The intervening months had seen the deaths first of Henry V of England and then of Charles VI. Now that the dauphin has become king, has the time not come to set aside reproach and criticism, however well merited, to look forward, and to see in the new reign the prospect of a new beginning? That mood of optimism was to prove short-lived, however. When we read the *Dialogus familiaris amici et sodalis*, composed in 1425 or 1426, we see that little had changed.[31] Chartier abandons the long speeches of the *Quadrilogue* in favour of a lively exchange, more akin to a conversation, between the Friend and his Companion. The Friend is a man of experience, pragmatic, inclined to take things as they come, and to see the present crisis as only the most recent in the long series of crises which France has weathered successfully. His Companion, almost certainly Chartier himself, is more reflective and more pessimistic, concerned lest the nation's sickness may be terminal. He describes a France riven by factions, where each section of society looks only to protect its own interests and where vice triumphs over virtue. Moral decay and national decline go hand in hand, argues the Companion, citing as examples the fall of Greece and Rome. Unless unity and lasting peace can be achieved, unless the nation as a whole repents and seeks divine forgiveness, France is in danger of suffering the same fate.

All these works were clearly intended for publication and circulation. The Latin works were no doubt directed at men and women of education, clerical and lay, 'opinion-formers', as today's publicists would call them. The *Quadrilogue*

---

be an important source for the sixteenth-century *Complaynt of Scotlande*. The Castilian version is in BL, Egerton MS 1868. See *Fifteenth-Century English Translations of Alain Chartier's 'Le Traité de l'Esperance' and 'Le Quadrilogue Invectif'*, ed. M. S. Blayney, 2 vols, EETS, Oxford, 1974, 1980, and M. S. and G. H. Blayney, 'Alain Chartier and *The Complaynt of Scotlande*', *Review of English Studies*, ns, Vol. IX, 1958, pp. 8–17.

29] *Quadrilogue Invectif*, p. 4.

30] *Œuvres latines*, pp. 225–44. The work concludes with *Metra super eodem*, forty hexameters on the same subject.

31] Ibid., pp. 245–325.

Invectif and other French works, such as the *Lay de Paix*,[32] were aimed at a wider audience, schooled above all in French, more lay than clerical, composed of nobles and bourgeois. We do not know how widely these works circulated in the 1420s, whether they were mainly read or heard south of the Loire, or whether they also penetrated into the north. It is striking, however, that the great majority of the surviving manuscripts are later copies, dating very often from the middle of the fifteenth century. Were these works prompted by Chartier's concern for the fate of France or were they commissioned by Charles VII, as we can now call him? One cannot be certain. What perhaps began as a personal initiative must have continued with Charles' encouragement.

Private and Public Thoughts 1427–29

The unfinished *Livre de l'Esperance*, begun probably in the second half of 1427, brings the reader closer to Chartier's private thoughts.[33] The work is an elaborate *prosimetrum*, in which passages of verse and prose alternate, on the model of Boethius' *De consolatione philosophiae*. In the opening poem, the author contrasts the past glories of France with her current plight. He is then visited by *Melencolie* (Melancholy), and soon afterwards by three monstrous apparitions who harangue him in turn: *Indignation* makes a violent attack on the court; *Defiance* (Distrust) argues that the situations of France and of the author himself are beyond help and hope; *Desesperance* (Despair) is more brutal still and recommends suicide. Horrified by that suggestion, *Nature* awakes *Entendement* (Understanding), who opens the door of memory and admits four more allegorical figures who bring welcome enlightenment and consolation. There follows a discussion between the author, *Entendement* and *Foy* (Faith), who takes the largest part and succeeds in putting *Defiance* and *Desesperance* to flight. *Esperance* (Hope) then comes forward and, in a parallel conversation, brings further comfort to the author and his troubled mind; like *Foy* before her, she emphasises the need for individuals and for the nation at large to have faith and trust in God, and to seek divine intercession through constant prayer. When *Foy* and *Esperance* first appear, they are accompanied by two other figures, a third lady and a damsel described as well-born and of good bearing.[34] While we can identify the third lady as Charity and can assume that Chartier planned to include a third conversation, the identity of the noble damsel is not revealed.

The composition of the *Livre de l'Esperance* must have overlapped with the preparations for the embassy to Scotland in which Chartier took part, as secretary and orator, in the summer of 1428. During the previous four years, he had

32] *Poetical Works*, pp. 410–20; *Poèmes*, pp. 211–20.
33] *Le Livre de l'Espérance*, pp. 1–179.
34] '… entrerent incontinent troys dames et une debonnaire et bien encontenancee damoiselle …' (ibid., p. 23).

gained wide experience as a royal envoy. A mission to the Emperor Sigismund early in 1425 attempted to secure imperial support for Charles VII's cause, and was associated with embassies to Venice and probably to Rome later that year. However, these diplomatic manoeuvres had little effect on the progress of the war. In April 1426, Chartier was one of Charles VII's envoys in an equally unproductive mission to the Duke of Burgundy.

In 1428, when his political and economic position was near desperate, Charles VII turned for help to James I of Scotland. The oration which Chartier delivered before the Scottish court is of particular interest.[35] Its tripartite structure and its opening text, *Salve, rex*, recall the famous sermon, *Vivat rex*, preached by Gerson on 7 November 1405 and often copied thereafter.[36] Chartier celebrates the institution of monarchy which has been ordained by God to enshrine virtue on earth. Monarchy is synonymous with *potestas*, *majestas* and *dignitas* ('power, majesty and dignity'), the three qualities which Chartier analyses in turn and which are embodied in James I. In flattering the King of the Scots, Chartier presents an ideal of monarchy which was as applicable to France as it was to Scotland; he no doubt hoped that Charles VII would hearken to at least part of his message. However, the embassy's immediate aim was to effect the renewal of the ancient alliances between the two countries. To that end, each section of the speech ends with a reference to their long-standing friendship and to the support they have brought to each other over the years. The oration concludes with a plea that Scotland should again come to France's aid and contribute to the final victory. Chartier's plea had positive results: in July 1428, James I agreed to the renewal of the alliance and to the marriage of his eldest daughter, Margaret, to the dauphin, Louis. He also promised to send further men-at-arms to reinforce Charles VII's army.

The optimistic notes struck by Chartier in his oration were grounded more in faith and hope than in reality. They reflect his passionate commitment to the recovery of France and his belief that God would in the end show compassion. Chartier lived long enough to see his prayers answered. *De Puella*, his last known work, was written in Bourges late in July or in August 1429, and was addressed to a foreign prince, probably the Duke of Milan.[37] It gives an enthusiastic account of the achievements of Jeanne d'Arc who had raised the siege of Orléans some three months earlier, on 8 May, and escorted Charles VII to Reims for his coronation on 17 July. Chartier's letter conveys his wonder at the divine intervention which had effected such an abrupt change in French fortunes.

* * * * *

35] *Œuvres latines*, pp. 206–18.
36] *Jean Gerson: Œuvres complètes*, ed. P. Glorieux, 11 vols, Paris, 1960–73, Vol. VII*, pp. 1137–85 (pièce 398).
37] *Œuvres latines*, pp. 326–29.

In the twenty years which he had spent in royal service, Alain Chartier had been no stranger to crisis. As he reflected on the events of that momentous spring and summer, he must have recalled the sombre days of Agincourt and Montereau, and perhaps above all the Treaty of Troyes by which the dauphin had been disinherited. As author, secretary and ambassador, Chartier had played a significant part in 'managing' these and many other crises. He had committed himself to the public service, as Dame France had enjoined in the *Quadrilogue Invectif*, and the words of his pen and his tongue had played their part in restoring French fortunes. Chartier no doubt hoped that it would not be long before his years of exile were over, allowing him to return to the Paris he loved; 'sans y estre, bon jour n'ay' ('unless I am there, no day is for me a good day'), he had written in the *Livre des quatre dames*.[38] Alas, that was not to be, for he died in Avignon on 20 March 1430.[39]

38] Line 3451. See n. 6, above.
39] What Chartier's business was in Avignon, and how long he had been there, is not known. See *Poetical Works*, pp. 15–18.

4

Intellectual Patterns and Affective Reactions in Defence of the Dauphin Charles, 1419–1422

NICOLE PONS

The double-monarchy created by the Treaty of Troyes was to cause contemporaries to ask many different questions regarding its implementation even before the premature and unforeseen death of Henry V while still regent of France. As Jean Favier has written, it is clear that the policies of Queen Isabeau, Philip the Good and Henry V were formulated on the understanding that the dauphin, Charles, should 'disappear from circulation'.[1] The reality would be very different: the dauphin still enjoyed much support, particularly in parts of the country south of the Loire, although this was a part of France which, generally speaking, contained few economic resources.

Among the causes leading to the final victory achieved by Charles VII may have been the death of Henry V. In seeking to impose his rule and to achieve the union of the two crowns of England and France, Henry held two trump cards: his military superiority and his political acumen. Nor did he lack admirers, even among the subjects of Charles VI. At the end of 1417 the humanist, Nicolas de Clamanges, addressed the King of England in an *Epistola exhortatoria ad iusticiam et alias virtutes*[2] in which he set out the king's numerous virtues – piety, a sense of justice, moderation, and a cultured mind (very important to Clamanges) – which made him into 'the person by whom the house of France shall be revived, rebuilt and recalled to its former greatness'.[3] On Henry's death, Jean Chartier, now responsible for writing the *Chronique de Saint-Denis*, painted this favourable image of the late king:

> he showed much magnanimity, valour in arms, prudence and wisdom: he was a great justiciar, and earned a reputation as such among the people: he was held in awe and honour by all ... In his lifetime, no other prince appeared more

1] J. Favier, *La Guerre de Cent Ans*, Paris, 1980, p. 457.
2] *Quoniam princeps illustris*, in *Nicolai de Clemengiis: Opera omnia*, ed. J. Lydius, 2 vols, Leiden, 1613, Vol. II, pp. 347–53 (Ep.cxxxvii).
3] F. Bérier, 'Remarques sur l'évolution des idées politiques de Nicolas de Clamanges', in *Pratiques de la culture écrite en France au XVe siècle*, ed. M. Ornato and N. Pons, Louvain-la-Neuve, 1990, pp. 45–79.

> capable than he of subduing or conquering a kingdom by the wisdom of his rule, by his good sense and the other qualities with which he was endowed.[4]

Not all, however, agreed with this view. Some regarded the king with a violent hatred which it would prove difficult to extinguish. In fact, the views of the first author of the tract known as *Débats et appointements* must have been shared by other people.[5] The work of two different authors, this pamphlet was composed in three parts. First, a chronicle intended to underline French sovereignty over all lands within France, and the futility of all English claims both to the crown of France and to their ancient possessions, namely Guyenne and Normandy. This was followed by a speech by 'Truth' ('Vérité') in which were set out the many complaints which Frenchmen could legitimately make against their enemy. The English were probably already well in control of Normandy by the time these two parts of the work were written, for 'Truth', addressing her king, tells him that the English 'have already taken both parts ["les deux pars"] of your land of Normandy and several other places in Perche and Maine',[6] which may suggest a date early in 1419, or even before. To these two sections a second author, writing between the murder of John the Fearless at Montereau (September 1419) and the Treaty of Troyes (May 1420) added a discussion between 'Truth' and 'France' in which reforms aimed at achieving eventual victory are proposed. Nothing is known about either author, nor may we assume that either was in the service of the king or of his son, the dauphin. One can only note that the first author, writing at a time when civil conflict between Armagnacs and Burgundians was at its height, refers only to the war against the English.[7] He prefers to remain uncommitted on matters of domestic concern, leaving open the possibility of a *union nationale*. His political sympathies remain hidden; only the crown is important. Yet whatever his opinions, he joined the dauphin's party after the Treaty of Troyes, thereby expressing his hostility to 'the ancient enemy of the kingdom'.

It is possible that the double monarchy might have succeeded if, on Henry V's death, Philip the Good had taken over the government of the kingdom in the name of the house of Lancaster. Instead, he was to see his ambition thwarted by John, Duke of Bedford. We know, however, that Philip enjoyed considerable support even outside his own lands: the example of the Parisians' attachment to the Dukes of Burgundy was not an isolated instance, and many living in the kingdom would certainly have been willing to obey him.

4] *Chronique du Religieux de St.-Denis*, ed. and trans. M. L. Bellaguet, 6 vols, Paris, 1839–52, Vol. VI, pp. 481–82.
5] *'L'Honneur de la Couronne de France'. Quatre libelles contre les Anglais (vers 1418–vers 1429)*, ed. N. Pons, SHF, Paris, 1990, pp. 45–79.
6] Ibid., p. 64, ll. 378–80. In all likelihood this refers to Upper and Lower Normandy, although the possibility that the author meant two-thirds of Normandy must be admitted.
7] Whether one accepts a date of 1418 or 1419, France was still in the throes of a civil war.

Many, indeed, but not all, as we learn from the tracts and pamphlets which sought to defend the dauphin's rights. From such we learn of the political convictions of at least some contemporaries. This section of public opinion, which did not lend its support to the conqueror and yet, in due time, would find itself on the winning side, expressed its views in all forms of works, long and short, literary, juridical and historical. Their number and diversity suggest that, even if all these writings were not entirely spontaneous, being, in some cases, clearly inspired by the authorities, they none the less reflect a body of opinion favourable to the dauphin, Charles. It is difficult to evaluate precisely the diffusion of such texts, who read them, and thus the weight of opinion which should be attributed to them. Nevertheless, we can be sure that these constituted a number whose influence was far from negligible.

Further, these texts indicate how contemporaries viewed political events as these unfolded; how they were judged and evaluated and, on occasions, what attempts were made to influence the outcome of events. All this casts a light which is, in one sense, closely related to the events concerned but which, in another, is more concerned to reflect the way that certain of the king's subjects viewed the monarchy and the kingdom. This evidence reveals the opinion and ideas of a part of the population, while also acting as a form of gauge of the state of mind of some Frenchmen at the time the events described or discussed took place, a formative factor in the creation of alliances and relationships between political sympathisers. This poses the problem of how we can learn what were the factors which created and influenced those sympathies: propaganda at a fairly low level of intensity which eventually overcame by force of arms, or views shared by a fairly large number of people?

At first sight, these texts appear easy to read. Yet they reflect many complex, sometimes contradictory, attitudes, which varied with time. Their contents are equally difficult to analyse in simple terms, making the creation of an unbiased synthesis very difficult. None the less, certain themes can be revealing. For instance, it is striking how, next to arguments based on law and history are to be found others which reflect views based on emotion and passion, in particular when the role of Burgundian policy is discussed. Here we have an important pointer on how we should understand the outcome of events of these years, and how they had an impact upon contemporaries. So, in order to appreciate the state of mind of one part of public opinion, we should note in particular how that opinion reacted to the actions of the Dukes of Burgundy and their party in texts written about 1420, in particular a number of anonymous pamphlets and certain works of Jean de Terrevermeille, Robert Blondel, Jean Gerson, and Alain Chartier. The fundamental problem remains that of the succession, which provokes denunciations of the treachery of the Burgundian dukes and the damage done by the rebellion which followed that treachery.

In the pages which follow, we shall examine briefly these three fundamental themes: the succession, treachery and rebellion. By way of conclusion I shall try to show how, by examining these themes, we may see how something more than a simple polemical point of view emerges from them; rather, they reflect a sense of 'belonging' which may explain the victory ultimately achieved by the dauphin's supporters.

The Succession to the Crown

This question, ever at the heart of the Anglo-French quarrel, was as old as the conflict itself. One could say that a plan to set up a personal double-monarchy had already existed for three-quarters of a century when, in 1419, Philip the Good, wishing to avenge his father's murder, undertook to put the direct Valois heir to the throne 'out of circulation' by recognising the King of England in his place. But it was only at that moment that the project finally appeared ready for realisation. This was particularly so from 2 December 1419, when Duke Philip, by letters patent issued at Arras, ratified the peace proposals put forward by Henry V, proposals which were later to form the basis of the Treaty of Troyes. That this development had long been in the planning is strongly suggested by the fact that, in December 1419 or January 1420, the defence of the dauphin's cause was taken up almost at once by an official of the *Parlement* of Poitiers in a Latin tract, *Super omnia vincit veritas*, intended to show the nullity of the future treaty. Soon afterwards, the same official, or perhaps one of his colleagues, rendered the Latin text into French, giving it the title *Réponse d'un bon et loyal François.*[8] Although these had much in common, each text had its own characteristics – one emphasised the legal arguments, the other appealed more to the emotions – so that one cannot really regard these two versions as simply the same tract, one in Latin, the other in French. Furthermore, their very structures are different, since they rely for their arguments upon another pair of closely related yet different texts: *Super omnia* upon the Latin letters patent issued at Arras, the *Réponse* upon a literal translation of only a part of those same letters.[9]

At the time that *Super omnia* was written, the attitude of Queen Isabeau to events was not yet clear: the dauphin and his followers could still hope for a reconciliation between mother and son, to counterbalance the Anglo-Burgundian accord, in particular as opinion in Paris was scarcely in favour of it.[10] Isabeau is not mentioned at all in *Super omnia*. In the *Réponse*, however, the queen was

8] '*L'Honneur de la Couronne*', pp. 113–33.
9] See T. Rymer (ed.), *Foedera, conventiones, literae...*, 17 vols, London, 1704–17, Vol. IX, pp. 816–18. The French translation of these letters includes only the content of the English proposals ('*L'Honneur de la couronne*', pp. 135–37).
10] P. Bonenfant, *Du meurtre de Montereau au traité de Troyes*, Brussels, 1958, pp. 110–30; B. Guenée, 'Les Campagnes de lettres qui ont suivi le meurtre de Jean sans Peur, duc de Bourgogne (septembre 1419–février 1420)', *Annuaire-Bulletin de la Société de l'Histoire de France,* 1993, p. 46.

given a certain prominence, a surprising fact given that, at the moment of composition (the second part, at least, was probably written in April or May 1420) she had totally cast her lot on the side of Henry V and Philip the Good. In spite of this, the author wrote that 'deboutee a tousjours, elle et ses hoirs, de l'onneur des fleurs de lis' ('she and her heirs were now excluded for ever from the honour of the fleurs de lis'),[11] while she and her daughter, Katherine, were detained under guard at Troyes, and acted as they did 'par espoventement et force de gens d'armes' ('only because they feared the power of the soldiery').[12] Did this willingness to ignore the realities of the queen's position, and her material indebtedness to the Duchess of Burgundy,[13] suggest a desire to influence the future, perhaps by giving the queen a way out of her dilemma? Or do these words stem from an emotional reaction to events so strong that one is convinced that the queen's actions can only be explained as being influenced by external constraint?

The reader of the tract is struck by the emotional aspect of its author's reactions. These are not simply those of a Frenchman roused to indignation, but that of a French heart weeping at the prospect of such a treaty: 'C'est grant horreur seulement de penser comme quelconque cuer françois, noble ou non noble, a peu et puet favoriser a tel traictié, veoir mais l'oïr sans detester' ('It is terrible to think how some French hearts, some noble others not, have supported or can support such a treaty, or can even consider or listen to its terms without hating it').[14] This text contains many comments intended to touch the hearts of the author's fellow-countrymen. The kingdom, he claims, will come 'en gouvernement et subjeccion totale non pas seulement des hommes anglois estrangiers desquelx on ne cognoist la langue, mais mesmement d'aucunes femmes anglesches' ('under the rule and complete subjection not only of unknown English soldiers whose language men do not know, but even of some English women').[15] Henry V has the impudence never to accord Charles VI his proper title, referring to him simply as his 'cousin de France'. (Is it in retaliation that the King of England is never given his title, being called simply 'Henri d'Angleterre'?) Furthermore, in taking advantage of the 'innocente pucelle' ('innocent maid'), the Princess Katherine, men are dishonouring her, leading to her fall into a state of mortal sin, thereby causing her to 'encourir crime de lese majesté humaine et divine' ('incur accusations of treason, both human and divine').[16]

Nevertheless, whatever the nature of their particular approach, each writer was seeking the same end, the defence of the dauphin's inheritance, principally

11] *'L'Honneur de la couronne'*, p. 125, ll. 111–12.
12] Ibid., p. 124, ll. 59–65.
13] A few days after the decision taken by the council on 17 January 1420 to denounce the dauphin as a 'parricide', the queen received a loan of 10 000 francs from Margaret, Duchess of Burgundy (Bonenfant, *Du meurtre de Montereau*, pp. 128–30).
14] *'L'Honneur de la couronne'*, p. 127, ll. 159–62.
15] Ibid., p. 126, ll. 120–23.
16] Ibid., p. 124, ll. 83–87.

by emphasising the argument summed up in the formula 'the son is necessarily the heir' ('quia filius est haeres'), and the idea intrinsic to it, the inalienability of the crown.

The year 1419 was not only the year which witnessed John the Fearless firmly established at the head of government until, that is, his elimination by the dauphin at Montereau. It was also a year of fundamental importance in the history of law, since it witnessed Jean de Terrevermeille, *avocat du roi* in the *sénéchaussée* of Beaucaire, rise against Burgundian pretensions by fixing the juridical rules regarding the devolution of the crown in his *Tractatus contra rebelles suorum regum.*[17] What are the points argued by Terrevermeille? First, he reiterates the principle, already set out by Charles V in his ordinance of 1374 concerning the royal coming of age, that 'according to nature, the father and his eldest son are regarded as one and the same person', a principle found, too, in the *Songe du Vergier* and in the works of Gerson.[18] Only a little later, at the time of the Treaty of Troyes, Robert Blondel would opine that 'Hii duo sunt et idem', which his translator was to render as 'the king and the dauphin are one and the same'.[19] It was, above all, the consequences which Terrevermeille attributed to this principle which marked a major step in the development of the law of succession: by reason of this perfect identity of nature, the dauphin himself might be called king. As *juvenis rex*, according to the *Decretum*, he already exercises a *jus coregnandi* and a *coadministratio* with his father, even in the latter's lifetime. Co-ruler with a king of sound mind, to him reverts by nature the full administration and government of the kingdom if the king is prevented from ruling through madness, absence, or any other reason. On the death of his father, or on his falling seriously ill, the son, in a sense heir to himself, does not require to be put in possession of what is already his.[20]

The officer(s) of the *Parlement* of Poitiers, author(s) of *Super omnia* and of the *Réponse,* did not make such elaborate legal claims. None the less their argument, put briefly, was that of their colleague from Beaucaire. As the author of *Super omnia* put it:

> the dauphin is the real sovereign lord of the kingdom of France because he is the king's only son and his legitimate heir; for, according to the Apostle [Paul], whoever is son, is heir; however young, even under age, he is no less

17] See J. Barbey, *La Fonction royale. Essence et légitimité d'après les Tractatus de Jean de Terrevermeille,* Paris, 1983.
18] 'Le filz est une mesme personne avesque le pere et le represente' (*Songe*): '[le dauphin] est comme une mesme personne avecquez le roi' (Gerson). On this theme, see J. Krynen, *L'Empire du roi. Idées et croyances politiques en France, XIIIe–XVe siècle*, Paris, 1993, pp. 140–52.
19] '... le pere et le filz sont tout un' (*De Complanctu bonorum Gallicorum* and *La Complaincte des bons François*, in *Oeuvres de Robert Blondel, historien normand du XVe siècle*, ed. A. Héron, 2 vols, SHN, Rouen, 1891–93, Vol. I, pp. 14, v. 315, 82, v. 833).
20] Krynen, *L'Empire du roi*, p. 152.

> sovereign lord. In the present condition of the king and of the kingdom, the dauphin is invested with public authority, and it is to him that power to rule belongs.[21]

Expressed more simply, the text of the *Réponse* also reflected the same line of thought: 'because the king, [the dauphin's] father, is dead in a civil sense, and is not capable of governing, his only son, according to all human and divine law, must have the rule in the place of his father – quia si filius et heres, qui est dominus omnium' ('because if he is son and heir, then he is lord of all').[22] Consequently, even if the king wishes to disinherit his heir, he cannot do so because he lacks the right to dispose of the kingdom: 'according to the law and approved customs of the kingdom, which are regarded as law, either the king's son or the male of the royal blood nearest to the king must succeed. Of his own will, the king cannot lawfully ordain anything contrary to this law.'[23] As the author of the *Réponse* wrote:

> how has the king in his sickness been able to consent and agree to so great a thing [as the perpetual alienation] of the kingdom of France, the right of the crown and the honour of the 'fleur de lis' ... against all laws, whether divine, civil, natural or canonical, and against the very custom of France ... for the good government of the entire kingdom requires it?[24]

Here again, however, the tone of the *Réponse* differs from that of the corresponding Latin text through the affective character of its argument. It is as a result of the 'natural love' between father and son that the disinheriting of the latter cannot be envisaged. The treaty will lead the king and queen to lose their position and dignity and, as a result, 'par mort naturele', the person whom they love the most in the world, their son, the dauphin.[25] The issue is not simply a matter of law; what is at stake is the law of nature and his parents' love for an 'innocent, tres bel et vertueux' dauphin. The treaty is said to be not only 'desraisonnable' and 'tres deshonneste'; it is 'desnaturel', too.[26]

The Treason of the Duke of Burgundy

In the eyes of the dauphin's supporters, the person responsible for this act of disinheritance so contrary to nature was the Duke of Burgundy, and what we observed in relation to the first point – an elaborate juridical argument in the

21] *'L'Honneur de la couronne'*, p. 114, ll. 37–43.
22] Ibid., p. 128, ll. 187–92. See also p. 123, ll. 34–37, where the dauphin's right to rule, in the event of his father's incapacity, is emphasised.
23] Ibid., p. 120, ll. 202–07.
24] Ibid., pp. 127–28, ll. 175–84.
25] Ibid., p. 126, ll. 129–32.
26] Ibid., p. 124, ll. 70–75.

work of Terrevermeille, with a much more summary one in *Super omnia* – will be found again when the role of the Duke of Burgundy is considered.

Terrevermeille wrote his *Tractatus* before the conclusion of the Anglo-Burgundian alliance. It was, therefore, against a rebel that he directed his attack. The duke dares to try to rival the king and the dauphin, the legitimate head of the mystical body which is the kingdom, while giving the hypocritical appearance of being a protector and a reformer of the kingdom. Trying to usurp the exercise of power to which he has no right, the duke is a tyrant, and those who support him are rebels. Tyranny and rebellion thus appear as the two perversions which, in Terrevermeille's view, destroy the kingdom and threaten the lives of its members.[27] The *avocat* from Beaucaire draws up a long list of indictments against this 'Antichrist', this *destructor regni* which falls into seven categories: homicide and other villainies; the destruction of the kingdom, its subjects and wealth; acts bringing dishonour upon the law; the inability to act in the interests of the kingdom; interference in royal government; usurpation of power through the use of violence; and above all, *lese majesté* reflecting his attacks upon the *status regni*.[28]

Writing after the Anglo-Burgundian accords had been made at Arras, the author of *Super omnia* attacks the Duke of Burgundy mainly as a disloyal vassal. Refuting the Burgundian letters patent, he sets out his arguments carefully. Naturally enough, he begins by questioning the very titles, 'Philippus dux Burgundie, comes Flandrie' borne by their writer; these, he argues, should be rejected, as Philip has been, or at least deserves to be, deprived of his Burgundian and Flemish lands on account of his betrayal (*crimen lese majestatis*) of the king and the dauphin, made manifest in the accord arranged with the English enemy.[29] What John the Fearless began has now been continued by his son, Philip, notwithstanding the many pacts made between his father and the dauphin, and the oaths sworn to the dauphin.[30] As we have already seen, it is the dauphin, invested with public authority, to whom the powers of government belong. This means that Philip, like any other vassal, should obey him as a superior power.[31] A vassal who conspires with an adversary of both king and kingdom should be deprived of his fiefs and declared a *hostis publicus*, a traitor whom all knights and all the king's faithful subjects should be ready to fight.[32] One may note that this Latin tract, doubtless because of its very juridical character, remains more strongly attached to the feudal model than its French counterpart; in the passage just cited, the term 'vassal' appears five times, whereas in the French text, which employs the terms 'subgiez du royaume' or 'ceulx et celles du royaume', it is

27] Barbey, *La Fonction royale*, p. 244.
28] Ibid., p. 244 n. 8.
29] *'L'Honneur de la couronne'*, pp. 113–14, ll. 18–28.
30] Ibid., p. 114, ll. 28–35.
31] Ibid., p. 114, ll. 45–48.
32] Ibid., pp. 114–15, ll. 42–60.

wholly absent.[33] However that may be, we should note that the tone of the author of *Super omnia*, in its reflection of dauphinist views of the Duke of Burgundy, is much less virulent in its language than is Terrevermeille, ending the tract with an appeal to the duke 'to return to the straight path of truth and justice'.[34]

By contrast, the animosity of Robert Blondel towards the Duke of Burgundy, while equal to that of Terrevermeille, is expressed in a very different way. Blondel, Norman by origin, was a *universitaire* who made a career for himself serving the house of Anjou, finishing up as *maistre d'escolle* to the second son of Charles VII. A forceful supporter of the dauphin, his *De Complanctu bonorum Gallicorum* constitutes important evidence of the feelings experienced by a strong upholder of the dauphin's cause towards the Treaty of Troyes. The poem, some 900 Latin hexametres long, is a work of rhetoric, comprehensible only to those with a certain degree of education. For this reason, it was immediately translated or, rather, adapted into French by a clerk called Robinet, with the title *La Complaincte des bons François*.

The text of the *De Complanctu* is relatively little known, for although published a century ago, the edition was faulty, largely because the editor used a late manuscript interpolated with rubrics taken from Robinet's French adaptation which often distort Blondel's original Latin.[35] The work begins with a long appeal to true Frenchmen that, rediscovering the virtues of their ancestors, they should come to the help of their country which is suffering from three disasters which have beset her simultaneously. The first is the rising of May–June 1418, at the end of which the Parisians expelled their natural lord in favour of a traitor who, allied to the English, would cause the capital to share the fate of Troy and Jerusalem. The second disaster is that of the English conquest, which France cannot resist as she must oppose another enemy (the third disaster), the Duke of Burgundy, a traitor and perjurer who, under the guise of helping the country, has led it to ruin by causing the death of Louis, Duke of Orléans, whose unpunished murder lies at the root of all the troubles experienced by France. The author draws attention to the similarity of the crimes perpetrated by John the Fearless and Henry IV of England (who caused his sovereign lord, King Richard II, to be killed), crimes which have helped to cement the Anglo-Burgundian alliance of today.

Already an attack upon John the Fearless for instigating the murder of Louis of Orléans,[36] the work is primarily an appeal for support for the dauphin's cause

33] Ibid., pp. 114–15, ll. 44, 47, 49, 54, 57; p. 125, l. 95. See also ll. 104, 109.

34] Ibid., p. 120, ll. 219–20.

35] N. Pons, 'Un lettré et son traducteur: du royaume de France de Robert Blondel à la Normandie du clerc Robinet', in *Identité régionale et conscience nationale en France et en Allemagne du Moyen-âge à l'époque moderne*, ed. R. Babel and J.-M. Moeglin, Sigmaringen, 1997, pp. 415–16. The title *De Complanctu* was not the choice of the author, but came from the French version. It should probably have been called *Desolatio regni Francie*.

36] See B. Guenée, *Un meurtre, une société. L'assassinat du duc d'Orléans, 23 novembre 1407*, Paris, 1992, pp. 14, 285.

and a violent denunciation of Burgundian actions both at the time of the Parisian uprising in 1418 and later, when the foundations of the Treaty of Troyes were laid.

A sort of lyrical outpouring, Blondel's work is little more than a succession of passionate reactions influenced less by reason and logic than by emotion and sentiment. For example, nothing is worse than to lose one's country, since love of it is something which catches fire in the full meaning of that term. That love has the characteristic of fire: more precious than gold, its ardour burns hearts and it cannot be extinguished.[37] This attachment to the land of one's birth – an attachment endowed with the strength and characteristics of fire – is presented as something involving the passions to a greater degree than the simple *amour naturel* of Alain Chartier for a land which gives a man 'his security, his peace, his refuge, his rest in old age and his final burial place'.[38]

Of particular interest to us is the way in which Blondel deals with the personalities of the dauphin and the Duke of Burgundy, both described in language of pure emotion. For Blondel, there is a direct biological line which conveys the characteristics of the royal house.[39] Similarly, a propensity to evil and to treason is inherited; reprehensible actions on the part of the father are normally reflected in the son, so that there is nothing surprising that a son should act like his father. Indeed, Blondel's translator, Robinet, added that it was natural for things to happen in this way.[40] In forming an alliance with Henry V, Philip the Good was almost predictably completing what had been initiated by his father, John the Fearless, when he ordered the assassination of Louis of Orléans. It was from this act that the present woes of France could be said to stem.[41]

Like the author of *Super omnia*, who described the accords made at Arras as a 'proditoria confederatione' ('treacherous alliance'),[42] Blondel attacks the 'leo proditor effrons' ('shameless traitor') responsible for them.[43] It is of interest that he regards John the Fearless, responsible for the tragic events of more than a decade earlier, as much a traitor as his son, Philip, who surrendered the king to his English rival, both father and son being referred to as 'perfidi' in the same passage.[44] This is far from being the only example of Blondel denouncing what he regards as Burgundian treason. So he refers to the 'treason which strives to reject the French lineage'; no greater betrayal ever having been committed, for it is one which has deceived consciences. He appeals to faithful vassals to give their help 'to their lord, whom treason has shamelessly betrayed to the enemy'.[45]

37] Blondel, *Oeuvres*, Vol. I, p. 18, vv. 407–10.
38] *Alain Chartier, Le Quadrilogue Invectif*, ed. E. Droz, rev. edn, Paris, 1950, p. 11.
39] Already emphasised by Krynen, *L'Empire du roi*, p. 335.
40] Blondel, *Oeuvres*, p. 30, vv. 664–65; p. 120, vv. 1757–60.
41] Ibid., p. 30, vv. 659–63; p. 120, vv. 1745–56,
42] *'L'Honneur de la couronne'*, p. 114, l. 26.
43] Blondel, *Oeuvres*, Vol. I, p. 30, v. 646.
44] Ibid., p. 30, vv. 652–54, 662–63.
45] Ibid., p. 30, vv. 646, 651; p. 31, vv. 671–72; p. 36, vv. 781–83.

The clerk, Robinet, the translator of Blondel's work, adds further attacks against the English adversary whom he denounces in passages which are of his own composition. It is only a traitor, he claims, who can rejoice at the English conquest of Normandy.[46] While Blondel reserves the term *proditor* for the Duke of Burgundy, Robinet uses it much more liberally, applying it not only to the duke, an even greater traitor than Ganelon who betrayed Roland, but to the Parisians, the Anglo-Burgundian allies, and the English as well.[47] In this regard it is important to underline how Blondel's translator makes explicit what, in the language of the educated, is normally expressed in metaphors and allusions. One such appears in the following passage. Blondel begs the French to take care that their division, always referred to as *scisma*, can only lead to a mountain where there are boulders, thorny bushes, brambles and dark caves; places, Robinet adds, where various wild animals live. It is here that his rendering becomes particularly interesting; the Burgundians are compared to wild beasts capable of murder, treachery and causing division, while the English are both 'heretics and the begetters of murder'.[48] So it is the treachery of Burgundy, and not the usual divisions commented upon by contemporaries, including both Blondel and Robinet, which is regarded as being the cause of war against the old enemy.[49]

Rebellion, the Fruit of Treason

The reason lying behind the hostility of certain of the dauphin's supporters towards Burgundian attitudes and actions is probably to be found in the events concerned with the entry of the Burgundians into Paris, and the subsequent slaughter of Armagnacs in May–June 1418. The impact of these events must have been such that they could be neither forgotten nor forgiven. That, at least, is what the attitude of Jean Gerson, chancellor of the university, leads one to suppose. In political matters, Gerson was not an extremist but a moderate reformer, who sought to achieve harmony between the three estates of the kingdom. Alone, his strong reaction against Jean Petit's justification of tyrannicide at the Council of Constance appears to belie this impression we have of him. Nevertheless, the tragic news from Paris (he was in Bavaria at the time, having recently left Constance) greatly provoked him, reminding him, as it must have done, of the Cabochian revolt in 1413 when his house next to Notre Dame had been pillaged. The most recent events stung him into composing a vehement *lamentatio*. Little

46] Ibid., p. 92, vv. 1066–68.
47] Ibid., p. 85, v. 887; p. 100, v. 1261; p. 103, vv. 1309, 1314; p. 104, v. 1346; p. 112, v. 1541; p. 116, v. 1656; p. 126, v. 1889.
48] 'Et premier leons ravissables / ours tirans et loupx homicides; / Ce sont Bourguignons decevables / Traystres, pervers et patricides; / Aussi sont tigres scismatiques / Semans par tout division / Et leopars qui sont heretiques / Anglois, peres d'occision' (ibid., p. 14, vv. 322–24; p. 83, vv. 851–64).
49] Ibid., p. 7, vv. 135–36; p. 65, vv. 442–43.

known, probably even to his contemporaries, this work merits our attention as reflecting the personal reaction of a man of intellectual and political influence to the momentous events of his time. Like the works of Blondel, Gerson's *Deploratio*,[50] written in difficult Latin, is essentially a rhetorical work, accessible only to the educated, in which we seek in vain for either logical or closely reasoned arguments. It is, albeit a little surprisingly, a violent denunciation of the rebellion, a fine example of a spontaneous and heart-felt reaction to events.

In this work Gerson makes frequent use of the word 'horror'. From the opening lines, he associates the popular movement with horror and acts of savagery.[51] Nothing sums up the tone of the work better than his use of telling adjectives to describe what has happened: 'frightful, horrendous, appalling, terrible, uncivilised, crime succeeding crime, no day without its horror', followed shortly by the statement: 'the horror is spreading';[52] rebellion is worse than any war,[53] associated as it is with envy, the self-interest of the tyrant, and civil unrest.[54] Formerly one of the glories of the world, Paris is now a city at the mercy of the mob, whose bestial fury has been responsible for many terrible crimes: children have been killed unbaptised, and the bodies of Christians have been left, unburied, to feed the birds and wolves.[55] 'Where is virtue', Gerson asks, 'where is piety? There is no animal that does not respect its own image; but this does not apply to these people, whose behaviour is scarcely human.'[56] Human nature itself has been denied; indeed, he claims, 'nature has changed'.[57]

The terrible crimes denounced by Gerson and by others, all of them acts against nature,[58] represented the ultimate in perversity. Such crimes cannot be forgiven and Robert Blondel, for one, cannot ignore them. In the light of the tone which he was to adopt in the *De Complanctu*, it comes as no surprise that Blondel's language, when describing the massacres in Paris, should be at least as

50] See G. Ouy, 'La *Deploratio super civitatem aut regionem que gladium evaginavit super se* (ms. unique Paris B.N. lat. 2049). Gerson est-il l'auteur de ce texte anonyme sur les massacres de juin 1418?', in *Miscellanea André Combes*, 2 vols, Rome, 1967, Vol. II, pp. 351–87. Also published in *Divinitas*, Vol. XI, 1967, pp. 747–84. The discovery of a second manuscript of this text enabled Gilbert Ouy to confirm its attribution to Gerson; see 'Problèmes d'édition des manuscrits autographes médiévaux', in *Les Problèmes posés par l'édition critique des textes anciens et médiévaux*, ed. J. Hamesse, Louvain-la-Neuve, 1992, pp. 405–06.

51] 'Consurrexit tumultus in populo, horror et rabies immanitatis' (*'Deploratio'*, p. 376, ll. 16–17).

52] 'Terribile, dirum, pestilens, atrox, ferum! Scelera sceleribus succedunt. Nulla dies horrore caret ... Crebescit horror' (ibid., p. 386, ll. 310–11, 316).

53] 'Bello gravior sedicio, rabies leonina' (ibid., p. 378, ll. 69–70).

54] Ibid., p. 377, ll. 37–38.

55] Ibid., p. 377, ll. 44–45; p. 381, l. 185; p. 380, ll. 130–37; p. 379, ll. 108–09.

56] Ibid., p. 381, ll. 175–78.

57] Ibid., p. 381, l. 184; 'mutata natura', p. 378, l. 84.

58] See C. Gauvard, *'De grace especial'. Crime, Etat et Société en France à la fin du Moyen Age*, 2 vols, Paris, 1991, Vol. I, p. 219. All attacks on pregnant women were regarded as sacrilege (ibid., Vol. II, p. 824).

strong as that of Gerson. 'Shame on you, Paris, for causing all these evils ... City of homicide, you have killed the prelates of God, and are steeped in the blood of kings; infants have fallen to your fury, and the unborn have died, unbaptised, in the wombs which bore them.'[59] Crimes such as these – he instances, too, the murder of royal officers – are born of treachery and rebellion.[60] In character, these represent acts associated with Nero and Herod. Blondel is not afraid to accuse the Duke of Burgundy, the target of these attacks, of being linked to these terrible crimes.[61]

The *De Complanctu* brings together the two accusations underlined above. For Blondel, as for the author of *Super omnia*, the Duke of Burgundy is a 'vassal felon', whose alliance with England is denounced in several passages.[62] Secondly, as Jean de Terrevermeille had already claimed, both Dukes of Burgundy were rebels, seducers of the people, propagators of every kind of evil which spread among the people, infecting towns with their venom of envy.[63] Above all, it is the so-called 'love' of John the Fearless which has broken fraternal bonds and sustained rebel vassals against their lord; that same love has deprived many mothers of their children, forced the just to submit to the torments of martyrdom, converted peoples and towns into rebels, so that sons now prepare to fight their fathers. Many are the rich who have become poor; many, too, are those forced to flee their country. That 'love' has also been responsible for acts of arson, theft, and pillage, as well as ambushes, rapes, murders and other betrayals. It is John the Fearless, above all, who is the cause of the divisions from which the kingdom suffers.[64]

If Blondel holds Duke John directly responsible for the Parisian massacres, Gerson is more circumspect. His *Deploratio* contains only a single implicit (and bitter) reference to the duke 'who governs through rebellion';[65] none the less, much of the language employed is clearly aimed at the Burgundians more generally. Likewise, following Blondel, he establishes a link between this rising and John the Fearless's first crime, the assassination of Louis of Orléans, whose blood cries out to heaven.[66] Although Gerson is not explicit in his hope for an act

59] 'Ve tibi Parisius! Nobis mala cuncta ministrans; / ... Prelatos tu necuisti / Urbs homicida, Dei; maduisti sanguine regum / Atque furore tuo pueri cecidere tenelli / Et cum ventre suo periit sine crismate fetus' (Blondel, *Oeuvres*, Vol. 1, p. 12, vv. 269, 274–77).
60] Ibid., pp. 7–8, vv 147–50; p. 9, vv. 184–85.
61] Gauvard, *'De grace especial'*, Vol. I, p. 226; Blondel, *Oeuvres*, Vol. I, p. 8, vv. 171–72.
62] For example, 'Teque vorare leo dominum vult et leopardus / Ambo feri socii sunt, sanguinis ambo rapaces' ('The lion and the leopard want to devour both your lordship and yourself: these two wild beasts, both avid for blood, are allies' (ibid., p. 13, vv. 292–93)).
63] 'Urbes invidie madefactas labe veneni / Inficiens' (ibid., p. 18, vv. 425–26).
64] Ibid., pp. 19–20, vv. 445–55.
65] '... ducem sedicione potentem' (Ouy, 'La *Deploratio*', p. 383, l. 229).
66] 'Vox effusi sanguinis fratris regii super terram / ... clamat ad Dominum' (ibid., p. 382, ll. 207–08).

of divine vengeance, is this not what he seeks? Certainly, as is well known, Blondel hoped for one, and he viewed the murder at Montereau as an act of justice: 'People, do not complain at the death of this hardened lion ... the only cause of the evils from which the world suffers; no man was ever born who caused so many evils as did this bloody tyrant'.[67]

But rather than linger on such evidence of Robert Blondel's hatred of the Duke of Burgundy, should we not ask what lay behind it? Did it stem from the duke's attitude at the time of the siege of Rouen (1418-19)? Having described the English conquest of Normandy, Blondel turns to make a virulent attack not, as might be expected, against Henry V but against John the Fearless. Faced with the English invasion, the people of Rouen, confident of the duke's support, expected him to defend them; instead, he was more concerned with seizing the lands and goods of his sovereign lord, the king.[68] Blondel then addresses the city of Paris to emphasise the harsh reality of the duke's so-called 'love', stressing that he has betrayed the people of Rouen, too; having promised to come to their aid, he left them to their fate, thus making himself responsible for the long drawn-out siege which claimed 30 000 deaths from starvation. A Norman in exile, Blondel cannot forget; nor can he forgive.

* * * * *

The arguments which we have considered are very different. Between them they cover a wide span of reactions to events, and a variety of ways of reasoning. When compared with the intellectual arguments, the role of those inspired by emotion and personal reaction is impressive. The sense of indignation, sometimes almost visceral in character, is brought to bear in support of the dauphin. But it is also found linked to arguments which are the product of an analysis of institutions and forms of government which we may regard as objective. This mixture becomes clear when Blondel or Terrevermeille refers to the person of John the Fearless, that 'tyrant' whose ambition it has been to usurp the government of the kingdom. Another example is to be found in the appeals from supporters of the dauphin to the University of Paris. After the dauphin's flight from Paris (May 1418), but before the settling of the Anglo-Burgundian accord (in December), his secretary, Alain Chartier, the well-known humanist, wrote to the university, asking for it to intervene, since it alone, he claimed, could restore peace among a divided people.[69] Even in this short text we find ideas already expressed by both Blondel and Gerson: the father and son are one, and the powers

67] Blondel, *Oeuvres*, Vol. I, pp. 32–33, ll. 700–06.
68] Ibid., p. 95, vv. 1137–56, a translation of *De Complanctu* (ibid., pp. 18–19, vv. 427–34).
69] *Les Oeuvres latines d'Alain Chartier*, ed. P. Bourgain-Heymerick, Paris, 1977, pp. 221–24, esp. p. 221, § 4. See the chapter in the present volume by James Laidlaw on this point.

of the crown are hereditary; all that is happening is contrary to nature.[70] That is why, when faced with a threat which could lead not only the king and his son, but the kingdom as a whole, into servitude, the university owes it to itself, as its sole responsibility, to preach a real peace, not a false one, and to lead the people towards harmony.[71] Chartier's appeal is both moral and political, but he gives it an institutional character. In so far as the university is, as Gerson claims it to be, the 'enseigneresse de verité' ('teacher of truth'), its role is to guide the government of the country.[72]

A similar appeal is made by Robert Blondel. In this case, however, we are playing on another register, using another vocabulary. Blondel begs the university to rally around the dauphin in order to help its 'brother', expelled from its high tower by rebellion.[73] Even if this expression has a meaning identical to that of the expression 'fille du roi' widely used at the time, its rarity (it does not appear elsewhere) reinforces its impact.

What conclusions may one come to? Any attempt to appeal to sentiment is not an effort to convince by argument, but an appeal to a sentiment already shared with others. Failing to take account of this leaves all the arguments in their different modes of expression without any meaning. The appeal to emotion is valid only when one has ceased to try to convince intellectually, but can yet achieve something by appealing to commonly-held assumptions, in the present case a particular sense of identity and membership of the national community which meant that, as a subject of that community, it was inconceivable that anyone should act as if he were not.

Therein lies the importance of the steps taken on behalf of the faction which, weaker than its opponents at the time, would none the less taste victory in the years to come. However, did it actually reflect the opinion of the majority or, at least, of the majority of those with influence over the control of government? Would it, on the other hand, be imposed by the victory of that action? Is the winning faction that which is able to impose its vision of things, or does it win precisely because it represents the most widely-held political ideas? The reply given by the texts is unequivocal, and any consideration of the development of national sentiment must take it into account.

Finally, we should notice that affective arguments do not hold sway for very long; their influence is soon lost. We have seen how the passionate expression of hostile opinion centred largely on John, Duke of Burgundy. Yet, even before the reconciliation brought about at Arras in 1435, the tone of the writings of Jean Juvénal des Ursins was already much more measured than that of Jean de

70] Ibid., p. 223, § 14; p. 222, § 9.
71] Ibid., p. 223, § 16.
72] 'Veniat pax' (Gerson, *Oeuvres complètes*, Vol. VII/2, p. 1100, no. 396).
73] 'Surge Minerva, juva fratrem ... Expulit ista tuum germanum turribus altis' (Blondel, *Oeuvres*, Vol. I, p. 10, vv. 214, 223).

Terrevermeille and Robert Blondel, closer to that of the official at the *Parlement* of Poitiers who compiled the very juridical tract, *Super omnia*. It is true that in *Audite celi* Juvénal des Ursins criticises Philip the Good for allying himself to the King of England, but the Treaty of Arras is largely a summary of the arguments put forward in favour of reconciliation with the King of France, so that the Duke of Burgundy shall no longer hesitate to place himself at his service: 'retournés a luy et le servés de tout vostre cueur' ('go back to him and serve him with all your hearts'), pleads Juvénal.[74]

The text *Pour ce que plusieurs*, drawn up to help in the negotiations of 1463, is even more significant. It contains a clear refutation, in four points, of the Treaty of Troyes: it was sealed when Charles VI was a sick man; he was a prisoner; he had no right to transmit the crown which was not his personal possession; and, finally, the papacy recognised Charles VII as the legitimate king from the moment of his succession.[75] There is no reference to John, Duke of Burgundy; indeed, his son, Philip the Good, himself possessed a copy of the work![76] This casting of the past into oblivion was certainly facilitated by the irrational character of the criticisms levelled against the dukes. Given the role played by the future King of France in the murder of John the Fearless at Montereau, one can also imagine that it was in the general interest to bury the past. Things were restored, or well on the way to being so.

74] *Ecrits politiques de Jean Juvénal des Ursins*, ed. P. S. Lewis, 3 vols, SHF, Paris, 1978–1992, Vol. I, p. 264.

75] *Pretensions des Anglois a la couronne de France*, ed. R. Anstruther, Roxburghe Club, London, 1847, pp. 40–42. On this matter see M. Harvey, *England, Rome and the Papacy, 1417–1464. The Study of a Relationship*, Manchester, 1993, pp. 133, 135.

76] Brussels, Bibliothèque Royale, ms 9469–70.

5

War, Propaganda and Diplomacy in Fifteenth-Century France and England[1]

CRAIG TAYLOR

I

Medieval rulers did not have the capacity to produce and circulate propaganda on a modern scale, nor could they benefit from the scientific analysis of psychology and sociology as a guide for such activities. Yet they were well aware of the basic means, such as the manipulation of words and images, symbols and public ceremony, of influencing the thoughts and actions of their subjects.[2] Indeed, during the Hundred Years War, the French and English governments made every effort to ensure public support for a conflict that placed an unprecedented burden upon the populations of both countries. In France, some of the greatest of all medieval writers contributed to this programme, consciously or unconsciously: Alain Chartier, Christine de Pizan, Jean Gerson and their colleagues were naturally hostile to the enemies of France, and called upon their countrymen to rally behind their king and accept reform as the price of victory.[3] At the same time, a number of polemical texts offered a more

1] This chapter offers a re-examination of the corpus of texts discussed by P. S. Lewis in his seminal article, 'War Propaganda and Historiography in Fifteenth-Century France and England', *TRHistS*, Fifth series, Vol. XV, 1965, pp. 1–21, repr. in idem, *Essays in Later Medieval French History*, London, 1985, pp. 193–213. I would like to express my thanks to Peter Lewis for the guidance that he has given me, and to Françoise Autrand, Pierre Chaplais, James Clark, Kathleen Daly, Jean-Philippe Genet, Michael Jones and Nicole Pons.
2] P. Contamine, 'Aperçus sur la propagande de guerre, de la fin du XIIe au début du XVe siècle: les Croisades, la Guerre de Cent Ans', in *Le forme della propaganda politica nel due e nel trecento,* ed. P. Cammarosano, Rome, 1994, pp. 5–27.
3] *Alain Chartier, Le Quadrilogue Invectif*, ed. E. Droz, rev. edn, Paris, 1950, together with the *Dialogus familiaris amici et sodalis*, and the *Letter to the University* and *Letter concerning Joan of Arc*, in *Les Oeuvres latines d'Alain Chartier*, ed. P. Bourgain-Hemeryck, Paris, 1977, pp. 245–325, 221–24 and 326–29; Jean Gerson, *De puella Aurelianensi* and *Vivat rex* in *Oeuvres complètes*, ed. P. Glorieux, 10 vols, Paris-Tournai, 1960–73, Vol. IX, pp. 661–65; Vol. VII, pp. 1137–85; Christine de Pizan, *Le Livre de la paix*, ed. C. Willard, The Hague, 1958. See also *Débat des hérauts d'armes de France et d'Angleterre, suivi de 'The Debate between the Heralds of England and France' by John Coke*, ed. L. Pannier, SATF, Paris, 1877; 'Le *Tragicum argumentum de miserabili statu regni Francie* de François de Monte-Belluna', ed. A. Vernet, *Annuaire-Bulletin de la*

direct analysis of the war, going beyond the traditional medieval concerns about the evils of the times and the need for moral reform, to examine 'the legal and historical truth about the quarrel between England and France', seeking 'above all to instruct [and] to present the argument against the enemy in a convincing yet viable form'.[4] According to André Bossuat, these polemical treatises were part of the royal plan to win over public opinion and thus reveal 'les voies mystérieuses qui permettent à la pensée des "clercs" de pénétrer insensiblement le peuple tout entier' ('the mysterious ways which allow the thought of "clerks" to become imperceptibly that of the whole people'). More recently, Nicole Pons has claimed that they were primarily designed 'pour convaincre, pour entraîner l'adhésion du plus grand nombre de lecteurs potentiels possible' ('to persuade, to secure acceptance by the greatest number of readers'); while Jacques Krynen has declared that 'Ce qui rapproche toutes ces oeuvres ... c'est le désir plus ou moins avoué de chacun de leurs auteurs d'obtenir la plus large audience possible' ('what unites all these works ... is the implicit desire to reach the widest possible audience').[5]

Without doubt, some of the polemical texts were intended for dissemination to a wide audience. Nicole Pons has recently highlighted the importance of a number of short pamphlets produced in the aftermath of the murder of John, Duke of Burgundy, on the bridge at Montereau in September 1419. For example, *Super omnia vincit veritas*, written by an officer of the *Parlement* or *Chambre des Comptes* and subsequently translated into French as the *Réponse d'un bon et loyal François*, was probably part of the intense propaganda campaign to win over the undecided to the defence of the dauphin against the Treaty of Troyes.[6]

Société de l'Histoire de France, 1962–63, pp. 103–63. I will discuss contemporary writing on the Hundred Years War in my forthcoming book.

4] Lewis, 'War Propaganda and Historiography', pp. 2–4, repr. in idem, *Essays in Later Medieval French History*, pp. 194–96. Colette Beaune (*The Birth of an Ideology: Myths and Symbols of Nationhood in Later Medieval France*, Berkeley, 1991, p. 257) claims that Robert Blondel referred to eleven treatises on Anglo-French relations, but I cannot find any trace of this; moreover, it is highly unlikely that he was aware of all of the texts that she considers to have been on this list.

5] A. Bossuat, 'La Littérature de propagande au XVe siècle: le mémoire de Jean de Rinel, secrétaire du roi d'Angleterre, contre le duc de Bourgogne (1435)', *Cahiers d'histoire*, Vol. I, 1956, p. 146; N. Pons, 'Latin et français au XVe siècle: le témoignage des traités de propagande', in *Le Moyen français. Actes du Ve colloque international sur le moyen français, Milan, 6–8 mai 1985*, Milan, 1986, Vol. II, p. 71; J. Krynen, *L'Empire du roi: idées et croyances politiques en France, XIIIe–XVe siècles*, Paris, 1993, p. 311.

6] *L'Honneur de la couronne de France': quatre libelles contre les Anglais (vers 1418–vers 1429)*, ed. N. Pons, SHF, Paris, 1990, pp. 83–137; B. Guenée, 'Les Campagnes de lettres qui ont suivi le meurtre de Jean sans Peur, duc de Bourgogne (septembre 1419–février 1420)', *Annuaire-Bulletin de la Société de l'Histoire de France*, 1993, pp. 45–65, esp. pp. 56–57. Robert Blondel's *De complanctu bonorum Gallicorum* and *Oratio historialis* are often cited alongside the polemical treatises, but in fact they do not offer any significant discussion of the legal issues of the war and thus belong to the wider category of war literature. Robert Blondel, *Oeuvres de Robert Blondel, historien normand du XVe siècle*, ed. A. Héron, 2 vols, SHN, Rouen, 1891–93. On this matter, the reader is referred to the chapter by Nicole Pons in this volume.

Yet there is very little evidence to suggest that the most important French polemical texts were intended to serve as direct propaganda for the wider population.[7] Rather, these treatises were produced by royal officials for their fellow administrators and diplomats, and perhaps also for the king and other members of the court, developing models provided by fourteenth-century diplomatic dossiers and legal memoranda. Jean de Montreuil, *notaire et secrétaire du roi*, composed two major works, *Regali ex progenie* (1406–13) and the *Traité contre les Anglais* (1413–16).[8] His colleague, Noël de Fribois, was almost certainly the author of the *Mirouer Historial* (1451) and the *Abrégé des chroniques* (1453–61), and *Pour ce que plusieurs* (1464) was composed by an anonymous royal official, perhaps Guillaume Cousinot II, their fellow *notaire et secrétaire*; while another, Louis Le Blanc, was almost certainly the author of *Pour vraye congnoissance avoir* (1471).[9] Jean Juvénal des Ursins drew upon Montreuil's work to produce two direct discussions of the legal issues of the war, *Audite celi* (1435) and *Tres crestien, tres hault, tres puissant roy* (1446); he was not a *notaire et secrétaire* but, as he declared to Charles VII, 'ay esté vostre advocat et conseillier en vostre court de Parlement, ou j'ay gardé a mon povoir les drois de la couronne et de vous' ('I have been your counsellor and adviser in your court of *Parlement* where I have maintained, as far as I can, the rights of the crown and of yourself'), and he certainly felt qualified to provide detailed advice on the chancellorship and the administration in general when his brother Guillaume was appointed to that office in 1445.[10] Taken together, these treatises provided an invaluable resource

7] Bernard Guenée famously remarked that it is 'abusif de parler de propagande à propos de ces petits traités confidentiels et produits au XVe siècle par des humanistes en mal d'écrire et répandues à deux ou trois exemplaires' (B. Guenée, 'Les Tendences actuelles de l'histoire politique du moyen âge français', *Actes du 100e Congrès National des Sociétés Savantes, Paris, 1975*, Paris, 1977, Vol. I, p. 59. See also P. S. Lewis' comments in Jean Juvénal des Ursins, *Les Écrits politiques de Jean Juvénal des Ursins*, ed. P. S. Lewis, 3 vols, SHF, Paris, 1978–93, Vol. III, p. 153.

8] Jean de Montreuil, *Opera*, ed. N. Grévy-Pons, E. Ornato and G. Ouy, 4 vols, Turin-Paris, 1963–86), esp. Vol. IV, pp. 304–18.

9] For Noël de Fribois, see the forthcoming edition by Kathleen Daly together with her articles 'Histoire et politique à la fin de la Guerre de Cent Ans: l'*Abrégé des chroniques de France* de Noël de Fribois', in '*La France anglaise au moyen âge'. Actes du 111e Congrès National des Sociétés Savantes. Poitiers, 1986*, Paris, 1988, Vol. I, pp. 91–101, and 'The *Mirouer historial abrégié de France*: Historical Culture and Politics at the Court of Charles VII', in *Vincent de Beauvais: intentions et réceptions d'une oeuvre encyclopédique au moyen âge*, ed. M. Paulmier-Foucart, S. Lusignan and A. Nadeau, Montréal, 1990, pp. 467–94. For *Pour ce que plusieurs*, see C. D. Taylor, '"La Querelle Anglaise": Diplomatic and Legal Debate during the Hundred Years War, with an Edition of the Polemical Treatise *Pour ce que plusieurs* (1464)', unpublished DPhil thesis, University of Oxford, 1999, together with my forthcoming edition of the treatise. For *Pour vraye congnoissance avoir*, see BNF, mss. fr. 15490 and 25159, together with K. Daly, 'Mixing Business with Leisure: Some French Royal Notaries and Secretaries and their Histories of France, c.1459–1509', in *Power, Culture and Religion in France, c.1350–1550*, ed. C. T. Allmand, Woodbridge, 1989, p. 101.

10] Jean Juvénal, *Ecrits politiques*, Vol. I, pp. 441–551; Vol. II, pp. 124–32.

for the Valois government, preparing officials for diplomatic negotiations and public assemblies within France. That the English lacked such texts is less an indication of their failure to recognise the value and possibilities of propaganda, than the unique intellectual culture of the Valois government.

II

The French royal administration forms the natural context for the polemical treatises. Most of the authors were *notaires et secrétaires du roi*, while the majority of surviving manuscripts of the polemical texts emanate from administrative circles. Many of Montreuil's manuscripts were destroyed by the Burgundians when they captured Paris, but a number remained in the *Chambre des Comptes*. For example, Jean Budé owned a manuscript that included Montreuil's *Regali ex progenie*, as well as another containing *Pour ce que plusieurs*; during the reign of Louis XI, an abridgement of Montreuil's Latin text of the *Traité contre les Anglais* was included in a chancellery formulary, together with a genealogy of the kings of France and a list of royal prerogatives. A number of texts produced in the chancellery demonstrate a direct knowledge of Montreuil's works: the *Genealogie des rois de France, Verite est que* was written between 1422 and 1431, perhaps in 1425, by an anonymous scribe of the chancellery based on Montreuil's *Résumé du Traité contre les Anglais*; *Pour vraye congnoissance avoir* was also inspired by Jean de Montreuil, as were the *Mirouer Historial* and the *Abrégé des chroniques* by Noël de Fribois. Both of Fribois' chronicles themselves circulated within the *Chambre des Comptes*, as Jean Le Bègue possessed a corrected manuscript of the *Abrégé des chroniques* that was evidently an early draft of the text that Fribois presented to the king in 1459; Etienne Chevalier, *notaire et secrétaire* and then *trésorier* to Charles VII and Louis XI, owned a manuscript of the completed text. In the next generation, Jacques Le Picart annotated one of the best manuscripts of the *Abrégé des chroniques* and, with Nicole Gilles, made extensive use of it in his own work. But perhaps the outstanding example of the use that these treatises served for the administrators was *Pour vraye congnoissance avoir*, which contained precise references to the location of supporting documents in the *Chambre des Comptes* and the *Trésor des Chartes*.[11]

The polemical treatises were invaluable to French officials as a source of materials for the defence of the 'droiz, preeminences et prerogatives' ('rights,

11] Montreuil, *Opera*, Vol. II, pp. 240–46; Vol. IV, pp. 15–17, 35–40, 44–46; N. Pons, 'Un exemple de l'utilisation des écrits politiques de Jean de Montreuil: un memorandum diplomatique redigé sous Charles VII', in *Préludes à la renaissance: aspects de la vie intellectuelle en France au XVe siècle*, ed. C. Bozzolo and E. Ornato, Paris, 1992, pp. 243–64; K. Daly, 'The "Miroir historial abrégé de France" and "C'est chose profitable": A Study of Two Fifteenth-Century French Historical Texts and their Context', unpublished DPhil thesis, University of Oxford, 2 vols, 1983, pp. 169–73, 189–90; idem, 'Mixing Business with Leisure', pp. 99–115.

privileges and prerogatives') of the French crown at a time when successive kings bemoaned the 'grant desordre' ('great disorder') of the royal archives: by the reign of Louis XI, chests and cupboards in the *Chambre des Comptes* were literally overflowing with documents. Thus the location of materials for the defence of the crown could be a difficult task: in 1457, the *trésorier*, Dreux Budé, and three other officials searched for past treaties between kings of France and the kings of Hungary or Bohemia, in preparation for negotiations between Charles VII and Ladislas, the reigning king of Bohemia; in the early 1460s, French officials undertook a wide-ranging search of royal and provincial archives to find documents for the dispute between Louis XI and Duke Francis II of Brittany over regalian rights; in 1478 Louis XI called for two separate searches of the archives for materials to support impending negotiations with the Duke of Austria at Cambrai, and with the English.[12] Under these circumstances, royal officials needed working instruments, such as the memorials of the *Chambre des Comptes*. Moreover, clerks began to collect documents for personal and professional purposes. In the early years of the reign of Louis XI, genealogies of past kings, together with a short account of their reigns, were incorporated into a chancellery formula probably prepared for a *notaire et secrétaire*. Jean Le Bègue recorded historical details from the memorials of the *Chambre des Comptes* in his manual, as did Pierre Amer; Louis Le Blanc made a personal collection of copies of documents from the archives of the *Chambre*, and was also commissioned to compile an inventory of documents in the *Trésor des Chartes*.[13] French officials also prepared a number of dossiers relating to diplomatic negotiations with foreign powers. At the start of the fourteenth century, officials like Pierre d'Etampes assembled collections of documents relating to very limited themes such as the negotiations for a treaty with Flanders in 1320.[14] Then, shortly before the visit of the emperor Charles IV to Paris in 1378, Gérard II de Montaigu, the future *Garde du Trésor des Chartes*, prepared a collection of 172 documents for Charles V. This dossier, the *Recueil des traités de la France*, gave the king easy access to particularly important documents on the subject of the sovereignty of the crown; it clearly served Charles V well, as he spoke for more than two hours before the emperor about the history of France and the crimes committed by the

12] P. Contamine, 'Méthodes et instruments de travail de la diplomatie française. Louis XI et la régale des évêchés bretons (1462–5)' and 'La Mémoire de l'état: les archives de la Chambre des Comptes du roi de France à Paris au XVe siècle', in *Des pouvoirs en France, 1300–1500*, ed. P. Contamine, Paris, 1992, pp. 147–67, 237–50. Also see O. Guyotjeannin, '*Super omnes thesauros rerum temporalium*: les fonctions du Trésor des Chartes du roi de France (XIVe–XVe siècles)', *Ecrit et pouvoir dans les chancelleries médiévales: espace Français, espace Anglais. Actes du colloque international de Montréal, 7–9 septembre 1995*, ed. K. Fianu and D. J. Guth, Louvain-la-Neuve, 1997, pp. 109–31.

13] Daly, 'Mixing Business with Leisure', p. 103; Contamine, 'La Mémoire de l'état', p. 239.

14] Another register was established in the *Trésor des Chartes* for matters concerning Flanders, England and Scotland.

English.[15] During the reign of Charles VI, an anonymous French official from the *Chambre des Comptes* prepared a collection of treaties, instructions and reports of conferences dating back to the reign of Jean II, together with political and administrative documents such as the famous instruction for the safeguard of royal rights over Montpellier, ceded to the King of Navarre in 1372. This collection even included a list of contents to facilitate quick reference to materials and was undoubtedly intended to provide diplomats with materials necessary for the negotiations with the English.[16] Two manuscripts of the mid-fifteenth century contained diplomatic materials concerning the conflict with the English, while another dossier included a comprehensive collection of original and copied documents relating to François de Surienne's attack upon Fougères in March 1449, and the subsequent abandonment of the truce by Charles VII. This collection may have been prepared in response to a royal instruction issued in 1479, calling for materials to defend the crown against English claims concerning the war.[17]

Perhaps the most interesting French dossier is the *Memoire abregée grossement*, originally prepared in 1390, presumably for use by diplomats at the meetings at Leulingham. This collection included the materials prepared by Gérard II de Montaigu and other documents such as the letter sent to the English on 11 May 1369 regarding breaches of the Treaty of Brétigny; it also contained a general position paper setting out the Valois case against Edward III.[18] Shortly afterwards, Jean de Montreuil produced the first polemical treatise, essentially an extended version of the *Memoire abregée grossement*, which he had copied into one of his working manuscripts. Most of the polemical treatises followed this model, offering a structured analysis of the French case against the English, rather than simply transcribing the original documents; the authors referred the reader back to the archives for those original materials, or occasionally included a limited number of *pièces justificatives*, such as Edward III's confession that he paid liege homage to Philip VI.[19] Montreuil and his colleagues developed the *Memoire abregée grossement* by drawing upon a second type of source, the

15] A. Artonne, 'Le Recueil des traités de la France composé par ordre de Charles V', in *Recueil de travaux offerts à M. Clovis Brunel*, 2 vols, Paris, 1955, Vol. I, pp. 53–63; F. Autrand, 'Les Livres des hommes de pouvoir: de la pratique à la culture écrite: I. Pratique diplomatique et culture politique au temps de Charles V', and N. Pons, 'A l'origine des dossiers polémiques: une initiative publique ou une démarche privée?', in *Pratiques de la culture écrite en France au XVe siècle: Actes du colloque international du CNRS*, Louvain-la-Neuve, 1995, pp. 199–204; 362–63.
16] BNF, ms. fr. 2699.
17] BNF, nouv. acq. fr. 6215 and 6224; ms. fr. 4054. The 1479 memorandum appears in ms. fr. 4054, fol. 241v.
18] Lewis, 'War Propaganda and Historiography', pp. 17–18, repr. in idem, *Essays in Later Medieval French History*, pp. 209–10; Montreuil, *Opera*, Vol. III, pp. 19–20, 51–110.
19] Brussels, Bibliothèque Royale ms. 10306–10307. See also, for example, Montreuil, *Opera*, Vol. II, pp. 106–08, 175–77, 232–34, 279–81; Jean Juvénal, *Ecrits politiques*, Vol. II, pp. 170–77.

academic discussions offered by the extensive legal encyclopaedia, the *Somnium viridarii*, written by Evrart de Trémaugon in 1376 (and translated by Jean Le Fèvre as the *Songe du Vergier* two years later), and the commentary on St Augustine's *De civitate Dei* by François de Meyronnes. The *Somnium viridarii* offered detailed discussion of the rules governing the royal succession, while its translation added a series of arguments against the Treaty of Brétigny, first expounded by Le Fèvre in a speech before the papal mediators in December 1376, and influenced in part by two earlier opinions written by John de Legnano and Richard Saliceto, doctors of the University of Bologna. Montreuil drew heavily upon this material for his own case on the royal succession and the Treaty of Brétigny, while the other polemical writers introduced additional material to support these arguments and also oppose the Treaty of Troyes.[20]

Thus the polemical texts offered a very useful tool for administrators, as demonstrated by the circulation of manuscripts of the works of Montreuil and Fribois within the *Chambres des Comptes*. In addition, many of the treatises also served an important role within the diplomatic sphere. *Tres crestien, tres hault, tres puissant roy* was written by Jean Juvénal in 1446 in preparation for the planned meeting between Henry VI and Charles VII. The author declared that he had followed the king's instructions to compose a treatise for 'la convention que devés avoir avec tres hault et puissant prince Henry, vostre nepveu et adversaire soy disant roy d'Angleterre' ('the meeting which you are going to hold with the very honourable and powerful prince, Henry, your nephew and adversary, so-called king of England'); he developed his earlier discussion of the English claims in *Audite celi*, itself based upon the work of Jean de Montreuil, and also provided his readers with a number of *pièces justificatives* copied from original documents in the registers of the chancellery.[21] Similarly, *Pour ce que plusieurs* provided information for French negotiators for a meeting to be held late in 1464 between the English and the French at Saint-Omer to arrange a marriage between Edward IV and a French princess. Three manuscripts of *Pour ce que plusieurs* also contained the *Vraie cronicque d'Escoce*, probably written

20] Montreuil removed almost all legal references and simply referred his readers to 'un autre traictié a part assez plus grant que c'est ycy' ('another treatise which is considerably bigger than this one'), which may well have been the *Songe du vergier* (Montreuil, *Opera*, Vol. II, pp. 195–96; *Somnium viridarii*, ed. M. Schnerb-Lièvre, 2 vols, Paris, 1993–97; *Le Songe du vergier: édité d'après le manuscrit Royal 19 C IV de la British Library*, ed. M. Schnerb-Lièvre, 2 vols, Paris, 1982; P. Chaplais, 'Jean Le Fèvre, Abbot of Saint-Vaast, and the *Songe du vergier*', in *Recognitions: Essays Presented to Edmund Fryde*, ed. C. Richmond and I. Harvey, Aberystwyth, 1996, pp. 203–28). Jean Juvénal used François de Meyronnes' commentary on Augustine's *De civitate Dei* in *Ecrits politiques*, Vol. II, pp. 42, 46.

21] Jean Juvénal, *Ecrits politiques*, Vol. II, pp. 13–14, 170–77. Nicole Pons regards this as 'un exemple de traité de propagande, joint à un recueil diplomatique' ('an example of a propaganda treatise, accompanied by a collection of diplomatic papers') (Pons, 'A l'origine des dossiers polémiques', p. 369).

shortly after December 1463 by John Ireland, a Scotsman at the University of Paris; this treatise offered an important tool for Louis XI's diplomats negotiating over Scotland's role in the debates between England and France in 1464.[22] The *Résumé du Traité contre les Anglais* was apparently written by Montreuil in two drafts between 1414 and 1416. According to Pons, 'cette oeuvre, assez courte, était certainement destinée à une grande diffusion' ('this short work was surely intended for a wide public') and reflected the wish of Montreuil to reach those outside the government. Yet the surviving copies testify to the dissemination of the work within diplomatic circles; the first draft appears in three English compilations of diplomatic materials belonging to Bishop Bekynton, and the one remaining copy of the second draft appears in a Norman manuscript, immediately before a memorandum on Charles VII's rights to Normandy, apparently used by French diplomats at Arras in 1435. The work, written in French rather than Latin, would seem to be an *aide-mémoire* for the French embassy, a working precis of Montreuil's larger *Traité contre les Anglais.*[23] In 1435, Jean de Rinel wrote a tract in support of the English cause, demonstrating that the Treaty of Troyes was valid and that Henry VI, rather than Charles VII, was the true King of France. Bossuat described this as a propaganda text, designed to persuade those who were unsure or uncommitted to the double monarchy. Yet the mémoire has the 'air more of a private official memorandum than propaganda' and should properly be associated with the diplomatic negotiations at the Congress of Arras.[24]

The value of these texts for diplomats is clear: they offered summaries of the complicated disputes with the English, and clear statements of the Valois position on most points that might be raised during negotiations. Unfortunately there is very limited information as to the materials used by diplomats, largely because so few documents survive. Beyond the official letters that ensured their safe conduct and defined and established the powers and the scope of their actions, diplomats would have required instructions and letters of credence, and occasionally original documents: the instructions given to the French ambassadors sent to Boulogne in April 1377 indicate that they were carrying copies of documents concerning the homage paid by Edward III to Philip VI, as well as letters by which Edward had confirmed all previous agreements made between the

22] K. Daly, 'The *Vraie cronicque d'Escoce* and Franco-Scottish Diplomacy: An Historical Work by John Ireland?', *Nottingham Medieval Studies*, Vol. XXXV, 1991, pp. 106–33; C. D. Taylor, 'Sir John Fortescue and the French Polemical Treatises of the Hundred Years War', *EHR*, Vol. CXIV, 1999, pp. 112–29.

23] Montreuil, *Opera*, Vol. II, pp. 44–46, 324–31; Pons, 'Un exemple de l'utilisation des écrits politiques de Jean de Montreuil', pp. 243–64.

24] Lewis, 'War Propaganda and Historiography', pp. 14–15, repr. in idem, *Essays in Later Medieval French History*, pp. 206–07; *English Medieval Diplomatic Practice. Part 1: Documents and Interpretation*, ed. P. Chaplais, 2 vols, London, 1982, Vol. II, pp. 648–52; Bossuat, 'La Littérature de propagande au XVe siècle', p. 141.

kings of France and England.[25] Yet diplomats would also benefit from shorter memoranda, setting out the central points in contention. As the English observed in 1418, their French counterparts were unfamiliar with the terms of the Treaty of Brétigny and, indeed, had limited geographical knowledge of the territories under discussion, potentially a serious problem given the importance of territorial arrangements in any genuine attempt to resolve the conflict.[26] Large embassies usually included an *orator* who would require a detailed knowledge of the issues between the two sovereigns: in both 1435 and 1439, Archbishop John Kemp and Regnault de Chartres, Archbishop of Reims, exchanged 'orations' regarding the respective claims of Henry VI and Charles VII to the French crown.[27] Diplomats might need background information, and in this context, it is significant that French officials provided an enormous collection of materials relating to the dispute with the Duke of Brittany in the early 1460s, and that for the conference at Chinon in October 1464 they also produced a brief memorandum which offered a readable summary of the key points. Similarly, Michel de Pons, the *procureur général*, composed a detailed treatise on the Burgundian succession in preparation for negotiations that culminated in the Treaty of Arras in 1482; this work survives in twelve copies, some of them illuminated, but the complexity of this work suggests that its primary role was as a manual for royal administrators and diplomats.[28] To a degree, these materials complemented and extended the instructions given to diplomats, which often contained the expression 'bailliee par maniere de memoire' ('drawn up in the form of a memoir') at the head of the text and followed a general format, whereby each article was preceded by an 'item' and separated from the subsequent point by one or two blank lines. The polemical treatises were often presented in the same form, sometimes with lists of contents to facilitate reference to specific sections within

25] *The Anglo-French Negotiations at Bruges, 1374–77*, ed. E. Perroy, in *Camden Miscellany*, Vol. XIX, RHistS, London, 1952, p. 80. Also see I. Le Bis, 'Pratique de la diplomatie. Un dossier d'ambassadeurs français sous Charles VI (1400–1403)', *Annuaire-Bulletin de la Société de l'Histoire de France*, 1985–86, pp. 97–209; J. Dickinson, '"Blanks" and "Blank Charters" in the Fourteenth and Fifteenth Centuries', *EHR*, Vol. LXVI, 1951, pp. 375–87.

26] C. T. Allmand, *The Hundred Years War*, Cambridge, 1989, p. 116. French diplomats regularly defined the boundaries of the Duchy of Guyenne as the *sénéchaussées* of Bordeaux, Landes and Bazadais, even though these were areas of customary law rather than administrative and judicial boundaries (M. G. A. Vale, *English Gascony, 1399–1453: A Study of War, Government and Politics during the Later Stages of the Hundred Years War*, Oxford, 1970, p. 103 n. 8). See also M. Desjardins, 'Les Savoirs des notaires et secrétaires du roi et la géographie de la France d'après le manuel d'Odart Morchesne et un index de chancellerie', *Ecrit et pouvoir dans les chancelleries médiévales*, pp. 87–97.

27] J. Dickinson, *The Congress of Arras, 1435. A Study in Medieval Diplomacy*, Oxford 1955, pp. 5–6, 114; C. T. Allmand, 'The Anglo-French Negotiations of 1439', *BIHR*, Vol. XL, 1967, pp. 10, 17.

28] Contamine, 'Méthodes et instruments de travail de la diplomatie française', pp. 166–67; P. Saenger, 'Burgundy and the Inalienability of Apanages in the Reign of Louis XI', *French Historical Studies*, Vol. X, 1977–78, pp. 13–26.

the text.[29] It is possible that they were intended for use during the meetings themselves, but it is more likely that they provided background information; the treatises did not set out the precise responses to be given to almost any conceivable argument put forward by the English.

Ultimately, the importance of the polemical treatises within the French royal administration was attested to by the repeated requests for such manuals to be updated.[30] In 1446, Jean Juvénal composed *Tres crestien, tres hault, tres puissant roy* in response to a royal request that 'je me transportasse en vos Chambres des comptes, du tresor de vos chartres, et ailleurs, pour veoir les lettres et chartes qui pourroyent estre necessaires ... et que d'icelles feisse transumptions soubz seel auttenthicque, et que je queisse toutez aultres choses servans a la matiere' ('I should go to your *Chambre des Comptes* and the *Trésor des Chartes* and elsewhere to see such letters and charters which might be required ... and to make copies of these under seal of authentication, and that I should look for other papers relating to the matter'); in the aftermath of the English attack on Fougères in 1449, Charles VII asked Jean Juvénal to provide him with a justification for renewing the war against the English.[31] On 16 August 1464, Louis XI commissioned Guillaume Cousinot II to prepare a defence of royal rights over the Duchy of Brittany; Cousinot was also the author of a memorandum supporting Louis XI's pretensions to Burgundy and the county of Mâcon upon the death of Charles the Bold.[32] In 1478, Louis XI again asked Cousinot to join five other men to draw up 'beaux, notables, grans' memoranda setting out responses to the English pretensions to the crown of France, to Normandy and to Guyenne. Perhaps the next year, a council memorandum indicated the importance of 'beaulx livres a perpetuel memoire pour estre mis tant en la Chambre des Comptes que ou Tresor des chartes ... [regardant] la querelle du roy a l'encontre du roy d'Angleterre' ('fine volumes holding records to be kept in the *Chambre des Comptes* and the *Trésor des Chartes* regarding amongst other things the king's dispute with the king of England').[33] Indeed, this effort was not confined solely to France; in 1459 the Duke of Burgundy instructed his chancellor to produce a memorandum on the French non-observance of the Treaty of Arras for the Burgundian ambassadors who were about to negotiate with them.[34]

29] Le Bis, 'Pratique de la diplomatie', pp. 105–23; *Anglo-French Negotiations at Bruges*, ed. Perroy, pp. 69–74. See also J. Ferguson, *English Diplomacy, 1422–1461*, Oxford, 1972, pp. 146–74; Dickinson, *Congress of Arras*, pp. xvi–xxii, esp. p. xx.

30] The repeated request to produce new treatises may also demonstrate the ephemeral nature of such texts: there is no surviving official, contemporary French copy of the *Résumé du Traité contre les Anglais* or *Tres crestien, tres hault, tres puissant roy*, and although the *notaire et secrétaire* Jean Budé had a copy of *Pour ce que plusieurs* by 1486, there is no trace of an earlier 'official' copy.

31] Jean Juvénal, *Ecrits politiques*, Vol. II, pp. 13–14; Vol. III, p. 79.

32] *Lettres de Louis XI, roi de France*, ed. J. Vaesen and E. Charavay, 11 vols, SHF, Paris, 1883–1909, Vol. II, p. 219 (no. cxxxv).

33] BNF, ms. fr. 4054, fols 240–43.

34] Dickinson, *Congress of Arras*, p. 242n.

III

Certain polemical texts may have been well received within the royal court. Essentially they provided summaries of more complex materials, including both original documents and legal memoranda: Montreuil avoided the use of detailed legal citations, emphasising his desire to be understood by laymen, while Fribois thought that the 'importance and verbosity' of such sources prevented investigation of the past by nobles, 'obstans la briefte et fragilite de ceste vie humaine et les grans affaires en quoy ilz sont souventesfoiz occupez pour le bien de la chose publique' ('considering the brevity and frailty of mortal life and the affairs in which they are all too often occupied for the sake of the common good').[35] Moreover, almost all the polemical texts were written or translated into the vernacular, and where sources were quoted in Latin, the writers were careful to provide translations. This accorded with Charles V's programme of translating highly academic materials into the vernacular. Clearly the most important audience for such works was the crown itself: Raoul de Presles translated Augustine's *De civitate Dei* into French 'tant pour plaire a vous [Charles V] comme pour profiter a voz subgéz' ('both for your pleasure and the benefit of your people'), and Gérard II de Montaigu provided both Latin and French copies of documents in the *Recueil des traités de la France* 'on the orders of the king'.[36] Fifty years later, the *Réponse d'un bon et loyal François* even attacked the English for composing the Treaty of Troyes (1420) in Latin, given that the king, the queen, Princess Katherine and the majority of the nobles could not understand that language.[37] Certainly, many of the polemical treatises would have held a genuine interest for the kings and great nobles, especially when couched in a more literary style that softened the form of the administrative and diplomatic text. Montreuil's treatise *Regali ex progenie*, and its translation, *A toute la chevalerie*, offered a commentary on the martial qualities and successes of the French. The text was originally dedicated to the dauphin of the day, Louis de Guyenne (d.1415), as an encouragement to emulate the examples of his predecessors; the discussion of the English claims was a mere appendix to *A toute la chevalerie*, which in 1413 Montreuil expanded into a fully-fledged discussion of the debates with the English. Fribois' *Abrégé des chroniques* was intended to encourage 'the kings and princes of France' to follow the example of their illustrious predecessors: the discussions of specific issues, such as the laws governing the royal succession and the validity of the Treaty of Troyes, were essentially detailed

35] Montreuil, *Opera*, Vol. II, pp. 162, 223, 265, 268–69; the *Abrégé des chroniques,* in B.L. Add. Ms. 13961, fol. 2.

36] J. Monfrin, 'Humanisme et traductions au Moyen Âge', in *L'Humanisme médiéval dans les littératures romanes du XIIe au XIVe siècle*, ed. A. Fournier, Paris, 1964, pp. 217–46; Artonne, 'Le Recueil des traités de la France', pp. 55–57.

37] *'L'Honneur de la couronne de France'*, pp. 122–23; note, however, that Louis XI, for example, was well trained in Latin.

reports within this glorious story.[38] Such materials, particularly the chronicles, would undoubtedly have appealed to the French kings: Charles VII read a chronicle during his visit to the Norman abbey of Ardenne, during the military campaign of 1450.[39] Moreover, there are certainly hints that individual kings were well-informed about such matters: in 1480, Louis XI reported that he had been told that if women were permitted to succeed to Flanders and Burgundy, then Charles of Navarre or the King of England would be the rightful ruler of France because apanages were subject to the same rules as the French crown.[40]

Perhaps the best examples of works prepared for the prince are the texts written on the eve of the Congress of Arras in 1435. Dream stories were a common means for French scholars to present complex works; the method was used by Evrart de Trémaugon in the *Somnium viridarii*, Philippe de Mézières in the *Songe du vieil pèlerin*, and by Honoré Bouvet in the *Apparicion maistre Jehan de Meun*. It is hardly surprising that in *Audite celi* Jean Juvénal presented his first discussion of the issues of the war through the medium of the strange vision of a mysterious woman who had seen three ladies, France, England and the Church, meeting at Arras in order to find peace; their discussions were influenced by the contributions of Ambition, Greed, Hatred, Vengeance, Sedition, Charity, as well of those of True Love and other positive virtues. Jean Juvénal wished to set out the legal issues of the war, but having witnessed the impact of the war upon his see of Beauvais, he also genuinely hoped that the forthcoming negotiations at the Congress of Arras would lead to peace. At the same time, a number of Burgundian councillors produced memoranda examining Philip the Good's obligations to Henry VI by virtue of the Treaty of Troyes; these texts employed a very literary style, particularly one that addressed the question through an excursion into the history of Persia under King Darius. In both cases, the authors approached complex problems through highly literary styles, demonstrating that they were intended to be read or heard by the king or duke. The Burgundian writers clearly hoped to placate any qualms that Philip the Good had about breaking the oath that he had made to uphold the Treaty of Troyes.[41]

Even the more dry, academic works may have served to prepare princes and

38] Montreuil, *Opera*, Vol. II, p. 11; Daly, 'Histoire et politique', pp. 91–101.
39] M. G. A. Vale, *Charles VII*, London, 1974, pp. 139, 198.
40] *Lettres de Louis XI*, Vol. VIII, pp. 275–77, discussed in Saenger, 'Burgundy and the Inalienability of Apanages', p. 12. In 1320, Edward II had a quick and detailed answer to a tricky question posed by the French regarding homage (H. Rothwell, 'Edward I's Case against Philip the Fair over Gascony', *EHR*, Vol. XLII, 1927, pp. 575–77).
41] Jean Juvénal, *Ecrits politiques*, Vol. I, pp. 96–98, 145–278; F. Schneider, *Der europäische Friedenskongres von Arras (1435) und die Friedenspolitik Papst Eugens IV und das Basler Konzils*, Griess, 1919, pp. 185–208, discussed in Dickinson, *Congress of Arras*, pp. 66–77 and 241–44. The Count of Foix and the Duke of Brittany had earlier wrestled with the same problems, and may have also sought the opinion of canon lawyers and the church.

great nobles for diplomatic meetings with the English. Normally such men played a very limited role in diplomatic parleys, perhaps because of their rank and also to avoid any embarrassment over precedence. But throughout the Hundred Years War, and particularly from the 1370s to the negotiations near Calais in 1439, specific nobles were heavily involved in negotiations, even if the surviving sources provide little information as to their precise roles.[42] During a preliminary meeting on 14 February 1390 to arrange a conference between the two kings, the English proposed an embassy composed of the royal uncles and four hundred knights and esquires, together with just two prelates or doctors as counsellors. But three years later, John of Gaunt and the Dukes of Gloucester, Berry and Burgundy agreed a provisional treaty and arranged a separate meeting of legal experts to resolve the continuing problems of sovereignty and resort over lands within France. The next year Montreuil himself took part in an embassy to England with Jean de Blaisy, and took the opportunity to write to John of Gaunt, seeking a rapprochement between the English and French crowns, and recommending the use of specialist counsellors to overcome the problems of sovereignty.[43] Presumably the expert diplomats would have been able to make use of compilations of documents, and perhaps even the complex legal opinions offered by the *Somnium viridarii* and the other legal memoranda of the war. But as Montreuil indicated in September 1416, the polemical treatises would be valuable for the great lords taking part in embassies:

> Les Anglois ayent livres les plus beaulx et les plus notables quilz pevent faire de ce quiulz demandent en France, lesquelz ils portent communement avecques eulx quant ilz doivent assembler avec les Francois pour traicter, et scavent par especial les grans seigneurs tout ce quilz cuydent qui face pour eulx, semble que veue la grandeur de ceste matiere, qui est celle du monde qui plus touche le roy, vous et tous le royaulme de France vous la devez scavoir, pour en parler en lieu et en temps et avoir a cueur pour y pourveoir sur toutes choses.[44]

> The English have the finest and the most outstanding books that they could have drafted regarding their claims in France, and they generally bring these

42] See, for example, J. J. N. Palmer, 'The War Aims of the Protagonists and the Negotiations for Peace', in *The Hundred Years War*, ed. K. A. Fowler, London, 1971, pp. 51–74, together with Dickinson, *Congress of Arras* (esp. p. 4) and Allmand, 'The Anglo-French Negotiations, 1439', pp. 1–33.

43] Montreuil, *Opera*, Vol. I, pp. 240–48; Vol. III, pp. 13–17, 32–41; the *Memoire abregée grossement* in BNF, nouv. acq. fr. 6215, fol. 32v; J. J. N. Palmer, 'The Anglo-French Peace Negotiations, 1390–1396', *TRHistS*, Fifth Series, Vol. XVI, 1966, p. 82.

44] Montreuil, *Opera*, Vol. II, p. 266, discussed in Lewis, 'War Propaganda and Historiography', p. 16, repr. in idem, *Essays in Later Medieval French History*, p. 208. In 1479, a council memorandum requested 'beaulx livres a perpetuel mémoire' ('properly drawn-up records') regarding, amongst other things, 'la querelle du roy a l'encontre du roy d'Angleterre' ('the king's quarrel with the King of England'). See n. 32, above.

> with them when they have to meet the French in order to negotiate; and, most notably, the great lords who represent them understand all that should be known about this subject. Considering the importance of this matter which, more than anything else in the world, affects the king, yourself [the dauphin] and the entire kingdom of France, it seems that you should be informed about it so as to [be able to] speak about it in [every] place and at all times, and to know it well enough to equip yourselves for all eventualities.

The polemical writers were able to meet the need for these 'beaulx livres': Montreuil offered the final draft of his *Traité contre les Anglais* to the new dauphin, Jean, clearly anticipating that he would play an active role in the inevitable negotiations with Henry V. Similarly, Jean Juvénal wrote *Tres crestien, tres hault, tres puissant roy* for Charles VII in 1446 in preparation for his personal meeting with Henry VI.[45]

It is also possible that some of the polemical texts may have served as briefing papers and propaganda for foreign princes and powers, particularly the Holy Roman Emperor, the Pope and the councils of the Church. For example, Montreuil addressed a brief letter to the Emperor Sigismund during his visit to France in March or April 1416, which included passages from his own *Traité contre les Anglais*, together with a genealogical tree demonstrating the true descent of the French crown to Charles VI; the Duke of Berry also lent the emperor a manuscript of the Latin chronicle of Guillaume de Nangis.[46] The French king was himself often the recipient of such works. In 1448, Charles VII was presented with a Latin history of Milan by Antonio Astesan, secretary to the Duke of Orléans, to persuade him to assist the duke in his pursuit of his claim to the Duchy of Milan; thirteen years later, a Florentine ambassador, Donato Acciaiouli, gave Louis XI an account of the life of Charlemagne, perhaps in the hope that Louis would emulate his illustrious predecessor by helping Florence.[47] Most interestingly, in 1468, Sir John Fortescue presented Louis XI with 'ung grant memoire declaratif des drois que le roy Edouart pretend a la couronne Dangleterre et apres a la couronne de france' ('a statement setting out the rights which King Edward claims to have to the crown of England and, consequently, to that of France'). This work has been lost but certain sections of his earlier pamphlets, *De titulo Edwardi comitis Marchiae* and *Defensio juris domus Lancastriae*, sound as if they were composed for foreigners. Moreover, in *De titulo*, Fortescue claimed that Pius II had issued a bull supporting resistance to

45] Montreuil, *Opera*, Vol. II, p. 265; see also n. 21, above.
46] In the aftermath of Sigismund's agreement with Henry V, Montreuil vented his spleen in a pamphlet against Sigismund called *Quatinus vestre maiestatis diffamationi* (Montreuil, *Opera*, Vol. II, pp. 335–45; Vol. III, pp. 17–18, 41–44). Also see H.-Fr. Delaborde, 'La Vraie chronique du Religieux de Saint-Denis', *BEC*, Vol. LI, 1890, p. 98 n. 3.
47] BNF, ms. lat. 6166; J. Monfrin, 'La Figure de Charlemagne dans l'historiographie du XVe siècle', *Annuaire-Bulletin de la Société de l'Histoire de France*, 1964–65, pp. 67–78.

Edward IV not only by all Englishmen but also by Louis XI, thus emphasising that the French king had a duty to support Henry VI.[48]

IV

The assumption that the polemical treatises served as propaganda for the Valois monarchy has led historians to emphasise an apparent contrast between France and England: 'the written word had little part to play in the public relations exercises undertaken by the English monarchy prior to 1450 ... those historical and biographical works that were produced within the court circle and express what might be called the official line were often intended for very specific, private consumption'.[49] In fact, the French did not use the polemical treatises as part of a wider 'public relations exercise', but rather as diplomatic and administrative manuals. Yet this raises the very difficult question of why the English rarely produced treatises examining the legal issues of the war. French historians have recently claimed that the English royal archives were far more organised than their counterparts across the Channel, so that one might assume that there was no need for manuals setting out the Plantagenet case.[50] Yet after the disappearance of the office of *custos processuum* in 1339, it is clear that the English administrators and diplomats made just as much use of dossiers concerning the legal issues of the Hundred Years War as their French counterparts.[51] The *Gesta Henrici Quinti* testifies to the existence of a *liber recordorum* containing materials relating to France, Scotland and the Empire. David de Montferrand, Archbishop of Bordeaux, sent Henry V transcripts of Anglo-French treaties relating to the Duchy of Guyenne, together with the *Livre des homages*, originally drawn up for the Black Prince. In May 1433, the English and Anglo-French councils met at Calais and had copies of past truces prepared in readiness for the meeting with Cardinal Albergati. In anticipation of a meeting with the French in July 1445, Henry VI ordered a search in the treasury for all agreements

48] J. Calmette and G. Périnelle, *Louis XI et Angleterre, 1461–1483*, Paris, 1930, p. 303; V. Litzen, 'A War of Roses and Lilies: The Theme of Succession in Sir John Fortescue's Works', *Suomalaisen tiedeakatemian tomituksia Annales Academiae Scientiarum Fennicae*, Vol. CLXXIII, 1971, pp. 15–16; *The Works of Sir John Fortescue*, ed. Thomas [Fortescue] Lord Clermont and Chichester Fortescue, 2 vols, London, 1869, Vol. I, pp. 506, 69*–70* and 74*.

49] W. M. Ormrod, 'The Domestic Response to the Hundred Years War' in *Arms, Armies and Fortifications in the Hundred Years War*, ed. A. Curry and M. Hughes, London, 1994, pp. 97–98.

50] Pons, 'A l'origine des dossiers polémiques', p. 364; F. Autrand, 'Les Artisans de paix face à l'état: la diplomatie pontificale et le conflit franco-anglais au XIVème siècle', in *War and Competition between State Powers*, ed. P. Contamine, Oxford, forthcoming.

51] G. P. Cuttino, *English Diplomatic Administration, 1259–1339*, 2nd edn, Oxford, 1971, pp. 50–51; V. H. Galbraith, 'The Tower as an Exchequer Office', in *Essays in Medieval History presented to T. F. Tout*, ed. A. G. Little and F. M. Powicke, Manchester, 1925, pp. 231–47; B. Wilkinson, *The Chancery under Edward III*, Manchester, 1929.

between Henry V and Charles VI.[52] Yet perhaps the most interesting compilations are those produced during the middle years of the reign of Henry VI, under the auspices of Thomas Bekynton, diplomat and secretary to the king between *c.* 1438 and 1443, and later Bishop of Bath and Wells and Keeper of the Privy Seal. Bekynton may well have been building upon an existing dossier developed earlier in the war: his dossiers contained a number of memoranda relating to Edward III's claim to the French throne, including materials produced in 1344, an extensive record of the treaties of Brétigny and Troyes, French texts responding to English claims, and even an *Extractum ab originali libro antiquo cronicarum Sancti Severini Burdegalensis*, setting out the ancient boundaries of Gascony and Guyenne.[53]

Thus English administrators and diplomats certainly had dossiers to match those produced in France, and also memoranda on very specific topics, such as the position papers prepared for Henry V before the negotiations at Alençon in 1418, and for the English embassy that met the French near Calais in 1439.[54] It may be that Montreuil was referring to this type of material when he observed, in September 1416, that English diplomats used 'beaulx livres' setting out their claims in France.[55] Yet there is only limited evidence of any English polemical texts to match those produced in France, or even the pro-Lancastrian pamphlets that Sir John Fortescue composed while in exile in Scotland in the early 1460s.[56] Royal clerks like Adam Murimith, James le Palmer and Thomas Hoccleve were clearly interested in writing and book collecting, but such men apparently did not see the need to develop defences of the rights of the English crown,

52] *Gesta Henrici Quinti*, ed. J. S. Roskell and F. Taylor, Oxford, 1975, pp. xxxix–xl (for *Liber recordorum*); Vale, *English Gascony*, pp. 78–79 (for Montferrand's collection); M. Harvey, *England, Rome and the Papacy, 1417–1464. The Study of a Relationship*, Manchester, 1993, pp. 155–56 (for May 1433); Ferguson, *English Diplomacy*, p. 28 (for 1445). For fourteenth-century dossiers, see F. Bock, 'An Unknown Register of the Reign of Edward III', *EHR*, Vol. XLV, 1930, pp. 353–72, and 'Some New Documents Illustrating the Early Years of the Hundred Years War (1353–1356)', *BJRL*, Vol. XV, 1931, pp. 84–99; *The Diplomatic Correspondence of Richard II*, ed. E. Perroy, RHistS, London, 1933, pp. vii–xxvii.

53] BL, ms. Cotton Tiberius B xii; mss. Harley 861, 4763; Oxford, Bodleian Library, ms. Bodley 885. For the *Liber abreviatus*, see *The Anglo-French Negotiations at Bruges, 1374–77*, ed. Perroy, pp. 1–85.

54] *English Medieval Diplomatic Practice*, ed. Chaplais, Vol. I, pp. 207–23; C. T. Allmand, 'The Anglo-French Negotiations, 1439', *BIHR*, Vol. XL, 1967, pp. 25–28; *Documents Relating to the Anglo-French Negotiations of 1439*, ed. C. T. Allmand, *Camden Miscellany* Vol. XXIV, RHistS, London, 1972, pp. 140–49.

55] Montreuil, *Opera*, Vol. II, p. 266.

56] These tracts may have enjoyed a wide dissemination. Edward IV later required Fortescue to issue a retraction, and the *Replicacion ageinste the clayme and title of the Duc of Yorke* was included amongst the manifestos and newsletters in John Vale's book (*The Works of Sir John Fortescue*, Vol. I, pp. 497–518 and 63*–90*; *The Politics of Fifteenth Century England: John Vale's Book*, ed. M. L. Kekewich et al., Gloucester, 1995, pp. 202–03).

particularly against the Valois kings of France.[57] Thomas of Walsingham wrote the *Ypodigma Neustrie* not so much to encourage Henry V to pursue his claim to Normandy, but rather 'as a call for greater caution, and an end to blind expansionism', while William of Worcester presented the *Boke of Noblesse* to Edward IV in order to glorify the past achievements of English kings against the French, and perhaps thereby persuade the king to emulate his forbears. Similarly, Humfrey, Duke of Gloucester commissioned Titus Livius da Forli to write a panegyric of his brother Henry V and also an account of the duke's own campaign in Flanders in 1435–36. Neither text examined the English claims in France in any detail.[58] Beyond this, there is a glorified genealogy originally compiled in 1461, and a series of Latin texts which set out briefly the English title to the overlordship of Wales, Aquitaine, Normandy, Ireland and Scotland, written by Andrew Aston, hosteler at Bury St Edmunds.[59]

It is possible that the English did produce polemical texts for the use of royal officials, but that they were subsequently lost. Thomas Bekynton was said to have composed a 'learned treatise in confutation of the Salique law, to prove the rights of the kings of England to the crown of France', though this may simply be a reference to one of his surviving dossiers. Similarly, the *liber recordorum* is only known to historians through the testimony of the *Gesta Henrici Quinti*; the survival of such manuals, if given to diplomats, would probably have depended upon their being returned to the royal archives.[60] Yet it is equally possible that the English never felt the need to produce polemical treatises. The collections produced by Bekynton contained everything that a diplomat or administrator would need, particularly given that the English claims during the war were relatively simple: Edward III had been the nearest male heir to the throne in 1328, and both the treaties of Brétigny and Troyes created situations which the English subsequently wished to continue. Moreover, English diplomats were

57] T. F. Tout, 'Literature and Learning in the English Civil Service in the Fourteenth Century', *Speculum*, Vol. IV, 1929, pp. 365–89; W. M. Ormrod, 'Accountability and Collegiality: The English Royal Secretariat in the Mid-fourteenth Century', *Ecrit et pouvoir dans les chancelleries médiévales,* pp. 81–83.

58] Thomas Walsingham, *Ypodigma Neustrie*, ed. H. T. Riley, RS, London, 1876; William of Worcester, *Boke of Noblesse*, ed. J. G. Nichols, London, Roxburghe Club, 1860) discussed in Lewis, 'War Propaganda and Historiography', pp. 14–15, repr. in idem, *Essays in Later Medieval French History*, pp. 206–07; A. Gransden, *Historical Writing in England, II. c.1307 to the Early Sixteenth Century*, London, 1982, pp. 210–13; J. Clark, 'Intellectual Life at the Abbey of St. Albans and the Nature of Monastic Learning in England c.1350 to c.1440', unpublished DPhil thesis, University of Oxford, 1997, pp. 302–03.

59] For the genealogies, see BL, Add. Ms. 10099, fols. 205–210v, together with fifteenth-century copies in BL, mss Harley 116 and 326, cited in Lewis, 'War Propaganda and Historiography', p. 15, repr. in idem, *Essays in Later Medieval French History*, p. 207. For the texts of Andrew Aston, see BL, ms Cotton Claudius A xii, fols. 145v–155v.

60] See n. 51 above, and J. Collinson, *The History and Antiquities of the County of Somerset*, 3 vols, Bath, 1791, Vol. III, p. 384.

clearly reluctant to examine these arguments too closely in public: in 1418, 1435 and 1439, they declared the subject too high a matter for mortal men to discuss, an argument also used by William Lyndwood at the Council of Basle in 1433.[61]

Ultimately, the absence of any English polemical texts highlights the fact that the French treatises were a unique development of the intellectual legacy of the court and chancellery of Charles V. Montreuil and many of the other scholars in the Parisian chancelleries were heavily influenced by the nascent humanism emanating from Italy, but this may not have been a central factor in the generation of the polemical texts. This was an intellectual culture that placed greatest emphasis upon Latin and classical knowledge, and the polemical treatises resemble the vernacular collections of sources produced by Italian chanceries in the fourteenth and fifteenth century, rather than the *Commentaries* which the great humanists subsequently developed from these materials. Thus it is perhaps not surprising that Montreuil was the only major French humanist of his generation to become directly involved in the intellectual defence of the crown against the English.[62] Rather, Montreuil was probably affected by his professional context, and particularly by the legacy of Charles V who had effected one of the most remarkable intellectual programmes of the late Middle Ages, translating a considerable body of scholarship into the vernacular. The polemical writers effectively continued this effort, drawing upon both archival records and complex legal arguments from sources such as the *Songe du Vergier*. This was a formula that had recently been employed by an acquaintance of Montreuil, Honoré Bouvet, whose *L'Arbre des Batailles* was a vernacular treatise that merged discussions of history and warfare with legal materials developed by John de Legnano in the *Tractatus de bello*, as well as matters of contemporary importance, such as the Angevin succession to the throne of Naples.[63] Thus the French polemical texts may reflect a unique intellectual culture within official Valois circles. It is perhaps not a coincidence that the only direct English equivalent to the French

61] Dickinson, *Congress of Arras*, pp. 131–32, 143; for 1439, see *Proceedings and Ordinances of the Privy Council, 1386–1542*, ed. N. H. Nicolas, 7 vols, London, 1834–37, Vol. V, pp. 352, 374, 390.

62] G. Ianziti, *Humanist Historiography under the Sforzas*, Oxford, 1988, pp. 11–12, 63. For general discussions of the French context, see E. Ornato, *Jean Muret et ses amis Nicolas de Clamanges et Jean de Montreuil: contribution à l'étude des rapports entre les humanistes de Paris et ceux d'Avignon (1394–1420)*, Geneva, 1969, and N. Pons, 'Les Chancelleries Parisiennes sous les règnes de Charles VI et Charles VII', in *Cancelleria e cultura nel medio evo (16 Congrezzo internazionale di scienze storiche)*, Vatican City, 1990, pp. 137–68.

63] Honoré Bonet, *The Tree of Battles*, ed. and trans. G. W. Coopland, Liverpool, 1949, discussed in M. Hanly, 'Courtiers and Poets: An International System of Literary Exchange in Late-Fourteenth Century Italy, France and England', *Viator*, Vol. XXVIII, 1997, pp. 317–21. The model offered by Montreuil may have found particular favour in the aftermath of the capture of Paris by the Burgundians, when royal officials were denied access to the archives. It was during this period that Odart Morchesne produced his famous formulary (Desjardins, 'Les Savoirs des notaires et secrétaires du roi', pp. 87–97).

polemical treatises was a tract produced by a Frenchman in the service of Henry VI: Jean de Rinel had originally served as secretary to the Duke of Guyenne from 1407 onwards and as *notaire et secrétaire du roi* in 1418. Thus he was intimately connected with the French chancellery and so may have produced his memorandum based upon his own familiarity with this tradition.[64]

V

In conclusion, the polemical treatises written by Valois officials in the fifteenth century were primarily intended to serve as manuals for administrators and diplomats. The writers themselves frequently implied that their texts were intended for a wider audience, but their testimony is far from convincing. For example, the abbreviated versions of Montreuil's texts, the *Resumé du Traité contre les Anglais* and the *Genealogie des rois de France, Verite est que* were clearly intended for a diplomatic context, yet both begin with a declaration that they were produced to resolve the confusion of people who were mistaken about the truth of the matters in question because of their ignorance of the law and the relevant facts. Similarly, the anonymous author of *Pour ce que plusieurs* argued that many people were unaware of the truth about the dispute between the kings of France and England because they did not have sufficient knowledge of the origins and circumstances of that quarrel; thus he claimed that he was writing 'to end their confusion, so that all might be informed [of the truth] clearly and unambiguously, and thus be properly informed [about it]'. Yet there is clear evidence that this work was written for diplomats, as a handbook for impending meetings with the English. The author of *Pour vraye congnoissance avoir* declared that he was not writing for the nobility and clergy who already understood the subject in question, but rather for ordinary people who wanted to guard and protect the crown. Yet this was a manual for clerks in the *Chambre des Comptes*, which even included precise references to supporting documents in archives. Thus there is a danger that claims to a wider audience were in fact a simple literary topos.[65]

The surviving manuscripts of these treatises offer little evidence that these works circulated beyond narrow, official circles. Excluding the author's own working drafts, there are only two contemporary manuscripts containing any versions of *A toute la chevalerie* and *Traité contre les Anglais* by Jean de Montreuil, and only five others from the second half of the fifteenth century; there is certainly no evidence that these works enjoyed a wider dissemination than the French and

64] *English Medieval Diplomatic Practice*, ed. Chaplais, Vol. II, pp. 648–52, discussed in Bossuat, 'Littérature de propagande au XVe siècle', pp. 131–46, and Pons, 'Les Chancelleries Parisiennes', p. 154. See n. 24 above.

65] Montreuil, *Opera*, Vol. II, p. 325; Pons, 'Un Exemple de l'utilisation des écrits politiques de Jean de Montreuil', p. 256. For *Pour ce que plusieurs*, see BNF, ms. fr. 5058, fol. 1; for *Pour vraye congnoissance avoir*, see n. 9 above.

Burgundian archives. *Tres crestien, tres hault, tres puissant roy* by Jean Juvénal, which was undoubtedly a manual for diplomats, survives in just two contemporary copies, with two more dating from the end of the century. There are ten manuscripts produced between 1435 and 1475 that contain his earlier work, *Audite celi*, and another five from the end of the fifteenth century. *Pour ce que plusieurs* survives in fifteen contemporary manuscripts. Thus the five most important treatises of the war survive in just forty manuscripts, of which the vast majority were either the authors' working drafts or copies made in the final quarter of the fifteenth century.[66] Very few of these manuscripts have marginalia or annotations that might show evidence of the reaction or interest of readers; those that do are invariably draft copies, or ones that circulated within the chancellery. Indeed, where it is possible to identify the original owners of manuscripts that originated outside official circles, they were generally either the princes themselves or great bibliophiles for whom such works merely formed an adjunct to their collections:[67] Charles d'Anjou 'Count of Maine' personally commissioned a copy of the *Mirouer Historial* but acted ambivalently enough in the War of the Public Weal in 1465 to arouse the suspicions of Louis XI, before being implicated in plots in 1472.[68] One interesting development was the production of dossiers with an anti-English theme. For example, the anti-English chronicle *Débats et appointements* appeared in six such manuscripts with a variety of materials, including genealogies of the kings of France and England, the *Recouvrement de la Normandie* by the Berry Herald, and extracts from the process of the Duke of Alençon. In eight manuscripts of *Pour ce que plusieurs*, the treatise appeared with other material of a polemical nature, such as the *Vraie cronicque d'Escoce*, the *Abrégé des chroniques*, *Audite celi* and the *Chronique de la traison et mort de Richart II*. For Nicole Pons, this demonstrates 'la diffusion d'une véritable conscience nationale', but the examples of this type of collection are very limited and mostly appear late in the fifteenth century. As she observes,

66] Montreuil, *Opera*, Vol. IV, pp. 15–47; Jean Juvénal, *Ecrits politiques*, Vol. I, pp. 93–142; Vol. II, pp. 1–11. For the manuscripts of *Pour ce que plusieurs*, see Taylor, '"La querelle Anglaise": Diplomatic and Legal Debate during the Hundred Years War', Appendix, section 1. The use of chapter headings and lists of contents in many of the polemical treatises may suggest that individual copies were principally intended to be read silently.

67] These owners included Jeanne de France, Duchess of Bourbon (*Audite celi* and *Pour ce que plusieurs*); Jacques d'Armagnac, Duke of Nemours (*Pour ce que plusieurs*); Louis de Bruges, Lord of Gruuthuse (*Pour ce que plusieurs*); Jean Budé (*Pour ce que plusieurs* and *Regali ex progenie*); and Pons d'Aubenas, lieutenant of the *sénéchal* of Beaucaire and Nîmes (*Audite celi*).

68] Daly, 'The "Miroir historial abrégé de France" and "C'est chose profitable"', pp. 201–02. Charles de France, brother of Louis XI, clearly felt that Cicero's *De Officiis* was more relevant to his position, and even underlined passages that justified rebellion (P. Saenger, 'Silent Reading: Its Impact on Late Medieval Script and Society', *Viator*, Vol. XIII, 1982, p. 412.

the variety of combinations shows that this is not merely mechanical copying, but it still remains possible that these collections are the work of bibliophiles or were put together for personal use.[69]

The real obstacle for historians is that the limited number of surviving manuscripts may indicate that these texts were not disseminated widely, or alternatively be caused by the fact that private individuals would have had less concern for the preservation of manuscripts than corporate bodies such as the government, colleges and chapters.[70] A more fruitful approach to the problem may be to consider an indirect channel through which the ideas presented by these treatises could have reached a wider audience: like their fourteenth-century precursors, the polemical texts may have served to prepare agents of the crown speaking at public meetings. Both Guillaume de Dormans, royal advocate, and his brother Jean, Cardinal of Beauvais and Chancellor of France, spoke at length at the *Parlement* in May 1369, justifying the receipt of the Gascon appeals by Charles V, and probably basing their discussion upon the position laid out in a letter sent to the English earlier in the year. As a result, the representatives of the Estates-General approved of the king's decision, and suggested that it be communicated to the pope, the curia, the emperor and all the *bonnes villes* and other places within the realm.[71] In 1375, Charles V convened a *grand conseil* of princes of the blood, nobles, prelates, clerks and scholars who declared that the king 'could not surrender any of his sovereign rights or powers without breaching his coronation oath, and thus imperilling his honour and his soul'; it is possible that this was the occasion upon which the principles outlined by Trémaugon in the *Somnium viridarii* were first developed.[72] Jean Juvénal may have spoken about the proposals for a treaty with the English at the Estates-General at Orléans in October 1439, and certainly composed a brief memorandum on the subject shortly afterwards.[73] In 1468, Louis XI convened the Estates-General at Tours

69] '*L'Honneur de la couronne de France*', pp. 33–36; Pons, 'A l'origine des dossiers polemiques', p. 377, together with P. S. Lewis, 'Jeu de cubes: reflexions sur quelques textes et manuscrits', in *Pratiques de la culture écrite en France au XVe siècle: Actes du colloque internationale du CNRS*, Louvain-la-Neuve, 1995, pp. 313–30.

70] Pons, 'Latin et français au XVe siècle', Vol. II, p. 81.

71] R. Delachenal, *Histoire de Charles V*, 5 vols, Paris, 1909–31, Vol. IV, pp. 136–45; *Les Grandes chroniques de France: chroniques des règnes de Jean II et Charles V*, ed. R. Delachenal, 4 vols, SHF, Paris, 1910–20, Vol. II, pp. 72–116. In 1359, at a meeting of churchmen, nobles and representatives of the *bonnes villes* convened by the regent Charles, Guillaume de Dormans complained that the terms of the second Treaty of London would lead to the loss of sovereignty and resort over lands conceded to the English (Vol. II, p. 236).

72] *Grandes chroniques*, Vol. II, p. 176; Delachenal, *Histoire de Charles V*, Vol. IV, pp. 573–74.

73] According to the abbé Legrand, Jean Juvénal 'soutint avec beaucoup de vigueur, que le roy n'estant que simple usufruitier de la couronne il ne pouvoit aliener la moindre partye de son domaine' ('argued with great force that the king, being only the usufructuary of the crown, could not alienate even the smallest part of his domain'). BNF, ms. fr. 6960, fol. 13v, cited in Jean Juvénal, *Ecrits politiques*, Vol. III, p. 161.

to win support for the crown against the Duke of Brittany and Charles de France. During this assembly, Jean Juvénal, Guillaume Cousinot and a number of other royal councillors spoke at length on the legal issues surrounding the status of Normandy, which Louis XI had been forced to cede to Charles de France during the War of the Public Weal. These arguments were clearly understood and accepted by the representatives, who not only drew heavily upon them when making their own statements at the end of the meeting, but also copied summaries of the speeches into their own registers.[74] The principles developed by Jean Juvénal and the other polemical writers continued to be invoked in public assemblies, such as the assembly of notables in December 1527, discussing the Treaty of Madrid. Indeed, the arguments invoked at this meeting had earlier been raised in a royal memorandum intended for international consumption, and may well have derived from the treatise composed by Michel de Pons before the Treaty of Arras in 1482.[75]

Ultimately, however, whether the polemical treatises influenced a wider audience thanks to the advent of printing or through public forums, their importance in the development of the ideology of the crown is unquestioned. *Pour ce que plusieurs*, also known as *La Loy Salicque premiere loy des françois*, set the seal on the myth of the Salic Law, while Jean Juvénal des Ursins in particular played a key role in the popularisation of the law of inalienability governing the crown.[76]

74] Two examples survive: Arch. Comm., Rodez, BB 3, fols 61v–66; Arch. Comm., Poitiers, carton 98, reg. 5, fols 115–19. See J. R. Major, *Representative Institutions in Renaissance France, 1421–1559*, Madison, 1960, p. 164 n. 39.

75] H. Hauser, 'Le Traité de Madrid et la cession de la Bourgogne à Charles-Quint', *Revue bourguignonne*, Vol. XXII, 1912, pp. 90–96; Saenger, 'Burgundy and the Inalienability of Apanages', pp. 13–26.

76] Taylor, '"La querelle Anglaise": Diplomatic and Legal Debate during the Hundred Years War', pp. 55–101 and 128–81.

6

History and the Literature of War: The *Boke of Noblesse* of William Worcester

CHRISTOPHER ALLMAND and
MAURICE KEEN

As they pursued a better future for their country, Englishmen of the third quarter of the fifteenth century sought ways of bringing about the recovery of a society which had experienced defeat abroad and weak rule, leading to civil conflict, at home. When William Worcester, to whom is attributed the *Boke of Noblesse*,[1] and Sir John Fortescue, author of *The Governance of England* and the *De Laudibus Legum Anglie*,[2] wrote what could be described as polemical works, each was prompted by a particular view of how best to overcome the 'sorrows' experienced by England at the time. Both men were deeply concerned for the public weal, the common profit of the realm; both, too, were anxious about the level of the crown's indebtedness, and concerned at the rise of civil discord. In his book, each laboured the importance to the king of sound and prudent counsel; each saw the restoration of 'dominion' – or proper rule – as vital for the future; each, too, would make use of historical evidence to bolster the arguments which he put forward.

Yet, while these two men shared a purpose, their works reflected a fundamental difference of approach. Fortescue would propose to achieve better things by concentrating upon necessary changes on the domestic scene; the former Chief Justice favoured the resumption of crown lands, a king endowed with a protected income, as well as reform of the royal council as means toward re-establishing the effectiveness, power and good name of the monarchy. While not denying the significance to be played by the king himself, Fortescue placed his principal emphasis upon the need to give greater power to the office of the crown

1] William Worcester, *The Boke of Noblesse, addressed to King Edward the Fourth on his Invasion of France in 1475*, ed. J. G. Nichols, London, Roxburghe Club, 1860. It has recently been suggested that Stephen Scrope, stepson of Worcester's patron, Sir John Fastolf, may have collaborated in the work (J. Hughes, 'Stephen Scrope and the Circle of Sir John Fastolf: Moral and Intellectual Outlooks', in *Medieval Knighthood, IV. Papers from the Fifth Strawberry Hill Conference 1990*, ed. C. Harper-Bill and R. Harvey, Woodbridge, 1992, p. 133.
2] Sir John Fortescue, *The Governance of England*, ed. C. Plummer, Oxford, 1885; *De Laudibus Legum Anglie*, ed. and trans. S. B. Chrimes, Cambridge, 1942.

through (in this case) institutional and financial reform. Here, perhaps, he was influenced by his legal training and inclinations. Worcester, on the other hand, had a different perception of how the common profit might be restored. Rather than concentrate on what might be done at home, Worcester chose to emphasise the need to recover those English possessions recently lost in France through human failure and divided command. What was needed was a ruler who, by providing personal leadership, could restore to the monarchy something of its historic glory, thereby giving back to both England and to her king a pride in their achievement. England was badly in need of a leader who would fight with the 'worshipfulle men of the Englisshe nacion'[3] to reassert his power through success in war. In the light of his experience and of his long association with a man who had devoted most of his active life to furthering and defending English interests in France, it is hardly surprising that Worcester should see things in this way.

Born in 1415, a student at Oxford at the age of eighteen, Worcester entered the service of Sir John Fastolf in his early twenties, remaining with him until the old soldier's death in 1459.[4] Living in France for part of that time, Worcester got to know what the English were trying to do, and what material interests made them seek to maintain their conquests. His links with Fastolf, who was not only a successful soldier but a patron of letters who brought back books from France, introduced Worcester to cultural interests which were almost certainly an important bond between master and servant.[5] Later, after Fastolf's death, Worcester became involved in the complicated consequences arising out of his former master's will (he appears, for example, in the famous *Paston Letters*),[6] and it may have been this experience and earlier administrative and secretarial assignments which taught him the value of evidence in making and maintaining a case.[7] Worcester's cultural interests ranged widely. His *Itineraria* show a man of enquiring mind, a view confirmed by even the briefest examination of College of Arms MS 48, for example, which reveals him as having a deep-seated, almost

3] *Boke*, p. 9.
4] On Worcester, see K. B. McFarlane, 'William Worcester: A Preliminary Survey', in *Studies Presented to Sir Hilary Jenkinson*, ed. J. Conway Davies, London, 1957, pp. 196–212, repr. in idem, *England in the Fifteenth Century*, London, 1981, pp. 199–224; A. B. Emden, *A Biographical Register of the University of Oxford to AD 1500*, 3 vols, Oxford, 1957–59, Vol. III, pp. 2086–87.
5] Hughes, 'Stephen Scrope', pp. 129–30; McFarlane, 'William Worcester', p. 205, repr. in idem, *England in the Fifteenth Century*, p. 208. Fastolf was closely associated with John, Duke of Bedford, one of the most important patrons and collectors of his day (see J. Stratford, *The Bedford Inventories. The Worldly Goods of John, Duke of Bedford, Regent of France (1389–1435)*, London, 1993, esp. pp. 91–96, 105–26).
6] *Paston Letters and Papers of the Fifteenth Century*, ed. N. Davis, 2 vols, Oxford, 1971–76, select index.
7] See P. S. Lewis, 'Sir John Fastolf's Lawsuit over Tichwell 1448–55', *Historical Journal*, Vol. I, 1958, p. 2, repr. in idem, *Essays in Later Medieval French History*, London, 1985, p. 216.

scholarly appreciation of the past and of what it could offer the present.[8] This approach would be found right through the *Boke of Noblesse*, whose author represented the point of view of those stunned by the English defeats of 1450 and 1453. Worcester was clearly a man of real learning, well read in the classics and sympathetic (like Fortescue) to the appeal of the Roman model, and with a deep appreciation of the history and traditions of his own country. The use which he made of his learning and, in particular, of his sense of history, is one of the work's outstanding characteristics.[9]

As we have it, the *Boke* is dedicated to Edward IV, although it has been argued (and seems likely) that Worcester was then working from an earlier draft, written in the early 1450s in the immediate aftermath of the loss of Henry VI's French territories.[10] By June 1475 (the date of the explicit at the end of the book), Edward was 'undisputed king of England, and, like his predecessors, the titular king of France'. He was ready to stake his claim to that country and to do so with the enthusiastic support of those 'burning for military fame', indignant at the losses incurred in France a generation earlier, and now ready to regain French lands through conquest. As its nineteenth-century editor, J. G. Nichols, put it, 'the Book of Noblesse was written to excite and inflame such sentiments and expectations'.[11]

Such was the view a century or more ago. Can one offer another which, if it does not entirely replace the first, adds considerably to it? While the *Boke* was the work of a man who understood, from first-hand experience, the resentment and sense of betrayal experienced by those English who had been the losers in the recent war against the French, it was surely more than an attempt to whip up approval for a war intended to reverse these losses.[12] Above all else, the *Boke* sought to explain the country's recent defeat. In that sense, it was first of all a form of post mortem. Basically, the author's reasoning reduces itself to two main arguments. The first is that, over a long period of time, Englishmen have been dealing with a people whom they cannot trust. Early in the work, Worcester writes of 'unjust dissimilacions' of which the French have been guilty during the

8] *Itineraria Symonis Simeonis et Willelmi de Worcestre*, ed. J. Nasmith, Cambridge, 1778; William Worcestre, *Itineraries*, ed. J. H. Harvey, Oxford, 1969. See also McFarlane, 'William Worcester', p. 124, repr. in idem, *England in the Fifteenth Century*, pp. 212–13.

9] 'The English claim and the French defence against it both [Worcester] and the authors of the French treatises saw as an historical problem' (P. S. Lewis, 'War Propaganda and Historiography in Fifteenth-Century France and England', *TRHistS*, Fifth Series, Vol. XV, 1965, pp. 15 and 19, repr. in idem, *Essays in Later Medieval French History*, pp. 207–08 and 211. On Worcester's learning, see ibid., p. 216.

10] See McFarlane, 'William Worcester', p. 210, repr. in idem, *England in the Fifteenth Century*, pp. 212–13; C. Allmand, 'France–Angleterre à la fin de Guerre de Cent Ans: Le "Boke of Noblesse" de William Worcester', in *La 'France Anglaise' au Moyen Age. Actes du 111e Congrès National des Sociétés Savantes, Poitiers 1986*, Paris, 1988, Vol. I, pp. 104, 109.

11] *Boke*, p. i.

12] On this, see Allmand, 'Le "Boke of Noblesse" de William Worcester', pp. 103–11.

period of the war.[13] Here Worcester is referring to the relatively recent past, to the Truce of Tours of 1444 which held 'till [the French] had conspired and wrought theire avauntage', and, even more recently, to the events surrounding the fall of Normandy in 1450. A look into the more distant past produces other examples to bolster his argument. In a long passage he deals, in chronological sequence beginning with Richard I and Philip Augustus, with a series of truces which the enemy has broken. History, therefore, provides him with the foundations upon which to build his argument. Marginal notes further underline the message he is conveying: 'Treugae pluries infractae' ('Several truces broken'), or 'Nota fallacias Francorum in rupcione treugarum, vide et attende bene' ('Note the deceits of the French in breaking the truces: see and take good note'). It is French trickery that has been largely responsible for English defeats.[14]

At the same time, conceding a point which has a bearing on the main theme, Worcester admits that the English themselves have been at least partially responsible for their own defeat since, as a nation, they have not acted with proper 'noblesse'. He lays the blame for the defeat at Formigny in April 1450 upon those guilty of political squabbling in England in the months leading up to that event; there is a strong hint that this should never have been allowed to happen, and that the responsibility for the defeat should be attributed more widely than simply among the political and military leaders of the day. Worcester is arguing that the defeat of 1450 was a defeat for the English nation as a whole.[15]

So far his purpose has been to explain how England's forces and settlers, many of whom have lived in France for two generations, have been expelled in what is nothing less than a national humiliation. How may this be reversed? It is clear that, in Worcester's mind, defeat is only temporary and is wholly retrievable; on the very first page of his work he begins a section intended to put the country to rights, optimistically entitled 'De remedio casus Reipublicae'. The argument which he then presents takes several directions. To accept the finality of defeat would be to abandon all hope in God who, on many notable occasions in the past, has supported the justice of the English cause in France. Later, there begins a further section in which a rapid survey of selected past events (in this case going back to 1066), based on what he calls 'divers cronicles ... [and] many other historialle bookis of auctorite', is brought to the reader's attention to demonstrate the claim of English kings to lands in France, a claim based not so much on legal or archival evidence as on the record of past events provided by the person whom he calls the 'historier', or historian.[16] Worcester shows his awareness of the strength of an argument based upon history, or at least history as he chooses to present it. Furthermore, the circumstances with which he is dealing enable him to reinforce

13] *Boke*, p. 4. See also pp. 8, 34, 36–39, 41, 49.
14] Ibid., pp. 34–39.
15] The theme is touched upon on pp. 30, 33, 48, 51–52, 56, 72–74.
16] Ibid., pp. 24–25.

his case by citing examples taken from a much earlier age. He turns to Roman precedent to find support for his belief that the recent defeat in Normandy is little more than a setback. The Romans, he shows, also experienced such setbacks. But these did not prevent them from going on to eventual victory and greatness;[17] their defeats constituted a trial, a challenge to be met and overcome. More recently, God has allowed the English to be tested; perhaps he is punishing them for their divisions and their inability to do what is required to defend the undoubted justice of their right in France. All this can be reversed, however, if proper measures are taken and appropriate attitudes adopted.

In spite of his apparent downheartedness regarding the situation in France, Worcester appears optimistic about the future. England can and must live to fight another day. Far from being lost, the past is retrievable. Basing his case on the need to revert to a state of justice, Worcester turns to history to provide him with the evidence of past English rule in France, rule not achieved by trickery or usurpation but, in Normandy, through legitimate descent from William, Duke of Normandy and King of England, and, in Aquitaine, through the marriage of Henry II to the Duchess Eleanor. In a long passage on the attempts of past English kings to reach agreements with their French counterparts, Worcester stresses the unreliability of the French in keeping to the terms of truces. Even the saintly Louis IX is not exempted from criticism. Worcester comes close to implying that Louis counted on the weakness of Henry III to impose upon him the terms of the Treaty of Paris (1259), whereby Henry surrendered a 'verray auncient enheritaunce tailed', something which he had no right to do without 'the auctorite of the parlement of thre astatis of his roiaume'.[18] The language may be anachronistic, but the argument would have meant much to those entrusted to negotiate with ambassadors from Valois France in the closing stages of the recent war. In any event, Worcester's reading of the historical evidence satisfies him that England's case in France is based on justice; for that reason, England has an

17] Ibid., pp. 26–27. Worcester was probably inspired by his reading of Alain Chartier's *Quadrilogue Invectif*. Compare the passage with one in the *Quadrilogue* (*Alain Chartier, Le Quadrilogue Invectif*, ed. E. Droz, rev. edn, Paris, 1950), p. 31. See F. Autrand, 'La Déconfiture. La bataille de Poitiers (1356) à travers quelques textes français des XIVe et XVe siècles', in *Guerre et Société en France, en Angleterre et en Bourgogne XIVe–XVe siècle*, ed. P. Contamine, C. Giry-Deloison and M. Keen, Lille, 1991, pp. 111–12; and McFarlane, 'William Worcester', p. 212, and n. 5, repr. in idem, *England in the Fifteenth Century*, p. 215, and n. 101. The *Quadrilogue* was twice translated into English during the fifteenth century (*Fifteenth-Century English Translations of Alain Chartier's 'Le Traité de l'Esperance' and 'Le Quadrilogue Invectif'*, ed. M. S. Blayney, 2 vols, Oxford, EETS, 1974, 1980).

18] *Boke*, p. 34. It may be noted that Worcester is arguing that a ruler has no right to 'gyve away his duchees or countees ne his demaynes that is his propre enheritaunces to a straunge parsone' without the approval of a sizeable number of spiritual and secular members of Parliament 'as it hathe bene accustumed; so in conclusion the relese of king Henry thrid to king Lowes was and is voide' (ibid., p. 35). For the later use of a similar argument by the French, see the chapter by Nicole Pons in the present volume, p. 59.

obligation to pursue it, if necessary through the use of force. Worcester is using the past both to legitimise future English intervention in France and to exhort Englishmen to turn again to the path of 'noblesse' followed by their predecessors which had allowed them to achieve the state of justice, and thereby to win glory for themselves and for England.

Worcester's purpose is to encourage Englishmen to emerge from the trough of despondency, to mould them into a new nation, and to do this by persuading them to fight with a good hope of success, thereby restoring the English to what his reading of the chroniclers makes him regard as their rightful inheritance in France. First of all, however, England must rediscover a pride in herself. What better way to achieve this than to look back into her past. Here Worcester turns again from the misery of England's relatively recent involvement in France to more distant times to demonstrate two factors which will support his historically-based argument. The first is that the English are a very ancient people, descended from the Trojans, thus making them one of the nations founded by Brutus.[19] The second is that they are also a very united one, their unity having been achieved in more recent times, as their history shows. Furthermore, they are a people whose leaders have, over the centuries, won renown the world over: beginning with Arthur, who defeated the Romans, and proceeding through Brennus, Edmund Ironside, William the Conqueror to, most recently, John, Duke of Bedford.[20] The list is a long one, and names of all post-Conquest kings who have acted succesfully in defending England's interests are included. Worcester is particularly interested in those with 'credits' for warfare to their names. So Henry I 'defende[d] his dukedom [of Normandy] ayenst the Frenshe partie', while his brother, Robert, justly won renown as a considerable crusader but 'never had grace of victorie after' trying to lay his hands upon the same duchy. Richard I, 'clepid Cuer de lion', is given credit not only as a crusader but as a defender of his large 'enheritaunce' in France. Edward I, too, was a crusader, a king who kept 'under subjeccion bothe Irelond, Walis, and Scotlond, whiche were rebellis and wilde peple of condition', as well as one who 'protectid and defendid the duchees of Gascoigne and Guyen, his rightefull enheritaunce'.[21] History can be used to emphasise the qualities of a nation in different ways: its ancient lineage; its unity achieved long ago; in particular its leaders who have stood up for their rights and have shown outstanding courage over the centuries. It is a nation of both moral and physical strength.

History is thus used to underline England's ancient claims in France. Worcester takes the argument a step further when he turns to the more recent past to show how successfully such claims have been pursued through war. This is surely the importance of the emphasis which he attaches to the glorious exploits of such as

19] *Boke*, pp. 2 and 43 in particular.
20] Ibid., pp. 9–19.
21] Ibid., pp. 10–11.

Edward III, the Black Prince, Sir John Chandos and the early members of the Order of the Garter which, by implication, were intended to establish true justice. More recently, such aims have been pursued by Henry V and, since his death, by one of Worcester's heroes, John, Duke of Bedford.[22] The duke's death in 1435, in his view, has marked the beginning of the setbacks from which England has since been suffering overseas. Divided leadership in France lies at the root of the trouble. Not only is the point made directly; it is given indirect emphasis, too, through the way Worcester emphasises what England has to gain from both the military reputation of its ruler and the benefits of undivided leadership which he can offer. In the past, England's successes have resulted from the greatness of her leaders who have taken upon themselves personal responsibility for actively pursuing her interests. Worcester appears to be saying that 'noblesse', among its many characteristics, must include a willingness to accept the moral obligation of seeking justice and of defending the honour of both the king and his people. True peace will come only when justice is achieved. Englishmen, therefore, must not stand back and allow the king's rights in parts of France to be taken away from him by the French through their manifest acts of deceit, which are tantamount to injustice. Here he shows himself particularly aware of the problems experienced by the civilian population in time of war. While admitting that the English are now reaping the penalty of their mistreatment of the Norman population whom they claimed to rule,[23] he shows great sympathy for the former English settlers, chiefly those of Maine and Anjou, who have had the ground cut from under their feet and have lost their 'livelihood' as the result of the recent turn of events. The last is an act of injustice perpetrated by the French, a wrong waiting to be righted. While not all war is lawful, war fought to redress injustice is legitimate. As he allows Cicero, one of his favourite authors, to remind the reader, it is natural to turn to war in such circumstances. Worcester cites this authority to his advantage by encouraging him to bolster the argument yet further. Not merely justice, but nature, too, demands that men defend their own.[24] As a reading of history clearly demonstrates, parts of France belong to the King of England. If necessary, he should use force to defend them.

In the final third or so of the *Boke*, the part in which his classical learning is most apparent, Worcester moves the argument on to a different plane through an appeal to the English people to abandon their particular interests in favour of the evident need for all to join in the defence of the general good.[25] The term which he uses to pinpoint his ideal is the familiar one, the 'res publica'. What is this, Worcester asks? Cicero is again given the right of reply: 'Res publica est res

22] Ibid., pp. 4, 43–44, 46–47.
23] Ibid., pp. 6, 30, 72–74.
24] Ibid., p. 25.
25] Quoting Cicero, *De Rhetorica*. For the cultural background, see Hughes, 'Stephen Scrope', pp. 130–36.

populi, res patriae, res communis' ('The common good is the good of the people, the good of the country, the good of the community'). Anyone intending to strive for this (it is still Cicero speaking) must be ready to defend and to increase the interests of the community. In order to do this with success, the whole of a society must be coordinated in action. To illustrate what he means, Worcester has recourse to the familiar image of the ship. The 'res publica' is, of course, the vessel itself. At the helm is the master (or the ruler) with advisers of age and experience to assist him. The crew members are younger; it is their strength which pulls up the anchor, and their activity which hauls up the sails and fastens them securely. All this is another way of showing that the good of society cannot be achieved unless master and sailors, king and subjects, work together for its achievement, avoiding the 'danger and rokkis' to bring their ship safely into port. Worcester is making the simple, even naive, yet politically important point that the good of society depends on cooperation and team effort.[26]

Unoriginal as this may seem, there may be greater originality in the implications which are then worked out. Since the achievement of the 'res publica', or common welfare, is the end towards which both society as a whole and every one of its members should be striving, every contribution, whether collective or individual, made towards the achievement of that end must be an expression of the best which there is in human nature. It is this positive contribution made towards the common welfare which Worcester associates with true 'noblesse'. Nor, it follows, should 'noblesse' be regarded as a virtue associated with the knight or the soldier (nor indeed with the male sex) alone. Since it exists in any form of human endeavour intended to achieve justice and the advance of the 'res publica', all who help that process, by whatever means, may be said to possess 'noblesse'. Faithful to his method, Worcester takes as an example the Roman, Cato, whose career, he reminds his reader, began in 'the office of a knight in excersising armes', after which he occupied himself, in turn, as a tribune (or judge), as an ambassador, and then as a consul.[27] As an example of 'noblesse', Cato is seen in his role as an upholder of the public good. With examples such as these, drawn from the distant past but still possessing practical application in his own day, Worcester defines and illustrates his view of true 'noblesse'.

It is essential for a proper understanding of the *Boke* to appreciate how Worcester's thinking on the nature of 'noblesse' develops through the pages of the work. Essentially, as he states in the opening words of dedication to Edward IV and then expands a little more fully in the opening paragraph, 'noblesse [is] for the avauncyng and preferryng [of] the comyn publique of the Royaumes of England and of Fraunce'.[28] His view is a broad one; whatever contributes towards the common good is an aspect of 'noblesse'. None the less, we should

26] *Boke*, pp. 57–58.
27] Ibid., p. 61.
28] Ibid., p. 1.

not forget that the immediate cause for writing this work is to bewail the defeat experienced by English arms in France, to seek reasons why this should have happened, and to set out remedies for the recovery of the 'res publica' of England which must include a political settlement in France satisfactory to English interests. While he is ready to praise the efforts of diplomats in bringing about peace, the *Boke* makes it amply clear that negotiation and treaties are of no use when dealing with the French, so deceitful and untrustworthy are they as a nation. This being so, the sole effective option now remaining is recourse to a war to be fought in the interest of the 'res publica' of England.

This is more easily said than done. It is one thing to wish for victory; quite another to achieve it. There are some important passages in the *Boke* in which Worcester, although himself not a soldier, none the less demonstrates a practical appreciation of what it needs to turn armed men into a successful fighting force. How is the war to be won? Worcester is clear about this. It will not do to encourage men into thinking that victory is achieved either by numbers or heroic deeds alone. Of course, these have their part to play. He tells the tale, plucked from Roman history, of the consul, 'that vaillaunt citezin' Publius Decius who, fighting with a force being beaten back by the enemy, decides to court certain death by riding fearlessly, even recklessly, into the fray. Predictably, he meets his death, while his men, duly inspired, fight back and carry the day. Although impressed, Worcester does not see this approach as one which will always bring success; a marginal note in the text reads: 'Publius Decius non est recomendandus in hoc negotio' ('Publius Decius is not to be recommended in this matter'). What does Worcester hold against this approach to fighting? He provides his answer when he cites certain words which he has heard Sir John Fastolf utter regarding the two kinds of fighting man. 'One', he reports his patron as having said, 'ys a manlye man called, another ys an hardye man; but he seyd the manly man ys more to be commended, more then the hardy man …' He then proceeds to tell us why. The 'hardy man' acts on impulse; he wants to make a good impression, 'to be halde courageouse' (as the young and ambitious Fastolf had doubtless felt when, so he claimed, he had been the first ashore at Harfleur in 1415, 'la mer jusques a la ceinture' ['the sea up to his belt']);[29] such a man tends to forget those who are fighting with him, and he is too little concerned with their fate in defeat. On the other hand, the 'manly man' approaches war in a very different way. He is thinking about the best way of defeating those who oppose him; he is also aware of the welfare of those who are fighting alongside him. He may be more careful, less given to extravagant acts, but he is more effective for it.[30] There is no mistaking the point being made here. The success of the group (the army) is more important than the glory of the individual.

29] *English Suits before the Parlement of Paris 1420–1436*, ed. C. T. Allmand and C. A. J. Armstrong, London, RHistS, 1982, p. 264.
30] *Boke*, pp. 64–65.

This point is worth developing further. Worcester makes it clear that he believes that courage and valour on their own are not enough to win a war. These inborn instincts must be complemented by other attributes which can be learnt. Soldiers are normally more effective when fighting in units or groups led by a man responsible for the wellbeing of the whole 'felyshyp'. And there are other military qualities to be developed and encouraged if victory is to be achieved. Worcester is aware of the practical significance of training the soldier.[31] Training counts because it ensures greater efficiency, and is likely to promote a higher level of morale. We recognise here that Worcester has a sufficiently good knowledge of the ancient historians and the writers on war – of Vegetius, in particular – for him to emphasise how much they insisted on proper preparation,[32] and how they appreciated the importance which morale could play in the outcome of war. Above all, an army cannot expect success unless it is properly organised, and the men are ready to fight. Normandy, Worcester asserts, was lost because the English army lacked both courage and organisation. Two-and-a-half centuries earlier, our author's reading of history told him, King John was driven out of the very same duchy largely because he, too, was not prepared.[33] Lack of readiness reflects a serious lack of advance thinking and, above all, of training. Worcester reflects on the wars between Rome and Carthage, and takes examples to show that large armies can suffer defeat at the hands of much smaller ones, better trained, organised, disciplined and led: 'men of armes welle lerned and excercised is of a grettir tresoure then any precious stones or riche tresour', he says.[34] The lessons of history should teach and inspire men to emulate them.

Finally, since in order to win, an army must learn to act together, so war for the common good must also involve the effort of an entire society. This view reflects a vision in which war may involve everyone, stressing the common dependence of each individual upon every other. The army is society's arm through which it defends itself. The army's effectiveness reflects a good deal else: preparation, training and efficiency, not to forget material support. It represents the unity of the country, a unity which implies a willingness on the part of those not fighting to support those who are. So, Worcester argues, all should be ready to give of their wealth for the common good.[35] This is the way that will lead to victory, outward proof of the unity achieved.

Worcester's *Boke of Noblesse* can be read at more than one level. At one such, it is an attempt to inspire a revival in the flagging fortunes of England at a particularly difficult time after the long war with France. It uses historical evidence, much of it taken from the previous two centuries, to show that things

31] See, for instance, ibid., pp. 62–63, 76–77.
32] *Boke*, p. 21.
33] Ibid., p. 33.
34] Ibid., p. 27.
35] Ibid., p. 84.

are not as well managed as they used to be (in the early 1450s, perhaps not an unfair comment from one born in the year of Agincourt). For this purpose Worcester uses history to emphasise the truth of his main point, the fact that English kings 'have continually be[en] possessid and seased' of parts of France, as all the world well knows.[36] Normandy, in particular, is held 'frely in souvereinte and resort of none creature but of God'.[37] Yet the French have regained possession, so that both the king and those recently settled there have been denied justice. God will surely help England redress so blatant a wrong. But he will do so only if the English help themselves.

Worcester's message, although directed primarily at the English people, may be read at a second level limited by neither time, nor space, nor circumstance. It has, for instance, much in common with Alain Chartier's *Quadrilogue Invectif*, written in 1422, in which, as in the *Boke of Noblesse*, the author enquires into the causes of defeat, going far beyond the impact of the English conquest of Normandy in order to raise important questions regarding the divisions within France which, according to him, have been the cause of this disaster. Worcester implies, at least, that he had read the *Quadrilogue*.[38] There are striking similarities between the outlooks of the two writers, which transcend immediate issues. In spite of the gloom which pervades both works, Chartier's text reveals a latent optimism in the ability of men to revive the fortunes of France, while Worcester is similarly optimistic about the future – for the English. More tangibly, each reveals himself to be deeply concerned with the divisions within his own society, divisions which Chartier, unlike Worcester, makes very explicit by the way he shapes his discussion between representatives of the orders of society regarding the problems faced by France. Even if Worcester does not use this approach, it remains clear that he feels that defeat stems from a lack of unity within English society, and its inability to appreciate adequately the importance of England's historic claims to France. Worcester appears to borrow from Chartier a theme which he then incorporates into the *Boke of Noblesse* – the need for men to look to what the Frenchman termed the 'commun salut du pays de vostre nativité et a la defense de celle seigneurie soubz laquelle Dieu vous a fait naistre et avoir vie' ('common weal of the country of your birth and of the defence of that lordship under which God caused you to be born and to have life').[39]

From Chartier, too, Worcester could have derived the idea that not only is it right in law for men to defend what is theirs; nature, too, demands that they do this.[40] The theme occurs in the *Quadrilogue*, and is backed up there by examples

36] Ibid., p. 25.
37] Ibid., p. 22.
38] Ibid., p. 25. This part of the text was added later.
39] *Quadrilogue Invectif*, p. 11. See also *Boke*, notably pp. 83–85, and *supra*, n. 17.
40] A few years later, William Caxton would refer to the knight's duty to defend not only his lord but also his 'naturel countrey' (*The Book of the Ordre of Chyualry*, ed. A. T. P. Byles, London, EETS, 1926, p. 33).

taken from Roman history, notably the well-known story (which Worcester does not, in fact, use) of how the women of Rome cut off their hair to make ropes for the weapons being used to defend the Capitol against enemy attack.[41] The defence of the very symbol of Roman society was a classic example of true 'noblesse' (as Worcester understood the term) since it placed the general interest before the particular. Finally, there is Chartier's insistence that only men who are properly trained for war will fight with success. This message is central to the *De Re Militari* of Vegetius which, although written a whole millennium earlier, was the chief work on military theory read at the time. We know that Sir John Fastolf owned a copy,[42] and Worcester may have derived his knowledge of the Roman theorist's teaching from reading it. Chartier's work, too, is deeply imbued with the practical message regarding the best way to approach war, and Worcester may well have appreciated the contribution of Vegetius to the thinking of Chartier, and its relevance to the work he himself was composing.

Whether one is concerned with the long passages, based on recent historical events, intended to inspire Englishmen to seek their rights in France, or whether one takes the final section which, because it is least expected, is the most significant in the entire work, it should be recalled that the *Boke* has a unity, a sense of being created as a whole, which comes from Worcester's use of the word 'noblesse'. Both here and elsewhere he makes clear his view that 'noblesse' is not limited to those who are 'noble', least of all simply to those who have been born so. In his *Itineraria* he quotes (presumably with approval) the proverb 'virtue, not lineage, constitutes nobility'.[43] In so doing he is firmly taking sides in the controversy regarding nobility, what it constitutes, and whether it can be achieved. He has no doubt that it can be. The basic reason for this is that nobility consists of two dependent factors. One is an attitude of mind towards justice and one's fellow men, in which being noble means giving part of one's self (for instance, a readiness to risk life and limb in martial action) and to be willing to do this for the common good which it will help to bring about rather than for the fame which it will win for him who does it. The other factor is that justice can be realised only by those sufficiently equipped for the task. The man of true 'noblesse' must be properly motivated; he must also prepare himself, through training, to become an effective servant of society and of his fellow men. This is the combination which leads to success, the attributes of the 'manly man' favoured by Sir John Fastolf.

41] *Quadrilogue Invectif*, p. 31, citing Vegetius, *De Re Militari*, Book IV, ch. 9. Worcester's analogue to this story of self-sacrifice (*Boke*, pp. 84–85) is that the Romans gave liberally of their money to help sustain the war, a story with an altogether stronger and more appropriate message for the times.

42] R. F. Green, *Poets and Princepleasers. Literature and the English Court in the Late Middle Ages*, Toronto, 1980, p. 145.

43] 'Virtus facit nobiles, non parentes' (*Itineraries*, pp. 364–65).

'Noblesse', then, is within the grasp of others than those whose profession is that of arms. Worcester shows that he regards the word as being fully expressive only when it is given a political and social sense. 'Noblesse' is about understanding what the common good is and how it can be achieved, in this case by defending the honour of the English people and securing justice (as they see it) and peace. Men and women can contribute in different ways towards achieving the common good, and none should be excluded from making their contribution. It was Worcester's recognition that people must be made aware of where the common good lies, and how it can be achieved, that led him to write his *Boke*.

From his study of history, Worcester believed he saw how the Romans had striven to achieve their common good, even in moments of difficulty and defeat. Turning to more recent times, he reminded his readers that it was to Henry, Duke of Lancaster, that young men were sent from many countries that they might learn one of the attributes of true 'noblesse', that of being ready for war if it should come. If people will do this again, then England's greatness may re-emerge. But they show little inclination to do so. Instead, they 'wastyn gretlie theire tyme in suche nedelese besinessse' as the study of law so as to make a good impression at the county court and at sessions, where they go to defend their particular interests.[44] It is this egotistic, self-seeking attitude, the reluctance to put the common good before self-advantage, which Worcester regards as being contrary to that attribute of true 'noblesse', proper public-spirited motivation. Without it England's future, particularly in France, is a bleak one. On the other hand, if she can regain it, then she has nothing to fear. As the author of a tract intended to revive England's historical sense of 'noblesse', Worcester is, understandably, optimistic about that.

As stated earlier, we cannot be sure when the *Boke of Noblesse* was originally composed. It would appear to reflect immediate reaction to the disasters of the years 1450–53. Yet the date of completion given is 15 June 1475, the dedicatee King Edward IV,[45] about to set out on the expedition which would lead him to his meeting with the French king, Louis XI, on the bridge at Picquigny, near Amiens. Do these circumstances make the *Boke* simply into a *pièce d'occasion* or has it a broader historical foundation? Almost certainly it falls into the second category. Broadly speaking, the *Boke* fits into the same pattern as much other late medieval political writing which is concerned with either weak government or the (consequent) need for rulers to further the public good. Chivalry was always concerned with that good, and the emphasis which Worcester (and the circle around Fastolf) put upon Rome and the Romans as models of chivalry brought the point into sharp perspective.[46] This strongly suggests that Worcester's

44] *Boke*, p. 77.
45] Ibid., pp. 85, 1.
46] Hughes, 'Stephen Scrope', pp. 130–37.

work, with its aim (shared with the works of Fortescue) of strengthening government, should be seen in the long tradition of works written on how best to secure that end, the principal method advocated in this case being an active military policy.

It was probably in the Parliament of late 1472 that a speech was made urging the king that the best means of defence was to take the war to France, just as the Romans had done against Hannibal. Since the Conquest, the speaker explained, peace at home had never lasted for long 'in any kings day but in suche as have made werre outward'. War was an activity which unified the different parts of the nation, who contributed in their different ways to its success. It had the further advantage that it occupied 'men of werre that have none other purveaunce' and who, at home, might promote disorder.[47] Would not Caxton say much the same thing a decade later when he called for more tournaments so that men could learn to use arms as many notable men in England's past had done?[48] If Worcester and Fortescue differed in their views on how to set their country on an even keel, Worcester and Caxton would surely have seen eye to eye that the pursuit of warlike activity under the king was the best way to resolve the ills which faced England in the second half of the fifteenth century. In their time, a good many would probably have agreed with them.

47] See J. R. Lander, 'The Hundred Years' War and Edward IV's 1475 campaign in France', in *Tudor Men and Institutions: Studies in English Law and Government*, ed. A. J. Slavin, Baton Rouge, LA, 1972, pp. 81–83, repr. in idem, *Crown and Nobility 1450–1509*, London, 1976, pp. 228–30, citing *Literae Cantuarienses. The Letter Books of the Monastery of Christ Church Canterbury*, ed. J. B. Sheppard, 3 vols, London, RS, 1887–89, Vol. III, pp. 274–85.
48] Caxton, *Book of the Ordre of Chyualry*, pp. 121–24.

7
Commynes on Kingship[1]

JOËL BLANCHARD

In a well-known passage of his *Storia d'Italia*, Guicciardini recalls the remarkable courage of the French at the Battle of Fornovo. He ascribes their determination and spirit to the presence of the king, for whom they had a particular religious devotion: 'the courage of the French was strengthened by the presence, by their side, of the King of France, endangering his own person (for, according to the ancestral custom of this nation, the majesty of kings is no less revered than the name of God is adored)'.[2] The sacred character of kings in France and in those principalities (such as fifteenth-century Burgundy) where the princes had imperial or royal ambitions is well attested. Though it was impossible to accept that a man, even a king or a duke, could identify himself directly with God, the religious element in the representation of the king is increasingly marked in the mentality of the time. A royalist ideology satisfies this need for transcendence, and scholars in their writings echo this maximalist logic.

In this context, it is surprising to see a fifteenth-century writer move against the tide. But Commynes was no ordinary writer; indeed, he acknowledged as much himself. For example, the statement in his *Mémoires* 'I do not follow the rules of historians'[3] should be understood to mean that he set little store by the literary stereotypes used by historians of his day to celebrate the monarchy. 'Those chroniclers usually mention only that which is in praise of those persons they write about':[4] Commynes was thus certainly debunking the undertaking of the monks of Saint-Denis, and specifically the *Grandes Chroniques de France*. The *Chroniques*, of which Commynes must have been aware, were elaborated in successive layers from the thirteenth century onwards, and had the enormous

1] This chapter is a revised version of a paper given at a 'Later Medieval France' seminar at All Souls College, Oxford, on 17 February 1998.
2] Francesco Guicciardini, *Storia d'Italia, 1492–1534*, ed. A. Gherardi, 4 vols, Florence, 1919, Vol. I, pp. 134–35. The translation is my own.
3] Philippe de Commines, *Mémoires*, ed. B. de Mandrot, 2 vols, Paris, 1901–03, Vol. I, p. 194, edited from the best manuscript (BNF, ms. nouv. acq. fr. 20960). A new edition, by the present author, is in preparation for the series 'Lettres Gothiques'.
4] *Mémoires*, Vol. I, p. 405.

benefit of presenting a sort of vulgate of royal history. As a written memory of kingship, they set out a coherent vision of the national past which became the 'authentic and authorised version' of French history with a division into three periods, those of the three dynasties or *races* or *generations*, consecrated with the instruments of the royal cult (the fleur de lis, oriflamme, and king's evil, for instance). There were very few historians who, at the end of the fifteenth and beginning of the sixteenth century, could free themselves from the demands of this 'univocal discourse'.[5] Commynes, however, was one of these.

Commynes' concept of kingship is interesting because it reveals an original standpoint in opposition to the historiography of his day, which remained attached to an image of sacred and efficient kingship. Political history has long had a teleological conception of kingship and royal absolutism as an irresistible process. This retrospective vision introduces an underlying determinism to the passing of time. Commynes, on the other hand, shows that the things we postulate today were actually not self-evident at the time. The question, then, arises: is Commynes' attitude unique? It is in the exceptional life of this turncoat that we must look for answers. He was a professional diplomat, was never firmly rooted in any country, but had a personal association with the French king. This association grew progessively stronger through what the memorialist calls 'la continuelle residance'[6] (tantamount to sharing the king's intimacy). Peter Lewis has taught us how difficult it was to find one's bearings in the intricate maze of the royal court.[7] The private conversations between Commynes and the king were one of the new realities of the court at the end of the Middle Ages. They were also the driving force behind his vision of kingship set out in the *Mémoires*. The way the confidant looks upon the private and intimate life of the king deprives the latter of some of his majesty.

'Kings are men like us.'[8] This statement from the *Mémoires* is revolutionary in the late medieval context in which the king's person is held sacred. Medieval scholars were always very much aware of the human tragedy of kingship, of the double 'condition' of kings. The king reigns, yes, but 'with man's misery as his ever present companion and counterpoint to every step of his destiny'.[9] Writers maintained this insuperable distinction between the man and his function. With

5] See B. Guenée, *Histoire et culture historique dans l'Occident médiéval*, Paris, 1980, passim. A recent analysis of the influence of the abbey of Saint-Denis on a contemporary of Commynes is to be found in F. Collard, *Un historien au travail à la fin du XVe siècle: Robert Gaguin*, Geneva, 1996, pp. 137–38, 193–94, 202–10.
6] *Mémoires*, Vol. I, p. 2.
7] See P. S. Lewis, 'Reflections on the Role of Royal Clienteles in the Construction of the French Monarchy (mid–XIVth/end–XVth centuries)', in *L'État ou le roi. Les fondations de la modernité monarchique en France (XIVe–XVIIe siècles)*, ed. N. Bulst, R. Descimon and A. Guerreau, Paris, 1996, pp. 51–67.
8] 'Ilz sont hommes comme nous' (*Mémoires*, Vol. I, p. 2).
9] E. Kantorowicz, *The King's Two Bodies. A Study in Mediaeval Political Theology*, Princeton, 1957, p. 37.

Commynes, on the contrary, it seems as if this double 'condition' disappears, leaving the king in a state of human contingency and dependence. In the *Mémoires*, Commynes removes the king from his pedestal, divesting his sacred body politic in order to uncover the man himself. Examination of one of those royal rituals, that surrounding the death of the king, will reveal this debasement. The notion of *travail* (with its medieval meaning of moral suffering) chosen by Commynes to evoke the suffering of the king on his deathbed provides a remarkable illustration of this new, inverted point of view on kingship.

What are the effects of the removal of the king from his pedestal upon the royal ideology set out in the *Mémoires*? We can still see some remnants of the prevailing ideology, but on all points the memorialist stands apart from other writers of his day. Some, such as Thomas Basin, a contemporary of Commynes, freely criticised the monarchy, but were very careful to offer an alternative image to that of bad, iconoclastic kings. The ambivalence of rituals made this type of reversal easy. Commynes, apparently wishing to confine himself to a more matter-of-fact experience of power, renounced these polemical and heroic strategies. Abandoning the field of exemplary morality, he opened up new perspectives for politics with more immediate aims. Monarchical ritual would now be replaced by criteria of utility more adapted to the new situations created by the development of the state, power and sovereignty at the end of the Middle Ages.

* * * * *

The word 'experience' is an ever-recurring one in the *Mémoires.* It bears reference to Commynes' particular position at court as he defines it in the prologue:

> Of his [Louis XI's] youth I can say nothing but by his own report. But from the time I entered his service until the hour of his death, at which I was myself present, I was more continually resident with him than any man of my estate that served him, being ever either of his privy chamber or employed in his weighty affairs.[10]

This introductory statement by Commynes is of paramount importance because it defines one of the essential aspects of the *Mémoires* as belonging to the historiographical genre, the main interest of which lies in the familiar image it gives of the king. This sharing of the king's everyday life suggests that Commynes was with the king all the time. It is not sufficient for the memorialist to say 'I heard' or 'the king told me'; the closeness must be perceived in its continuity and should be seen as part of a normal way of life. Here, the contrast with Joinville is very significant. The author of *La Vie de Saint Louis* also proudly referred to his closeness to the king. We all remember the famous scene in which the king

10] *Mémoires*, Vol. I, p. 2.

unexpectedly laid his hands on Joinville's head.[11] The royal contact came as a surprise and as proof that it was impossible to foresee and penetrate the king's thoughts because the king never gave himself away.

The difference between the man who lives on familiar terms with the king (like Joinville, as a member of his household) and the confidant (Commynes) lies precisely in the latter's 'continuelle residance', that is to say this sort of in-camera session of the memorialist with the king. This experience corresponds to the reality of the world of the court, the closeness of the confidant being a very particular link among other types of relationships. In the court society of the time, various sociological and political realities could be observed. Describing the evolution of courtly circles at the end of the Middle Ages, Philippe Contamine has written about the organisation of the Chamber, a confined inner space reserved for important characters such as chamberlains, counsellors and minions.[12] We must admit that it is not easy to tell these persons apart; neither was it so for contemporaries. In his prologue, Commynes describes himself as counsellor and chamberlain;[13] in other places he is said to be the king's *mignon*[14] – the word being used without any derogatory or sexual connotation. The chamberlain and the *mignon* belonged to the same category of *familiarissimi*, as the monk of Saint-Denis called them in his *Chronique*. Their presence answered the need for privacy felt by the king, this closed circle providing him with intimacy and security. The distinction between those groups was not a product of institutional differences but was part of an attempt to exercise a certain ascendancy over the king. If counsellors enjoyed room to manoeuvre in the political field because the king trusted them, the influence of the confidant was not limited by the attribution of any particular power. The counsellor enlightened the king on his obligations, whereas the confidant was the guardian of the king's secrets. In the *Mémoires*, the confidant's influence is linked to a genuine sharing of day-to-day existence. One striking example was the way the king had Commynes dress like him on important occasions such as high-level diplomatic meetings.[15] This was not mainly a matter of security but rather a public token of familiarity for everybody to recognise (a familiarity expressed in the *Mémoires* by the word *pratiquer* [to frequent], a turn of phrase peculiar to Commynes). Nor should we confuse the confidant with the 'mediator' who, in practice dating back to the feudal society of the early tenth and eleventh centuries, was the official placed in

11] Joinville, *Vie de Saint Louis*, ed. J. Monfrin, Paris, 1995, p. 212.
12] P. Contamine, 'Pouvoir et vie de cour dans la France du XVe siècle: les mignons', *Académie des Inscriptions et Belles-Lettres, Comptes rendus des séances de l'année 1994*, pp. 541–54.
13] *Mémoires*, Vol. I, p. 1.
14] 'Not very long ago, certain friends of mine acquainted me with the fact that the king had given to one of his mignons whose name I do not know ...' (*Les La Trémoille pendant cinq siècles*, ed. L.-C. de la Trémoille, 5 vols, Nantes, 1892–96, Vol. II, pp. 23–24).
15] *Mémoires*, Vol. I, p. 316.

charge of the regular proceedings inside the *colloquium familiare* or *secretum*.[16]

We may think that the memorialist, wishing to enhance the value of his testimony in the eyes of the reader, attempted to exaggerate or magnify his intimacy with the king, but generally speaking, it turns out to be based on historical truth. A precise chronology of the time Commynes spent with the king, undertaken elsewhere,[17] emphasises that his claims to intimacy were entirely justified.

* * * * *

The *continuelle residance* provided Commynes with the inspiration for his literary project, that is to say a treatise on the personalities of princes. This treatise broke with the traditional way of speaking about kings. The chroniclers of the time had an a priori awareness of the majesty of kings, whereas Commynes, more radically opposed to them than it may seem, reduced the distance between the person of the king and the man who wrote about him.[18] This distance suddenly vanishes because of the familiarity induced by a life entirely devoted to the daily service of the king. We can find this same perspective in the account of the death of Louis XI, and in the insistence on the king's 'natures' which deprive him of his majesty and lay bare a certain form of human weakness in him. The narrative underlines a particular aspect of the king's personality as he nears death: his fear of losing any of his authority. This comes as an echo of a theme which appears here and there in the *Mémoires*, but which is taken up again at this point in a most striking manner through what the memorialist says of the king's 'passions', that is to say, his sufferings. Although the king died on a particular day, in a sense he had already been 'dead' for some days. The latent or imagined disobedience of some of his entourage or, even worse, of his family was to cause great suffering to the man who was conscious of being deprived of his power, and who could see that the body politic was already ceasing to be what it had previously been. Physical death was preceded by other 'deaths'. According to the ritual saying, 'the king never dies' but, in fact, because of this humiliation, the king was already 'dead' before his actual death.

The turning point in the narrative is the moment when the relationship between the king and his physician is described. Louis XI has forbidden anyone to mention 'this cruel word of death' in front of him, but Coictier speaks very

16] G. Althoff, *Spielregeln der Politik im Mittelalter. Kommunikation in Frieden und Fehde*, Darmstadt, 1997, pp. 157–84.

17] J. Blanchard, *Commynes l'Européen. L'invention du politique*, Geneva, 1996, pp. 29–70, 137–46.

18] Unlike Commynes, chroniclers, when drawing the portrait of a prince, did not intend to give a familiar or intimate picture of him: their business was to praise or to blame according to what was required or forbidden by royal majesty; the chronicle developed on a background of due reverence. See B. Guenée, 'Le Portrait de Charles VI dans la *Chronique du Religieux de Saint-Denis*', *Journal des Savants*, 1997, pp. 125–65.

bluntly to his dying patient: 'no one would tell a knave ... "you haven't got eight days left ...!"'[19] 'Considering the great respect he had always had from so many good people and famous men',[20] for he was in truth 'a master with whom one had to toe the line',[21] this sudden lack of courtesy, the infringement of the rules of hierarchy, disobedience or fear of it, greatly mortified the king. This situation merely increased the 'imaginations' (that is to say the over-excitement) of the king who acted to protect his authority and to give the illusion of power preserved. Commynes describes the measures taken at some length. Considerable precautions were taken for the king's security: for instance, to prevent surprise attack (however improbable) by his feudal lords, the king began to fortify his castle of Le Plessis. He himself remained almost completely out of sight. Yet, despite living as a recluse, he nevertheless sought to give the illusion that he had preserved his power intact. Terrified by the idea that people might think that he had been laid low by illness, he resorted to all sorts of means to keep up appearances. He dressed in the finest vestments 'such as he was never accustomed to do before', sent for the rarest animals, reindeer and elks, that he had bought from Sweden and Denmark, and *adives*, a type of wolf no bigger than a fox, all of which he had purchased at well above their normal value.[22] He made sizeable donations to churches, and there was no charm he did not covet or on the use of which he did not seek information. For Louis XI, this represented a way of staying alive. Commynes' long account finally provides the answer to an essential question: what is the death of a king like? On the one hand, by giving his son his final recommendations and having the seals, emblems of the king's function, conveyed to him, the king divested himself of royalty. On the other hand, he clung on to power, desperately striving to keep its outward appearances alive.

The account of Louis XI's death is the exact opposite of other accounts of royal deaths. In hagiographies, or even in chronicles, whether one thinks of the death of Saint Louis or of Charles V, the king imposes himself more in death than in life. The inevitable themes of illness, of the death agony and of death itself within these accounts, constitute purple patches, accompanied by copious references to the good Christian death. Emphasis is placed on the preparation of the dying man for death, and particularly on appropriate devotional gestures.[23]

19] *Mémoires*, Vol. II, p. 77.
20] Ibid.
21] Ibid., Vol. II, p. 43.
22] W. Paravicini, 'Des animaux pour un roi mourant: Louis XI et les Hanséates de 1479 à 1483', *Commerce, finances et société (XIe–XVIe siècles). Recueil de travaux d'histoire médiévale offert à M. le Professeur Henri Dubois*, ed. P. Contamine, T. Dutour and B. Schnerb, Paris, 1993, pp. 101–21.
23] L. Bornscheuer, *Miseriae regum. Untersuchungen zum Krisen- und Todesgedanken in den herrschaftstheologischen Vorstellungen der ottonisch-salischen Zeit*, Berlin, 1968, pp. 93–121; H. M. Schaller, 'Der Kaiser stirbt', in *Tod im Mittelalter*, ed A. Borst, G. v. Graevenitz, A. Patschovsky and K. Stierle, Constance, 1993, pp. 59–75; F. Autrand, *Charles V*, Paris, 1994, pp. 847–51.

Indeed, every effort is made to limit everything which may jeopardise the exemplary nature of the ritual. The account of the death of Louis XI is the inverted image of the apotheosis of gestures and pronouncements expected at the end of a royal life. Admittedly, devotional manifestations and preparations for death are not entirely absent from the *Mémoires*. However, emphasis on ritual gives way to something that may best be described as a final settling of accounts. The harmonious balance of the natural body with that of the immortal body politic disappears, as does the fiction of all manner of royal prerogatives. What is left is the image of a king which, based as it is on an individual, cannot be predetermined.

Does this mean that the portrayal of Louis' death is offensive? Commynes' narrative is not strictly speaking a medical one, even if, on occasions, we are given information about the king's illness. Admittedly, it records the opinions of the king's doctor, Angelo Cato, but details of the king's physical deterioration form a relatively minor aspect of the narrative. Commynes' account remains well within the bounds of that of the Italian ambassadors regarding the pathological manifestations of the various afflictions from which the king was suffering. For instance, they mention the stomach pains or haemorrhoidal growths that contributed to the king's profound irritability.[24] The *Mémoires* do not actually offer any new revelations on the king's physical deterioration, as other contemporary chroniclers or the clinical narratives in official or semi-official chancellery documents do. In fact, the memorialist's attention is focused on the affective and moral repercussions of the illness, rather than on the illness itself. The prime objective is to investigate the constitutions of princes when confronted by the testing realities of power.

The great originality of Commynes' work is to have introduced, if not to have considerably deepened, the concept of *travail* to unmask what had come to be recognised as one of the touchstones of the world of the court. The concept appears elsewhere in the medieval tradition. In his *Arbre des Batailles*, Honoré Bouvet, one of the leading intellectuals of the reign of Charles VI, expounds on the theme of the moral suffering of princes, starting with examples drawn from Valerius-Maximus or from the Bible.[25] However, the notion is much more

24] J. Chmel, 'Briefe und Actenstücke zur Geschichte der Herzoge von Mailand von 1452 bis 1513', *Notizenblatt, Beilage zum Archiv für Kunde österreichischer Geschichtsquellen herausgegeben von der historischen Commission kaiserlichen Akademie der Wissenschaften in Wien*, Vol. IX, 1856, p. 193.

25] Honoré Bonet, *L'Arbre des Batailles*, ed. E. Nys, Brussels, 1883, p. 152. The notion of *travail* appears in other texts of the fourteenth and fifteenth centuries; for instance, in the *Songe du Vergier*, ed. M. Schnerb-Lièvre, 2 vols, Paris, 1982, Vol. II, p. 267, and, above all, in the famous account of the death of Charles V by Christine de Pizan. On his deathbed the king had two crowns brought to him, the crown of thorns and the royal crown. Contrasting them, he spoke of the second as 'the vilest of all things, considering the weight, labour, anguish, torments and sufferings of heart, body and conscience it causes to those who carry it, besides jeopardising their souls ...' (*Livre des fais et bonnes meurs du sage roy Charles V*, ed. S. Solente, 2 vols, SHF, Paris, 1936–40, Vol. II, pp. 187-88).

fundamental to the *Mémoires* which, while not ignoring the literary background, rely mainly on the personal experience of the author. Although the idea of *travail* in Commynes' text occasionally refers to the idea of physical suffering or struggle, it is above all interpreted as the moral suffering of kings. Commynes refers to the *travail d'esperit* (spiritual suffering) when evoking the fears of Louis XI or the melancholy of Edward IV.[26] Each prince follows the particular path of his own constitution, but each initially experiences the corrosive force of power in a spiritual sense before suffering any physical effects. The origin of this argument is the idea that princes are 'en nécessité et en affaire' (always under constraint and overworked);[27] in other words, they are embroiled in inextricable situations of their own making. This is the case, for example, when they have to pledge their word to other princes or to meet them. It is impossible for them to *s'asseurer*[28] (that is to say, to be in control of their own situation). Thus, they are drawn into making promises that they will not keep, or to say and write 'so many things that are almost the direct opposite of their actual thoughts'.[29] The effort required to meet such situations leads to tension and physical and mental fatigue, the result of which is that the lives of princes are necessarily shortened 'through taking on so much pain and suffering'.[30]

These situations in which princes are engaged are given a specific name in the *Mémoires*. The term used by Commynes is *brouilliz* (embroilments),[31] one that clearly expresses its meaning and appears on several occasions in the sense of intrigues. The *brouilliz* are situations which inextricably implicate princes, and over which they cannot gain control. They are overwhelmed by the complexity of reality, and are unable to direct the course of events which they themselves have set in motion. Louis XI 'tormented himself'[32] in vain to prevent a reconciliation between the princes and Charles the Bold in 1471, since it was clear from the outset that the latter would never give his consent to the marriage of his daughter, the young Mary of Burgundy, who was the prize in all these *pratiques* (politickings). Equally to no avail was the corrosive disquiet experienced by Edward IV when doing all he could to prevent the marriage between Marie de Bourgogne and Charles de France, Louis XI's brother, since this union of 'so many domains united to the crown' would, he feared, have catastrophic consequences for the future of his own kingdom. He is described as 'truly taking this matter to heart'.[33] No prince is free of such taxing, yet pointless, anxieties.

Let us stay with Edward IV for a moment. Commynes depicts that king's life

26] *Mémoires*, Vol. I, pp. 221, 291.
27] Ibid., Vol. I, p. 83.
28] Ibid., Vol. I, p. 314.
29] Ibid., Vol. I, p. 291.
30] Ibid.
31] Ibid., Vol. I, p. 226; Vol. I, p. 47, variant: *brouilles*.
32] Ibid., Vol. I, p. 221.
33] Ibid., Vol. I, p. 227.

as a series of failures and misfortunes. He is reduced to fleeing his country in the most adverse conditions, to living in discomfort and even to being persecuted by his own servants. His life is a long succession of frustrations, defeats and betrayals, at the end of which he dies. His death can be attributed to a variety of factors, among which Commynes gives particular prominence to melancholy.[34]

It is this emphasis on the moral and psychological dimension of power that makes Commynes' analysis so remarkable. His account of the suffering of princes brings out a certain disposition that is perculiar to them. When Commynes tells us that 'princes are men like us', we have to be clear what is meant by the notion of 'humanity', since it is a concept that leads easily to confusion. The idea that kings share the moral and physical suffering common to all is not a new one; indeed, debates on the notion of natural equality can be found in biblical commentaries as early as the twelfth century.[35] These writings suggested that kings, although exalted by office and unction, nevertheless participated in common humanity founded, both before and after the Fall, on equality. Commynes, however, does not evoke this 'natural equality'. On the contrary, he addresses 'complexions' and 'conditions' that are specific to royalty, in particular the immeasurable suffering of princes who, *mutatis mutandis*, bear intolerable suffering way beyond the experience of their subjects.[36]

The conclusion so far is as follows: Commynes elaborates the concept of *travail* to evoke the suffering of princes, and this represents a new stage in the process of individualisation and personalisation which, as historians have noted, was occurring towards the end of the Middle Ages. It would, however, be going too far to postulate that this concept owes its elaboration to Commynes alone. The influence upon Commynes of cultural traditions which were like screens between reality and him (who, paradoxically, refers to himself as a 'non lettré' ['unlearned'])[37] cannot be doubted. One striking example of this is the powerful impression made by the religious tradition found in works of hagiography. As Jacques Le Goff has demonstrated with regard to Saint Louis, the image of the king going through his passion is a fruitful one. However, the extent of the difference between the accounts of the death agony of Louis XI by Commynes

34] Ibid., Vol. I, p. 454; Vol. II, p. 63.
35] P. Buc, *L'Ambiguïté du livre. Prince, pouvoir, et peuple dans les commentaires de la Bible au Moyen Age*, Paris, 1995, pp. 327–28.
36] 'In an earlier section I started to make a comparison between the sufferings which the king had inflicted on some people, among them many who lived under him and his authority, and those similar in nature which he endured before his death (for if they were neither as great nor as long lasting, as I mentioned in that section, they were none the less very considerable, particularly in view of his nature, which demanded more obedience than did any other in his day, and had obtained more of it; for the slightest word of opposition to his will was for him a very great torment hard for him to endure). I referred to how his imminent death was announced to him with a minimum of sensitivity' (*Mémoires*, Vol. II, p. 75).
37] Ibid., Vol. I, p. 439.

and that of the 'Christ king' by Joinville cannot be exaggerated. For the latter, to use Le Goff's own words, the path of pain places kingship above and beyond any tribulations.[38] Characteristically, it is Purgatory (that place of expiation) which is evoked in the account of the death agony of Louis XI. The *Mémoires* state that 'he lived out his purgatory on earth',[39] with the emphasis on the king's dark side rather than any presentation of a Christ-like transfiguration. One might even wonder whether, at the dawn of the modern age, Commynes, with his secular vision of the royal sphere, had not exposed a process of sacred ritualisation inherent in the establishment of any form of absolutism. In this light, the framework within which royal majesty finds expression in the *Mémoires* becomes more blurred than ever.[40]

* * * * *

Commynes' description is a real desacralisation since it gives a very detailed portrait of the king and his weaknesses which contrasts sharply with the expected hieratic image of a monarch. Taking this line of enquiry to its limits, one may even wonder what remains of royalty in the *Mémoires.* Commynes evinces a certain reserve when addressing any issue related to 'the religion of royalty', whereas for all his contemporaries this element was an essential facet of the picture. He says nothing about the rite of the Holy Ampulla (used to anoint French kings at their coronation), about the *privilegia Franciae*, or about the possession of the coat of arms with the fleur-de-lis of the royal standard – although these symbols underwent spectacular developments at the end of the Middle Ages.

Commynes is interested neither in the anointing nor in any other royal rituals. Yet he evokes the use of the Holy Ampulla on one occasion, when the king, in the face of death, asks to have his whole body anointed with the contents of the sacred phial which he has had specially brought from Reims. In Commynes' account, however, the ritual is distorted by what is apparently an inversion of the established order: the thaumaturgic king using *ad usum proprium* the health-giving properties intended for the sick, of whom Commynes notes

38] J. Le Goff, *Saint Louis*, Paris, 1996, p. 886.

39] *Mémoires*, Vol. II, pp. 72, 77, 79.

40] In this analysis of royal rituals which are debased in the *Mémoires*, we could add another example: that of the death of Charles VIII. The *Mémoires* give the only consistent account of the circumstances of this death. Charles VIII died at the castle of Amboise, in degrading circumstances, on a bed of straw, in the midst of garbage strewn over a gallery, from which he was watching a game of real tennis; 'it was the filthiest place in the castle, for everyone pissed there' (*Mémoires*, Vol. II, p. 381). The king met a miserable death, and it seems, even though the memorialist did not mention it, that people went on playing without taking heed of the king's fate. The 'simple body of the king', deprived of its royal dignity, was a grievous sight over which Commynes dwells at length.

elsewhere that 'there were many'![41] If the death of a king is supposed to be in the tradition of a model death that is also politically beneficial, then it is clear that the perspective of the *Mémoires* offers something altogether different.

The personality of Louis XI was undoubtedly very important in this sort of debunking of royal ritual. The king's lack of enthusiasm for the official aspects of royal life is well documented. The Milanese ambassadors, for example, were surprised by the simplicity of his household 'where only the horseflesh was up to royal standard'.[42] In addition, there were few ceremonies, few *entrées royales* into towns. On the contrary, Louis favoured customs which did not defer to royalty, promoting a familiarity which suppressed the respect due to a monarch, a practice so disconcerting to the Italians.[43] Such developments are echoed in the works of Basin and Chastelain.[44] Yet while these chroniclers are scandalised and make the most of the occasion to expose Louis XI's guile, Commynes is not in the least troubled. He cares as little as the king himself for ritualised demonstrations of royalty. He is unreceptive to the dominant doctrinal tendencies of his day, and appears to lack interest in the beliefs on which the traditional representation of the political and social world was founded. It seems to us that it is in this light of informality that Commynes' tolerant attitude towards the political illegitimacy of the Italian princes should be understood.[45] Most Italian princes, whether Visconti or Este, were illegitimate sons. Commynes' lack of interest in this case is indicative of his general disregard for the legitimist and nationalist theories developed by chroniclers of his own time. Above all, he refutes the theory of the royal blood upon which the representation of the sovereign was based at the end of the Middle Ages. One could argue that Commynes was not alone in his enthusiasm for illegitimate sons; their rise to the heights of public office was not limited to Italy.[46] True as this may be, the fact

41] *Mémoires*, Vol. II, pp. 67–68 ; Vol. II, p. 41.

42] P. M. Kendall, *Louis XI, the Universal Spider*, London, 1971, p. 116.

43] See *Mémoires*, Vol. I, p. 298: 'the said Lord was not so stately, or vain, as to have either herald or trumpet in his train, as many other princes have'. Contemporary chroniclers, and above all Italian ambassadors intent on giving in their dispatches an account of the idiosyncrasies of the king, testified to Louis XI's prejudice against ceremonial. See references in Blanchard, *Commynes l'Européen*, pp. 101, 139 n. 5, 189, 275–76. The king's dislike of ritual is to be contrasted with what can be noted in the state of Burgundy where most elaborate forms of ceremonial, far from being a sort of romantic escapism, as has often been said, were used intentionally by the princes as an instrument of power in order to enhance and proclaim their legitimacy. On this see W. Prevenier and W. Blockmans, *Les Pays-Bas bourguignon*, Antwerp–Paris, 1983, and P. Arnade, *Realms of Ritual: Burgundian Ceremony and Civic Life in Late Medieval Ghent*, Cornell, 1996, pp. 13ff.

44] For Chastelain, see G. Small, *George Chastelain and the Shaping of Valois Burgundy. Political and Historical Culture at Court in the Fifteenth Century*, Woodbridge, 1997, p. 182.

45] *Mémoires*, Vol. I, p. 437.

46] M. Harsgor, 'L'Essor des bâtards nobles au XVe siècle', *RH*, Vol. CCLIII, 1975, pp. 319–54.

remains that Commynes does distance himself from controversy over the legitimacy of princes, preferring to devote his attention to their material and professional success. This would explain the barely restrained admiration – a feeling shared by Louis XI – shown for men such as Francesco Sforza, whose cobbler ancestry did not prevent that 'his virtue deserved high regard and was worthy of the noblest princes who reigned in his day'.[47] The same interest is shown in the Earl of Warwick, whose successes in the fields of property and finance are described in detail by the memorialist.[48] Just like Louis XI, these men were political adventurers who dared to defy the customs of their times, who could count only on themselves, and who knew how to seize the opportunity when it occurred. In this context Commynes was the only writer (as far as I know) to evoke the qualification 'holy' used by Italians to refer to Giangaleazzo Visconti, Duke of Milan, who was 'a great and wicked tyrant, but nonetheless honourable'.[49] It was from the mouth of a monk, during a visit to the Charterhouse of Pavia where the duke was buried, that Commynes garnered this startling characterisation, whereas other chroniclers, driven by the traditional opposition between *tyrannus* and *rex*, did not hesitate to call him a usurper.[50] Was the relating of this anecdote in the *Mémoires* simply humorous? Possibly so, but at least it corresponds to an attitude which transgresses the limits inside which the history of princes and reigning monarchs was conventionally organised. Commynes' political thought develops on a large scale, which enables him to correct or at least attenuate the sometimes suffocating effects of official propaganda. He imposes an alternative measure of legitimacy judged by the yardstick of his own experience as diplomat, traveller and renegade. His is the judgement of a man who is free (or who has been freed) from ideological constraints that were still, for the most part but not entirely, feudal, and who, having known personally all the princes in Europe, was in a position to make comparisons and relative judgements.

There is, therefore, in Commynes an absence of any reference to the majesty of the king, to that absolute, untouchable grandeur 'which is, as it were, the

47] *Mémoires,* Vol. I, pp. 125–26.
48] Ibid., Vol. I, p. 196.
49] Ibid., Vol. II, p. 156.
50] The qualification of 'holy' would require a vast development, too long for a simple footnote. No other example of applying the term to a tyrant is to be found in Italian or French texts, yet its use may be significant in the more general perspective of a valorisation of seigniorial regimes in Italy. These regimes enjoyed durability and evinced a will to make private interest and public welfare meet (notably through their emphasis on town planning, as in the quotation from the *Mémoires* devoted to the tastes and architectural achievements of Giangaleazzo Visconti). On the values of monarchy and tyranny in northern Italy, see P. Gilli, 'Dictature, monarchie et absolutisme en Italie aux XIVe et XVe siècles', *Revue Française d'Histoire des Idées Politiques*, Vol. VI, 2nd semestre, 1997, pp. 275–89. Commynes may have been influenced by these trends of thought because of his practical experience in Italy.

exterior touchstone upon which the whole institutional edifice was founded',[51] namely all the beliefs and dogmas on which authority and submission depend. With Commynes there is a change of attitude towards royalty. This description lacks the commonplaces of the doctrine of monarchy meticulously mentioned by other contemporary ideologists. For instance, there is nothing in the *Mémoires* on the organic concept of power so dear to theologians and lawyers, nor on the indispensable stability of the limbs of the body politic; nothing, either, on the fidelity, love and obedience of the subjects, nor on the emotion generated by a physical encounter with the king. In place of all this, and through the use of the expression *continuelle residance*, Commynes offers an alternative depiction of proximity to the king which is more familiar and less solemn. This impression of a demythologisation of royalty remains dominant, even though Commynes does take the trouble to recall the vitality of loyalty to the king and the feeling of national community that existed at the close of Louis XI's reign.[52] Furthermore, his work contains nothing on the greatness of the French in battle (a theme inspired by the works of Caesar that were being translated at the time), on the religious grandeur of the crown, nor on the fact that the monarch was *naturel* (that is to say, legitimate by birth). Neither is there anything on the love of motherland which, as a component factor in national unity, was a deeply ingrained element in people's consciousness at the end of the fifteenth century. On the contrary, in the *Mémoires* we find a rather fluid image of the notion of *fides*. For Commynes, fidelity is the virtue of those who, little concerned by feudal or national demands, settle their own personal situation in a contractual way, offering their services to the highest bidder or to those to whom they are genuinely attracted.

These are just a few points from a list which could be drawn up if one were to carry out an examination of the various accounts of the Estates General of 1484. If there are similarities between the *Mémoires* and the speeches of the notables present at that assembly, it is equally true that there are also many differences. The themes broached by the likes of Jean de Rély, Guillaume de Rochefort and Philippe Pot, all of whom Commynes met at the Estates, belong exclusively to the movement aimed at developing the clerical perspective of monarchy. Their speeches, filled with quotations from the Scriptures, deal with theoretical problems concerning kingship, and are devoted above all to the 'virtues' which are traditionally expected of a king. At the time, morality and politics were considered a fruitful combination. For example, the need for a good king is reiterated in the numerous tributes to Charles VII which, as has been clearly demonstrated, reduced the impact of the protests made at these

51] J. Chiffoleau, 'Amédée VIII ou la majesté impossible?', in *Amédée VIII–Félix V, premier duc de Savoie et pape (1383–1451). Colloque international Ripaille-Lausanne, 23–26 octobre 1990*, Lausanne, 1992, p. 47.
52] *Mémoires*, Vol. I, p. 445–47.

assemblies.[53] This kind of theoretical vision was beyond Commynes. Indeed, the very idea of theory, so different from his pragmatic view of history, was probably alien to him.

This analytical difference is most noticeable in the ways in which the memorialist deals with those royal occasions fraught with symbolism. In order to illustrate this concept, let us examine the idea of hunting, a royal theme if ever there was one. The canonical position, which perceives in hunting a manifestation of tyranny and an initiation into homicide, is well known. This is backed up by examples such as Nimrod, the archetype of a hunter prince, who exhibited a certain tendency to cruelty.[54] By contrast with the heavenly King of the Eucharist, a tyrant does not give of himself; on the contrary, he devours his subjects. This biblical example, developed through the Roman model, was used by Basin to denounce the excesses to which hunting led Louis XI: for instance, he restricted this pastime for others, depriving high-ranking lords and noblemen of an activity which was perceived as an inalienable right – the right to hunt.[55] A fellow cleric, Robert Gaguin, took up the metaphor of bleeding flesh with which both hunting and tyranny were associated, by reporting the rumour according to which Louis XI was said to have drunk the blood of sacrificed children in order to prolong his life.[56] Commynes, unaware of the scholastic background and its symbolic content, mentions none of this, and simply notes that the king hunted deer, but that it was a source not of pleasure but of annoyance to him, since 'it caused him great pain'.[57] Commynes is interested in hunting only to the extent that it throws light on the royal temperament: that is, the suffering caused by an activity that is both frustrating and disappointing for him who practises it.

Everything in Commynes' work evinces a pragmatic spirit which refuses to force the royal personality into the framework of general models or systems. On the contrary, Commynes was a practical man, attentive to the king's individual characteristics. His curiosity, which corresponds to a turn of mind far removed from that of the mirror of princes, keeps him apart from the doctrines that surround the royal person, so much so that it undoubtedly leads to a relativism that is critical in spirit. The famous passage from the *Mémoires* in which Commynes cannot help recalling the extraordinary moment of the physical

53] J. Krynen, *L'Empire du roi. Idées et croyances politiques en France, XIIIe–XVe siècles*, Paris, 1994, pp. 183–85.
54] T. Szabo, 'Die Kritik der Jagd – von der Antike zum Mittelalter', in *Jagd und höfische Kultur im Mittelalter*, ed. W. Rösener, Göttingen, 1997, pp. 170–74.
55] Thomas Basin, *Histoire de Louis XI*, ed. and trans. C. Samaran, 2 vols, Paris, 1963, Vol. I, p. 123.
56] Robert Gaguin, *Compendium de origine et gestis Francorum*, Paris, 1521, fol. cclxxxviii *v*°. On drinking human blood as a remedy at the end of the Middle Ages, see L. Thuasne, *Djem-Sultan, fils de Mohammed II, frère de Bayezid II, 1459–1495, d'après des documents originaux. Etude sur la question d'Orient à la fin du XVe siècle*, Paris, 1892, p. 113 n. 3.
57] *Mémoires*, Vol. II, p. 84.

transformation of young Charles VIII at Fornovo is well known. Commynes notes that the king, despite being slight of stature and normally timid, suddenly appeared 'to be carried away by a nature entirely other than his own ... looking so imposing on horseback'.[58] This description of another being surging within him indicates that this transformation is a direct inheritance of scriptural commentaries evoking the imposing stature of Saul, God's anointed.[59] Through unction, the king becomes the repository of a sublimating force which makes him look taller and nobler. The same image evoking the sacred can be found in Joinville's representation of Saint Louis during the battle on the road to Cairo: Saint Louis stood a head taller than anyone else, with a golden helmet on his head and a German sword in his hand.[60] In Charles VIII's case, prophecies (for instance those of Savonarola) accompanied this process of sanctification, so that Commynes, in drawing attention to this transcendence of the human state within the body of the king, is not very far from becoming a participant in the same process. However, no sooner is the sacred image depicted than it is being debunked with irony. Such irony is of a very Italian flavour linking, within the space of a few lines of the *Mémoires*, the portrayal of the holy king with the trivial depiction of the prince as 'a man of such meagre proportions', who in addition 'was not very clever'.[61] Here the memorialist is close to the often cruel jibes of the Italians about the ugliness, the lack of culture of this barbarous dwarf-king who was 'more like a beast than a man'.[62] Was the reason for this that Commynes was a man of free thought and free speech?

The narrative certainly illustrates the contradictory tendencies in the conflict of interest between, on the one hand, ritualisation and, on the other, the individual royal personality. Consider again the section describing the death of Louis XI. Everything seemed to unfold normally. Louis XI sent the 'dauphin', Charles, his recommendations and then his seals; only at the very end did he dismiss his personal guard and send away everything related to his greatest passion, hunting. Louis XI no longer addressed himself to the 'dauphin' but, in a strikingly original formula, 'to the *King*, his son'.[63] It only remained for him to die, which he did on 30 August, while the man who had, as it were, already succeeded him, had all the instruments of power at his disposal. More than ever

58] Ibid., Vol. II, p. 267.
59] For a different reading of this passage, see D. Crouzet, 'Désir de mort et puissance absolue de Charles VIII à Henri IV', *Revue de synthèse*, 4th series, 1990, pp. 423–41.
60] Joinville, *Vie de Saint Louis*, pp. 112–13.
61] *Mémoires*, Vol. II, p. 340.
62] C. de Frede, 'Più simile è mostro ch'è uomo. La bruttezza e l'incultura di Carlo VIII nella rappresentazione degli Italiani del Rinascimento', *Bibliothèque d'Humanisme et Renaissance*, Vol. XLIV, 1982, pp. 545–85; J. Blanchard, 'Political and Cultural Implications of Secret Diplomacy: Commynes and Ferrara in the Light of Unpublished Documents', in *The French Descent into Renaissance Italy, 1494–95. Antecedents and Effects*, ed. D. Abulafia, Aldershot, 1995, p. 239.
63] *Mémoires*, Vol. II, p. 71.

in the history of the kingdom, 'le mort saisit le vif' (to quote the French legal saying conveying the immediate effect of a succession).[64]

In fact this episode, in keeping with the demands of ritual, is exceptional in Commynes' narrative. It is as if the memorialist had crossed a border and was stepping for a short moment on to foreign ground. The reader is interested only in the omnipresent image of the king locked in a desperate struggle against death. Louis XI was traumatised by a nightmarish memory of the death of his father, Charles VII, who, forcibly fed and 'tormented by imagining that he was the victim of a plot to poison him at his son's request', died 'shortly after being forced to eat'.[65] The fact that Louis had 'always' condemned this treatment provides an explanation for his paranoid reaction after falling ill. The theme of fear strongly linked to family relations is a recurrent one in the *Mémoires* in which several accounts of such violent episodes are to be found. The 'particularly horrifying act' committed by Adolf of Guelders (who took the life of his father), although an extreme case, is revealing: whereas other chroniclers make but a brief allusion to it, Commynes provides a much fuller account.[66] This violence distorts the order of natural causality which would normally control the relationship between father and son, and sets little store by the reassuring image of the transfer of monarchy that the memorialist had sketched elsewhere.

* * * * *

It must be admitted that ritual is presented in an unfavourable light by Commynes, whose recollections of Louis XI are linked to episodes that had a great impact on him. The memorialist's approach can be interpreted as belonging to the process, familiar to historians, of the personalisation of royal power: Commynes' history goes a long way in that direction. What is the extent of this desecration? I do not intend to present Commynes either as a profane or impious figure, still less as an unbeliever. Rather than seeing him as a critic of the monarchical institution, I would characterise his approach primarily as one of neutrality. The image of monarchy is not totally absent from the *Mémoires*; it is simply that its main lines are attenuated and its lustre dimmed. The same type of neutrality can be observed towards military institutions, to which the destiny of royalty is intimately bound. As noted,[67] Commynes seems almost indifferent to the lyrical nature of war that finds emphatic expression, for example, in the *Chroniques* of Froissart.

64] J. Krynen, '"Le Mort saisit le vif". Genèse médiévale du principe d'instantanéité de la succession royale', *Journal des Savants*, 1984, pp. 187–221.
65] *Mémoires*, Vol. II, p. 42.
66] Ibid., Vol. I, pp. 259–62. Commynes was very well informed about the affair of Guelders. He even acted, so he tells us, as mediator in the attempts of the Duke of Burgundy to reconcile father and son (ibid., Vol. I, pp. 260–61).
67] Commynes, *Mémoires*, ed. P. Contamine, Paris, 1994, p. 26.

What, then, are the origins of this rejection of the phraseology employed with such rapture by his contemporaries? Does this lack of concern for customary ritual not have its roots in the foreign influence mentioned above? Was Commynes perhaps receptive to the severe judgements passed on the monarchy by Italian humanists? On several occasions, one can find in his work a muted echo of the *ad hominem* criticisms addressed to French monarchs, criticisms which must be seen in the light of the diplomatic context of the fifteenth century, in which the threat of French intervention weighed heavily.[68] Plausible as this sounds, however, I would prefer a less contextually-based explanation, by illustrating a long-term evolution to which the *Mémoires* bear witness. For, in Commynes' writing, are we not confronted by the manifestation of a certain resistance to, not to say an outright suspicion of, the efficacity of ritual itself? Commynes is giving voice to a disquiet regarding the essential frailty of ritual, which, as has been recently demonstrated,[69] ran right through the Middle Ages. Caught in the impossibility of bringing together earthly and celestial happiness, the two 'cities' of Augustinian terminology, kings were abandoned to the fate of their human condition. This sort of Augustinianism, which Commynes demonstrated, wont as he was to evoke the downfall of princes, easily accommodated this point of view.[70] His suspicion of ritual was also reinforced by a fundamental crisis of belief which implicated the whole symbolic order of social practices.

The difficulty with this theory is that, being a man of such contradictions, Commynes can only partially be made to fit this providential explanation. The abandonment, in the *Mémoires*, of traditional points of reference to the sacred does not leave the king totally vulnerable. The space relinquished by ritual opens the way for a rationalisation of power, out of which royalty emerges strengthened. It is particularly his diplomatic experience that helps Commynes find new footholds: 'there is more than one side to a man'.[71] This observation, bearing the stamp of a prudent relativism, settles the concepts of the useful and the useless in a field that had previously been dominated by 'universals'. Aristotle had conceived change in spatial terms. The pragmatic ambition of intellectuals of the fourteenth century, keen to account for diversity in the social world, corres-

68] P. Gilli, *Au miroir de l'humanisme. Les représentations de la France dans la culture savante italienne à la fin du Moyen Age*, Rome, 1997, pp. 31–106.
69] P. Buc, 'Writing Ottonian Hegemony: Good Rituals and Bad Rituals in Liutprand of Cremona', *Maiestas*, Vol. IV, 1996, pp. 3–38; idem, 'Martyre et ritualité dans l'antiquité tardive. Horizons de l'écriture médiévale des rituels', *Annales, ESC*, Vol. LII, 1997, pp. 63–92.
70] We may note that Commynes owned a copy of the translation of *The City of God* by Raoul de Presles. The influence of Augustinianism was very strong at the end of the Middle Ages. The providentialist conception of war in the *Mémoires*, in accordance with the theocratic vision inspiring the discourse on 'righteous war', is only one example among many of an influence prevailing over the writers of his time. See Blanchard, *Commynes l'Européen*, pp. 313, 326, 339.
71] *Mémoires*, Vol. I, p. 118.

ponded to this progress. Significantly, Commynes conceived this change in temporal terms, which had the specific advantage of bringing the relativity of 'conditions' and human individuality into the heart of an apparently homogeneous world. To use Commynes' own terminology, the 'art' and 'science'[72] of kingship take this dimension of uncertainty in history into account. For Commynes' prince, goodness is to be found in utility, and even God becomes subordinate to success. In a hostile environment, prudence and cunning may dispense with moral concerns in order to overcome misfortune. The author's intentionally down-to-earth point of view is ground-breaking. The desacralisation that occurs in this account is, therefore, not the result of principles. Rather, it is the natural consequence of pragmatic reason, of the daily companionship that brings out the king's humanity and all the relativism, the enemy of dogma, that Commynes strives to evince. This perspective, which lays bare royal ritual, creates a history that provides new information for the anthropology or sociology of beliefs at the end of the Middle Ages, and opens the way to a progressively larger, Machiavellian view of the king as prince and of the body politic as his stage.

72] Ibid., Vol. I, pp. 99, 94.

8

'Centre', 'Power' and 'Periphery' in Late Medieval French Historiography: Some Reflections

KATHLEEN DALY

The image of history as a mirror, in which the past reflected, guided and justified the present, and against which the virtues and the vices of contemporary society could be measured, was a familiar one to moralists, chroniclers and political thinkers in the Middle Ages. In recent years, historical writing has been studied not only in its own right, but also as a source of reflection on attitudes towards the medieval state.[1] It therefore seems appropriate to link two themes on which Peter Lewis has contributed his own particular insights: the complex realities of political relationships and 'power distribution' between the king and his subjects; and historiography in late medieval France.

The title of this chapter was inspired by Peter Lewis' article entitled 'The Centre, the Periphery and the Problem of Power Distribution in Later Medieval France', published in 1981.

> 'The centre of the kingdom', he wrote, 'was wherever the king, his court or the great departments of state happened to be ... The centre itself could seem remote ... [but the] periphery ... did not lack its lines of communication, both moral and physical, with the centre'.[2]

1] On the use of historiography during the Hundred Years War see P. S. Lewis's seminal article, 'War Propaganda and Historiography in Fifteenth-Century France and England', *TRHistS*, Fifth Series, Vol. XV, 1965, pp. 1–21, repr. in idem, *Essays in Later Medieval French History*, London, 1985, pp. 193–213, and the works of Bernard Guenée, notably his collected essays: *Histoire et culture historique dans l'Occident médiéval*, Paris, 1980, and *Politique et histoire au Moyen Age*, Paris, 1981. See also references given below. For examples of the earlier use of histories as well as romances as indices of contemporary opinion, see G. Doutrepont, *La Littérature française à la cour des ducs de Bourgogne*, Paris, 1909; and articles cited by Lewis, 'War Propaganda'.

2] P. S. Lewis, 'The Centre, the Periphery and the Problem of Power Distribution in Later Medieval France', in *The Crown and Local Communities in England and France in the Fifteenth Century*, ed. J. R. L. Highfield and R. Jeffs, Gloucester, 1981, pp. 34, 36, repr. in idem, *Essays in Later Medieval French History*, pp. 152, 154.

'Centre', therefore, may, but does not necessarily have to, be geographical: it is, above all, political. Parts of the kingdom may be 'isolated', particularly in time of war, but have contact, through a 'multiplicity of agents'. One such line of moral and affective communication could be found in historiography: this, too, has been seen in terms of 'centre' and 'periphery'. But which is which?

According to recent studies, the 'centre' is epitomised by the *Grandes Chroniques de France*. To summarise a complex problem, this composite historical text stems from a late thirteenth-century vernacular translation of a corpus of Latin chronicles initially collected or composed at the abbey of Saint-Denis; the vernacular text was continued to the late fourteenth century using material produced within and outside the abbey (the 'vulgate' or 'edition of 1380'), and, with the addition of further material taking it into the fifteenth century, was among the first vernacular texts to be published in Paris (1477).[3] Although the influence of this particular text has not been systematically studied, it can none the less be detected in later histories of France.

It has been argued that the *Grandes Chroniques* mirror the development of French royal power, supplanting alternative interpretations of French history. Gabrielle Spiegel, for instance, proposed that the genesis of the *Grandes Chroniques* should be seen in the context of a political and cultural conflict during the reign of Philip Augustus (1180–1223) between the interests of the crown and a small but politically and culturally significant group of northern French nobility, in the throes of crisis. According to this interpretation, the *Grandes Chroniques* represent a conscious attempt to assimilate the nobility within a royalist model of the kingdom's past, in which the role of the king is necessarily dominant.[4]

This interpretation has been influenced by, and accords well with, the analysis made, a decade or so earlier, by Bernard Guenée's studies which concentrated on the later history of the text. Guenée argued that, by the fifteenth century, history centred on the crown had triumphed. For Guenée, the popularity and dissemination of the *Grandes Chroniques* are both symptomatic, and perhaps the best example, of a more general trend in national history, which is focused on the king as the chief expression of national identity. Historiography thus reflects broader political processes, whereby power was vested in the king.[5]

3] G. M. Spiegel, *The Chronicle Tradition of Saint-Denis: A Survey*, Brookline, Leyden, 1978, for a survey of the literature and a discussion of the relationship between the Latin and French traditions. The difficulties surrounding the later history of the text have been illuminated by P. S. Lewis, 'Some Provisional Remarks upon the Chronicle of Saint-Denis and upon the [Grandes] Chroniques de France in the Fifteenth Century', *Nottingham Medieval Studies*, Vol. XXXIX, 1995, pp. 146–81.

4] G. M. Spiegel, *Romancing the Past: The Rise of Vernacular Historiography in Thirteenth-Century France*, Berkeley, 1993, passim, but esp. pp. 316–19.

5] B. Guenée, 'Histoire d'un succès', in *Les Miniatures de Fouquet: Les Grandes Chroniques de France*, ed. F. Avril, M.-T. Gousset and B. Guenée, Paris, 1987, pp. 83–

In such a model, where is the 'periphery'? Until recently, prime candidates would have been Brittany and the Burgundian dominions, where history was invoked not as a support for *French* national identity, under the leadership of the crown, but in an attempt to create, or to channel, pre-existing sentiments of regional loyalty for the benefit of the local prince, who could be considered to embody it. In 1971, for example, Yvon Lacaze proposed that the historical traditions extolled in works of history, epic and romance composed or modernised in the Burgundian dominions, particularly in the reign of Philip the Good, are evidence of a deliberate attempt to create an 'ideological' and affective basis for the Burgundian state, composed of heterogeneous principalities. For Lacaze, anti-French 'regionalist' sentiment was expressed in the revival of interest in the ancient Burgundian kingdom, predating the ascendancy of the Merovingian Franks, and defended against the Pippinids and Carolingians – a 'type' of Philip's own conflicts with Charles VII.[6]

In his study of Breton historiography from the late fourteenth to the early sixteenth century, Jean Kerhervé described how the Montfort dukes of Brittany inspired and fostered a distinctly Breton 'national' sentiment (a theme also explored by Michael Jones). Kerhervé argued that this survived even the duchy's annexation to France, and attributes to it characteristics analogous to those ascribed by Guenée to the *Grandes Chroniques.* He notes evidence in Breton historiography of the fidelity of a people to their *païs* – a multi-layered term, which could range in meaning from 'birthplace' to region to political community or 'state' – and to their *nacion*, which distinguished them from their neighbours by mythical or real common origins and common attributes. This was underlined by loyalty to their prince or 'natural' lord, the Montfort dukes, thus reflecting and reinforcing, in Kerhervé's view, the political aspirations of the dukes 'to become rival monarchs to the kings of France'.[7]

Such studies in turn appear to have influenced Guenée, who claimed that 'in a country where the power of the king clashed with that of numerous and powerful lords, it was normal for historians to be encouraged to write the history of a

---

138; 'Les *Grandes Chroniques de France*: le *Roman aux roys* (1274–1518)', in *Les Lieux de Mémoire: La nation*, ed. P. Nora, Paris, 1986, pp. 189–213; S. Citron, *Le Mythe National: l'Histoire de France en Question*, Paris, 1987, has argued that the influence of some aspects of the centralist paradigm found in the *Grandes Chroniques* could be detected in certain French school text books even in the 1980s: see n. 9 below.

6] Y. Lacaze, 'Le rôle des traditions dans la genèse d'un sentiment national au XVe siècle: la Bourgogne de Philippe le Bon', *BEC*, Vol. CXXIX, 1971, pp. 303–85. For the historiographical background to this interpretation, see G. Small, *George Chastellain and the Shaping of Valois Burgundy. Political and Historical Culture at Court in the Fifteenth Century*, Woodbridge, 1997, pp. 1–6.

7] J. Kerhervé, 'Aux origines d'un sentiment national: les chroniqueurs bretons de la fin du moyen âge', *Bulletin de la Société Archéologique du Finistère*, Vol. CVIII, 1980, pp. 165–206. Kerhervé's interpretation is more nuanced in a recent article: see n. 12 below.

few great families, or great seigneuries ... situated most frequently on the periphery of the kingdom'. By implication, seigneurial historiography was more or less marginalised, as the power of the great princes was eroded by the crown in the aftermath of the Hundred Years War.[8] One might consider an alternative interpretation. 'Peripheral' these might be with regard to 'royalist' or 'centralist' traditions; yet these 'peripheries' might have their own political and historiographical 'centres' focused on their prince.

Another model, however, lays greater emphasis on 'conciliation' than on 'conflict'. Colette Beaune's *Naissance de la Nation France* considered the historical past and its interpretation through historical writing as one element in a wide range of evidence. Seeking to delineate the main trends which contributed to the creation of a sense of national identity at the end of the Middle Ages, she concluded that 'there is not one France, but many; not a single national sentiment but many national sentiments, of which the components and the intensity are eminently variable'.[9]

For Beaune, historical texts such as the *Grandes Chroniques* essentially reflect northern French traditions, which spread outwards from the heart of the Capetian royal domains around Paris with the territorial acquisitions of French kings, gaining wider currency from the third decade of the fifteenth century with the enforced exile of Charles VII south of the Loire. The Hundred Years War, and the fifteenth century in particular, formed a key period in this process. Older traditions were revived; ancient texts, such as the Salic Law, formed the basis of new traditions, which justified the claims (and implicitly explained the survival) of the Valois dynasty, in the face of Plantagenet claims to the throne. Beaune suggested that, alongside the long-recognised role of the court, and particularly Charles VII's co-exiles in the kingdom of Bourges, other areas on the periphery of the kingdom may have contributed their own traditions, reinforcing the bonds of the remoter regions with the crown, the political 'centre' of the kingdom.[10] Although she does not analyse seigneurial historiography *per se*, she presents an interpretation of 'national sentiment' which emphasises what was held in common, within which can be accommodated a whole range of loyalties characteristic of late medieval society.

The theme is taken up again in a recent collection of essays on regional identity and national consciousness in France and Germany. The emphasis here

8] '... dans un pays où le pouvoir du roi se heurtait encore à celui de nombreux et puissants seigneurs, il était normal que des historiens fussent encouragés à écrire l'histoire de quelques grandes familles, ou de quelques grandes terres...situées d'ailleurs le plus souvent à la périphérie du royaume' (Guenée, 'Histoire d'un succès', esp. pp. 83, 89, which develop ideas expressed in his 'Les *Grandes Chroniques de France*', pp. 189–213).
9] C. Beaune, *Naissance de la Nation France*, Paris, 1985, p. 341, reviewed, with Citron (n. 5 above) by D. Bell, 'Recent Works on Early Modern French National Identity'; *Journal of Modern History*, Vol. LXVIII, 1996, pp. 84–113 (esp. pp. 97, 99–104).
10] Ibid., pp. 165–66.

is on the coexistence of regional and national sentiment in historical writing and the sense of the past, even in works originating in 'peripheral regions', in fifteenth-century terms, such as Normandy under English occupation, and Flanders.[11] Even for Brittany, Jean Kerhervé modified his earlier views, recognising (as Michael Jones had already argued some years earlier) that Breton sentiment did not necessarily exclude French sentiment.[12] The trend therefore seems to be to continue to recognise a 'geographic' and 'political' periphery, away from the court and the centres of the great offices of state (Paris or the Loire), while emphasising an affective 'pull' towards a sense of French national identity, reflected in historiography.

Some historical works, however, can also give insights into attitudes towards the nature and distribution of power both within the kingdom and in the particular region where the work was produced. In the remainder of this chapter I shall examine a series of such texts, produced during what Guenée has termed a renaissance in historical writing in fifteenth-century France, by authors either at the 'centre' of power (the royal court) or in the household or entourages of great princes.[13]

11] *Identité régionale et conscience nationale en France et en Allemagne du Moyen Age à l'époque moderne: Actes du colloque organisé par l'Université de Paris XII, 6–8 octobre 1993*, ed. R. Babel and J.-M. Moeglin, Sigmaringen, 1997, especially 'Introduction', pp. 7–11; F. Collard, 'Identité régionale et histoire nationale dans le *Compendium de origine et gestis francorum* de Robert Gaguin', pp. 429–41; N. Pons, 'Un lettré et son traducteur: du royaume de France de Robert Blondel à la Normandie du clerc Robinet', pp. 413–27. See in particular M. Morineau, 'Régions et nations entre trois colloques', pp. 445–53, which emphasises the 'longue durée' (long historical view) and the need to isolate the characteristics of various stages in the process 'd'assimilation, d'intégration volens nolens à une nouvelle entité, d'identité maintenue ou changée et dans quelles conditions' ('of assimilation, of eventual integration into a new entity, of identity preserved or changed, and of conditions causing these to happen'). However, Small (*George Chastellain*, pp. 162–90) demonstrates how French royalist traditions in historiography could be adapted and subverted by a skilful historian.

12] See J. Kerhervé, 'Entre conscience nationale et identité régionale dans la Bretagne à la fin du Moyen Age', in *Identité régionale*, pp. 219–43; M. Jones, 'Mon pais et ma nation. Breton Identity in the Fourteenth Century', in *War, Literature and Politics in the Late Middle Ages*, ed. C. T. Allmand, Liverpool, 1976, pp. 144–68; and 'Bons Bretons et bons François: The Language and Meaning of Treason in Later Medieval France', *TRHistS*, Fifth Series, Vol. XXXII, 1982, pp. 91–112, repr. in idem, *The Creation of Brittany. A Late Medieval State*, London and Ronceverte, 1998, pp. 283–307, 329–50. During a discussion which took place after the delivery of this paper, Michael Jones distinguished attitudes towards France in Breton historiography in the fourteenth and early fifteenth, from those of the late fifteenth and early sixteenth century, when historians perforce tried to take into account the new political framework created by the marriage of the Duchess Anne to Charles VIII and Louis XII of France.

13] Guenée, 'Histoire d'un succès', p. 89.

Authors and Texts

My first example comes from the political 'centre' of the kingdom. Noël de Fribois trained in canon and civil law, and served as notary and secretary to Charles VII from about 1423 until his resignation in 1444, as notary of the Council of the Gallican church convened at Bourges in 1438, then as a royal counsellor from at least 1452. Fribois definitely composed an *Abrégé des chroniques de France* completed by 1459 for Charles VII; and a strong case can be made for his authorship of two others: a *Mirouer Historial Abregié de France* (1451) and a short chronicle of the reign of Charles VII extracted from the chronicle of the monk of St Denis, Michel Pintoin, focusing on the rivalries between the dukes of Orléans and Burgundy, and the civil wars of the early fifteenth century.[14]

My second example links the political 'centre' – the king and court – to the 'periphery': in this case, the province of the Dauphiné. Mathieu Thomassin, the author of several historical works, was born in 1391 within the 'kingdom', son of a prosperous Lyon draper. He studied civil law at Orléans, becoming a 'docteur es lois' in 1446, and 'chevalier' about 1450. He also spent seven years in Paris, the 'administrative' and, in the early fifteenth century, still the 'political' capital of the kingdom. The rest of his career, however, was spent in the Dauphiné, an imperial fief acquired for the eldest son of the King of France, through the 'transport' of 1349. Geographically remote by virtue of its situation on the eastern frontier of the kingdom, and within the empire, even its lord must have seemed distant, until the future Louis XI (as Louis II) began his intensely active personal government of the Dauphiné.[15]

Thomassin served both Charles VII and Louis, as *avocat general* from 1422, delphinal counsellor from 1428, and again from 1446, and counsellor in the

14] Close study of the texts indicates that the author produced, or supervised, more than one version of each text. The details are given in my edition of the *Abrégé*, in preparation for the Société de l'Histoire de France. Meanwhile, see bibliography in Daly, 'Mixing Business with Leisure: Some French Royal Notaries and Secretaries and their Histories of France, c. 1459–1509', in *Power, Culture and Religion in France c. 1350–c. 1550*, ed. C. T. Allmand, Woodbridge, 1989, p. 100 n. 4. The versions used and cited here are the fullest text of the *Mirouer Historial*, as represented by Oxford, Bodleian Library, ms. Bodley 968, and the *Abrégé des Chroniques*, Vatican Library, ms reg. lat. 829, the basis for my edition. For Fribois' authorship of the translation of part of Pintoin's chronicle, see N. Pons, 'Michel Pintoin et l'historiographie orléanaise', in *Saint-Denis et la royauté. Etudes offerts à Bernard Guenée*, ed. F. Autrand, C. Gauvard and J.-M. Moeglin, Paris, 1999, pp. 237–59.

15] On 28 July 1440, Louis was granted the government of the province, but he did not come to the Dauphiné until 1446, and entered Grenoble on 12 August 1447 (N. Mietton Géroudet, 'Mathieu Thomassin, Juriste et Dauphinois au Service de Louis II', unpublished thesis, University of Grenoble, TER 1972, p. 3. I am grateful to the author for allowing me to consult this work).

Parlement of Grenoble, created from the delphinal council in 1453, clarifying through his writings the status of the dauphin vis-à-vis his vassals and neighbouring lay and ecclesiastical princes. When he compiled his longest work, the 'Registre delphinal', commissioned by Louis on 20 May 1456, Louis' relations with Charles VII were approaching breaking point. The dauphin's attempts to impose the *taille* and other taxes on allodial landholders, clergy and towns also aroused opposition, and he may have been seeking a more definitive juridical and historical basis for his rights. However, when on 30 August 1456, Louis fled the province for the court of Burgundy, most delphinal officials, including Thomassin, abandoned their former master and were retained in their offices by Charles VII.[16] In his later years, Thomassin therefore experienced the impact of a strong local 'political centre' in the person of the resident dauphin, and increasing political pressure on this geographically peripheral province from a 'national' centre of power – the king.

My third example comes from Foix-Béarn, where Michel du Bernis, *procureur* and notary in the county of Foix, composed a short chronicle of the ruling house in 1445. Bernis' text, the first substantial example of historiography for the house of Foix to survive, was commissioned by Eleanora of Navarre, wife of Gaston IV, Count of Foix and Vicomte of Béarn.[17] Like the Dauphiné, Foix-Béarn was on the geographical periphery, in this case the south-western frontier of the kingdom. Its rulers had interests outside France: their territories drew them into the orbit of the Spanish kingdoms of Aragon and particularly Navarre, of which Eleanora was later briefly to be queen in 1479. Plantagenet-Valois rivalry had allowed the rulers of Béarn to withdraw this principality from the suzerainty of the English dukes of Gascony, technically their immediate overlords, until their final expulsion in 1453, but also enabled them to evade paying homage to the kings of France.

My fourth example, the *Chronique du bon duc Loys de Bourbon* (Louis II), was composed in 1429 at the command of Louis' grandson, Charles, Count of Clermont (the future Charles I, Duke of Bourbon), probably on the occasion of his marriage. The author, Jean dit Cabaret D'Orreville, a Picard, relied on the reminiscences of Jean de Chateaumorand, sire de Poligni; indeed, Chazaud, the

16] E. Pilot de Thorey, *Catalogue des actes du Dauphin Louis II…relatifs à l'administration du Dauphiné*, Grenoble, 1899, Vol. I, pp. xviii–xix.

17] Miguel des Verms (Michel du Bernis), 'Cronique dels comtes de Foix et senhors de Béarn', *Choix de chroniques et mémoires sur l'histoire de France*, ed. J. A. C. Buchon, Paris, 1838, pp. 575–98. The only known copy of the text prefaces an inventory of the Foix archives made between 1446 and 1452. Gaston IV himself commissioned a chronicle in 1456 from his treasurer, Arnaud Esquerrier, which was better known and more widely consulted than that of Bernis. See *Chroniques romanes des comtes de Foix composées au XVe siècle par Arnaud Esquerrier et Miégeville*, ed. F. Pasquier and H. Courteault, Foix, 1895, pp. viii, xii–xiv. For a comparison of these works, see also K. Daly, 'Some Seigneurial Archives and Chronicles in Fifteenth-Century France', *Peritia*, Vol. II, 1983, pp. 59–73.

nineteenth-century editor of the text, considered Chateaumorand to be the text's real author.[18]

My fifth and final example is Perceval de Cagny, a native of the Beauvaisis, author of a genealogy and memoir of the counts and dukes of Alençon. When he composed his texts, between 1434 and 1438, he had served three counts or dukes of Alençon for 46 years, as *panetier*, *écuyer d'écurie* and, finally, *maître d'hotel*. Unusually, Cagny's work was not commissioned, and there is no direct evidence that the Alençon family possessed a copy. It seems to have been intended for Cagny's own descendants: 'so that his successors might see, know and understand how and with which lords he lived much of his life'.[19]

The authors varied in their relationships with rulers, from Fribois, writing his texts for the king, to Cagny's more personal intentions for his work. How did their different perspectives affect their analysis of power?

From 'Centre' to 'Periphery': King and Dauphin

For Noël de Fribois, power was centred on the French crown and those he regarded as its rightful heirs, the Valois dynasty. In his texts, relationships between the king and his subjects form part of a broader vision of the French kingdom, defined by the special relationship between God and the crown of France, and the divine prerogatives which embody it. These in turn justify the special juridical status of the French king; not subject to the emperor, he is himself emperor in his own kingdom.[20]

Fribois highlights most potential sources of political conflict and opposition to royal power in late medieval France. In the *Mirouer Historial* they are the pope and the emperor; in the *Abrégé des chroniques*, the English; and in the abridgement of Michel Pintoin's chronicle, the factions in the Armagnac-Burgundian civil war. A recurrent theme is, however, royal relationships with the nobility.[21]

'The king of France is judge in his own cause, for he is exempt from the empire, although he must judge according to truth', and 'all inhabitants within the kingdom of France are under the power and lordship of the king of France and subject to his power and jurisdiction', Fribois claims in the *Abrégé*, osten-

18] A copy of the text was in the ducal library at Moulins until 1523. *La Chronique du bon duc Loys de Bourbon*, ed. M. A. Chazaud, SHF, Paris, 1876, pp. x–xi, xvi, xx–xxi. On this text, see O. Matteoni, 'Portrait du prince, idéal et idéologie nobiliaire dans la "Chronique du bon duc Loys de Bourbon"', *Studi francesi*, fasc. CXV, gen.–aprile 1995, pp. 1–23.
19] Cagny calls the work a 'memoire', although the rubric describes it as a 'chronique'. The text was edited from a seventeenth-century copy made by Duchesne of a lost original, as the *Chroniques de Perceval de Cagny*, ed. H. Moranvillé, SHF, Paris, 1902, pp. i–xiv, 31.
20] On this theme, see J. Krynen, *L'Empire du roi. Idées et croyances politiques en France XIIIe–XVe siècle*, Paris, 1993, esp. pp. 384–428.
21] See nn. 14 above and 25 below for references.

sibly following Baldus de Ubaldis and Guy de Baisy.[22] In the *Mirouer Historial*, the geographical context of royal government is particularly stressed, the frontiers ascribed to the kingdom being those of the Franks and of the Carolingian empire. Attention is focused primarily on Aquitaine and Gascony, conquered from the Arian Goths through divine aid by Clovis, the first Christian king. At key points in the text their frontiers are described, with the clear implication that their inhabitants are subjects of the King of France.[23]

While the supremacy claimed for the French crown had implications for the King of England, it was also an implicit denial of the claims to special status put forward by French princes such as the rulers of Burgundy and Foix to rule 'by the grace of God', or to the exercise of royal prerogatives stemming from the Breton dukes' claim that Brittany had once been a kingdom.[24] For example, the assertion contained in the *Mirouer* that the ancient frontiers of France extended to the Pyrenees meant that they encompassed Béarn (despite its vicounts' claim that the principality was allodial land). Brittany's independence is explicitly denied in the *Mirouer Historial*; and, in the *Abrégé*, Fribois asserts that the duchy is an appendix of Normandy and dependent upon it.

The *Mirouer* records the conquests of the kingdom of Burgundy by Clovis. In the *Abrégé* Fribois stresses the dubious origins of the county of Flanders. He emphasises that the county was granted as the result of the rape of Judith, daughter of Charles the Bald, and cites canon law, that ravishers should not benefit from their crimes but should be punished by death.

Fribois' desire to elevate the status of French kings and denigrate that of the English (a familiar diplomatic trick) leads him to blur the distinction between their roles as English kings and as French princes. In the *Abrégé,* he treats England as if it were a fief of the French crown analogous to Normandy: with the death of the direct descendants of William the Conqueror, he claims, it should have reverted to the King of France, which would make Charles VII rightful King of England.

22] K. Daly and R. E. Giesey, 'Noël de Fribois et la loi salique', *BEC,* Vol. CLI, 1993, pp. 28–29.

23] K. Daly, 'The *Mirouer Historial Abregie de France:* Culture and Politics at the Court of Charles VII', in *Vincent de Beauvais: Intentions et réceptions d'une oeuvre encyclopédique au Moyen Age*, ed. M. Paulmier-Foucart, S. Lusignan and A. Nadeau, Montreal, 1990, pp. 467–94.

24] Note, for example, *Abrégé,* Vatican Lib., ms. reg. lat. 829, fols 65v–66: 'Les empereurs sont roys, et n'est aucune dignité, puissance ou dominacion oultre ou pardessus la dignité royal... *Cellui doncques n'est pas roy qui est subgiet a autre roy, car il n'est pas entierement franc, qui est subgiet au roy*, pour ce que necessairement il lui convient obeir et servir / a son seigneur' (my italics). ('Emperors are kings and no dignity, power or domination is superior to that of the royal dignity ... *So he who is subject to a king is not himself a king, for anyone subject to a king is not entirely free*, for he must necessarily obey and serve his lord [the king]. (My italics)).

Fribois' venom is reserved particularly for the English, rather than for the nobility as a whole. While the punishment of rebellious or traitorous princes, particularly of the royal house, is underlined, the texts emphasise the benefits of cooperation and harmony, particularly between princes of the royal family:[25]

> Princes et grans seigneurs ... en administration publique sont participativement diz roys ...

> Princes and great lords ... through their participation in government are called 'kings' ...;

but

> le principal acte ou fait du roy est de mectre et faire lois et constitucions au bien de la chose publique, et se ceste chose est convenable a aucuns, ce n'est que en tant qu'ils participent du gouvernement du roy. Ceulx doncques qui en ce royaume ouquel le roy est *supremus monarcha* font de leur auctorité privee et indeue lois et constitucions et establissemens contre et ou prejudice de la chose publique en sont a pugnir a l'exemple de tous autres.

> The principal act or deed of the king is to enact or make laws in the public interest, and if making law is [also] appropriate for others, this should only be to the extent that they share in royal government. In this kingdom, where the king is supreme monarch, those who through their personal and unwarranted authority make laws against or to the prejudice of the public interest should be punished, as an example to all others.[26]

Although princes have their place in power, their glory is a reflection of that of the crown, and their role is only legitimate when countenanced by royal authority.

Members of the nobility owned manuscripts of the *Mirouer Historial* and the *Abrégé des chroniques*: one copy of the *Mirouer* was dedicated to Charles d'Anjou, Count of Maine, and the interests of the Count and the house of Anjou, as well as those of the king, are reflected in the text. A manuscript of the *Mirouer* was later prepared for Antony of Burgundy, 'le grand bâtard' (1421–1504), while a member of the house of Épinay-Montauban owned a manuscript of the *Abrégé*. Clearly, one has to be cautious in interpreting this evidence, when none of these noble owners left evidence of what they read into, or even whether they

25] *Mirouer Historial*, Oxford, Bodleian Lib. ms. Bodley 968, fols 25–27v. See K. Daly, 'Culture and Politics', *Vincent de Beauvais*, pp. 467–94; idem, 'Histoire et politique à la fin de la Guerre de Cent Ans: *L'Abrégé des Chroniques* de Noël de Fribois', in *La 'France Anglaise' au Moyen Age. Actes du 111e Congrès National des Sociétés Savantes [Poitiers 1986]*, Paris, 1988, Vol. I, pp. 91–101, for an analysis of the major themes discussed here.
26] *Mirouer Historial*, fol. 110r–v (1451); *Abrégé*, fol. 81 (1459).

read, the text. Nevertheless, the sentiments expressed by the texts on the relative distribution of power within the kingdom could well have been compatible with the views of their noble owners. Charles d'Anjou had benefited from Charles VII's favour (as Antony of Burgundy was to do later, under Louis XI), as well as sharing kinship with, and the reflected glory of, the royal house, while the Breton house of Montauban had French sympathies.[27]

In contrast to Fribois, Mathieu Thomassin's major concern is to anchor the dauphin's powers firmly in provincial history, by providing genealogies of its former rulers, from the kings of Burgundy to the counts of Vienne and the dauphins, to Humbert II. His attachment to his *païs* is also reflected in his record of events which were important for the province, echoing his comments in an earlier work, that in spite of its moderate size, the Dauphiné was fruitful in its warlike nobility and humble and obedient subjects who are distinguished by loyalty to their prince.

The province, however, is also linked to the the kingdom of France, and derives considerable honour from this association. In terms analogous to Fribois' works, Thomassin lists the special attributes of the French crown: its king is 'most Christian', 'leader of Christendom', and is entitled to use the term 'by the grace of God' in his letters. French kings have never erred from the true faith; they have restored the papacy to Rome and are its 'principal protectors'. The king has been ordained and established by God 'son vicaire en la temporalité en son tres noble et tres puissant royaume de France ... estably en la temporalité de Dieu le pere et sans souverain, si ce n'est Dieu seulement' ('his vicar in temporal matters in his most noble and powerful kingdom of France, established ... by God the Father, with no sovereign other than God').[28] French subjects cannot therefore claim equality with their king.

Thomassin had spent much of his career propounding a case for the dauphin against secular and ecclesiastical lords, and the association between the dauphin and the crown could be applied to the dauphin's status vis-à-vis the inhabitants of Dauphiné. In his *Breviaire des anciens droiz ... du Dauphiné*, composed for Louis II between 1453 and 1456, and something in the nature of a dry run for the 'Registre', Thomassin had even drawn a direct analogy between royal and

27] Daly, 'Culture and Politics', idem, pp. 491–94; 'Histoire et politique à la fin de la Guerre de Cent Ans, La "*France Anglaise* (sic)"', pp. 99–100. For the Epinay-Montauban manuscript, BNF, ms. fr. 10141, fol. 1, see Daly's edition (*supra*, n. 14), and E. W. Inglis, 'Jean Fouquet as a Painter of National History', unpublished doctoral thesis, Institute of Fine Arts, New York University, 1998, p. 150. I have not found convincing evidence, however, to support Dr Inglis' assertion that Charles VII or Louis XI 'would have been eager to distribute Fribois' text for propaganda purposes'. For further background to Fribois' work, the reader is also referred to the chapter by Craig Taylor in the present volume.

28] For these two paragraphs, see the 'Registre delphinal' (Grenoble, Bibliothèque municipale, ms U909–10, fols iii^{r-v}, fols 58^{v}–63^{r}); 'Seigneurial Archives', p. 70, n. 1.

delphinal power. Just as the king was emperor in his kingdom, 'le Daulphiné qui a este translaté a la tres crestienne maison de France ne recongnoit point ... de souverain que le prince daulphin seigneur du pays', even though the Dauphiné was 'selon le commun langaige ... a la part de l'empire' ('the Dauphiné, which was transferred to the most Christian house, recognises no other sovereign than the prince, dauphin and lord of that land', even though the Dauphiné was 'according to common speech ... part of the empire').[29] In 1450, in a conflict with the Archbishop of Vienne, Louis II had moved from principle to practice by subjecting allodial lands to new fiscal measures. It is probable that the inclusion of a short treatise in the 'Registre' on the relationship between secular and ecclesiastical powers was intended to prove the dauphin's superiority in disputes with local prelates.[30]

In the case of Savoy, whose prince was a 'foreign' ruler ('etranger'), Thomassin cites the Treaty of Paris, of 5 January 1355, which he believed was not territorially to the advantage of the dauphin, but alleges that 'proffitable fut d'acquerir l'ommaige et la confederation du dict conte et de ses successeurs pour les tenir en crainte et subjection ... qui ... avoient esté contraires aux roys et aux daulphins' ('it was advantageous to gain the homage and alliance of the count [of Savoy] and his successors and keep them in awe and subjection, as they had opposed [French] kings and dauphins').[31]

Nevertheless, association with the crown of France could be a double-edged sword for the dauphin, who was suspected by Charles VII of trying to create a virtually autonomous principality. In the 'Registre', no doubt under the pressure of worsening relations between Charles and Louis, Thomassin posed the question: was the real ruler of the Dauphiné the king, or his son? In other words, how was power distributed between them?

Nicole Géroudet notes a development in Thomassin's attitude in the 1450s. There was no established rule of succession and, by custom, the dauphin only obtained power by act of the king, even if he held the title. Thomassin tries to distinguish between two ideas of sovereignty: public power, which rested with the dauphin, and supreme authority, which was vested in the King of France. However, he declares himself unable to resolve the question of who is the real lord and proprietor of the Dauphiné, the King of France or his son, preferring to leave the issue to jurists.[32]

29] 'Breviaire', Grenoble, Ms U909–10, fol. 155.
30] In 1450, for example, Louis attempted to secure the homages of the Archbishop of Vienne, and the bishops of Gap, Die and Grenoble (Géroudet, 'Mathieu Thomassin', pp. 3, 4, 13, 24).
31] 'Registre delphinal', fols 83v–84. By the treaty, all the land west of Guiers was ceded to the Count of Savoy, together with Faucigny, for which he paid homage. Géroudet ('Mathieu Thomassin', p. 18) suggests that Thomassin may have wished to make succeeding conflicts between the dauphin and Savoy seem like felony.
32] Géroudet, 'Mathieu Thomassin', pp. 25–30.

It is interesting that the Dauphiné's association with the Empire is relegated to a very inferior register: there is no attempt on Thomassin's part to build up the empire as a counterpoise to French royal power. He prefers to emphasise its early connections with the future kingdom of France, as part of Gaul, and then its conquest by Clovis, which freed the province from the Roman empire. His interest in the imperial rulers of the Dauphiné is thereafter confined to the descendants of Charlemagne. Sensitive to the danger that, because Charlemagne was emperor, later kings of France are subject to imperial authority, Thomassin denounces the tactless action of the emperor Sigismund in dubbing a plaintiff in the *Parlement* of Paris in 1416: the only emperor in France is the king, who acts as such in his kingdom. As if turning the tables, he regrets the 'ingratitude' of the Roman church, which allowed the empire to be separated from the kingdom of France (rather than vice versa), even suggesting that had the expedition of French troops led by the dauphin to Nancy in 1444 been successful, the empire might have been restored to the French crown in the person of the dauphin, Louis.

His attitude to the kingdom of Burgundy is more equivocal. After listing those rulers he can identify, Thomassin explains: 'I wished to speak of this kingdom as it was a fine [one] ... to encourage [Louis II] or another of the house of France to restore it [de le remectre sus]'. From the context, however, it seems unlikely that Thomassin envisages a new kingdom as the power base for the dauphin, but rather an increase in delphinal prestige.[33]

In Thomassin's eyes, there are clearly two political and affective 'centres' : the *païs* de Dauphiné and France. Indeed, the affective pull of the kings of France seems to exceed that of the dauphins, including Louis himself. Although aware that the Dauphiné is part of the Empire, he minimises the connection, while emphasising that with France. Far from being on the periphery, his *païs* is at the emotional 'centre' of the kingdom. The Dauphinois have given their lives in 'la deffense de la chose publique du Daulphiné et aussi du royaulme' ('defending the public interest of the Dauphiné and the kingdom') at the battle of Anthon but, unlike at the battle of Verneuil, their sacrifice has not been recognised as it should. By doing their duty against the 'Burgundians' and Louis de Chalon, Prince of Orange, they have saved the Dauphiné, and perhaps the kingdom

33] For this and the preceding paragraph, 'Registre delphinal', fols xx, xxii^{v}–xxiii^{v}, xxv, xxvi. On the kingdom of Burgundy, see fol. xliiii: 'De ce royaulme j'ay voulu parler pour ce que c'estoit ung beau royaume ... pour donner affection a Monseigneur ou a quelque autre de l'ostel de France de le remectre sus. Et mieulx le peuent faire que le daulphin Humbert qui se perforça de le faire ...' By an agreement dated 16 April 1335, the emperor Louis of Bavaria invested Humbert II with the Viennois, and promised to erect this into a kingdom (A. Leroux, *Recherches critiques sur les relations politiques de la France avec l'Allemagne de 1292 à 1378*, Paris, 1882, p. 250). For the Lorraine expedition, see 'Registre delphinal', fol. 113.

itself.[34] Thomassin's works thus highlight the real dilemma and conflict of loyalty which confronted him and his fellows when the dauphin decamped and the king, Charles VII, took back direct government of the Dauphiné.

Prince, 'Centre, Periphery': Foix-Béarn, Alençon and Bourbon

Relations between the house of Foix-Béarn and the crown of France had been variable. Gaston IV had been knighted by Charles VII in 1442 after the siege of Dax, and named lieutenant-general in Gascony and Guyenne in 1443. However, he had earned the king's displeasure by aiding his uncle, Mathieu, Count of Comminges, against the Count of Armagnac so that, in 1443, he was accused of usurping rights of the royal domain, and claiming to rule 'by the grace of God', a title which the king had already forced other southern noblemen to relinquish, and which Gaston himself was obliged to surrender in 1448.

As a seigneurial official, Michel du Bernis had played an active part in defending the count's rights, including his title to rule 'by the grace of God'. There is a faint echo of the dispute in the chronicle: Bernis notes that Count Roger Bernard II had used the formula when paying homage to King Louis IX of France in 1229. However, Bernis' main aim is to establish the comital succession, presumably for the benefit of the Countess Eleanora. His chronicle presents short biographies of all whom Bernis could trace, with the apparent intention of glorifying the comital house.

Initially Bernis focuses on local events and, in accordance with the historical record, scarcely mentions the kings of France. However, from the time of Roger Bernard II, these play a more prominent role, particularly with the accession of Alphonse of Poitiers, Louis IX's brother, as Count of Toulouse.[35] The way in which Bernis describes this transfer of allegiance is instructive, emphasising the *personal* bond between the king and his new vassal rather than its juridical implications. Roger Bernard is presented as a model of knightly virtue: worthy, brave, beyond reproach and loyal to his lord, the Count of Toulouse. According to Bernis, Louis IX attempted to win over the Count of Foix because of his reputation for bravery and loyalty; while Count Roger Bernard finally resolves this conflict of allegiance by gaining the express consent of the Count of Toulouse to the change.[36]

34] 'Registre delphinal', fols 96v–97 (on the plan for the dauphin to retire to the Dauphiné 'en attendant la grace Dieu'); 'Registre delphinal', fols 106v–110 (for the Battle of Anthon, 1430). Thomassin's account is criticised by E. Payet, 'L'Aggression du Dauphiné par le prince d'Orange et la vérité sur la bataille d'Anthon (11 juin 1430)', *Bulletin de l'Académie Delphinale*, Sixième Série, 1953, pp. 39–51.

35] In contrast, Arnaud Esquerrier sets the history of Foix-Béarn within a French context, drawing on the *Grandes Chroniques de France* (Esquerrier, *Chroniques*, pp. xi–xii).

36] Buchon, *Choix de Chroniques*, pp. 577–78.

There is no reference, however, to the involvement of the counts in the Albigensian heresy during the thirteenth century. It seems highly unlikely that Bernis was misled by his sources: only a few years later, in his *Chronique des comtes de Foix*, written for Gaston IV, Arnaud Esquerrier specifically castigates Roger Bernard for destroying the patrimony of the house of Foix through his association with the heretics.[37]

Did Bernis wish to present an almost uniformly chivalrous, loyal and crusading lineage of counts for Eleanora? The later counts are depicted as ideal vassals: more than 'fizel', they are 'vertadier sosmes' or 'fidel sosmes'; Gaston Febus is the loyal greyhound of Charles VI, and carves royal fleur-de-lis on his hôtel 'as a sign of humility and obedience to the crown of France'.[38] In return, through the graciousness and benevolence of Charles VI, the count and countess are maintained in their possessions. Needless to relate, Gaston IV conforms to this pattern of loyal service with regard to Charles VII. The context is emotional, personal and chivalric: it does not reflect 'regional' sentiment pitted against a royal 'centre'.

This emphasis could be interpreted in different ways. War against the English in the service of the king, like war against the counts of Armagnac, was a way of achieving honour. The emphasis on the loyalty and submission of the counts, however, might seem unusual: Esquerrier was more assertive about the independence of the vicomtes of Béarn. In a text intended for the king, it might reflect the count's desire to divert the king's attention from his actions in the affair of Comminges, or to win support for the count's ambitions beyond the Pyrenees. In a work evidently intended for the comital house itself, however, this seems unlikely; it is far more probable that Bernis' account reflects genuine value systems and idealised relationships which often sat uneasily with the practical exigences of survival in the troubled conditions of the fifteenth century. Gaston IV seems to have acknowledged this dilemma in 1448 when acceding to Charles VII's demands for him to relinquish his claim to rule 'by the grace of God'. As a reflection of the count's prestige in his locality, justified by documents going back to the thirteenth century, it could not withstand the restoration and expansion of the crown's prestige and material resources.

The houses of Bourbon and Alençon had also suffered during the Armagnac-Burgundian feuds; Jean I of Bourbon and Jean I of Alençon were captured at the Battle of Agincourt, and Jean II of Alençon became a prisoner after the Battle of Verneuil in 1424. Jean II of Alençon and Charles (I), both as Count of Clermont

37] Esquerrier, *Chroniques*, p. 28.

38] Buchon, *Choix de chroniques*, pp. 589, 592, where he asserts that whereas Count Bernard of Armagnac has been made governor of Languedoc 'against the king's will', Jean I, Count of Foix, acts 'in the service of the King of France and in his obedience' by fighting with the Burgundian faction in the Languedoc.

and Duke of Bourbon, were active in court faction. In 1440, Bourbon's hostility to the military reforms of the royal *ordonnance* of 1439 led to the Praguerie, in which Alençon also took an active role: it ended ignominiously with their acknowledgement of the king's sovereign rights in their lordships. Alençon's intrigues, particularly with the English, eventually led to his condemnation in 1458 at the *lit de justice* at Vendome. Although this disgrace lay in the future, it is striking how much emphasis each text places on the issue of loyalty to the crown. Perceval de Cagny was inspired to write by his ardent wish to show how 'par tout pais fussent dictes tres honnorables et bonnes parolles à la louenge et recommendation de leur dit hostel' ('most honourable and fine words should be said in praise and recommendation of their house in every land').[39] The feats of arms and worthy life of Louis II are likewise held up to the Count of Clermont (the future Charles I) as a guide for the count's own conduct, as lieutenant for the King of France and custodian of the Bourbonnais in the absence of the duke, so that the count could fulfil the requirements of his office ('dignité') properly.[40]

The genealogies which begin each text emphasise the extent to which each family's prestige depends on its royal ancestry, and above all from 'the very glorious line of St Louis': in the case of Bourbon, through Louis IX's son, Robert of Clermont. Cabaret even attributes the erection of the county of Bourbon into a duchy in 1327 to the reign of St Louis.[41] For the house of Alençon, the link is through Louis' grandson, Charles of Valois, to Charles, Count of Alençon and Perche; it is even suggested that the house of Alençon had been deprived of the rightful portion of the kingdom of France when Charles' eldest son became Philip VI of France.[42] The honour of each house is particularly dependent on relations with the King of France. One of Cagny's chief aims is to show how members of the house of Alençon 'ont tous estez tres obeissans et loyaulx a la couronne de France' ('have all been very obedient and loyal to the crown of France').[43] In both texts, honour includes valour in battle against the English.[44] Cagny also exonerates the house of Alençon by blaming Burgundy's 'falseness and treason' in murdering the Duke of Orléans, the king's brother, in 1407, for all the wars and troubles in the kingdom. The treaty negotiated by the princes with Henry IV of England in 1412 is presented as an essential move 'pour obvier aux mauvaises malices des entreprinses du duc de Bourgoigne' ('to counter the

39] Cagny, *Chroniques*, p. 31.
40] Cabaret, *Chronique*, p. 1.
41] Ibid., p. 3 and n. 1.
42] Cagny, *Chroniques*, p. 5.
43] Ibid., p. 31. For the importance of honour and loyalty in the chivalric code expressed in literature, see M. Keen, 'Chivalry, Heralds and History', in *The Writing of History in the Middle Ages: Essays presented to R. W. Southern*, ed. R. H. C. Davis and J. M. Wallace-Hadrill, Oxford, 1981, pp. 393–414, repr. in idem, *Nobles, Knights and Men-at-Arms in the Middle Ages*, London, 1996, pp. 63–81.
44] Cabaret, *Chronique*, pp. 31–33, 41, 58; Cagny, *Chroniques*, p. 13.

machinations of the Duke of Burgundy's plans').[45] Princes, like Alençon, who opposed Burgundy were therefore only fulfilling their duties to the king 'so that he could govern his kingdom in true [bonne] justice, peace and tranquility'.[46]

Although there is clearly a good dose of simplification here, Cagny's text does reflect a genuine dilemma. Françoise Autrand's comment that the French princes were not merely leaguers competing for pensions, but leaders defending the interests of their country, is borne out by Cagny's references to the hardships suffered by the house of Alençon. As well as seeing his *païs* conquered by the English, Jean II, captured by the English at the Battle of Verneuil in 1424, was forced to accept only half of what his inheritance of Fougères was worth from the Duke of Brittany, described as his 'relative but not his friend'.[47]

In contrast, Charles VII is reproved for his failure to listen to Jeanne d'Arc, for his preference for giving away the inheritance of the crown rather 'than arm[ing] himself and prosecut[ing] the war', and for failing to avenge the injury to the house of Orléans, and compensate Alençon for his losses. The Duke of Brittany is criticised again for violating royal rights, denying that his duchy was held of the crown, adopting the title 'by the grace of God' and striking gold money.[48] Nevertheless, even loyalty to the house of Alençon cannot prevent Cagny from criticising Jean II, with other princes of the blood, for failing to protect the people from the English and from robbers.[49]

The complex relationship between the prince, his *païs* and the crown is also portrayed through the account, given by Cabaret (or Chateaumorand), of the actions of Louis II of Bourbon. The text emphasises the high status of Bourbon's 'parents', and the honour which they bestow on him. In turn, Louis' valour reflects glory on his family, the 'hostel de France', while his service to the crown as a 'preudomme' results in the 'monté [de] ung lignaige'. He aids those who ask for help through 'affinité de linaige', while he and his vassals are bound by reciprocal ties of affection.[50] He is the ideal lord, who governs with the counsel of his vassals.[51]

45] Cagny, *Chroniques*, pp. 41, 71, 72. Cf. Matteoni, 'Portrait du Prince', p. 23, for the more favourable treatment of Burgundy by Cabaret, possibly explained by the rapprochement of the ducal houses in 1429.

46] Cagny, *Chroniques*, pp. 49, 74–75.

47] Ibid., p. 23; F. Autrand, *Charles VI*, Paris, 1986, pp. 451–64.

48] Cagny, *Chroniques*, pp. 206, 209, 211, 228–29.

49] Ibid., p. 253.

50] Cabaret, *Chronique*, pp. 4–5, 320, 322. Comparable emphasis on the virtue of aiding 'amics' can be found in du Bernis' chronicle (Buchon, *Choix de Chroniques*, pp. 577–78).

51] On his return from captivity in England he is greeted by an assembly of nobles to whom he expresses his hope of governing 'through you and with your counsel, those matters which concern my lands and the good of this kingdom ... I wish to live and die with you, and I believe that you would do the same for me' (Cabaret, *Chronique*, pp. 7–8).

There is an interesting contrast between the values presented by Thomassin, with his fierce defence of delphinal rights, and the image of a seigneurial official portrayed in the chronicle of Louis de Bourbon. The latter text emphasises how the duke punishes Huguenin Chaveau, who has recorded the encroachments of his vassals on his rights, during Louis' captivity in England as a hostage for King Jean II. Instead of being rewarded for his pains, Huguenin, *procureur* of the Bourbonnais, is depicted as an enemy of the nobility, and is forced to watch seven years' work burn with his register of ducal rights.[52]

This incident surely reflects the noble *moeurs* of Jean de Chateaumorand, mediated by Cabaret, and a less than subtle attempt to persuade Charles, Count of Clermont, to value and not to oppress his vassals. However, it also idealises the relationship between lord and vassals. Louis is willing to sacrifice his financial interests to increase the love of his knights. It underlines the purpose attributed in the text to the foundation of Louis' order of the Écu d'Or (Golden Shield), which bound the duke and his vassals together through mutual affection in the service of God and defence of the *païs*.[53]

Cabaret's King of France, like Cagny's, is unable to fulfil the obligations of lord to vassal; although he has married Bourbon's sister, Charles V cannot recompense him for the sums Bourbon has taken from his *païs* during his captivity in England.[54] The duke is compared favourably with the Duke of Brittany, whose traitorous conduct in allying with the English against 'his rightful lord' is singled out for particular opprobrium.[55]

Both the Bourbon and the Alençon chronicles reflect the problems posed by the presentation of idealised norms for imitation by contemporary rulers, princes as well as kings. The exercise of power in both cases depended on the acceptance of those norms by the subjects, and the good will of the king, which included generosity in distributing the offices, favours, and funds upon which the nobility had come increasingly to depend for their economic survival. It was a balance which civil war and foreign invasion had made particularly difficult to maintain.

52] Ibid., pp. 10–12. This episode merits comparison with Froissart's attitude to evil counsellors. See P. Ainsworth, *Jean Froissart and the Fabric of History: Truth, Myth and Fiction in the Chroniques*, Oxford, 1990, pp. 100, 195–96.
53. '… and let us all be united in defending our lands, and thereby able to win the perfect honour of chivalry' (Cabaret, *Chronique*, p. 13).
54] Bourbon is hostage 'at his cost and expense for the sake of his sovereign lord', whereas Bourbon's own vassals raise his ransom, 'the king had not given the duke any help' (ibid., pp. 4–5).
55] Ibid., pp. 38–39.

Conclusion

I conclude by returning to Peter Lewis' article:

> th[e] sense of isolation was ... a product of war: under anything like the normal [situation], coming and going of agents, either of the centre or of members of the community, was the pulsing lifeblood of later medieval politics ... One played the system: one did not try to break it if one had any sense. Individual nobles or groups of nobles, it is true, sometimes rebelled about the way in which the system seemed at some particular moment to be stacked against them ...[56]

All the examples considered here can be analysed for evidence of local and/or national sentiment. I think, however, that they are of greater interest for their reflection of attitudes to power. Of course, they represent particular points of view at specific times and in specific places; other chroniclers could suggest alternative views of the relationship, shifting the balance more in favour of the local prince than the crown. However, with this caveat, the texts do mirror the magnetic pull of the crown as a source of honour, material favours, and support or protection against rivals. Few enjoyed the luxury of retaining power in their own locality if they were exiled from the 'centre'. It is no coincidence that battles with regional or national rivals feature so prominently in the texts. In such conflicts, proximity to a glorious lineage (particularly the crown), loyalty, services rendered in blood and money all justified a right to a prince's moral and material recognition. Yet even those (such as Alençon and Clermont) enjoying royal favour when these texts were written could not guarantee it would last. Servants such as Cagny and Chateaumorand appear to have regarded that favour as only a just, yet clearly an insufficient recognition of blood and status, and a reward for past services rendered by the houses of Alençon and Bourbon. The dauphin Louis himself, heir to the French crown, was not exempt from royal displeasure and its consequences. Thomassin's emphasis on the reflected glory of the French crown may be thought to portray Louis' vulnerability more clearly, for even ten years' residence in the Dauphiné could not enable the dauphin to withstand the crown.

Philippe Contamine has argued that the period from the noble leagues of 1314–15 to the Estates General of 1484 witnessed the transformation of the French nobility 'from power to privileges': great princes preferred to try and secure a place in the royal council and assure themselves pensions than lead assemblies, or challenge royal actions, in spite of the demand of disaffected

56] Lewis, 'The Centre, the Periphery', pp. 46–47; idem, *Essays in Later Medieval French History*, pp. 164–65.

magnates for the summoning of the Estates General in 1439, 1442 and 1465.[57]

Concomitant with this transformation, one may detect the princes' loss of the moral 'high ground' by too overt a search after self-interest. Unlike Cagny a chronicler of the house of Alençon, writing in the sixteenth century, had to exonerate Jean II from treason. The ideological framework which he presents is, in many respects, similar to that of Cagny's chronicle, which may have served in part as his source. He emphasises the 'proximité de lignage', or 'close blood relationship' of Jean II to Charles VII; 'les grandes aydes et faveurs qu'il luy avoit faictz contre lesdicts Anglois ses adversaires et ennemis cappitaux' ('great assistance and favour he had given him against his adversaries and principal enemies, the English'); and his gradual loss of hope that Charles, 'par remords de conscience ou aultrement' ('through remorse or for other reasons'), would recompense him. He even attributes twinges to the ducal conscience over the reconquest of Normandy, 'veu que la plus grande partie des habitans ... de Normandye ... tenoient pour chose certaine que ledict duchie de Normandye appartenoit par heritaige audict roy d'Angleterre, heritier...au duc Guillaume le Bastard' ('given that most Normans were convinced that the duchy of Normandy belonged by inheritance to the King of England, heir to William the Bastard [the Conqueror]'). He was nevertheless forced to deplore the damage which the count's actions brought on his heirs and the family's honour, and to resort to blaming Alençon's evil counsellors for inciting him to treason.[58]

On the other hand, if the princes were vulnerable, so was the crown, particularly in time of war. Fribois, 'at the centre', shares many of the assumptions and fears of chroniclers nearer 'the periphery'. Just as the seigneurial chroniclers we have considered emphasise the potential harmony between nobles and kings, historians 'of the centre', like Fribois, emphasise the role of magnates as 'pillars' of the monarchy. If rebellious magnates are castigated, unworthy kings also merit their share of criticism, particularly for imposing unjust tributes and taxes. The problem, as always, was to find the balance between, on the one hand, impoverishing the nobles, the 'nerf et force du royaume' ('nerves and strength of the kingdom') (thereby depriving them of their rightful privileges, as the *cahier* of the nobility claimed at the Estates General of 1484), and, on the other hand, of impoverishing the crown to provide them with pensions, or risk their rebellion. The authors we have considered can to some extent be seen as the 'moral fixers',

57] P. Contamine, 'De la puissance aux privilèges: doléances de la noblesse française envers la monarchie aux XIVe et XVe siècles', in *La Noblesse au Moyen Age, XI–XVe Siècles: Essais à la mémoire de Robert Boutruche réunis par Philippe Contamine*, Paris, 1976, pp. 235–57; and, more recently, idem, *La Noblesse au Royaume de France de Philippe le Bel à Louis XII: Essai de Synthèse*, Paris, 1997, pp. 316–26, for the complex relationships between crown and nobility, and the idea that obedience to a sovereign is a necessary component of chivalry.
58] BNF, ms. fr. 4794, fols 57–59.

equivalent to the political fixers described by Peter Lewis, trying to reconcile conflicting interests, with an appropriate 'spin' to their interpretation. However, although their texts reflect realities, like Thomassin they preferred in the main to leave practical problems to the realm of practical politics.

9
Centre and Periphery in Late Medieval France: Tournai, 1384–1477[1]

GRAEME SMALL

A patriotic local historian may have been exaggerating when he claimed that Tournai was once 'la quatrième bonne ville du royaume' ('the fourth *bonne ville* [the technical term used in correspondence between the king and his more important urban communities] of France'), but a recent demographic study estimates the city's population was as great in the second half of the fourteenth century as that of Bruges, and consequently greater than that of most important regional centres in later medieval France.[2] The ancient episcopal city was at the very least a prominent element in the 'ossature urbaine' ('urban backbone') of the realm.[3] The destruction by German air-raid in May 1940 of the remarkable municipal archive and manuscript collection may explain why Tournai, unlike some comparable French cities, has not been the subject of a major monograph in recent times.[4] But much may still be attempted.[5] Under-used

1] I wish to thank friends in the *Vakgroep Middeleeuwse Geschiedenis* of the University of Ghent for their hospitality and advice while working on this chapter. At Liverpool, my fellow conference participants made many valuable suggestions when it was delivered as a paper, as did Sam Cohn who kindly read drafts. I am grateful to the Royal Society of Edinburgh and the Caledonian Research Foundation for the award of a European Visiting Fellowship which enabled me to carry out much of the research.

2] The claim is in P. Rolland, *Histoire de Tournai*, Tournai, 1956, p. 163. See C. Dury, 'L'Évolution démographique de Tournai au XVe siècle', in *Autour de la Ville en Hainaut: Mélanges d'Archéologie et d'Histoire urbaines offerts à Jean Dugnoille et à René Sansen*, Paris, 1986, pp. 185–203.

3] Tournai lies at the upper end of urban communities helpfully categorised in M. Pacaut, 'Naissance et renaissance d'une petite ville: Louhans du XIIIe au XVIe siècle', in *Villes, bonnes villes, cités et capitales: études d'histoire urbaine (XIIe–XVIIIe siècles) offertes à Bernard Chevalier*, ed. M. Bourin, Caen, 1993, pp. 123–32.

4] On the losses, see L. Verreist, 'La Perte des archives du Hainault et de Tournai', *Revue belge de Philologie et d'Histoire*, Vol. XXI, 1942, 186–93; P. Rolland, 'L'État actuel des grands problèmes tournaisiens', *RBAHA*, Vol. XVIII, 1949, pp. 125–43. On other cities, see B. Chevalier, *Les Bonnes villes de France du XIVe au XVIe siècle*, Paris, 1982; and A. Rigaudière, 'Bilan', in *Gouverner la ville au Moyen Âge*, Paris, 1993, pp. 6–13.

5] An important survey in G. Preud'homme, 'Les Finances de la commune de Tournai de 1188 à 1522: perspectives de recherche', in *Recueil d'études d'histoire hainuyère offertes à Maurice A. Arnould*, ed. J.-M. Cauchies and J.-M. Duvosquel, Mons, 1983, pp. 231–51.

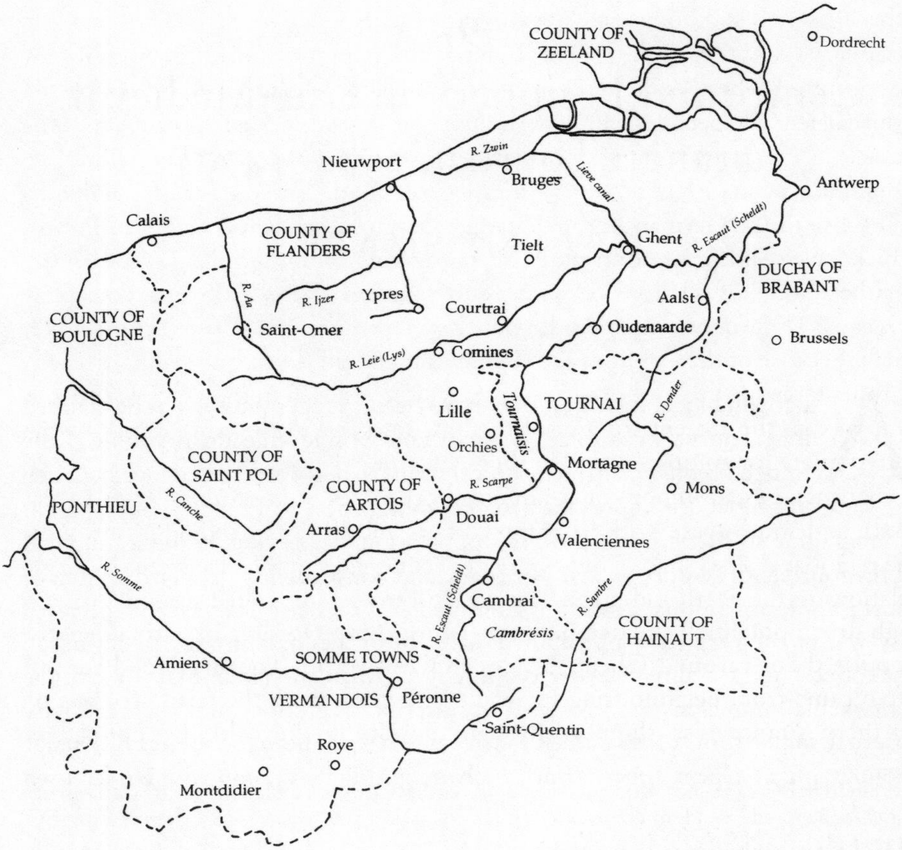

sources include published extracts of the registers of the deliberations of the *Consaux* (members of the urban council) of Tournai, an incomplete but none the less very rich collection stretching back to 1385.[6] There is also an impressive

6] Earlier than many cities in France, and earlier than any other in the Low Countries. For indications of further unpublished material and a general discussion of the strengths and weaknesses of the source material and editions, see G. Preud'homme, 'Extraits des registres des Consaux de la ville de Tournai (1455–72): complément à l'édition de la Grange', *MSRHAT*, nouv. sér., Vol. I, 1980, pp. 297–341 (hereinafter RC 1455–72); to which should be added idem, 'Extraits des registres des Consaux de la ville de Tournai (1489–99)', ibid., Vol. II, 1981, pp. 91–106. The main editions cited below are: 'Extraits analytiques des anciens registres des Consaux de la ville de Tournai, 1385–1422', ed. H. Vandenbroeck, *MSHLT*, Vol. VII, 1861 (hereinafter RC 1385–1422); 'Extraits analytiques des anciens registres des Consaux de la ville de Tournai, 1422–30', ed. idem at ibid., Vol. VIII, 1863 (hereinafter RC 1422–30); 'Extraits analytiques des anciens registres des Consaux de la ville de Tournai, 1431–1476', ed. A. de la Grange at ibid., Vol. XXIII, 1893 (hereinafter RC 1431–76); 'Extraits des registres des Consaux de Tournay (1472–1490, 1559–1572, 1580–1581)', ed. L. P. Gachard, *BCRH*, Vol. XI, 1846, pp. 327–473

tradition of chronicle-writing which requires closer study.[7] Drawing on this and other material, and borrowing as our guide the productive theme of centre and periphery from the work of Peter Lewis, this chapter explores the question of 'rapports ville-État' ('city-state relations') in later medieval France from the Tournaisien perspective.[8] Should the city be considered an 'exception communale' ('exception among communes'), comparable to the 'villes libres de Lombardie et aux *Freistädte* de l'Empire germanique' ('free cities of Lombardy and those of the German Empire') rather than to other *bonnes villes* of France which have seemed, by contrast, to be more tightly bound to the monarch?[9] Or is either model of relations between centre and periphery really appropriate in this case? These questions and others are posed for the period from 1384 to 1477, partly because of the extent of the sources mentioned above but mainly because of the interesting geo-political circumstances of Tournai in these years, situated as it was on the ancient frontier of the kingdom and in close proximity to the Burgundian dominions – a city, in short, on two peripheries.

Tournai was an important commercial centre for royal communities to the south and south-west, with its biannual fairs and its commanding position on the regional river system.[10] But of greater economic significance were the city's relations to the north and north-east within Europe's so-called second 'zone of high urban potential' situated between Tournai and Dordrecht, with a densely populated core around Ghent, Bruges and Antwerp.[11] Tournai's food supply often came from neighbouring Hainault, and grain from the fertile regions of northern France was shipped through the city to be sold to populations

---

(hereinafter EC 1472–90); 'Extraits des registres des Consaux de la ville et cité de Tournai (1477–1482)', ed. F. Hennebert, *MSHLT*, Vol. III, 1856, pp. 57–285 (hereinafter EC 1477–1482).

7] *Croniques de Franche, d'Engleterre, de Flandres, de Lile et espécialement de Tournay*, ed. A. Hocquet, Mons, 1938 (hereinafter Hocquet, *Croniques*); *Chronique des Pays-Bas, de France, d'Angleterre et de Tournai*, in *Recueil des Chroniques de Flandre*, ed J.-J. de Smet, Brussels, 1856, Vol. III, pp. 111–570 (hereinafter de Smet, *Chronique*); and *Kalendrier des guerres de Tournay (1477–1479) par Jehan Nicolay*, ed. F. Hennebert, in *MSHLT*, Vol. II, 1853 and Vol. III, 1856 (hereinafter Nicolay, *Kalendrier*). On the second of these works, see C. Van Loo, 'Historiografische studie van "La Chronique des Pays-Bas, de France, d'Angleterre et de Tournai" (1294–1483)', 2 vols, University of Ghent, unpublished *Licentiaat* thesis, 1987.

8] Rigaudière, 'Bilan', p. 10; P. S. Lewis, 'The Centre, the Periphery, and the Problem of Power Distribution in Later Medieval France', in *The Crown and Local Communities in England and France in the Fifteenth Century*, ed. J. R. L. Highfield and R. Jeffs, Gloucester, 1981, pp. 33–50, repr. in idem, *Essays in Later Medieval French History*, London, 1985, pp. 151–68.

9] P. Rolland, 'L'exception communale et ses causes', *RN*, Vol. XX, 1934, p. 300. Cf. H. Sée's thesis that Charles VII and Louis XI had imposed an 'étroite tutelle administrative' ('tight administrative control') upon their *bonnes villes* (H. Sée, *Louis XI et les villes*, Paris, 1890, p. 367).

10] Rolland, *Histoire de Tournai*, p. 86; *Tournai: une ville, un fleuve (XVIe–XVIIe siècle)*, ed. F. Thomas and J. Nazet, Brussels, 1992, esp. p. 70.

11] J. De Vries, *European Urbanization 1500–1800*, London, 1984, pp. 158–61.

downstream.[12] Tournai also established itself as a centre for the sale of French wines in Flanders.[13] The city's industries and the careers of those involved in them further underline the degree of integration within a wider regional economy. Cloth production benefited from Ghentish expertise, and black Tournai stone, although it was sold in many parts of Europe, was a primary material in Flemish building sites until changing preferences in Ghent sparked off a decline in exports.[14] Apprentices from Tournai sometimes learned their trade in Flemish towns and vice versa, while the business interests and connections of entrepreneurs in the city – men such as the foundry owner Michel Le Maire, or the tapestry maker Pasquier Grenier – could extend deep into Flanders.[15] Tournaisiens acquired land and property in neighbouring regions, a phenomenon which further contributed – despite royal objections – to the inevitable circulation in the city of coins minted outside the kingdom.[16] At the fundamental level of civic finances, outsiders invested in Tournai and Tournaisiens invested in other towns, not least Ghent and Saint-Omer, through the issuing and purchasing of *rentes*.[17] It is true

12] de Smet, *Chronique*, p. 365; RC 1422–30, pp. 38–39; RC 1431–76, p. 177; G. Bigwood, 'Gand et la circulation des grains en Flandre, du XIVe au XVIIIe siècle', *Vierteljahrschrift für Sozial- und Wirtschaftsgeschichte*, Vol. IV, 1906, pp. 397–460. The authorities in Ghent were particularly anxious that political conflict between the Duke of Burgundy and the king should not disrupt this essential trade: RC 1385–1422, pp. 44–46, 114, 125.

13] But less important a centre than Arras or Valenciennes: J. Craeybeckx, *Un Grand commerce d'importation: les vins de France aux anciens Pays-Bas (XIIIe–XVIe siècle)*, Paris, 1958.

14] *Ordonnances*, Vol. IV, pp. 588–89; L. Nys, *La Pierre de Tournai: son exploitation et son usage aux XIIIe, XIVe et XVe siècles*, Tournai–Louvain-la-Neuve, 1993, pp. 7, 152–53.

15] Like the man from Tournai resident in Bruges in 1426 to learn his trade along with Flemish (de Smet, *Chronique*, p. 397) or, a century earlier, the boy from Courtrai placed by his father in Tournai to learn his trade as a baker (L. Verreist, *Les Luttes sociales et le contrat d'apprentissage à Tournai jusqu'en 1429*, Brussels, 1912, pp. 45–46). On Le Maire and Grenier, see respectively P. Rolland, 'La Chapelle funéraire de Michel de Gand en l'église Saint-Piat à Tournai', *RBAHA*, Vol. III, 1933, p. 356; J. Lestocquoy, *Deux siècles de l'histoire de la tapisserie (1300–1500): Paris, Arras, Lille, Tournai, Bruxelles*, Arras, 1978, pp. 72, 74.

16] Examples of Tournaisiens owning fiefs or other property in neighbouring principalities can be found in RC 1385–1422, p. 421; RC 1422-30, pp. 40–41. The penetration of Burgundian coin into northern France was a feature of the first half of the fifteenth century (P. Desportes, 'Monnaie et souveraineté: les monnaies durant la période de la domination bourguignonne à Amiens (1435–75)', in *Commerce, finances et société (XIe–XVIe siècles): recueil de travaux d'histoire médiévale offert à M. le Professeur Henri Dubois*, ed. P. Contamine, T. Dutour and B. Schnerb, Paris, 1993, pp. 201–16). In 1456 a royal initiative to ban such practices was rescinded in Tournai's case because the city 'n'estoit point pareille aux autres villes du royaume' ('was not the same as the other towns of the kingdom') – exceptional circumstances which the crown also had to recognise in 1390 and 1413: RC 1431–76, pp. 224–33; *Ordonnances*, Vol. VII, p. 371; ibid. Vol. X, pp. 179–80. The circulation of different moneys in Tournai could encourage speculation and produce profit, particularly in times of devaluation (de Smet, *Chronique*, p. 370).

17] M. Boone, '*Plus dueil que joie*: les ventes de rentes publiques par la ville de Gand pendant la période bourguignonne: entre intérêts privés et finances publiques', *Bulletin trimestriel du Crédit communal*, Vol. CLXXVI, 1991–92, pp. 3–25; M.-J. Alibart, 'Les

that for all Tournai's connections within surrounding economies, interventions from the royal centre could have serious repercussions upon the city's fortunes.[18] But this was because Tournai, like Arles and Marseille in Provence or St Malo in Brittany, was part of an economic network that extended considerably beyond the boundaries of the political centre to which it gave allegiance.[19]

As the seat of an extensive bishopric stretching across Flanders to the coast, Tournai was an important spiritual centre in its own right. Cases from the county were dealt with in the bishop's court, and each year large numbers of Flemish penitents participated in the *grande procession* at Tournai.[20] These and related circumstances further conspired to draw the city within the Burgundian orbit. Since the bishopric incorporated several densely-populated cities and centres of ducal authority, successive dukes sought to exercise their influence over the see.[21] All five bishops of Tournai in our period owed their position to Burgundian influence and a substantial proportion of the canons of the cathedral chapter held benefices and offices in the duke's lands.[22] This was not entirely to Tournai's disadvantage. Compared with some other French cities which benefited little from their status as the seat of a bishopric, Tournai could at least exert a degree of leverage at the Burgundian centre through the intermediary of its politically-active ecclesiastics.[23] In April 1426, for example, Philip the Good set aside his threat of military action against the city 'à la prière de Mons. l'évesque de Tournai qui s'en estoit agenoulliés devant [luy]' ('at the pleading of the

---

Rentes à vie et les rentiers de la ville de Saint-Omer au XVe siècle', *Bulletin trimestriel de la Société académique des Antiquaires de la Morinie*, Vol. XXI, 1969, pp. 247–49; RC 1422–30, pp. 11, 64; RC 1431–76, p. 221.

18] RC 1431–76, p. 312.

19] Cf. W. P. Blockmans, 'Voracious States and Obstructing Cities: An Aspect of State Formation in Preindustrial Europe', in *Cities and the Rise of States in Europe, A.D. 1000 to 1800*, ed. C. Tilly and W. P. Blockmans, Boulder–Oxford, 1994, p. 244; L. Stouff, *Arles à la fin du Moyen Âge*, 2 vols, Aix-en-Provence–Lille, 1986, Vol. I, pp. 478-79; N. Coulet, *Aix-en-Provence: espace et relations d'une capitale (milieu XIVe–milieu XVe siècle)*, 2 vols, Aix-en-Provence, 1988, Vol. II, pp. 60ff; J.-P. Leguay, *Un Réseau urbain au Moyen Âge: les villes du duché de Bretagne aux XIVe et XVe siècles*, Paris, 1981, p. 77.

20] M. Boone, 'Les Gantois et la grande procession de Tournai: aspects d'une sociabilité urbaine au bas Moyen Âge', in *La Grande Procession de Tournai: une réalité religieuse, urbaine, diocésaine, sociale, économique et artistique*, ed. J. Dumoulin and J. Pycke, Tournai–Louvain-la-Neuve, 1992, pp. 51–58.

21] On ducal policy generally here, see R. Vaughan, *Valois Burgundy*, London, 1975, pp. 57–59; W. P. Blockmans and W. Prevenier, *De Bourgondiers: De Nederlanden op Weg naar Einheid 1384–1530*, Amsterdam, 1997, pp. 133–35.

22] J. Pycke, 'De Louis de la Trémoille à Ferry de Clugny (1388–1483): cinq évêques tournaisiens au service des ducs de Bourgogne', in *Les Grands Siècles de Tournai (12e–15e siècles)*, ed. J. Dumoulin and J. Pycke, Tournai–Louvain-la-Neuve, 1993, pp. 209–38; O. de Waele, 'Étude prosopographique des chanoines de Tournai (1378–1460)', 2 vols, Catholic University of Louvain-la-Neuve, unpublished *Mémoire de Licence*, 1992–93, Vol. I, pp. 41ff.

23] Cf. Stouff, *Arles*, Vol. I, pp. 184ff; M. Bourin, 'L'Évêque et sa ville: Pierre Joannis et Carcassonne', in *Villes, bonnes villes, cités et capitales*, ed. Bourin, pp. 269–77.

Bishop of Tournai, who had gone before him on bended knee').[24] During times of crisis negotiations between Tournai and the duke were regularly conducted through influential members of the chapter such as Raoul Lemaire and Guillaume Arnaldi.[25] But it would be a mistake to overestimate the influence which the Tournaisien authorities could hope to exert through men whose first political allegiance, when they had to express one, was usually to the Burgundian dukes. All five bishops of Tournai served on the ducal council, four of them at its head. Two were also chancellors of the Order of the Golden Fleece. Episcopal consecrations and enthronements were occasions for the Burgundian court to deploy its magnificence in the city.[26] In such circumstances it is hardly surprising to find that royalist Tournai was at times marginalised within its largely Flemish bishopric, and that the leading ecclesiastics of the town, when they did involve themselves in political matters, were patrons rather than agents of the city.[27]

The circumstances briefly outlined above gave successive dukes an impressive range of options when they had to bring pressure to bear on Tournai. Trade embargos, the seizure of goods, the arrest of merchants and moratoria on the payment of debts owed to Tournaisiens by ducal subjects are the most common tactics which appear in our sources in times of crisis.[28] Indirect military pressure could be exerted through the depredations of Burgundian soldiery in the surrounding region and by menaces proferred by major Burgundian servants who were no doubt acting with ducal permission, perhaps even under ducal instruction.[29] In discussions held with the estates of Flanders in August 1471, Charles the Bold contemplated a suitably Herculean initiative that would surely have dealt a fatal blow to the obstructive city.[30] The Tournaisien *Consaux* learned

24] RC 1422–30, p. 203.
25] de Waele, 'Étude prosopographique', Vol. II, nos 23, 118.
26] J. Cousin, *Histoire de Tournay ou troisième et quatrième livres des chroniques, annales ou démonstrations du Christianisme de l'évesché de Tournay*, Douai, 1619–20; repr. Tournai, 1868, pp. 197, 225, 237, 245.
27] During the early stages of the Schism, for example, Tournai was a Clementist enclave in largely Urbanist Flanders. Urbanist canons and others, 'Flamens et touttes langhes' ('Flemings and men of all languages') were arrested and their goods confiscated (Hocquet, *Croniques*, p. 256; A. d'Haenens, 'Les Relations de l'abbaye de Saint-Martin de Tournai avec la papauté au XIVe siècle', *Bulletin de l'Institut historique belge de Rome*, Vol. XXXI, 1958, p. 119).
28] RC 1385–1422, p. 95; de Smet, *Chronique*, p. 365; RC 1385–1422, pp. 38–39, 48–49; RC 1431–76, pp. 44, 48–49, 53–54, 60, 152–53, 177, 309–10, 311–14.
29] RC 1385–1422, pp. 70–73, 134–35, 161, 241; RC 1422–30, pp. 62, 222; RC 1431–1476, pp. 5, 15, 334–39.
30] *Handelingen van de Leden en Staten van Vlaanderen (1467–77): Excerpten uit de rekeningen van de Vlaamse steden, kasselrijen en vorstelijke ambtenaren*, ed. W. P. Blockmans, Brussels, 1971, pp. 135–37; RC 1455–72, p. 337. Cf. M. Boone, 'Destroying and Reconstructing the City: The Inculcation and Arrogation of Princely Power in the Burgundian-Habsburg Netherlands (14th–16th Centuries)', in *The Propagation of Power in the Medieval West*, ed. M. Gosman, A. Vanderjagt and J. Veenstra, Groningen, 1997, pp. 1–33.

in October of the means by which their nemesis might be achieved: Charles was prepared to 'ôter à la ville le cours de l'Escaut, et autres nouvellités' ('divert the course of the Escaut away from Tournai and other strange measures'). In the end, the first town to experience the consequences of Charles' ambitions to re-route rivers was Neuss during the siege of 1474–75.[31] Tournai avoided this outcome and no doubt much other inconvenience by means of a 'traictié perpétuel' ('everlasting treaty') in 1472. The municipality agreed to pay an annual sum to Charles and a pension to his half-brother, Anthony, to guarantee peaceful relations and freedom of commerce between Tournaisiens and the duke's subjects.[32]

The treaty of 1472 remained in force until the death of Charles the Bold.[33] It marked a return to a similar accommodation which his father had reached with the city in 1424, and which was renewed annually at increased cost through a series of negotiations until 1434.[34] During periods of conflict between dukes and French kings, the treaties were intended to achieve certain basic objectives, above all the neutralisation of the potential threat which Tournai posed to the economy and – bearing in mind the fact that the city, like so many in frontier settings, had a highly developed military sector – the security of the Burgundian dominions.[35] Ducal willingness to resort to treaties with Tournai throws interesting light on any grander designs they may have had. As Jacques Paviot has perceptively observed: 'that the dukes sought to integrate Tournai within their dominions seems undeniable, but that they ever intended to take possession of it, even by force, is inconceivable … it would have been necessary for the sovereign lord, that is to say the king, to invest the Duke of Burgundy with the fief of Tournai and the Tournaisis, which was unimaginable'.[36] As we shall see, the

31] R. Vaughan, *Charles the Bold*, London, 1973, p. 325.
32] For the terms see RC 1431–76, pp. 322–27.
33] It has been stated that the Treaty of Soleuvre rendered null and void the terms of Tournai's agreement with Charles the Bold (J. Paviot, 'Tournai dans l'histoire bourguignonne', in *Les Grands Siècles*, p. 77). However, Tournai was still raising money to pay Charles by the treaty's terms in February 1476; only when it was quite certain Charles was dead, in February 1477, did the *Consaux* agree to cease payment: RC 1431–76, p. 352; EC 1472–90, p. 342.
34] Houtart, *Les Tournaisiens et le Roi de Bourges*, Tournai, 1908, pp. 501–07; RC 1431–76, p. 21.
35] By the terms of their agreements with the duke, the Tournaisien authorities also agreed not to host a royal garrison. On the military sectors of frontier towns, see D. Menjot, 'La Ville frontière: un modèle original d'urbanisation?', in *Les villes frontière (Moyen Âge-époque moderne)*, Paris–Montreal, 1996, pp. 5–14. On fortifications and the arms industry, see P. M. Vêche, 'La Fortification urbaine à Tournai au Moyen Âge', *Publications extraordinaires de la SRHAT*, Vol. II, 1985, pp. 41–67; E. Soil de Moriamé, *Armes et armuriers tournaisiens: contribution à l'histoire des métiers d'art et à l'histoire militaire de Tournai, du XIIIe au XVIIIe siècle*, Antwerp, 1913.
36] 'Qu'ils aient cherché à l'intégrer dans leurs domaines semble indéniable, mais qu'ils aient cherché à en prendre possession – même par la force – ne semble pas concevable … il aurait fallu que le seigneur, c'est-à-dire le roi, investît le duc de Bourgogne du fief de Tournai et du Tournaisis, ce qui n'était pas pensable' (Paviot, 'Tournai', p. 70).

possibility of alienation from the crown with Valois consent may not have seemed quite so unlikely to contemporaries in Tournai, at the Burgundian court or even its royal counterpart. Philip the Good was, in fact, granted Tournai to be held in fief under the jurisdiction of the *Parlement* in September 1423, along with all profits save those of the mint.[37] The grant was made by the Duke of Bedford, however, not by the dauphin, and was a convenient way of settling an outstanding debt to Philip whilst encouraging him to bring the delphinal city into the Anglo-Burgundian fold. Philip the Good's decision to opt for a financial settlement with Tournai is readily explained. The intervention in 1424 of Humfrey of Gloucester in Hainault on behalf of Jacqueline of Bavaria distanced Philip from the English.[38] The duke was subsequently too busy in Holland to concern himself greatly with Tournai. Although the grant of 1423 was never put into effect, and was formally annulled by the Treaty of Arras in 1435, it is clear that the treaties of 1424 and 1472 brought Tournai closer than ever into the Burgundian orbit for as long as their terms were observed.[39] There is one telling illustration of this fact. Tournai's regular financial contribution to the royal centre consisted from 1383 onwards of a *composition* of 6000 *livres tournois*, an arrangement struck with the monarchy by some other towns in the north of the Artois and in the Boulonnais.[40] During the period of the treaties it becomes clear in the *registres des Consaux* that the city began to default on its annual settlement with the monarchy, and that eventually Charles VII, and later Louis XI, 'had consented to the non-payment of the annual 6000 *l.t.* for as long as it was necessary for the town to buy peace from my lord of Burgundy'.[41] In other

37] Houtart, *Les Tournaisiens*, pp. 236–38, 486–89.

38] A Tournaisien contingent joined the Burgundian and Brabantine forces which recovered Hainault from the English for Jacqueline's estranged husband, John IV of Brabant (RC 1422–30, p. 171; Houtart, *Les Tournaisiens*, pp. 289–300).

39] E. Cosneau, *Les Grands traités de la Guerre de Cent Ans*, Paris, 1889, pp. 140–41; the payments were scheduled to end in 1440 (RC 1431–76, p. 34).

40] M. Rey, *Le Domaine du roi et les finances extraordinaires sous Charles VI, 1388–1413*, Paris, 1965, p. 171; A. Allard, 'Le Premier bailliage de Tournai-Tournaisis, 20 juin 1383–janvier 1423 (n. st.): contribution à la biographie des jurisconsultes Jehan Boutillier et Jacques d'Ableiges', *Annales du Cercle archéologique de Mons*, Vol. XXV, 1896, pp. 8–10.

41] '[Le roy] avoit consenti non payer à luy les vj. m. l.t. par an tant qu'il convenist la ville accater paix audit Monseigneur de Bourgogne' (RC 1422–30, p. 344), The dauphin had already allowed Tournai to use the annual *composition* for purposes of defence in 1422 (Houtart, *Les Tournaisiens*, pp. 477–80). In 1424–25 it appears the city was attempting to meet its payments to the crown, partly because the arrangement with Philip the Good still seemed temporary (ibid., pp. 104, 106, 154; see Houtart, *Les Tournaisiens*, pp. 179, 516, 518–19). Before January 1427 the authorities had clearly given up (RC 1422–30, pp. 229–30, 247). Insistent royal demands in 1429 led to the raising of a small amount of finance, and further demands were made in 1431 (ibid., pp. 305–06, 343–45, 349–50, 367–68; RC 1431–76, pp. 1–2, 7). However, in 1434 the Tournaisien authorities were seeking to use the king's money to pay Philip the Good, and as late as 1444 royal ambassadors were still discussing 'se le temps est expiré de la grace des vj^{m}' ('if the days of grace for the payment of the 6000 *livres* had expired') (ibid., pp. 22–23, 116). Closer inspection of some

words, for nearly one quarter of the period under consideration here, the closest financial relationship which Tournai had with any political centre was with the Burgundian dukes, and this by royal consent.

The coercive power of the Burgundian centre was strong, and at times its financial relationship with the Tournaisien periphery was close. It was perhaps inevitable under these circumstances that affinities should have emerged between groups in power within the town and the decision-taking elites of the surrounding Burgundian dominions. The family connections and career of Simon de Saint-Genois – a member of an old Tournaisien family and prominent municipal office-bearer in his own right – may serve as an illustration.[42] Simon de Saint-Genois acquired the status of *conseiller et chambellan* of Charles VII. His eldest son was an *échanson* of Louis XI and lieutenant of the royal *bailli* of Tournai-Tournaisis. By marriage, however, Saint-Genois was allied to the Burgundian de Gouy family. His father-in-law, Arnoud, was a servant at the court of Philip the Good and *haut-bailli* of Ghent. Simon contracted a marriage for his daughter Agnès within the de la Howardrie family, members of which served in the main military campaigns fought by the dukes from the 1430s onwards. Saint-Genois acquired a reputation as a leading member of the pro-Burgundian faction in Tournai in the early 1420s. He found it necessary to emigrate before he was banished from the city during the so-called 'democratic revolution' of 1423 which brought the deacons (*doiens*) of the guilds to power alongside older patrician families. When Saint-Genois returned to the city in 1429, it was with the blessing of Charles VII, despite the fact that the king had not yet made his peace with the duke whom Simon was believed locally to support. The former exile later served his monarch at the head of a Tournaisien contingent of crossbowmen at the siege of Pontoise in 1441.

The ambiguous position of men like Saint-Genois is understandable when it is remembered that the Burgundian dukes to whom they were drawn were not simply powerful neighbours in their own right. Philip the Bold first came to the region as the agent of French royal expansion. As late as 1438, Philip the Good – 'si grant et puissant prince, et prochain à la couronne' ('a great and powerful prince, and close to the crown') as a Tournaisien record then thought fit to describe him – claimed his right as 'per et doyen des pers de France' ('a peer and the senior peer of France') to pardon exiles on entering the city.[43] Those, such as Jean de Lannoy or Jean de Melun, whom Philip the Good most commonly employed in

surviving Tournai accounts, now in the Archives Générales du Royaume in Brussels, will shed further light on the matter (C. Pantens, 'Rapport sur les comptes dits généraux de la ville de Tournai (1397–1427)', *BCRH*, Vol. CXXIX, 1963, pp. ic–ci).

42] For what follows, see Houtart, *Les Tournaisiens*, pp. 27, 33, 125, 138, 190–92, 215, 225, 354, 373, 387, 448, 450, 462; P.-A. du Chastel de la Howarderies-Neuvireuil, *Notices généalogiques tournaisiennes dressées sur titres*, 4 vols, Tournai, 1881–1910, Vol. III, pp. 415ff; Vol. I, p. 450; Vol. II, p. 493.

43] RC 1431–76, pp. 372–73.

his dealings with Tournai also had careers or landed interests that brought them into contact with both royal and ducal milieux.[44] In Gerald Aylmer's words, 'it was desirable, if not essential, that [the] municipality and its senior officials should enjoy good relations with any powerful noble neighbour as patron or protector, unless they had effective direct access to the ruler and his court'.[45] Tournaisien access to the royal centre was, as we shall see, intermittent. By contrast, Burgundian influence at the king's court could be considerable in our period, during the reign of Philip the Bold and for long periods under John the Fearless, but also for brief spells under Philip the Good, notably before the death of Charles VI in 1422 and for a time after the accession of Louis XI in 1461. Such factors may explain the presence of an impressive number of old Tournaisien families in the membership lists of the *Cour amoureuse* of Charles VI. This literary society was founded in Paris in 1400 by Philip the Bold and John, Duke of Berry.[46] Its precise functions require further research, not least because of the impressive array of princes of the realm, members of the upper nobility, royal administrators and townsmen who belonged to it. The Tournaisien presence within the *Cour amoureuse* far exceeded that of any other *bonne ville*, indicating that the city's power elites had found a niche within networks of sociability linking the royal and Burgundian courts early in the fifteenth century. There is a similar correlation between periods of Burgundian influence at the royal court and direct ducal interventions in the political life of the city and its region. The first three dukes all requested financial or material support from Tournai during such periods.[47] John the Fearless succeeded in appointing Burgundian *baillis* in the Tournaisis, and as late as 1461 Philip the Good profited from warm relations with the new king, Louis XI, to place a trusted equerry, Hervé de Meriadec, in the same post.[48] In this respect as in others, the pull exerted by the Burgundian centre could at times be strong: that of the royal centre to the south was often much weaker.

Tournai formed part of more or less distant *bailliages* until the creation, one

44] W. Ossoba, 'Jean IV de Melun, seigneur d'Antoing' and 'Jean, seigneur de Lannoy, Lys et Wattignies', in *Les Chevaliers de la Toison d'Or: notices bio-bibliographiques*, ed. R. de Smedt, Frankfurt-am-Main, 1994, pp. 72–73, 109–10.

45] G. E. Aylmer, 'Centre and Locality: The Nature of Power Elites', in *Power Elites and State Building*, ed. W. Reinhard, Oxford, 1996, pp. 65–66.

46] The membership lists are published in *La Cour amoureuse dite de Charles VI*, ed. C. Bozzolo and H. Loyau, 2 vols, Paris, 1982–92. See also their two studies, 'L'Histoire de la ville de Tournai vue à travers les armoriaux de la Cour amoureuse dite de Charles VI', in *Actes du 2e Congrès de l'Association des cercles francophones d'Histoire et d'Archéologie de Belgique (Nivelles, août 1984)*, Vol. IV, 1987, pp. 253–64; and 'Princes, prélats, barons et autres gens notables: à propos de la Cour amoureuse dite de Charles VI', in *Prosopographie et genèse de l'état moderne*, ed. F. Autrand, Paris, 1986, pp. 159–70.

47] See, for example, RC 1385–1422, pp. 52, 61–62, 141–42, 171–72, 194–95; RC 1431–76, pp. 32–33.

48] G. Dupont-Ferrier, *Gallia Regia ou état des officiers royaux des bailliages et sénéchaussées de 1328 à 1515*, 6 vols, Paris, 1942–66, Vol. IV, pp. 50–52.

year before the start of our period, of the *bailliage* of Tournai-Tournaisis.[49] As its name implies, this area incorporated both the city and the narrow hinterland no more than seven or eight miles wide which stretched to the north and south over a distance of roughly thirty miles along the left bank of the Escaut.[50] The Tournaisiens did not let this situation last for long, and in 1389 the city secured its former juridical independence from the *bailli* at a cost of 10 000 *l.t.* Thereafter the *registres des Consaux* chronicle the mostly successful efforts of the authorities to fight off any perceived encroachment on the city's privileges by the officers of the *bailli*. Twice, indeed, they attempted to have the post of *bailli* abolished altogether, and once, in 1423, they were temporarily successful.[51] This course of action was pursued despite the fact that the small number of officers connected to the *bailliage* appear in the main to have been locals, as was often the case, and that in moments of crisis they sought permission to take refuge in the surroundings of the city itself.[52] Like their counterparts in Lyon, the authorities in Tournai preferred to keep the *bailli*'s men at a safe distance.[53] Needless to say, the local estates that gradually emerged within the framework of the *bailliage* were heavily dominated by Tournai itself. The process of deliberation and consultation which could establish relationships and hierarchies among urban communities of the same region and obedience remained even more intensely local than usual.[54] Only once was Tournai the setting for a regional meeting of estates involving representatives from other urban communities of a significant size.[55]

Ultimately, relations between centre and periphery depended less on the crown's officers in the locality than upon the frequency and nature of the contacts between the civic authorities and the king in his council.[56] Tournai

49] Unless otherwise stated, what follows is based on Allard, 'Le Premier bailliage de Tournai-Tournaisis'. For the earlier period, see P. Rolland, 'À quels baillis ont ressorti Tournai et le Tournaisis durant le XIIIe siècle?', *RN*, Vol. XIII, 1927, pp. 249–74; H. Waquet, *Le Bailliage de Vermandois aux XIIIe et XIVe siècles: étude d'histoire administrative*, Paris, 1919, pp. 12–13, 47ff.

50] A. d'Herbomez, *Géographie historique du Tournaisis*, Brussels, 1892.

51] Houtart, *Les Tournaisiens*, pp. 155–59; *Inventaire analytique des Archives de la ville de Tournai, 3e fascicule*, ed. A. Hocquet, Tournai, 1939, p. 61; RC 1431–76, p. 91.

52] *Ordonnances*, Vol. XIII, pp. 18–20; RC 1385–1422, pp. 116, 129–30; RC 1422–30, p. 70; RC 1431–76, pp. 387–88. The Tournaisien authorities were also hostile on occasion to the office of the royal *tabellion*, established by 1367 to arbitrate in civil cases (H. Nélis, 'Études diplomatiques sur le *tabellionage du roy* de Tournai au Moyen Âge [1367–1511]', *BCRH*, Vol. LXXIII, 1904, esp. pp. 9–26, 78–90. See also RC 1422–30, p. 71.)

53] J. Deniau, *La Commune de Lyon et la guerre bourguignonne, 1417–35*, Lyon, 1934, pp. 214–15.

54] G. Wymans, 'Les États de Tournai et du Tournaisis', *APAE*, Vol. XXXIII, 1965, pp. 163–80.

55] Tournai hosted a gathering of the Estates of Artois in March 1415, a meeting summoned – significantly by John the Fearless (C. Hirschauer, *Les États d'Artois de leurs origines à l'occupation française, 1340–1640*, 2 vols, Paris, 1923, Vol. I, pp. 46, 86; Vol. II, p. 15).

56] B. Chevalier, 'The *bonnes villes* and the King's Council in Fifteenth-Century France', in *The Crown and Local Communities*, ed. Highfield and Jeffs, pp. 110–28.

received only one royal visit during our period.[57] In the course of preparations for the entry which eventually took place in 1464, Pierre Doriole, the king's secretary, recalled accurately that the last royal visit had occurred in 1382, and then wholly inaccurately that no monarch had visited Tournai for more than three hundred years before that, 'car les rois de France n'avoient gaires accoustumés de venir en icelle ville' ('for kings of France were scarcely accustomed to visting that town').[58] Such a lapse in the political memory might be taken as a sign that a great distance separated the Tournaisien periphery from the royal centre. Compared with some parts of the realm, such as the Languedoc before 1390, Tournai was not strictly speaking one of the 'longtaines parties du royaume' (distant parts of the kingdom).[59] From the second quarter of the fifteenth century, the distance to the king 'outre Loire' ('beyond the Loire') increased, but up to that point news commonly reached Tournai from Paris within three or four days (or even less when the news was especially pressing).[60] During difficult times, however, the distance to the royal centre could become very great indeed. One entry in the *registres des Consau*x for 1424 records how the authorities were then having to send envoys to Charles VII via Geneva and Lyon.[61] The following year Charles allowed the suspension of appeals from Tournai to the *Parlement* at Poitiers because the road was too perilous.[62] The sense of isolation we find in correspondence between centre and periphery can be striking, including a royal letter of 1428 describing how Tournai remained 'seule oultre la rivière de Seine en nostre obéissance' ('the only town beyond the Seine in our obedience'), its citizens 'esloignez de nous par grans distances et intervales' ('separated from us by a long distance'). Even when communication was less dangerous, the Tournaisien authorities could describe their city to the king as 'éseulée et eslongiée des aultres villes de France' ('isolated and distanced from the other towns of France').[63]

Tournai also faced the perennial problem of how to gain secure and regular access to the decision-taking core. Like many other *bonnes villes*, the city employed a quasi-permanent group of experts in Paris, 'le conseil de la ville à Paris' (the council of the city in Paris), to handle affairs at court and in other

57] A. de la Grange, 'Les Entrées des souverains à Tournai', *MSHLT*, Vol. XIX, 1885, pp. 7–321, esp. pp. 32–69.
58] RC 1455–72, pp. 320–21.
59] Cited in F. Autrand, 'L'Allée du roi dans les pays de Languedoc', in *La Circulation des nouvelles au Moyen Âge: XXIVe Congrès de la S.H.M.E.P (Avignon, juin 1993)*, Paris–Rome, 1994, p. 86.
60] News of John the Fearless's murder at Montereau, sent from Paris to Tournai on 13 September 1419, took two days to reach the city (RC 1385–1422, pp. 180–81). See also Paviot, 'Tournai', p. 59.
61] RC 1422–30, p. 96.
62] *Ordonnances*, Vol. XIII, pp. 103–04.
63] The first document is published in Houtart, *Les Tournaisiens*, pp. 553, 555; the second in RC 1431–76, p. 226.

institutions based in the capital.[64] Their tasks were wide-ranging and sufficiently demanding to require full-time employment – this much the city authorities demanded so that its representatives would not carry out legal work that conflicted with or impeded the pursuit of Tournai's interests.[65] The occasional surviving letter reveals how these 'expert fixers' operated in court circles with a mixture of guile and well-targeted largesse.[66] They were also expected to act as the eyes and ears of the periphery at the centre.[67] For all their undoubted value to the city – a value which was recognised by the fact that their salaries were left untouched in municipal cost-cutting exercises – these confident jurisconsults also had their limitations.[68] So long as the annointed king was primarily based in and around Paris, it was worth Tournai's while to maintain such men in the capital.[69] In the reigns of Charles VII and Louis XI, however, the benefit must have seemed less obvious. Moreover, all too easily these men could become agents of the centre whenever it wished to exert control over the periphery. In March 1412, for example, Jacques Bacheler was summoned into Charles VI's bedchamber to be told the king wanted 2000 *écus* from 'ses boins subgés et amis de Tournay' ('his good subjects and friends in Tournai').[70] Bacheler conveyed the request along with a list of benefits he believed he could negotiate in return. In 1418, Jacques Courre had to be dismissed for spying on the city and reporting back to the Armagnacs in power in the capital.[71] Regular representation in Paris was not without its perils.[72]

A second tactic was to acquire the services of men who were already well-established at the centre in another capacity and who were thus well-placed to help Tournai achieve its goals. To secure the release of the city from the jurisdiction of the *bailli* in 1389, for example, delegates were authorised to spend

64] Houtart, *Les Tournaisiens*, pp. 37–38.
65] RC 1385–1422, pp. 9, 97–101.
66] The term is from Lewis, 'The Centre', p. 40, repr. in idem, *Essays in Later Medieval French History*, p. 158.
67] For example, letters from the *conseil* first warned Tournai of Louis of Orléans' designs on the town in 1402 (RC 1385–1422, p. 51).
68] RC 1385–1422, p. 9; Houtart, *Les Tournaisiens*, p. 37 n. 4. On these men generally and their value to towns, see A. Rigaudière, 'L'Essor des conseillers juridiques des villes dans la France du bas Moyen Âge', *Revue historique de droit français et étranger*, Vol. LXII, 1984, pp. 361–90: repr. in idem, pp. 215–51.
69] Cf. B. Guenée, 'Paris et la cour du roi de France au XIVe siècle', in *Villes, bonnes villes, cités et capitales*, pp. 259–65.
70] RC 1385–1422, pp. 88–89. A revealing letter from one *conseiller* to the Tournai authorities, detailing an interview with Charles VI in 1406 'ou petit gardin devant sa chambre' ('in the little garden outside his chamber'), was published in L. Mirot, 'Lettres closes de Charles VI conservées aux archives de Reims et de Tournai', *MA*, deuxième sér., Vol. XXX, 1919, p. 28 n. 2.
71] RC 1385–1422, pp. 155–59; Houtart, *Les Tournaisiens*, pp. 35–36.
72] Or its expenses: in 1407 the Tournai authorities had to appoint a special committee to look into the extravagant expense claims of Jacques Bacheler (RC 1385–1422, p. 66).

up to 1000 or 1200 *écus* to acquire friends at court.[73] They were to do so with the help of a former governor of Tournai, Enguerran Doudin, who had already won favour in the city by refusing to publish a royal demand for a hearth tax for fear of the public reaction it might provoke.[74] The *registres des Consaux* are not as good a source for the study of Tournai's dealings with powerbrokers as a full set of municipal accounts would have been, but there is none the less enough evidence to show that Tournai adopted a range of measures, including speculative generosity towards great men who might be of some assistance in the future (such as the metropolitan, Jacques Juvénal des Ursins, who received wine in 1445); and regular gifts to men whom they could not afford to neglect (such as the chancellor and others, 'jusques à cent ou environ' ('up to the number of one hundred'), who received gifts in 1394).[75] Such activities might create a natural constituency of sympathisers inclined to act in Tournai's favour.[76] But such sympathy was difficult to guarantee or control, and once more we touch upon the inherent difficulty of the informal means at the periphery's disposal to achieve its goals at the centre. Tournai's authorities may have felt that they could resolve this matter by relying on powerful men whose roots lay in the region. Of all the powerbroking relationships which emerge in the registers, these appear to have been the most problematic.[77] Philippe de Commynes' patrimony originally lay about twenty miles from Tournai, so it is not surprising to find him striking up a relationship with the city's authorities – a relationship which became increasingly unsatisfactory as Commynes' demands increased.[78] But at least he did not fleece Tournai as badly as Olivier le Daim, the barber from Tielt. After the death of Louis XI's favourite in 1484, the Tournaisien authorities tried to recover what they could of the money demanded or extorted by him over the years.[79]

73] Allard, 'Le Premier bailliage', pp. 18–19.

74] de Smet, *Chronique*, p. 251.

75] RC 1431–76, p. 120; RC 1385–1422, p. 20.

76] Evidence of 'friends at court' occurs in 1424, for example, when it was reported back to Tournai that several royal councillors had spoken out against men whom the city had banished, and who were seeking royal support against the city's decision (RC 1422–30, pp. 102–03).

77] Research for this chapter did not throw up a great deal of evidence of local men establishing themselves at the royal court, but see E. Soil de Moriamé, 'Lettres de remission pour Guillaume de Moriaumez, échanson du roi Charles VI (1416–17)', *ASRHAT*, nouv. sér. Vol. I, 1986, pp. 157–79; Houtart, *Les Tournaisiens*, pp. 188–89 (Gui V de Moy); du Chastel de la Howarderies-Neuvireuil, *Notices généalogiques*, Vol. I, p. 7; Vol. III, pp. 556–57 (Guillaume de Thouars). The subject clearly deserves further study. For valuable comment on relations with men at the royal centre, see B. Chevalier, *La Ville de Tours et la société tourangelle, 1356–1520*, 2 vols, Lille, 1974, Vol. I, pp. 138–40.

78] RC 1431–76, pp. 362–64; EC 1472–90, pp. 341, 342, 364–65, 373; *Lettres et négociations de Philippe de Commynes*, ed. J. Kervyn de Lettenhove, 3 vols, Brussels, 1867–74, Vol. I, p. 128.

79] EC 1472–90, pp. 373–74; see also pp. 349, 366, 367; V. Van der Haeghen, 'Les Députés de Tournai auprès de Louis XI et d'Olivier le Dain en juillet 1477', in *Mélanges Godefroid Kurth*, 2 vols, Liège, 1908, Vol. I, pp. 207–12.

The third means open to the periphery was the dispatch of ambassadors to the centre to discharge a specific mission.[80] Some of these missions could be lengthy and clearly involved a watching brief, but their purpose was generally restricted and of limited value in widening and deepening the relationship between ruler and ruled. Indeed, in some circumstances the authorities of Tournai, no doubt like many other cities in later medieval France, were extremely cautious about sending ambassadors to the centre. For example, when it came to the sensitive task of sending envoys to Charles VII to secure recognition of the new place the guilds had won for themselves in the government of Tournai in 1423–24, the *Consaux* obliged their ambassadors to swear they would make no undertakings on behalf of the city; that they would only require reasonable expenses; that they would reject any offices or other rewards given to them; and that they would otherwise do nothing that went against the privileges of Tournai.[81] Aware that they might be required to accept the Treaty of Troyes if they sent a deputation to a meeting of the estates in Paris in 1421, the *Consaux* were advised by representatives of one parish to send a few men with no experience of municipal government 'adfin qu'ilz ignorassent les dites requestes' ('so that they could ignore the said demands').[82] Earlier that year, the *Consaux* had decided to send no envoys to Paris, partly for the same reason and partly because 'on ignorait si la ville estoit en grâce ou non' ('it was not known whether the town enjoyed the king's favour or not'). In their estimation, envoys might be interrogated and forced to give away the true condition of the city, 'entiere et le moins damagiée des autres boines villes du royaume' ('intact and of all the cities of the kingdom the least affected').[83] It is usually assumed that peripheries sought to be heard by the centre, but sometimes they wished to hide from it, too.

The pull from the royal centre thus appears to have been intermittent, and this in contrast to the pressures Tournai experienced as a consequence of its position on the Burgundian periphery. And yet through every change of regime in the city, through every twist of fortune at either pole of attraction, Tournai never once left the royal obedience.[84] This fact is worth emphasising in view of the more varied experience of other French cities.

80] In this respect it would be more accurate to speak of royal *centres* and to emphasise, following M. Hébert's study of the county of Provence, the diversity of 'lieux d'échanges' (points of contact) between 'centre' and periphery (M. Hébert, 'Communication et société politique: les villes et l'état en Provence aux XIVe et XVe siècles', in *La Circulation des nouvelles*, p. 237). The destruction of the municipal accounts makes it difficult to follow Tournai's envoys, but see the details of the many sent out to different destinations to discuss matters with the king or his officers in 1422–23 (RC 1422–30, p. 74 n. 1).
81] Ibid., pp. 96–97.
82] RC 1385–1422, p. 211.
83] Ibid., pp. 202–03.
84] Setting aside the periods covered by the treaties discussed above, and indeed prefiguring them in several respects, the only other episode that springs to mind here is the cautious support Tournai felt obliged to give to John the Fearless during his campaigns in France in 1417–18. The treaty which Tournai, like many other French

Kings could express in the strongest possible terms their wish to hold on to Tournai. In 1470, Louis XI informed Jean Dauvet, president of the *Parlement*, that he was in danger of losing the king's confidence by continuing to obstruct a case Tournai had brought against royal officers in the *bailliage*. He reminded Dauvet: '[v]ous avez esté à Tournay, et congnoissez la situacion, et comme la ville est au meillieu des pais de monseigneur de Bourgongne, et savez qu'il m'est bien besoing de les entretenir' ('you have been to Tournai and know the position, and how the town is situated among lands belonging to my lord of Burgundy; and you know, too, how very much I need to keep it on my side').[85] But kings were not always masters of their own actions, let alone of their kingdoms; they could find themselves having to concede what they were unwilling to concede or to sanction a state of affairs they had been powerless to prevent. Had any of the reported plots to make Tournai over to Burgundian dukes come to fruition, it is conceivable that the long-term outcome might have been an attempt to negotiate annexation to the Burgundian dominions rather than full restoration of the king's rights over the city.[86] More significantly, Tournai was surrounded by towns which kings of France had ceded to local rulers. Lille, Douai and Orchies were granted in 1369 to the Count of Flanders at the time of Philip the Bold's marriage to Margaret of Male.[87] The Somme towns and the strategically important town of Mortagne, on Tournai's doorstep, were ceded by the Treaty of Arras in 1435 to Philip the Good.[88] These communities were recovered with finance in 1463, but were ceded once again by the Treaty of Conflans of 1465.[89]

towns, sealed at that time was eventually presented as an act of obedience to the pseudo-regent Isabeau. Within the royal council it was acknowledged that 'il n'estoit pas possible de faire autrement' ('it was not possible to do otherwise') (RC 1385–1422, p. 142, R. Vaughan, *John the Fearless*, London, 1966, pp. 215ff). This was precisely the position which both Charles VII and Louis XI took with regard to the treaties of 1424 and 1472.

85] *Lettres de Louis XI, roi de France*, ed. J. Vaesen and E. Charavay, 11 vols, SHF, Paris, 1883–1909, Vol. IV, pp. 101–02, 115–17.

86] This is a speculative point since reports of plots to make Tournai over to the dukes appear to have had little substance. In 1414 and 1416, three prominent aldermen were accused and exonerated of planning to sell the city to John the Fearless (RC 1385–1422, pp. 115–16, 127, 130–32; de Smet, *Chronique*, p. 361). In October 1426 a plot was discovered involving prominent *bourgeois* and their supporters expelled from the city by the new regime in 1423. Led by Simon de Saint-Genois and others based in Oudenaarde, their main aim was to overthrow the increasingly radical guilds and re-establish themselves in the city (Houtart, *Les Tournaisiens*, pp. 354–60). Finally, in an important but little-known clash in August 1453 between the deacons of the guilds and the *Consaux*, Jean Boutepoix, *souverain prévôt*, claimed his enemies among the guilds had spread the rumour that there were 200 men in the city who wished 'que icelle feust en l'obéissance de Philippe, duc de Bourgoingne' ('that the city were in the obedience of Philip, Duke of Burgundy') (de Smet, *Chronique*, pp. 520–25; RC 1432–76, pp. 199–202).

87] R. Vaughan, *Philip the Bold*, London, 1962, pp. 5–6.

88] Cosneau, *Les Grands traités*, pp. 136ff.

89] Vaughan, *Philip the Good*, pp. 355–57, 390–91; A. Bocquillet, 'Mortagne pendant la Ligue du Bien Public', *RT*, Vol. III, 1907, pp. 171–75.

In the case of St Quentin, for long the nearest royal town to Tournai, the situation remained fluid beyond 1465: recovered by Louis XI in 1471, the town was ceded once more to Charles the Bold four years later.[90] Although no Valois monarch relinquished his hold of Tournai in our period, few later medieval French cities confronted the possibility of alienation more often. In 1402 it was rumoured that Charles VI was planning to give Tournai in apanage to Louis of Orléans.[91] In 1465, news reached Tournai that Louis XI had granted the city to his brother, Charles de France.[92] Just ten years later it seemed likely that Louis would cede Tournai to Charles the Bold.[93] Four times in 14 years the Tournaisien authorities felt it necessary to secure letters from Charles VII guaranteeing non-alienation, the last occasion occurring ten months after the promulgation of the Treaty of Arras which had stipulated that Tournai would remain 'ès mains du Roy' ('in the hands of the king').[94] Letters guaranteeing non-alienation were also requested from Louis XI in July 1461 and November 1474.[95] By right of their claim to the throne of France, kings of England felt entitled to dispose of Tournai as they saw fit – not just in 1423 as we have seen, but also in 1474, when Edward IV presumed to grant the city to Charles the Bold by the terms of the Treaty of London, and in 1513, when Henry VIII took it by force.[96] The Tournaisien authorities repeatedly expressed and maintained their adhesion to monarchs who, even if they were not inclined to do so, always had the power to sign the city away. In the decision-taking process at the heart of successive regimes in Tournai – that is to say, within the *Consaux* themselves and the deacons of the guilds who established their authority in 1423, among the 300 *élus* whom these groups consulted on sensitive issues, and among the heads of household organised by parish whose views were sought in the last resort – the royal centre repeatedly emerged as the centre of choice.

As many historians have found, it is not impossible to explain Tournai's adhesion to the monarchy in terms of the patriotism of its citizens – albeit with

90] Vaughan, *Charles the Bold*, pp. 68, 352, 413 n. 1.
91] RC 1385–1422, p. 51.
92] RC 1431–76, pp. 284–85; RC 1455–72, p. 324; H. Stein, *Charles de France, frère de Louis XI*, Paris, 1921, pp. 113, 546.
93] RC 1431–76, pp. 350–51. Philippe de Commynes received a gift of tapestry for helping to ensure Tournai was not ceded 'comme on doubtoit que les Bourgongnons désiroient' ('as it was feared that the Burgundians wished it to be').
94] *Inventaire analytique*, ed. Hocquet, pp. 60, 61; Houtart, *Les Tournaisiens*, pp. 480–82; RC 1422–30, pp. 343–45; RC 1431–76, pp. 35, 366–69; Cosneau, *Les Grands traités*, p. 140.
95] RC 1455–72, p. 317; EC 1472–90, p. 341.
96] T. Rymer, *Foedera*, 20 vols, London, 1704–35, Vol. XI, p. 810; C. Davies, 'Tournai and the English Crown, 1513–1519', *The Historical Journal*, Vol. XLI, 1998, pp. 1–26. In 1433, Charles of Orléans promised that if he failed to secure terms for a general peace, he would try to obtain Tournai and a number of other strategically important cities for Henry VI (G. du Fresne de Beacourt, *Histoire de Charles VII*, 6 vols, Paris, 1881–91, Vol. II, p. 463).

the necessary proviso that it is difficult to plot the fluctuations of national sentiment in the context of a specific locality where evidence is often circumstantial and conflicting.[97] As Edward Shils reminds us, the centre is more than a geo-political reality: 'The center, or the central zone, is a phenomenon of the realms of values and beliefs'.[98] From the centre to the periphery, the means by which 'l'état a créé la nation' ('the state created the nation') are as evident in Tournai as elsewhere in later medieval France.[99] Processions mobilising the population in support of the king's cause or to mark significant dynastic events were common.[100] We have seen that royal visits were few and far between, but royal correspondence with the city is plentiful and is couched in historical terms which emphasise at every turn Tournai's ancient devotion to the monarchy.[101] In one memorable letter influenced by a reading of Livy's account of the Punic Wars, Charles VII compared Tournai to Petelia, a city which remained steadfastly loyal to Rome in the face of Carthaginian aggression.[102] Even if doubts arose and letters guaranteeing non-alienation seemed necessary, the official language of loyalty between the king and his *bonnes villes* was not – could never be – equivocal.[103]

The crown certainly encouraged Tournaisiens to live up to the example set by their ancestors and to act as good and loyal Frenchmen. It is fair to say, however, that the expression of such sentiments was a more complex issue bound up with local circumstances. In the fourteenth century, the domination of municipal

97] M. Houtart, 'Le Patriotisme dans l'histoire de Tournai', *RT*, Vol. I, 1905, pp. 80–115. Cf. C. Billot, *Chartres à la fin du Moyen Âge*, Paris, 1987, p. 36.
98] E. Shils, 'Center and Periphery', in his *Center and Periphery: Essays in Macro-sociology*, Chicago–London, 1975, p. 3. I am grateful to Dr Stuart Airlie for the reference.
99] The phrase is from B. Guenée, 'État et nation en France au Moyen Âge', *RH*, Vol. CCXXXVIII, 1967, pp. 17–30, (repr. in his *Politique et historique au Moyen Âge: recueil d'articles sur l'histoire politique et l'historiographie médiévales [1956–81]*, Paris, 1981).
100] RC 1385–1422, pp. 28–29, 91–92, 173, 175, 199; RC 1422–30, pp. 62, 71, 295, 337; RC 1431–76, pp. 44, 95, 126, 134, 139, 141–42, 148, 153, 188–89, 197, 203, 266, 302, 309, 311, 357–58.
101] Royal *ordonnances* in the fifteenth century often look back 'neuf cens ans ou environ' ('nine hundred years or so') to locate the origins of Tournai's loyalty to the crown, perhaps on the basis of the Life of St Eligius (Rolland, 'Exception communale', pp. 301–03). The cathedral chapter and (less plausibly) the crossbowmen's guild both located their origins under Merovingian kings (RC 1422–30, pp. 257, 378–79; RC 1431–76, p. 135). For other important dates in the history of the town's relationship with the monarchy, see *Ordonnances*, Vol. XIII, pp. 18–20; RC 1455–72, pp. 312–15, 324; EC 1472–90, pp. 385–86. The linked historical culture of city and monarch is also emphasised in the impressive series of Tournai origin legends (G. Small, 'Les Origines de la ville de Tournai dans les chroniques légendaires du bas Moyen Âge', in *Les Grands Siècles*, pp. 81–113).
102] RC 1431–76, pp. 180–81. The letter was sent in 1452. The source was Book XXIII of Livy's *History of Rome from its Foundation*. On the wide readership of Livy in fourteenth- and fifteenth-century France, not least at the royal court and around Charles VII himself, see B. Guenée, *Histoire et culture historique dans l'Occident médiéval*, Paris, 1980, pp. 28, 108, 223, 229, 290, 316.
103] A. Rigaudière, 'Qu'est-ce que c'est qu'une *bonne ville* dans la France du Moyen

government by the 'gros bourgeois' ('wealthy burghers') had already led some among the populace to prefer direct royal rule.[104] Later, the excluded expressed their political agenda in strong royalist terms, above all during the 'democratic revolution' brilliantly studied by Maurice Houtart and mentioned on several occasions above.[105] The radical period of the new regime was brought to an end in 1428, but the emotions it had excited remained close to the surface. In the records of prosecutions carried out that year by a municipal commission to restore social peace, the popular party in Tournai was strikingly described as 'plus français que le roi' ('more French than the king'), its members as 'doubles franchois' ('doubly French').[106] In July 1429, a coal porter objected to the aldermen reading out a letter from Jeanne d'Arc because 'la puchielle avoit escript et envoyé ses lettres aux bons franchois, et non point à ceux de la Loy' ('the Maid had written and sent letters to the loyal French and not to the men of the town council').[107] Overt expressions of Burgundian sympathies during times of conflict between dukes and the king can be cited, but they are few and far between.[108]

Âge?', in his *Gouverner la ville*, pp. 53–112, esp. p. 80. It is instructive here to compare the language employed by Tournaisien authorities with that found in the correspondence of another frontier town, Épinal. In 1463, a letter from the authorities in Épinal to Louis XI stated they would prefer 'qu'on nous abattit noz murailles et nos maisons sur nos testes que jamais nous dussions avoir aultre seigneur que le roy; et ainsi voulons vivre et mourir' ('that the walls and our houses should be knocked down on our very heads rather than we should ever have to have any other lord than the king: and this is how we wish to live and die') (Sée, *Louis XI et les villes*, pp. 184–85). In 1457, a Tournaisien orator told Charles VII's ambassadors that his fellow citizens were ready to 'abandonner leurs biens, femmes et enfans, et leur corps exposer à mort, et ameroient mieux estre tous mors et la ville estre en feu et destruite que avoir pensé de faire chose qui fut au contraire ... au roy' ('abandon their possessions, women and children, and expose their bodies to death, and they would prefer all to be dead and the town burned and destroyed rather than entertain thoughts of doing anything against the king') (RC 1455–72, p. 311).

104] Verreist, *Les Luttes sociales*, pp. 19–20.

105] This stands in contrast to some of the fourteenth-century evidence which reveals that Tournaisien weavers sympathised with their Flemish counterparts who resisted royal expansion. Following the battle of Courtrai in 1302, a series of 'manifestations anti-françaises' ('anti-French protests') involving the drapery guilds had to be suppressed by the Tournaisien aldermen (ibid. pp. 11–13). After the French victory at Roosebeke in 1382, some Tournaisiens turned against the victors and liberated Flemish captives and property – an act which led Charles VI to impose the *composition* of 1383 and create the *bailliage* of Tournai-Tournaisis mentioned above (Hocquet, *Croniques*, pp. 253–54). By contrast, as this last source shows, Tournaisien groups in power supported the monarchy. One of their number, Olivier le Maire, captured a Flemish coat of mail and proudly left it in his will to a nephew (A. de la Grange, *Choix de testaments tournaisiens antérieurs au XVIe siècle*, *ASRHAT*, nouv. sér., Vol. II, 1897, p. 118). Similar sympathies were to emerge in 1452, as we shall see below.

106] Houtart, *Les Tournaisiens*, pp. 216 and n. 1, 405 n. 1

107] Ibid., p. 430 n. 3. See also RC 1422–30, pp. 334–35.

108] Before the 'democratic revolution' erupted in 1423, two royal ambassadors reported that they had been insulted in the streets for bearing the dauphin's arms. Three years later, members of a Tournaisien contingent which had participated in the campaigns of John IV,

Popular taunting of the duke and his supporters was, by contrast, a dangerous sport at which some Tournaisiens excelled.[109] It is important to note that elements in municipal government which had developed affinities with the Burgundian elite, or which were suspected of having done so, also affirmed their loyalty to the monarchy. The exiles in Oudenaarde who attempted to oust the guilds in 1426 took as their rallying cry 'Vive le roi, bourgeoisie et marchandise!' ('Long live the king, the bourgeoisie and commerce!').[110] Marc Villain, one of the aldermen exonerated of the charge of plotting to sell the city to John the Fearless in 1416, left provision in his will for weekly masses 'afin que Dieu, par sa grâce, veuille tenir la bonne ville de Tournai toujours en bonne et seule obéissance de la noble couronne de France' ('so that God, by His grace, may keep the city of Tournai loyal and obedient to the noble crown of France').[111] There was no fundamental paradox in such expressions of loyalty. For the bulk of our period, the alternative to royal rule supposedly envisaged by such men was government by princes who, even when they did not perform homage for the lands they held of the monarch, still recognised the French king as their sovereign. Witness, for example, the enthusiasm with which 'bons et loyaux français' ('good and loyal Frenchmen') at the Burgundian court followed the victories of Charles VII over the English in the early 1450s.[112] The Tournaisien authorities celebrated the same events in 1455 by hosting a shooting match for contingents from towns of the Burgundian dominions accompanied by a competition of dramatic work written and performed by rhetoricians. Tournaisien theatre groups were not permitted

Duke of Brabant against the English in Hainault were punished for crying 'Vive Bourgogne!' ('Up with Burgundy!') and bearing the cross of St Andrew in the streets upon their return to the city (RC 1422–30, pp. 28, 171). The authorities imprisoned a certain Jean Gobinet in January 1426 for 'propos tenus contre la personne du roi' ('for having spoken against the person of the king') (ibid., p. 190).

109] Charles the Bold was the particular victim of Tournaisien critics. In April 1466, the *Consaux* banned seditious songs about any prince, and in September the ban was repeated on songs mocking Burgundian troops returning from the attack on Liège. Charles subsequently refused to order his troops to cease despoiling the Tournaisis 'à cause des injures proférées contre lui par plusieurs de la ville' ('because of the insults hurled against him by many from the town'). In July 1476, the authorities had to ban plays and songs concerning the Burgundian defeat at Murten (RC 1431–76, pp. 287–88, 291, 360; RC 1455–72, p. 325).

110] Houtart, *Les Tournaisiens*, p. 357.

111] Ibid., p. 32. Another striking example was to be found not far from Villain's tomb of 1425 in the same church of Saint-Piat, where Jean de Crespin was laid to rest just six years later. Crespin's son Jacquet had been killed at Agincourt. The father made provision in his will for 'un obit annuel pour les ames des vrais et loyaulx français qui pour soutenir l'honneur de la couronne de France demoureremt en la bataille qui se fit contre les Anglois' ('an annual service for the souls of the true and loyal French who, to maintain the honour of the crown of France, died in the battle fought against the English') (University of Ghent, Fond Van den Bemden, ms G 18214, fol. 41. I am grateful to Dr Ludovic Nys for the reference and astute comments on related points.)

112] G. Small, *George Chastelain and the Shaping of Valois Burgundy*, Woodbridge, 1997, pp. 59–60.

to compete for any prize in this last event, but the theme set for writers and players from the ducal towns was none the less triumphantly royalist: '[Les] haulx, miraculeux et victorieux fais des rois de France, et espécialment de ceulx qui estoient advenus en la réacquisition de Normendie, de Bourdelois et de Baionne' ('the great, miraculous and victorious deeds of the kings of France, and especially those that came to pass in the reacquisition of Normandy, the Bordelais and Bayonne').[113] In a frontier zone where loyalties often differed in hue rather than colour, Tournaisiens were able to revel in the unadulterated quality of their fidelity to the king of France: 'le roy, mon seul seigneur sur la terre' (the king, my only lord on earth'), as a local chronicler put it.[114] Ideas and sentiments which the centre would have wished to see prevail throughout the realm were often strongest on the periphery.[115] In this respect, Tournai was no more exceptional than many other towns on the frontiers of the kingdom.

Some towns (such as Épinal, Millau, Villefranche and Villeneuve in Rouergue) ceded by the crown to a local prince, rebelled against their fate.[116] Following Aylmer once again, the change of ruler risked fulfilling the 'worst-case scenario' which such communities naturally feared: 'to live under an oppressive local lord and to lack any alternative access to higher authority'.[117] The actions of successive regimes in Tournai contained a strong element of *realpolitik*. The advantages accrued came at a cost, above all the substantial payments linked to the treaties with the dukes. But how great was the cost? The treaties are frequently seen as a major factor in Tournai's economic decline in the fifteenth century; the Tournaisien authorities themselves cited the 'innumérables finances' ('enormous sums') spent on the treaties as the cause of municipal impecunity.[118] But we should beware of special pleading, and many other factors also had a bearing on Tournai's fortunes. Moreover, the question of how much the city actually paid, as well as how these sums were raised, deserves closer attention. According to Paul Rolland, the total cost of the treaties from 1424 to 1440 amounted to 'sept millions de francs d'or' ('seven million gold francs').[119] It

113] F. de Reiffenberg, 'La Fête de l'arbalète et du Prince d'Amour à Tournay, en 1455', *BCRH*, Vol. X, 1845, p. 260. Tournai is one of the few cities known to have celebrated the feast day established by Charles VII in honour of the reconquest of Normandy (C. Beaune, *Naissance de la nation France*, Paris, 1985, p. 186; idem, *The Birth of an Ideology. Myths and Symbols of Nation in Late Medieval France*, Berkeley, 1991, p. 150 and n. 74).
114] Nicolay, *Kalendrier*, p. 1.
115] C. Gauvard, 'L'Opinion publique aux confins des états et des principautés au début du XVe siècle', in *Actes du IVe colloque de la Société des historiens médiévistes de l'enseignement supérieur public (Bordeaux 1973)*, Bordeaux, 1979, pp. 127–52. This article contains much interesting material on Tournai from registers of the *Parlement* of Paris.
116] Sée, *Louis XI et les villes*, pp. 184–87.
117] Aylmer, 'Centre and Locality', p. 66.
118] G. Wymans, 'Le Déclin de Tournai au XVe siècle', *APAE*, Vol. XXII, 1961, 113–34; RC 1422–30, p. 381; RC 1431–76, pp. 114, 183.
119] Rolland, *Histoire de Tournai*, p. 161, accepted by Wymans, 'Le Déclin', p. 128.

is impossible to verify Tournaisien sources used to establish this figure. A calculation of the sums received by Philip the Good from 1430 to 1435 – nearly one-third of the period in question, at a time when the annual payments were at their highest level – suggests Rolland's estimation is several times greater than the total that actually changed hands.[120] The Tournaisien authorities were able, as we have seen, to limit their financial obligations to the king for the duration of the treaties. They also succeeded in spreading the cost of the payments between the city, the communities of the *bailliage* of Tournai-Tournaisis and, despite the protests which ensued, the cathedral chapter and the local abbeys of Saint-Martin, Saint-Nicholas and Saint-Amand.[121]

If we should not overestimate the cost of the treaties, nor should we underestimate their value. Our understanding of the 'état bourguignon' (Burgundian state) as a fiscally intrusive, determined and effective opponent of urban particularism has emerged enhanced from a number of recent studies. In Dijon, the powers of the municipal government were suspended on at least fifteen occasions in the fourteenth century. In 1386 the city failed in its attempts to prevent ducal officers from auditing the municipality's accounts. Such direct ducal interventions ceased in the following century, but municipal autonomy was nonetheless restricted since many *Dijonnais* who made a career in ducal service also occupied key posts in the city.[122] Much closer to Tournai, and therefore more likely to have served as a point of comparison for its inhabitants, was Lille. Here was a city – according to Denis Clauzel – whose coffers and privileges were greatly depleted through prolonged contact with the Burgundian regime, partly through high taxation, partly by the presence of several key ducal officers and organs of government.[123] Downstream from Tournai, Ghent provided further

120] Philip received over 100 000 *saluts* in this period (Vaughan, *Philip the Good*, p. 19). According to the *registres des Consaux* (cited conveniently in Paviot, 'Tournai', pp. 76–77), the annual sum agreed in 1424 was 2000 *écus*. This rose to 4700 *couronnes* in 1425, 7000 *écus* in 1426 and 15 000 *écus* in 1427. In 1428, the treaty was renewed for six years for a total of 73 500 *couronnes*. A similar arrangement was reached for the following six years, to 1440, for a total of 65 000 *saluts*. Even accounting for additional payments made to Jean de Luxembourg, Rolland's estimation is far greater.

121] Philip the Good tried unsuccessfully to prevent Tournai from forcing the chapter to contribute. The municipal authorities obtained royal letters in their favour. The city also defaulted on the 'cense perpétuelle' (tax payable in perpetuity) it was required to pay to the chapter, much to the latter's irritation. Tournaisiens who held fiefs in the Burgundian dominions were the most difficult group to pin down as they could easily absent themselves and avoid payment, but the municipal authorities had some success here too (RC 1422–30, pp. 200–03, 212, 237, 242–43, 247, 248, 256, 271, 272–73, 306–07, 378–79).

122] T. Dutour, 'Les Relations de Dijon et du duc de Bourgogne au XIVe siècle', *PCEEB*, Vol. XXXIII, 1993, pp. 5–19; A. Leguai, 'Les Ducs Valois et les villes du duché de Bourgogne', ibid., pp. 21–33.

123] D. Clauzel, *Finances et politique à Lille pendant la période bourguignonne*, Dunkirk, 1982; A. Derville, 'La Fiscalité d'état dans l'Artois et la Flandre wallonne avant 1569', *RN*, Vol. LXXIV, 1992, pp. 25–52; D. Clauzel, 'Le Roi, le prince et la ville: l'enjeu des réformes financières à Lille à la fin du Moyen Âge', *PCEEB*, Vol. XXXIII, 1993, pp. 75–90.

salutary lessons. No city in the Low Countries set such store by its political autonomy.[124] For a time, the dukes made allowances and reached a *modus vivendi* with the regime of the Three Members. From 1435 onwards, however, the fiscal noose tightened. Philip the Good's unsuccessful efforts to impose a *gabelle* in 1447 culminated in the devastating war of 1452–53. In the course of a bitter conflict which left Ghent with diminished privileges and a heavy burden of debt, the civic authorities tried and failed to encourage French royal intervention in their favour.[125] Even a city like Ghent was vulnerable when left to confront princely power alone.

Whatever the sentiments and related local circumstances which lay at the root of Tournai's adhesion to the monarchy, there were clearly other strong incentives, despite the cost, to keep the duke at arm's length. Over the long term, Tournai's policy brought one further set of advantages which should not be overlooked. On the frontiers of the kingdom, as successive kings knew well, loyalty could not simply be counted in coins. In cities like Tournai 'obéir au roi d'une part, payer l'impôt d'autre part, sont encore deux impératifs étrangers l'un à l'autre' ('obedience to the king on the one hand and the payment of taxes on the other were two imperatives which still remained quite separate').[126] Royal taxation could be onerous in fifteenth-century France, and every town tried to avoid the full weight of the king's demands so far as it could.[127] On the periphery, the tactics of delay, bargaining or outright refusal were more successful. Outside the periods governed by the treaties, Tournai remained remarkably adept at limiting its contributions to the monarchy. Between the Treaty of Arras in 1435 and the accession of Louis XI in 1461, we know of twelve demands for financial contributions to the king's wars considered by the *Consaux*. In one case the full sum was accorded, an *aide* of 10 000 *l.t.* towards the cost of the recovery of Bordeaux in 1453. This was the greatest royal achievement in living memory. Rejection or negotiation may have seemed indefensible.[128] The *Consaux* accorded grants of 2000 *l.t.* for the ransom of Charles of Orléans in 1440 and the supplying of Dieppe in 1443, although in each case the award was only made after an initial

124] M. Boone and W. Prevenier, 'The "City-State" Dream', in *Ghent: In Defence of a Rebellious City*, ed. J. Decavele, Antwerp, 1989, pp. 81–105; M. Boone, *Gent en de Bourgondische hertogen, ca. 1384–ca. 1453: een sociaal-politieke studie van een staatsvormingsproces*, Brussels, 1990.

125] M. Boone, 'Diplomatie et violence d'état: la sentence rendue par les ambassadeurs et conseillers du roi de France, Charles VII, concernant le conflit entre Philippe le Bon, duc de Bourgogne, et Gand en 1452', *BCRH*, Vol. CLVI, 1990, pp. 1–54.

126] Gauvard, 'L'Opinion publique', p. 28.

127] Cf. D. Angers, 'Le Redressement difficile d'une capitale régionale après la guerre de cent ans: Caen, 1450–1550', in *Commerce, finances et société*, pp. 188–89; M. Le Mené, 'Ville et fiscalité à la fin du Moyen Âge: l'exemple d'Angers', in *Villes, bonnes villes, cités et capitales*, pp. 89–104; Chevalier, *La Ville de Tours*, Vol. I, p. 143.

128] RC 1431–76, p. 202. The *Consaux* did manage to avoid giving any money to Charles VII after his coronation, however, much to the fury of the king's ambassadors (RC 1422–30, pp. 343–61).

refusal and the grant amounted to a fraction of the total requested.[129] Tournai responded to three other demands with the award of a paltry sum or gift, and in the remaining six cases the *Consaux* declined to give the king or his envoys any money at all.[130] During the same period, Tournai was asked on four occasions to provide crossbowmen for the king's armies. Only once was a contingent provided.[131] Alongside this evidence we should set the concessions which the king granted to Tournai in view of its particular circumstances. These included exemption from the *imposition foraine* traditionally levied on goods sold outside the kingdom and the suppression of the *droit d'aubaine* which discouraged foreigners from settling in France.[132] It is easy to see why, in the words of one royal *ordonnance*, it appeared to the centre that Tournai was 'pourveu de plusieurs beaux droiz ... privileges et libertez, plus largement que nulle autre ville de nostre royaume' ('provided with many precious rights, privileges and liberties, more than any other town in the kingdom'). Under royal protection the city maintained access to Flemish markets, preserved relative independence from the Burgundian dukes, and was privileged by its distant rulers.

Before our period, when Tournai was not surrounded by the Burgundian dominions, royal interventions could put an end to demands or dissent on the periphery. Both Philip VI and Charles V suspended the commune and established direct royal rule over the city. Earlier, in 1325, a conflict with Charles IV had threatened the same outcome.[133] It was difficult for later kings to act so

129] RC 1431–76, pp. 85–86, 99–100.

130] Ibid., pp. 49–50 (1437), 56 (1438), 65 (1439), 78 (1440), 113–17 (1444), 123 (1446), 139 (1449), 153–54 (1451). For two further cases, see du Fresne de Beaucourt, *Histoire de Charles VII*, Vol. V, p. 335.

131] RC 1431–76, pp. 30 (siege of Dieppe, 1435); 32–33 (siege of Calais, 1436); 33–34 (siege of Creil, 1436); 87–89, 374–76 (siege of Pontoise, 1441).

132] *Ordonnances*, Vol. VIII, pp. 487–91 (the quotation in the next sentence comes from this document); Vol. XVI, pp. 136–40. Exemption from the *imposition foraine* does not appear to have been constant after it was reinstated by the first of these documents in 1402 (see RC 1431–76, pp. 129, 131; *Ordonnances*, Vol. XIV, p. 40; Beaucourt, *Charles VII*, Vol. IV, p. 380). The value of the *droit d'aubaine* must be seen in relation to the cosmopolitan nature of Tournai's population, another common feature of frontier communities, particularly large ones (Menjot, 'La Ville frontière', p. 11). On Tournai as a city 'peuplée et habitée de gens de diverses nacions' ('inhabited and peopled by persons of many nations'), including a group of indolent Scots who had to be expelled in 1470, see Rolland, 'L'Exception communale', pp. 310, 313; *Ordonnances*, Vol. VII, pp. 20–24; RC 1431–76, p. 311. The evidence of one study indicates that immigrants often came from royal France (C. Dury, 'Topographie et structures sociales à Tournai en 1455–56', unpublished *Mémoire de Licence*, Catholic University of Louvain-la-Neuve, 1976, p. 153). The documents cited here suggest Tournai's attraction also extended to the north and further afield. Clearly, further study of the subject must be linked to the matter of political loyalties discussed above.

133] A. d'Herbomez, 'Notes et documents pour servir à l'histoire des rois fils de Philippe le Bel', *BEC*, Vol. LIX, 1898, pp. 520ff; idem, 'Les Constitutions de Tournai sous Philippe de Valois', *Nouvelle revue historique de droit français et étranger*, Vol. XXX, 1906, pp. 353–81, 453–76; Rolland, *Histoire de Tournai*, pp. 132ff.

directly, a point best illustrated in the unfolding events of a surprisingly neglected period of direct royal intervention in the middle of the fifteenth century.

In July 1452, Charles VII's ambassadors came to Tournai with a formidable range of powers, including permission to '[m]ettre en la main du Roy toute la loy, juridicion, recepte, revenus [et] gouvernment d'icelle' ('place in the king's hands the laws, jurisdiction, receipts, revenues and government of the city').[134] Even the *registres des Consaux* were closely inspected.[135] The main concern of the king's ambassadors was the appointment of a local commission with wide-ranging powers to reform Tournai's finances. Although these powers were directly comparable with those granted to the commission of 1428 to establish social peace in the city, they were now deemed to be against the king's 'seignourie et souveraineté, car il estoit seigneur naturel et direcq de cestedite ville' ('lordship and sovereignty, for he was the natural and direct lord of this town').[136] Another bone of contention was the fact that banners and a call to arms had been raised in Tournai during the Ghent war, ostensibly to protect the city from Burgundian troops assembling for the conflict. The ambassadors observed that '[c]'estoit chose périlleuse de se mettre en armes ... et appartenoit au Roy de savoir s'il estoit necessité ou non' ('it was a serious matter to take up arms, and it was for the king to decide whether it was necessary to do so'). A first consequence of the king's intervention was the arrest of the 'grand doien' (deacon) of Tournai and the confiscation of the guild banners in September 1452.[137] In June 1453, royal letters effected an important change in Tournai's constitution. Thenceforward, the consent of three of the four colleges of the *Consaux* would be sufficient to reach a decision. In the past, any proposal not unanimously approved could be presented to the wider community. By these means it became easier to limit the decision-taking process to groups in power and, at the same time, to bypass the college of the deacons who had risen to authority in 1423. The deacons were also the group most likely to turn to the wider populace for support.[138]

At first glance, Charles VII's intervention appears to be a striking assertion of central authority over local affairs. Tournai was confronted by a recently-victorious king at the height of his powers ('depuis Charlemaine, n'avoit heu Roy de France plus puissant de lui' ('since Charlemagne, no king of France had been more powerful than he'), as the royal ambassadors put it to the assembled *Consaux*).[139] From the perspective of the locality, however, it is clear the

134] RC 1431–76, p. 187.
135] Although this was only permitted in the hall where the volumes were kept because the civic authorities used them daily (ibid., p. 188).
136] For this matter and the next, see ibid. pp. 154–56, 179, 184–85.
137] For this sentence and the next, see ibid. pp. 189, 195, 196–97, 198–99.
138] Houtart's study clearly demonstrates the recourse of the deacons to popular support. In moments of crisis, the other three colleges of the *Consaux* tended to keep sensitive information from the populace.
139] Ibid., p. 181.

distribution of power between centre and periphery was much more evenly balanced. If Charles was disturbed at the creation of a commission with powers to effect radical change in the city's finances, his main concern in July 1452 was popular Tournaisien support for Ghent in the conflict with Philip the Good referred to above.[140] Ghent's direct appeal to the monarchy for assistance, now combined with Tournaisien sympathies for Ghent, risked jeopardising good relations between king and duke.[141] The deacons of the guilds were implicated in both the reform of civic finances and in the controversial raising of banners in Tournai.[142] Although they had strongly supported the monarch during the 1420s and had provided a counterbalance to patrician elements with suspected Burgundian sympathies during that period, the actions of the deacons now threatened local and regional stability. Hence Charles' measures against his former allies in September 1452. The king's position was further weakened in the following month by the revolt in the Bordelais. With stability in Tournai more important than ever, Charles took the additional step of ordering the constitutional reforms of June 1453 which marginalised the deacons. As the king set about reducing Gascony to his obedience, the protests of the deacons of Tournai fell on stony ground. A veritable purge orchestrated by the *Consaux* soon followed. Several lesser guildsmen were banished, and among those executed were Bertrand de le Cambe, 'grant doien' , Jehan Carvin, 'grand soubz-doien' ('chief sub-deacon'), and Jehan du Sollier, 'doien des foullons' ('deacon of the fullers' guild').[143]

The king had his own reasons for reducing the political influence of a group once known as his strongest supporters in Tournai. His intervention did not guarantee the automatic compliance of those who now controlled the city. A dispute over the extent of the jurisdiction of royal officers and the nature of municipal privileges led Charles VII to place a number of restrictions on Tournai, and to threaten the suspension of the commune in February 1456.[144] In July,

140] Vaughan, *Philip the Good*, p. 325. Military preparations in Tournai in April 1452 may have been interpreted by the duke as hostile rather than defensive, as is suggested by the trade embargo placed on the town later that month or early in May and the report that he was 'indignés [sic] sur ceulx de la ville' ('angry with the people of the town') (RC 1431–76, pp. 172–77).

141] The ambassadors sent to negotiate a peace between Philip the Good and Ghent were also charged with carrying out the king's wishes in Tournai (Boone, 'Diplomatie et violence d'état', pp. 24–26).

142] An appeal against the suspension of the commission to reform the city's finances in December 1451 was supported by the deacons but not the other colleges of the *Consaux* (RC 1431–76, pp. 168–69). The guilds brought their banners forth to serve as a rallying point for the population during the military preparations of April 1452 (ibid., pp. 175–76).

143] de Smet, *Chronique*, pp. 523–25.

144] The dispute dated back to 1452 when the king pronounced on the jurisdiction and privileges of Tournai, as he did again in 1455. In September of this last year, Tournai was asked to justify some of the privileges contested by local royal officers (*Ordonnances*, Vol. XIV, p. 373; RC 1431–76, p. 215). The municipal authorities were the subject of 'charges diffamatoires, injures et blasphèmes' ('slanderous, insulting and blasphemous

however, the political situation changed dramatically with the unexpected flight of the dauphin Louis to the Low Countries. Franco-Burgundian tension increased and had almost reached the point of open warfare by Charles VII's death in 1461. Tournai's loyalty was once again of critical importance to the king. Once more the centre's grip relaxed. A royal ambassador to Tournai in September 1456 praised the citizens on Charles' behalf, 'entre ses autres loyaulx subgés les plus singuliers de son temps' ('among his other loyal subjects, the most exceptional').[145] The *Consaux* commended the city to the king's good grace and raised the matter of the limits placed recently on their privileges, a request they resolved to pursue in February 1457. By November, a high-level royal commission was in Tournai to enquire into the matter, and in March 1458 the city's privileges were restored.[146] The next royal ambassador to visit the city was Richard Olivier, Bishop of Coutances, early in 1460. His instructions from the king were simple: to 'visiter et veoir les bonnes gens' ('visit his good people') of Tournai and to ask if they had any grievances they wanted the king to resolve.[147] The change of tone could hardly be clearer.

The most significant royal intervention in Tournai in the fifteenth century serves as a reminder that if the centre wished to exercise meaningful control and effect change on the periphery, it would have to choose its moment well. Royal pressure which seemed excessive in the locality could produce an equal and opposite reaction. In his letter to Tournai in 1452, the king had taken particular exception to 'aucuns langaiges' ('certain complaints') uttered in the city to the effect that 'le Roy n'estoit que gardien de la ville et non point seigneur souverain' ('the king was only guardian of the town, not its sovereign lord'). This was 'lèze-maiesté ou prumier degré' ('treason in the first degree') from the centre's perspective. Given the broader context of Tournai's circumstances and the immediate dispute with the king's men, it is possible to understand how such thoughts could occur on the periphery.[148] In royal charters written when relations were less strained, Charles had himself emphasised how the Tournaisiens had submitted 'de leur volenté à nostredite seigneurie' ('of their own volition to our rule'), and how, before that, 'se gouvernèrent de eulx mesmes sans congnoissance de quelque souverain' ('they had governed themselves without recognising any superior

accusations') uttered by the local *bailli* in a session of the king's council in January 1456 (RC 1455–72, p. 308). It was early in the following month that the king threatened to suspend the commune and restricted its privileges (*Ordonnances*, Vol. XIV, pp. 371–75).

145] RC 1455–72, pp. 309–10.

146] For the embassy, see ibid. p. 311; RC 1431–76, pp. 244–45; *Ordonnances*, Vol. XIV, p. 451; Beaucourt, *Charles VII*, Vol. VI, pp. 148–49, 380. On the restoration of privileges, see RC 1431–76, pp. 245, 376–77. It was briefly feared that the *procureur-général* would oppose confirmation of this last document (RC 1455–72, p. 311).

147] Ibid., p. 312; RC 1431–76, pp. 249, 377–79; Beaucourt, *Charles VII*, Vol. VI, pp. 271–72.

148] RC 1431–76, p. 181.

lord').[149] From here it was but a short step to the view expressed by a representative of Tournai in a case before the *Parlement* in 1456 that the *Consaux* 'sont seigneurs de ladicte ville' ('are lords of the said town') beneath the king. It was the king's responsibility to maintain them in this position, 'ou sinon nous [Charles VII] pourrions perdre nostre souveraineté et seigneurie directe' ('or we [Charles VII] could lose our sovereignty and direct lordship over them').[150] This extreme view suggests that Tournaisien groups in power had come to believe in a relationship of mutual obligation. The king as sovereign enjoyed his subjects' loyalty and he guaranteed their privileges, while the city governors ruled Tournai on his behalf. The concept of the geographical decentralisation of royal power had taken root early on this periphery.[151] A sudden switch from established norms of political behaviour could provoke a contretemps, or worse.

For much of our period, the relationship between centre and periphery functioned much as the *Consaux* appear to have understood it. Like some other towns in Artois and Picardy, Tournai exercised 'justice haute, moyenne et basse' ('high, middle and low justice') beneath the *Parlement* once the authorities had secured exemption from the jurisdiction of the *bailli* in 1389.[152] Municipal pride was identified with the royal function: the Tournaisien envoys who obtained the concession considered they had acquired the equivalent of 'loy d'empereur, considéré que le Roy nostre sire est empereur en son Royaume' ('sovereign rule, considering that our lord the king is emperor in his kingdom').[153] The mint in Tournai produced royal coin and responded to orders from the centre, but the *Consaux* also took a hand in fixing the value of coinage, in disposing of the profits of the mint, in deciding the periods of production and in appointing and dismissing the personnel.[154] A royal institution was thus effectively subject to a very large measure of local control.[155] The civic militia of Tournai was a royal

149] *Ordonnances*, Vol. XIII, pp. 18–20, (1423); Rolland, 'L'Exception communale', p. 302 n. 27. Other instances, including a rejection of this argument by a royal procurator in the *Parlement* in 1411 on the grounds that Tournai had submitted to King Pharamond, can be found in Gauvard, 'L'Opinion publique', pp. 10–11.

150] *Ordonnances*, Vol. XIV, pp. 371ff.

151] B. Guenée, 'Espace et état en France au Moyen Âge', *Annales ESC*, Vol. XXIII, 1968, pp. 744–58, repr. in idem, *Politique et histoire au Moyen Âge*).

152] Except for crimes reserved for royal justice, such as the bearing of arms, *lèse-majesté*, banishment from the realm or coining (G. Testaud, *Des juridictions municipales en France (des origines jusqu'à l'Ordonnance de Moulins, 1566)*, Paris, 1901, pp. 7–9).

153] Allard, 'Le Premier bailliage', p. 19. The Tournaisiens also referred to this political concept in 1398: RC 1385–1422, p. 45; cf. Davies, 'Tournai and the English Crown', p. 2.

154] RC 1385–1422, pp. 20, 170–71, 180, 193–95, 196, 219–20; RC 1422–30, pp. 27–30, 65, 76, 139, 228, 252, 297, 306, 350, 383–84; RC 1431–76, pp. 4, 15, 19, 30–31, 116.

155] For further pertinent comment, see G. Preud'homme, 'La Ville de Tournai eut-elle une politique monétaire autonome au XVe siècle?', in *XLVe Congrès de la Fédération des cercles d'archéologie et d'histoire de Belgique. Congrès de Comines. Actes*, Comines, 1980, Vol. I, pp. 197–98; P. Spufford, *Monetary Problems and Policies in the Burgundian Netherlands, 1433–96*, Leiden, 1970, pp. 89–95; M. Hoc, *Histoire monétaire de Tournai*, Brussels, 1970, pp. 70–120.

institution since – as both Charles VI and Charles VII affirmed – its members had the honour of serving as the king's personal bodyguard on campaign and were to be considered 'domestiques de l'ostel ... soubz le grant maistre d'hostel et son estendart' ('servants of the household ... under the grand master of the household and his banner').[156] The privileges of Tournai were a royal institution and were even to be protected against wayward royal officers or dubious decisions emanating from the centre.[157] An unfortunate royal sergeant from Lille discovered this to his cost when he went to Tournai to take a suspect to Paris for trial. Believing the arrest to be against the privileges of the city 'que les Roy[s] nous ont donné, dont Dieu en ait les âmes' ('given us by kings whose souls we pray God to keep'), a mob of angry Tournaisiens beat the unfortunate sergeant to within an inch of his life. The *Consaux* stated that they had been instructed by the king to release the prisoner, but, they assured the mob, 'vous avez bien fait de ce que vous ne l'avez point souffert' ('you did well not to allow it'). The city of Tournai kept the king's peace, another royal institution and an ancient function of the *bonne ville*.[158] Last, but not least, the coat of arms of Tournai was itself a pure royal symbol. In 1429 the *Consaux* objected to efforts to include three golden *fleurs de lys*, with royal consent, on their arms and seal. This was not 'honnourable pour la ville' ('honourable for the town'); the existing coat of arms was the clearest sign that Tournai 'a esté tousjours francement tenue et gardée entière ens et soubz la subgection et seulle obéissance des roys de France' ('has always been freely held and loyally maintained under the rule and in the obedience of the kings of France').[159]

The bond between royal centre and Tournaisien periphery was thus grounded in the guarantee of loyalty and the respect of privilege. To invert Philippe de Beaumanoir's famous comment on how rulers should treat their towns, this was a grown-up relationship which accepted responsibilities on both sides.[160] It was also a relationship which strongly resembled those described by Bernard Chevalier in his analysis of 'le roi et ses bonnes villes au temps de leur accord parfait' ('the king and his *bonnes villes* at the time of their perfect entente'): the period he situates between 1450 and 1550 when 'les villes et l'État

156] E. Jopken, 'L'Organisation militaire de la commune de Tournai', in *Fédération archéologique et historique de Belgique. Compte-rendu des travaux du Xe Congrès tenu à Tournai du 5 au 8 août 1895*, ed. E. Soil de Moriamé, Tournai, 1896, pp. 551–70; Houtart, 'Le Patriotisme', p. 85.

157] For what follows, including the quotation, see de Smet, *Chronique*, pp. 236–37; Hocquet, *Croniques*, pp. 153–55.

158] Cf. B. Chevalier, 'La Politique de Louis XI à l'égard des bonnes villes: le cas de Tours', *MA*, Vol. LXX, 1964, pp. 482–83.

159] RC 1422–30, p. 328. See also A. de la Grange, 'Les Vraies armes de la ville de Tournai', *ASRHAT*, New Series, Vol. III, 1898, pp. 107–34.

160] Towns should be treated 'aussi comme on feroit à l'enfant sous aagié' ('as one would an under-age child') *Les Coustumes du Beauvoisis par Philippe de Beaumanoir*, ed. A. A. Beugnot, 2 vols, SHF, Paris, 1842, Vol. II, p. 268.

coopérent de loin, sans se rencontrer souvent' ('the towns and the State cooperated at a distance without maintaining too close contact'), when 'l'État respecte parfaitement l'autonomie des bonnes villes tandis que celles-ci font preuve à son égard d'une loyauté à toute épreuve sans chercher en rien à en contrôler son action propre' ('the State acknowledges the autonomy of towns while in return the latter demonstrate a high degree of loyalty without trying to oppose its powers in any way'); a period, finally, when 'ce n'est plus l'État qui intervient dans les affaires de la ville, mais sa puissance qui est mise au service du pouvoir local' ('it is not so much that the State intervenes in urban affairs, but rather that its power is placed at the disposal of the local authority').[161] Tournai emerges from this discussion, not as an 'exception communale' ('exception among communes') but rather a *bonne ville* which, through its particular circumstances, developed an understanding with the monarchy that would later become more widespread in later medieval France. The neglected case of this great French city serves as a reminder that understanding the periphery is central to understanding the wider polity.

161] B. Chevalier, 'L'État et les bonnes villes en France au temps de leur accord parfait, 1450–1550)', in *La Ville, la bourgeoisie et la genèse de l'état moderne, XIIe–XVIIIe siècles)*, ed. N. Bulst and J.-P. Genet, Paris, 1988, pp. 72, 82.

10

'Decayed Feudalism' and 'Royal Clienteles': Royal Office and Magnate Service in the Fifteenth Century[1]

GARETH PROSSER

'The patrons of later medieval France', wrote Peter Lewis in 1964, 'had no less need of service, support and following [than their English counterparts]; but their attitude to the problem has not received analysis.' Thus he opened a trail into this quintessential political problem of the period, now familiar to all historians of late medieval France.[2] Much more recently, he has hailed the accumulation of evidence that royal government was infused with clientage, a system which articulated and energised the crown's formal structures, and ensured that the dynamic of politics often came from below. His 'Reflections on the Role of Royal Clientèles' will become as familiar as its predecessor to students of the period.[3]

The indifference to these issues in French historiography of the fifteenth century is attributable to the *Annales* school. In repudiating the clash between Republican nationalism and authoritarian traditionalism, the *annalistes* recast the debate about national identity through a polemical silence over state construction and territorial aggregation. Ironically, this silence permitted the state to retain its centrality in the historiography. *Annaliste* methodologies have canalised political history towards institutional, ideological and prosopographical studies, as a glance at the programmes of recent CNRS colloquia shows.[4]

1] Short versions of this chapter were delivered as papers at the Anglo-French colloquium at the University of York in April 1997, and at the Institute of Historical Research, University of London, in February 1998. I am grateful to Cheryl Aldridge for her support in its writing.

2] P. S. Lewis, 'Decayed and Non-Feudalism in Later Medieval France', *BIHR*, Vol. XXXVII, 1964, pp. 157–84, repr. in idem, *Essays in Later Medieval French History*, London, 1985, pp. 41–68.

3] P. S. Lewis, 'Reflections on the Role of Royal Clientèles in the Construction of the French Monarchy (Mid-XIVth/End XVth Centuries)', in *L'Etat ou le roi. Les fondations de la modernité monarchique en France (XIVe–XVIIe siècle)*, ed. N. Bulst, R. Descimon and A. Guerreau, Paris, 1996, pp. 51–67.

4] See the bibliography of the work of the 'Action thématique programmée' organised by the Centre National de la Recherche Scientifique on the 'Genèse de l'Etat Moderne' in *L'Etat moderne: Genèse. Bilans et perspectives*, ed. J.-P. Genet, Paris, 1990, pp. 308–50.

This would be more appropriate if the consensus on the political narrative was based on more than shared ignorance. Sadly, our understanding of fifteenth-century politics remains erratic.

Take, for instance, the Armagnac-Burgundian wars, the most serious period of French political and social dissolution between the 1350s and the 1560s. We still have no proper understanding of the nature of the Armagnac cause, its constituency, regional and social; its ideological and institutional underpinnings; its survival into the 1420s, or its convergence with royal Valois politics.[5] 'Burgundianism' has responded better to the Parisian bias in the historiography, but large gaps remain. Françoise Autrand's view that it had no legacy is implausible, but the research remains to be done. Less titanic upheavals, such as the Praguerie of 1440, the *Bien Public* of 1465, and the *Guerre Folle* of the 1480s, all await their historians. Our knowledge of the royal household is in its infancy, and the charge is being led by *seizièmistes* rather than medievalists.[6] The Valois princely houses lack modern monographs, and the most important – Burgundy and Anjou, but also Orléans and Alençon – have always been severely understudied. There is still no detailed study of the reign of Louis XI, and the research that would permit one has yet to gather momentum.

Against such a background, it is hardly surprising that current debates over patronage, clientage and affinity have not extended to the French fifteenth century. Yet a revival of interest in the late medieval French nobility is under way: in 1994, Marie-Therèse Caron argued that the nobility were at the heart of a newly developing problematic of the 'state'.[7] She had contributed substantially to this with her monograph on the Burgundian nobility,[8] while Michel Nassiet would subject the Breton petty nobility to intense analysis.[9] Philippe Contamine's excellent book on the French *noblesse* summarises a large body of research and local studies.[10] None the less, the perspective remains relentlessly *annaliste*: the political behaviour of French magnates and their followers remains a minority – and largely anglophone – interest.

5] 'Le "parti" armagnac est le plus mal connu des historiens et sans doute le plus insaisissable' (F. Autrand, *Les Armagnacs et les bourguignons*, Paris, 1986, pp. 458ff). Henneman's speculations about the continuities between the 'Western' aristocratic/officer coalition described by Cazelles, the Marmousets, the household of Louis d'Orléans and the Armagnacs remain to be confirmed, but this sketch of a political genealogy offers a useful starting hypothesis (J. B. Henneman, *Olivier de Clisson and Political Society in France under Charles V and Charles VI*, Philadelphia, 1996).

6] For a recent original contribution and summary of research, see D. Potter, *A History of France 1460–1560. The Emergence of a Nation State*, London and Basingstoke, 1995, pp. 57–89.

7] M.-T. Caron, *Noblesse et pouvoir en France, XIIIe–XVIe siècle*, Paris, 1994, p. 11.

8] M.-T. Caron, *La Noblesse dans le Duché de Bourgogne, 1315–1477*, Lille, 1987.

9] M. Nassiet, *Noblesse et pauvreté. La petite noblesse en Bretagne, XVe–XVIIIe siècles*, Rennes, 1993.

10] P. Contamine, *La Noblesse au royaume de France de Philippe le Bel à Louis XII. Essai de synthèse*, Paris, 1997.

Exceptions can be cited, of course. The 1986 CNRS round table, *L'Etat et les aristocraties*, held in Oxford, was one.[11] Pierre Charbonnier has discussed the entourage of Guillaume de Murol in terms of clientage, *familiarité* and *fidelité*.[12] Michel Harsgor and Werner Paravicini continue to make their contributions. Twenty years ago, Paravicini urged a Weberian focus on the processes of professionalisation which displaced the prince from the centre of his state. His concluding remarks sounded a note of doubt, however, for among the various impediments to the 'rationalité et collégialité au sein des institutions' he gave pride of place to the countervailing force of patronage.[13] Institutional studies, recently exemplified in a long-overdue collection of papers on the *Chambre des Comptes*, continue to appear, but without reference to the clientage models that figure in comparable studies for later periods.[14] Even more strikingly, the English debate on bastard feudalism, now over fifty years old, has no French analogue. K. B. McFarlane has not crossed the Channel.

'Decayed and Non-Feudalism' was the bridge he might have taken. Peter Lewis argued that in France, the degradation of the feudal tie had proceeded from fee assigned on land to *fief-rente*, rather than directly to a non-feudal indentured contract on the model proposed by McFarlane. But when homage disappeared from the terms of such a *fief-rente*, the residual feudal element quietly evaporated, 'a final, insignificant fracture'.[15] These views were echoed by the late J. Russell Major. He summarised the key relationships through which the late medieval and renaissance nobility was articulated. He partnered the English indenture with the French *lettre de retenue* as an instrument of retaining for life, one of the most important vertical ties holding the aristocracy together. He tracked its development from the *fief-rente*, defeudalising into the homage-less pension, and found in this nexus the origins of the patron-client relationship.[16]

11] *L'Etat et les aristocraties, XIIe–XVIIe siècle (France, Angleterre, Ecosse)*, ed. P. Contamine, Paris, 1989, especially the chapters by M.-T. Caron and M. Jones.

12] P. Charbonnier, *Guillaume de Murol. Un petit seigneur auvergnat au début du XVe siècle*, Clermont-Ferrand, 1973. For an exception to prove the rule, see his study of Auvergnat rural lordship covering everything from changing modes of vassalage to dry-stone walling (Charbonnier, *Une autre France: la seigneurie rurale en Basse Auvergne du XIVe au XVIe siècle*, Clermont-Ferrand, 1980, pp. 547–84).

13] W. Paravicini, 'Administrateurs professionels et princes dilettantes: remarques sur un problème de sociologie administrative à la fin du moyen âge', *Histoire comparée de l'administration (IVe–XVIIIe siècles)*, ed. W. Paravicini and K. F. Werner, Munich, 1980, pp. 168–77.

14] *La France des principautés: les Chambres des Comptes. XIVe et XVe siècles. Colloque tenu aux Archives départementales de l'Allier, à Moulins-Yzeure, les 6, 7 et 8 avril 1995*, ed. P. Contamine and O. Mattéoni, Paris 1996.

15] Lewis, 'Decayed and Non-Feudalism', p. 160, repr. in idem, *Essays in Later Medieval French History*, p. 44. Compare 'Une particularité des institutions féodales auvergnates est en effet la distinction entre l'hommage et la fidelité ...' (Charbonnier, *Une autre France*, p. 407).

16] J. Russell Major, *From Renaissance Monarchy to Absolute Monarchy: French Kings, Nobles and Estates*, Baltimore and London, 1994, pp. 61–75.

This is an advance on the statist account of the transformation from a feudal France to a 'France des fidelités' which, following Roland Mousnier, was created by Michel Harsgor. Harsgor posited the emergence of *fidelité personnelle* from vassalage from the fourteenth century, but it was the Hundred Years War which propelled minor nobles like Pierre de Brézé, Antoine de Chabannes and Odet d'Aydie to the top, and emerging state structures, with their 'vocation centralisatrice', which humbled magnates who could not 'correctly analyse the relationship of forces'. Such an account is as condescending to the victors as to the victims of late fifteenth-century French politics, and assumes what has to be proved, the political unimportance of *fidelités* in earlier crises.[17]

* * * * *

Pending necessary research, all these positions remain schematic. The *alliances* of Louis d'Orléans and the Burgundians cited by Lewis may be as difficult to extrapolate to lesser men as the indentures of John of Gaunt.[18] The evidence Major adduced was slight and scattered in space and time, chronologically vague and confined to those of princely rank. The pensioners of French princes, in particular of kings, have always attracted attention, but the question is still open as to whether, at lower levels of the nobility, effective dependence was mediated by *fief-rente* or pension. Estate records show pensioners as a banal feature of seigneurial life. Every lord of regional standing would have them, but they might be of relatively low status and contingent function: typically, legal counsel and estate administrators. There is no evidence that even so great a man as Jean, Count of Dunois, assigned pensions on his county of Longueville to any but lawyers; while in the 1450s his contemporary, Louis d'Estouteville, pensioned only two nobles (excluding lawyers) in the Caux, a heartland of his territorial possessions.

This may be an argument from silence, for the French *noblesse seconde* is poorly served by surviving accounts at household, receiver-general or controller-general level. But *lettres de retenue* are equally rare, and the English parallels are suggestive. After 'Decayed and Non-Feudalism', the French historian interested in affinity had to look at office, pension, chivalric orders, brotherhood-in-arms and other miscellaneous elements of *alliance*.[19] In England, the fracture of the consensus derived from McFarlane has generated similar emphasis on the diversity of retaining. In Michael Hicks' synthesis, the indenture has become but one of the means by which a 'connection' was constructed: the household, estate administration and tenantry have re-emerged, and relegated 'extraordinary

17] M. Harsgor, 'Fidelités et infidelités au sommet du pouvoir', *Hommage à Roland Mousnier. Clientèles et fidelités en Europe à l'époque moderne*, ed. Y. Durand, Paris, 1981, pp. 259–77.
18] Lewis, 'Decayed and Non-Feudalism', p. 158; repr. in idem, *Essays in Later Medieval French History*, pp. 42–43.
19] Ibid., pp. 173–78; 57–62.

retaining' to an exalted, but secondary and perhaps chronologically rather aberrant position.[20] A similar fate may befall the French pension.

Neither the status nor the numbers of d'Estouteville's pensioners laid the basis for the clientele which he deployed on the accession of Louis XI in 1461, interposing men between captains and their companies, seizing strong places, confronting town councils with the need for immediate submission. The men who can be identified as his agents – 'ses gens' as the king described them – were actually members of his family, household and *ordonnance* company. Jean Pevrel oversaw the first musters under Louis XI of the Breton companies of Geoffroi de Couvran and Olivier de Broons, Robert de Flocques' garrison company at Honfleur, and secured the allegiance of troops on Jersey formerly in the service of the disgraced Pierre de Brézé.[21] A longstanding *serviteur et familier*, he was listed in all surviving musters of his garrison on Mont-Saint-Michel, and he went on to serve his sons.[22] Accounts show him as one of the triumvirate of servants administering the family's seigneuries in the pays de Caux.[23]

The crown's military reforms from the 1440s weakened the imperative for magnates to have at hand the means of raising a noble retinue for military service. Membership of an *ordonnance* retinue became subject to processes of venality and provision by a patron – in this case, the captain.[24] It is surely excessive to conclude that the *ordonnance* was an instrument of the domestication of the nobility, as Contamine implied.[25] It merged into the sea of royal office, the common stock of maintenance available to magnates and courtier-officers. Christopher Stocker has pointed out the ubiquity of the expectation that they would provide their own people.[26] In the 1440s and 1450s, Robert de Flocques

20] M. Hicks, *Bastard Feudalism*, London and New York, 1995, pp. 43–68.
21] BNF, ms. fr. 21497, nos 158–61; Coll. Clairambault 235, p. 117.
22] He was d'Estouteville's *procureur*, or witnessed his private acts, in 1448, 1453, 1455, 1458, 1460, 1463, and for his sons in 1465 and 1470 (G. de La Morandière, *Histoire de la Maison d'Estouteville en Normandie*, Paris, 1903, pp. 367, 467; Arch. Dép. Seine-Maritime 33 J 415, *dossier Maison d'Estouteville* (unnumbered documents dated 11 March 1452 [sic] and 9 June 1460); ibid., *dossier duché d'Estouteville* (unnumbered document dated 18 May 1455); ibid., 2 E 1/188, *sub* 7 June 1458; P. Le Cacheux, *Actes de la Chancellerie d'Henry VI concernant la Normandie sous la domination anglaise*, Rouen and Paris, 1935, pp. 5–6; BNF, Pièces Originales 1083, *d'Estouteville* 24901, no. 193.
23] Arch. Dép. Seine-Maritime 33 J 847, *Comptes d'Estouteville*.
24] For instances of venality in Dunois' retinue, see Arch. Dép. Seine-Maritime 2 E 1/191, *sub* 17 May 1462 (Guillaume des Hayes' sale of his place as *homme d'armes*); compare with L. Merlet, *Registres et minutes des notaires du comté de Dunois. Inventaire sommaire*, Châteaudun, 1886, p. 33 (accord between Thomas Dubois, *homme de guerre*, and Bertrand du Fresne, *écuyer*, over replacing Dubois in Dunois' service). See R. Harris, *Valois Guyenne: A Study of Politics, Government and Society in Late Medieval France*, Woodbridge, 1994, p. 39.
25] P. Contamine, *Guerre, état et société à la fin du moyen âge. Etudes sur les armées des rois de France 1337–1494*, Paris and The Hague, 1972, p. 442.
26] C. Stocker, 'Office as Maintenance in Renaissance France', *Canadian Journal of History*, Vol. VI, 1971, pp. 21–44.

wove his *ordonnance* retinue into local office through the patronage which he wielded as *bailli* of Evreux.[27] He was transgressing neither contemporary norms nor breaking new institutional ground.

The expense of the *ordonnance* induced a countervailing emphasis on more traditional forms of service, and the *ban* was revitalised and formalised in the same period. In a lawsuit over his nobility in 1492, the Avranchin gentleman Etienne le Bis was said to have responded to every royal summons over thirty years; witnesses frequently, if baldly, described his equipment and mounts.[28] He had fought at Montlhéry and been blockaded within Paris in 1465, besieged Granville in 1466, and defended Mont-Saint-Michel in 1467–68. In all these actions and on subsequent expeditions into Brittany, France, Picardy, Artois and Hainault, he had ridden with the hundred or so active adult Avranchin nobles. Le Bis was not a professional soldier but a lawyer, man of affairs and petty royal officer. His experience shows how militarised the nobility of which he claimed membership still was.[29]

Recurrent warfare, the crown's requirement for and imposition of service, the use of attendance at musters as a criterion of *noblesse*, and the payment of royal wages to those who served, combined to shift the burden of maintaining a military retinue on to the royal budget and the *petite noblesse* itself. Le Bis served under various notable captains, including Main Goyon and Berthin de Silly, both *baillis* of the Cotentin, Raoul, seigneur de Brully, Jean Pigache and Jean Cholet, seigneur de la Choletière. But politics, arms and landholding had made this d'Estouteville country. Le Bis had made his debut under Louis d'Estouteville, mustering with the other nobles of the *bailliage* on the strand beneath the church tower at Genêts, looking across the bay to Mont-Saint-Michel. The military prestige of the great Louis and his sons, Bricquebec and Moyon, is apparent in the testimony.

The creation of cadres of assembly, leadership, discipline and logistics for the *ban* did not attenuate the leadership role of leading local families. This is part of the explanation why, in Normandy, the pensioning of the *petite noblesse* by the *noblesse seconde* failed to survive the civil wars and the English occupation on any scale. The concentration of the much grander *ordonnance* companies in the province after 1450 also had major consequences – it transmitted the structures of alliance, cooperation and dependence of the marcher warfare of the 1440s into the post-Reduction settlement, and over the longer term it provided the Norman nobility with a bonanza of royal military patronage.

This is important in the light of Robert Harding's influential work on the

27] G. Prosser, 'After the Reduction: Re-structuring Norman Political Society and the *Bien Public*, 1450–1465', unpublished PhD thesis, University of London, 1996, pp. 102ff.
28] Arch. Dép. Seine-Maritime 3 B 1126, *dossier particulier le Bis* (testimony of Bertrand Brouault, and particularly Jean de la Bignolaye).
29] Ibid., 3 B 1126, *dossier particulier le Bis*.

patronage networks of sixteenth-century provincial and lesser governors.[30] In arguing that these men were the archetypal political agents of the crown in the provinces, and that thereby they enjoyed real power, Harding had recourse to the informal attributes which explain and accompany the provision of a given magnate in office: name, status, a substantial clientele on the one hand, and a share in and influence over the disbursal of royal favour on the other.[31] *Ordonnance* companies were instrumental in the interface of their private clientage networks and their public role, and the same is true of fifteenth-century *chefs de guerre*. Among the many indicators of Dunois' political importance from the 1420s to the 1460s is the status of members of his *ordonnance* who, after 1450, shared five royal *bailliages*, four *vicomtés* or major *prévôtés*, eight major captaincies, two *verderies* and three *élections* – and this list covers only the weightier royal offices in the Ile de France and Normandy.[32]

The fifteenth-century captain's household was at the centre of every large company. Charles VII allowed Jean d'Estouteville, seigneur de Torcy, to keep four of his 'lances' in his hotel. The 1454 Norman *Echiquier* excused Hutin de Guebienfay, one of Torcy's *hommes d'armes*, from the attendance he owed as *verdier* of Eawy on the grounds that, as his *maître d'hôtel*, he was in continuous service about his captain's person.[33] Commensality interacted with service in the *ordonnance* in other ways: Charles de Hermanville, another *hommes d'armes*, settled with Lancelot de Haucourt, lieutenant of Torcy's *ordonnance*, over the marriage of his daughter – then living in the household of Torcy's wife – to Haucourt's brother.[34] Young men whose wardships Torcy had acquired moved

30] R. Harding, *Anatomy of a Power Elite. The Provincial Governors of Sixteenth-Century France*, Yale, 1978.
31] Ibid., pp. 26–37.
32] The *baillis*: Thibaut d'Armignac, Chartres; Arnaud-Guilhem de Bernède, Mantes; Jacques de Clermont, Caen and then the Caux; Florent d'Illiers, Chartres; Guillaume de Prunelé, the Caux. In addition, Jean Brochet was *vicomte* of Alençon 1456–58; Bernède was captain of Houdan in the Vexin; Prunelé was captain of Bonneval in the Chartrain from 1447; Clermont was captain of Montivilliers; Rigault de Fontaines was captain of Compiègne in 1457; Ussel, Dunois' lieutenant of Harfleur in the 1450s, was to be captain of Meulan, 1465–70. Cardin le Fevre held the office of *verdier* of Roumare in 1452/53–1462, and was pensioned at 120 *l.* until 'il lui ait meulx pourveu d'autre etat ou office que ladite verderie' ('he had provided him with a better office than that of verderer'). Jehannequin de Gaillarbois was to be *vicomte* of Beaumont-le-Roger by 1470–71. Jean de la Grange, *écuyer*, was *élu* of Montivilliers in 1452. Jean Hardi was *verdier* of Longchamp. Jean le Jeunehomme's homonym was *élu* of Montivilliers in 1474. Jean Chenu was *élu* of Caen and captain of 100 lances in 1474; Jean Cholet, seigneur de la Choletière, was briefly captain of Vire in the late 1460s, and was qualified as *conseiller et maître d'hôtel* when he discharged his commission to muster the nobles of the Evreçin in 1470. Perrot Dany rapidly obtained advancement under Louis XI, securing the captaincy of Laon in 1461 and Fismes in 1462. Jean de Ligny was later captain of the *franc-archers* of the *élection* of Paris.
33] Arch. Dép. Seine-Maritime 1 B 29, fol. 17; AN, AB XIX 3122, pp. 15, 27; 3120, p. 359; 3121, p. 133.
34] Arch. Dép. Calvados 7 E 94, *sub* 24 April 1457, fol. 95v; 7 E 95, *sub* 14 August 1460, p. 126. Jean de Haucourt was to die before the marriage could be celebrated.

into his company: Jean de Saint Mard, vicomte de Blosseville, was raised in Torcy's household, along with Robinet le Sénéchal, and they both entered his service.[35]

This was probably typical. Great men had arrangements tailored to their own situations. Dunois was allowed to detach up to twenty lances from his company, and the king had dispensed six lances from the musters as 'il lui est besoing mener et tenir avec lui continuellement six gentilshommes d'armes' ('he always needs to have six armed gentlemen in his company').[36] Admiral de Bueil had obtained a comparable concession.[37] It is difficult not to see such dispensations as a means of subsidising captains' households. A case can be made that the section of the Rouen garrison which shared the lodgings in the château of the *Grand Sénéchal*, Pierre de Brézé, was effectively his household in arms at royal wages.[38]

There are difficulties, however, in transplanting Harding's model back into the formative years of both governorships and the standing military companies of the crown. The companies which Louis XI found on his accession, and upon which he imposed new captains in defiance of existing clientage ties, were the products of political contingencies already antiquated. Princes did not yet figure largely among their captains – Bernard Chevalier calculated that as late as 1483–1520, only nineteen governors out of 43 were *ordonnance* captains.[39] The crown's primary agents in the localities were still the *baillis* and *sénéchaux*, men who held office in the localities and in the royal household. These men's formal role was defined by custom, but their significance derived from their Janus-like position, depending on personal contact with the ruler and networks of

35] AN, AB XIX 3116, p. 27; 3180, p. 117.

36] BNF, ms. fr. 20382, nos 8, 14. Dunois' personal retinue was to be paid by the *trésorier des guerres* on his simple quittance (e.g., no. 9, quarter ending June 1451).

37] From March 1453, Charles VII permitted de Bueil to 'mener et tenir avec lui continuellement quatre gentilz hommes d'armes' ('to lead and have with him at all times four armed gentlemen') of his company, naming them as René de Scépaux, Jean d'Allières, Pierre Simon and Pierre Bonin. The *généraux* were to pay these men on Bueil's simple quittance, notwithstanding non-attendance at the musters (BNF, Coll. Clairambault 825, no. 58). In 1456 he obtained further letters patent to the *généraux des finances* after he had requested that his *hommes d'armes*, René de Scépaux, *chevalier*, Guillaume du Périer, Louis Auve and Jean du Parc, *ecuyers*, be paid their wages for early that year. These men, it was claimed, were ever in his service ('se tiennent continuellement avec luy pour le accompaigner'). The *généraux* had refused, 'obstant que pour la continuelle residence quilz font avec icellui nostre cousin ilz ne soient aux monstres' ('because they were continually with our said cousin, they were not at the musters') (BNF, ms. fr. 20587, no. 67). Du Périer gave quittance for his wages as head of the company in July 1461, although he does not appear in the musters (L. Delisle, *Les Collections Bastard d'Estaing à la Bibliothèque Nationale. Catalogue analytique*, Nogent-le-Rotrou, 1885, p. 97, no. 879).

38] Prosser, 'After the Reduction', pp. 135ff.

39] B. Chevalier, 'Gouverneurs et gouvernements en France entre 1450 et 1520', *Histoire comparée de l'administration (IVe–XVIIIe siècles)*, p. 305.

influence among the ruled. Mediation by provincial governors or equivalents was still unusual and unsystematic.

In the regularity of their appointment and in the myths which legitimised them as a corps, the provincial governors belong to the sixteenth century, and only sporadically to the mid-fifteenth century. Only in the south or in emergencies did provincial governors or royal lieutenants interpose themselves between court and locality. In Normandy their importance was ephemeral save where they possessed local significance derived in other ways, such as in the cases of Richemont as *Connétable* and d'Estouteville as *Grand Sénéchal*. Dupont-Ferrier's remarks on the governors, made almost a century ago, still stand for the mid-fifteenth century: they were unable to construct 'une autorité constante, normale, sensiblement pareille en temps de paix à ce qu'elle était en temps de guerre' ('an established and accepted authority effective in times of peace and war'), and had yet to achieve 'une fixité réelle' ('real stability') in geographical terms.[40]

Lay courtier-officers may have founded politically important affinities on a number of bases: departments of the royal household; great charges such as the admiralty or forest office; the opportunities for maintenance and provision supplied by patrimonial jurisdictions; brokerage with a princely house; even (as perhaps in the case of d'Estouteville) autonomous influence over ecclesiastical patronage. Most such clienteles are currently invisible, and many are likely to remain so. However, where the patron in question was an *ordonnance* captain and the musters of his company survive, we do have a route into the affinity. By interrogating these lists by means of other sources, we can show in detail what kinds of links gave coherence to certain circles, sample the character of and classify particular relationships, and develop prosopographies fitting service to a courtier magnate into a wider career. Where evidence of lawsuit and property transaction, estate or household survives, we can widen our scope to include commensals, legal and administrative officers, as well as kin and allies.

This methodology shows Pierre de Brézé recasting his career as he drifted away from close personal service to Charles VII after the late 1440s, to re-emerge as a key figure in the administration of Normandy, in Channel warfare and in Anglo-French relations. At the same time, he modified his affinity on the basis of a portfolio of military and judicial office. Those who served and followed Brézé included household men and estate officers, kinsmen, longstanding associates and occasionally tenants. Overall, however, his was an affinity built on patron-client relationships. Those with places in his *ordonnance* company all served at royal wages, but it was not the king who had given them place or would lead them in battle, but Brézé himself. It was Brézé as lord or patron who would

40] G. Dupont-Ferrier, *Les Officiers royaux des bailliages et sénéchaussées et les institutions monarchiques locales en France à la fin du Moyen Age*, Paris, 1902, p. 234. See Chevalier, 'Gouverneurs', pp. 291–307.

broker their disputes, assist them in debt and even advance them in marriage. It was to him, as intimate of king and Angevin princes, that they would look for intercession at court. It was to him as Valois *chef de guerre* that they would look for provision to lieutenancies of garrisons and companies, and other military charges. It was to him as *grand sénéchal* of Normandy that they would look for maintenance in their lawsuits with rivals and with their own tenants.[41]

It was this latter office which gave Brézé that reach into the Rouennais legal milieu which would endure right through to 1499, when the *sénéchaussée* counsellors of his grandson, Louis de Brézé, were advanced into the standing *Echiquier* which was to replace both it and the *Echiquier* of commission. This interpenetration of urban elite, royal government cadre and aristocratic affinity was unusual only in the size of the city and the prominence of the institution, which would become the *Parlement* of Rouen. There is a line of descent from the influence of Pierre through Louis de Brézé and his widow Diane de Poitiers to the strength of their Guise descendants in the Norman capital.[42]

In 'Royal Clientèles', Peter Lewis revised the conclusions he vouchsafed in *Later Medieval France: The Polity* (1968), which were frankly sceptical of the significance of clientage. Accepting the saturation of royal government with clientage, he sought to turn away from the means of retaining to its function: 'the essential thing was a community of interest, durable or temporary'. The Brézé instance shows that affinity might be durable indeed, despite disasters – the disgrace of Pierre in 1461–62, his death and the treason of his widow in 1465, and his son's slaying of a wife who was also the king's bastard sister in 1474. Such durability was part of what Bernard Guenée called 'dynamism in the base'. An existing client network could not be wished away, but even decapitated it was part of the local situation which had to be faced and adapted by courtiers, royal officers and magnates. In Normandy, this was true of the rupture of 1449, when Brézé took over a circle of Lancastrian administrators. Even Lancastrian curial ecclesiastics, whose careers Susanne Saygin has shown being made in the 1420s and 1430s by Cardinal Branda di Castiglione, were later to focus their loyalties on Guillaume d'Estouteville, Cardinal-Archbishop of Rouen.[43]

Jean de Montauban, Breton magnate, companion and counsellor of the dauphin, Louis, benefited dramatically from his accession to the throne in 1461. He stepped into the charges of Charles VII's courtier-magnates, de Bueil, the *amiral*, and Guillaume d'Harcourt, Count of Tancarville, *Grand Maître des Eaux et Forêts.* He delegated military office in Lower Normandy, admiralty office in the Atlantic ports, and forest charges in Normandy and across northern

41] Prosser, 'After the Reduction', pp. 128–60.

42] S. Carroll, *Noble Power during the French Wars of Religion: The Guise Affinity and the Catholic Cause in Normandy*, Cambridge, 1998, pp. 53–88.

43] Unpublished paper given at the Institute of Historical Research, University of London, March 1997.

France in 1461–65. He quickly asserted himself in Lower Normandy, an area where the Breton dukes had been influential in the previous decade. He displaced second-ranking Breton captains like Guillaume de Rosnivinen, Olivier de Broons and Geoffroi de Couvran, and men associated with Duke Francis II's mistress, Antoinette de Maignelais, notably the *bailli* Odet d'Aydie. He built a new regional connection out of disparate elements, buying the service of lesser captains who had previously served de Bueil and d'Aydie, and bringing in Breton aristocrats who were either kinsmen and allies of some importance, or lesser men who were longstanding Delphinal commensals. He also patronised a number of members of the Norman *noblesse seconde*, such as Jean de Montenay and his kinsmen the Malet de Graville, and borrowed men from the d'Estouteville circle. This developing affinity was still fragile four years later when it was disrupted by the war of *le Bien Public*. With difficulty, elements of it weathered the crisis, before being reshaped by Louis, bastard of Bourbon, to become a key cadre of the influence of Louis Malet de Graville later in the century.[44]

In one sense, this instance is local to Lower Normandy and, where it is of wider importance, institutionally confined within the admiralty. But it also relates to more important matters. One is the institutional coalescence of the *Table de Marbre*, the seat of admiralty and forest justice. Bourbon and Malet were Montauban's successors in both offices; all three created or recreated these as effective jurisdictions, waged struggles with rival jurisdictions in the Norman ports, strove to annex other great maritime charges such as the captaincy of La Rochelle, and to assert the sovereignty of the *Table de Marbre* against the Rouen *Echiquier* and other jurisdictions. Admiral de Bourbon triumphed in the 1470s, establishing for a long generation the sovereignty of his *Table de Marbre* at Paris.[45] The evolution of the Lower Norman entourage of the admirals of France across the later fifteenth century can also be used to illustrate a key political fact

44] Prosser, 'After the Reduction', pp. 174–82, 249.

45] A. Floquet, *Histoire du Parlement de Rouen*, Rouen, 1840, p. 262. In Normandy, the jurisdictional boundaries of forest and admiralty were defined in the fourteenth century (*Ordonnances*, Vol. II, p. 408). The attendance of *verdiers* and admiralty lieutenants at the *Echiquier* was still routine in the 1450s, and works in the *cohue du Roi* at Rouen 'pour le fait de l'Echiquier' ('at the Exchequer'), in 1463, extended to the 'parc et banquet de la juridiction des eaues et foretz' (jurisdiction of the 'waters and forests') (Arch. Dép. Seine-Maritime 1 B 31, fols 2–6; R. N. Sauvage, *Catalogue des manuscrits de la Collection Mancel à Caen*, Caen 1906, no. CCCIV[1]). On Bourbon's campaign, see C. Bourel de la Roncière, *Histoire de la Marine française*, 6 vols, Paris, 1899, Vol. II, pp. 47–48, 439–40; and for Rouen's recovery in 1507, see C. de Robillard de Beaurepaire, *Dernier recueil de notes historiques et archéologiques concernant le département de la Seine-Inférieure et plus specialement la ville de Rouen*, Rouen, 1892. The cursory overview of the admiralty given by F. Lot and R. Fawtier (*Histoire des Institutions françaises au moyen âge*, 3 vols, Paris, 1957–62, Vol. II, pp. 539–44) should be supplemented with Bourel de la Roncière, *Histoire de la Marine*, Vol. II, pp. 439–44, and the series of fourteen articles by J. Darsel in *Annales de Normandie*, 1969–1981, collecting the scattered material on admiralty jurisdiction port by Norman port. His focus, however, is on the sixteenth century and later.

of the 1440–80 period, the replacement of the Anjou by the Bourbons as the most centrally influential princely house. The operation of such processes is comparable across levels of status and abstraction.[46]

So royal office was not the plaything of the patron. The institutional efflorescence of Valois France in legal, fiscal and military terms has impressed all French historians. Yet the machinery of government was not machinery: it was persons, each with kinship and personal connections, career strategies and collective interests. For the later period, Sharon Kettering has developed a clientage model around this point.[47] By the fourteenth century, the inalienability of the royal demesne and the administrative practices of great *corps d'état*, such as the *Parlement* and the *Chambre des Comptes*, began to obstruct the largesse of princes. This is a sign that clientage as such had already become an issue in the fourteenth century. At the end of that century came the attacks on *bendes*, the legislation against venality and the retaining of royal officers.[48] This was followed by the privileging of election to office over impetration, a notion which became orthodox after Charles V, was annexed by the Burgundians, and became conventional again by the mid-fifteenth century.[49]

In the last decade of his life, Charles VII, that least Burgundian of kings, was strong enough to pay more than lip-service to such ideals. His successor, however, was never sufficiently secure to permit real debate over the choice of great commensal officers. The purges of royal office and of the court, and the reforms in royal fiscality which marked the early years of the reign of Louis XI, were echoes of an earlier 'Burgundianism'. They were largely token, however, and later critiques, such as the assault of the Estates upon the king's pensioners in 1484, owed little to 'Burgundian' tradition. There was more vitality and continuity in the ideologies of sovereignty nurtured in institutions such as the *Parlement*, and in the particularist myths that sustained provincial customs and the local institutions that embodied them. Both disciplined courtier-magnates in terms of what they could expect, the price they would pay and with whom they could deal.

These constraints, and entrenched unregulated venality, helped make the manipulation of royal institutions more dependent on technical and everyday

46] As Charbonnier observed in different language (*Une autre France*, p. 567).

47] S. Kettering, *Patrons, Brokers and Clients in Seventeenth-Century France*, New York/Oxford, 1986.

48] C. Gauvard, 'Les Officiers royaux et l'opinion publique en France à la fin du Moyen Age', *Histoire comparée de l'administration*, ed. Paravicini and Werner, p. 587.

49] Paravicini, 'Administrateurs professionels', ibid., pp. 171–76; Gauvard, 'Les Officiers royaux', pp. 586, 589ff; F. Autrand, 'Offices et officiers royaux en France sous Charles VI', *RH*, Vol. CCXLII, 1969, pp. 285–338; idem, 'Rétablir l'état: l'année 1454 au Parlement', in *La Reconstruction après la Guerre de Cent Ans. Actes du 104ᵉ Congrès National des Sociétés Savantes, Bordeaux 1980*, Paris 1981, Vol. I, pp. 7–23; R. Cazelles, *La Société politique et la crise de la royauté sous Philippe de Valois*, Paris, 1958, pp. 338–40; S. Luce, 'L'Élection au scrutin de deux chanceliers de France sous le règne de Charles V', *RH*, Vol. XVI, 1891, pp. 91–102; B. Guenée, *Tribunaux et gens de justice dans le bailliage de Senlis à la fin du moyen age*, Paris, 1963, p. 168.

processes of management. Innovation and the adjustment of the balance between competing institutional complexes were circumscribed by a profound legalism and local specificities. Higher authority was either reactive or was propagated through mechanisms outside the formal institutions of royal government. Some of these mechanisms could achieve regularity, as with the *maîtres des requêtes*, but *ad hoc* commissions were ubiquitous. We often find Louis XI in his letters ordering his *commis* to take aid from the men of such and such a magnate. Even when they were royal officers themselves, the talents, independence and clientage connections of *commissaires* were easily tailored to local situations. As the court elite stabilised in the 1480s to become the court of the *maîtres du royaume* described by Michel Harsgor, so governors appeared in other provinces as instruments of devolved control and intervention.[50] The court was scaling up a conventional solution to an old problem.

So Françoise Autrand's insight as to the distinction between office and commission may be fundamental in a technical and legal rather than in a practical sense – a position first advanced by Dupont-Ferrier.[51] Moreover, royal pensions were regarded as in some sense substitutes for specific office, as we see in the perennial grants of pension pending provision to office of equivalent value. The service such favour implied was no less real for being unspecific, as we see in the facility with which royal counsellors shuffled pensions, offices, gifts, favours, *dons de mariage*, debt repayments and assignations of all kinds following the crisis of *le Bien Public*.

Royal councillors annotated their accounts with suggestions for retrenchment: 400 *livres tournois* might be shaved off the pension of Pierre Pongnant, as 'depuis il a eue l'office de maitre des requetes' ('he has since had the office of master of requests'); 1500 *l.t.* might come off the 5000 *l.t.* pension of Louis de Laval, seigneur de Châtillon, since he had both the *maîtrise des eaux et forêts* and the governorship of Langres, the latter worth about 500 *l.t.*; 400 *l.t.* could be deducted from the pension of the newly rehabilitated Antoine d'Aubuisson, seigneur de Monteil, since he had the *bailliage* of the Caux and the captaincy of Arques. Annotations of a precisely similar character were made on the assignations given on places and *recettes générales*. Jean du Fou, premier *échanson* and captain of Cherbourg, had 2000 *l.t.* assigned in Normandy and the same in Languedoc – 'semble le Roy y peut prendre mille livres' ('seems that the king can take 1000 *livres*')[52]

50] M. Harsgor, 'Recherches sur le personnel du conseil du roi sous Charles VIII et Louis XII', unpublished doctoral thesis, University of Lille, 1980; idem, 'Maîtres d'un royaume. Le groupe dirigéant français à la fin du XVe siècle', *La France de la fin du XVe siècle. Renouveau et apogée*, ed. B. Chevalier and P. Contamine, Paris, 1985, pp. 135–46.
51] Autrand, 'Offices et officiers'; G. Dupont-Ferrier, 'Le Rôle des commissaires royaux dans le gouvernement de la France spécialement du XIVe et XVIe siècles', *Mélanges Paul Fournier*, Paris, 1929, pp. 171–84.
52] BNF, ms. fr. 20498, nos 58–62.

For the king's accountants, their ingenuity stretched beyond breaking point by royal largesse, it was perforce the cash values that mattered. This is to extend only slightly Stocker's points about the uses of royal office as maintenance.[53] It is also consistent with contemporary criticism of the exploitation of institutional complexes for personal profit rather than for political objectives – for such were Thomas Basin's attacks on the *maîtrise des eaux et forêts*.[54] But office also inscribed a man in the market of favour, and afforded influence over those making disbursals. With the crown always over-assigning on particular *recettes*, this was an important consideration.[55]

The king's councillors clearly expected their materialism to be shared by those benefiting from the king's patronage. But if cash was in some crude sense the bottom line, it was only one way of mediating service and favour. The capacity to place a client, influence a lawsuit, and impede or expedite the execution of royal letters all came together to shape local credit. This did not derive from position in some notional royal office hierarchy. Any great man might be able to dominate a local situation out of his own resources, even make the acts of central organs irrelevant, especially where others were ignorant or indifferent. But this would be powerfully supplemented by a capacity to provide access to, and to trade favours with, powers outside the structure of royal office, including ecclesiastics, municipal authorities and secular lords. The capacity to exploit royal rights at a local level and to influence local royal courts, to provide access to fountainheads of royal authority at the centre, to influence greater officers and coerce lesser ones was, for a magnate or courtier-officer, a vital extra dimension of power on the ground, a local counterpart to factional processes at court, in which place was both an index of, and instrumental in, competition.

The importance of courtier-officers derived from delegations of royal powers, the light of sovereignty shining on royal servants. But their local usefulness to the crown was partly dependent upon their landed wealth and local credit, and what this implied about their capacity to mobilise men at any level appropriate to the action required. They needed to be able to influence the centre and to exercise lordship in the locality.

Variations in this symbiosis were a matter of the particular balance struck between the different components of local importance. Charles VII had not had to take any of these components as he found them. Not the least interesting contrast between him and Louis XI is the price each paid for service. Louis' later reputation as a prince prepared to woo men with exorbitant rewards compares

53] Stocker, 'Office as Maintenance', pp. 21–44.

54] Thomas Basin, *Histoire de Louis XI*, ed. C. Samaran, 2 vols, Paris, 1963, Vol. I, pp. 34–36. See also Dupont-Ferrier, *Officiers royaux*, p. 280; Floquet, *Parlement de Rouen*, pp. 257, 268.

55] The more placid operations of the fiscal machinery are best seen in Etienne Petit's *Estat* for the last year of Charles VII's reign, for he is at pains to explain normal procedure to the incoming regime in rather full *marginalia*, BNF (ms. fr. 20498, pp. 77ff).

with his father's sobriquet of *le Bienservi*, which exalted the talents of his servants while stressing how hard they were worked. From the 1430s, the Valois drive northwards liberated much royal patronage, but the military revival focused royal generosity on to the royal captains doing the work. This was less true of the great conquests of 1449–53, a fact which may help to explain how firmly Charles VII's regime was stabilised upon the basis of Norman and Gascon patronage. Charles was just as capable of providing the landed and local context for his servants as his son would be. In Normandy he did this for Dunois in exempting his county of Longueville from his revocation of many other pre-Reduction grants. Other grants of lands and revenues do not have to be envisaged as maintenance defined only as reward for services rendered. In the usufructuary grants of *vicomtés* to an Angevin admiral, a Limousin marshal and Breton constable, we see the king giving his men the tools for the job. In the fifteenth century, the courtier-magnate was already a patron and a broker of patronage, but still remained a lord.

The debate on clientage in the period after 1500 is built on longer interest and a far better documentary base than the fifteenth century can look to. Its horizons have expanded correspondingly.[56] If the political importance of clientage networks in the French fifteenth century attracts investigation, the debate on the later period will be modified in so far as its clientage model emerged in distinction from a medieval past supposedly characterised by the mediation of independent landed power between crown and nobility. Focus on the fifteenth century's provincial princely 'states' itself emerged as an alternative to the teleology of royal state-building, an alternative for which Edouard Perroy may stand representative.[57] Yet the notion of the state is dependent upon a binary opposition, public-private, which had not mastered, let alone monopolised, contemporary political culture. The attraction of focus on affinity, patronage, clientage and service is that it reconciles noble culture with royal and princely institutionalisation. But it is not at all certain that the royal and princely states of present historiography will survive a turn to the pluralism of power stressed by Peter Lewis.

56] The sixteenth-century debate is summarised from a somewhat hostile standpoint by K. Neuschel, *Word of Honor: Interpreting Noble Culture in Sixteenth Century France*, Cornell, 1989, pp. 1–37. See also M. Greengrass, 'Noble Affinities in Early Modern France: The Case of Henri I de Montmorency, Constable of France', *European History Quarterly*, Vol. XVI, 1986, pp. 275–311; Potter, *History of France*, pp. 187–206; Carroll, *Noble Power*, pp. 53–88. French historians are also now turning to the subject: see L. Bourquin, *Noblesse seconde et pouvoir en Champagne aux XVIe et XVIIe siècles*, Paris, n.d.; Charbonnier, *Une autre France*, pp. 1074–1109.

57] E. Perroy, 'Feudalism or Principalities in Fifteenth-Century France', *BIHR*, Vol. XX, 1943–45, pp. 181–85, repr. in idem, *Etudes d'histoire médiévale*, Paris, 1979, pp. 177–81; P. S. Lewis, 'The Centre, the Periphery and the Problem of Power Distribution in Late Medieval France', *The Crown and Local Communities in England and France in the Fifteenth Century*, ed. J. R. L. Highfield and R. Jeffs, Gloucester, 1981, pp. 33–50, repr. in idem, *Essays in Later Medieval French History*, pp. 151–68.

11

Justification and Theory of the Death Penalty at the *Parlement* of Paris in the Late Middle Ages

CLAUDE GAUVARD

Our perception of the Middle Ages is influenced by what we regard as acts of cruelty carried out in the name of justice, the most significant of these being the death penalty. Historians associate it with the gallows which, from the twelfth century, feature prominently on the social and political scene. This approach has been developed partly as a result of the researches of Michel Foucault, who has underlined the large increase in the number of executions carried out since that time. The philosopher would argue that capital punishment was a political instrument (*operateur politique*) which emphasised the power of the ruler. But Foucault's conclusions were largely based on specific cases, above all political crimes, and those concerned with treason, and on the penalties which came to be associated with them.[1] Could one really apply the same punishments associated with particular crimes, such as those meted out under Philippe le Bel to punish the lovers of the king's daughter-in-law who were flayed alive before being quartered, beheaded and hanged, or those imposed during periods of civil unrest when traitors were beheaded and their bodies exposed at the gates of towns (some of these being on the very frontiers of the kingdom) to the majority of criminal cases which might theoretically end in the passing of a death penalty? Various types of crime are often considered together, and the inevitable conclusion of terrible repression is all too readily drawn. However, Michel Foucault took care to distinguish treason (*lèse majesté*), a crime whose character would be developed in the late Middle Ages, from more 'everyday' crimes such as homicide or theft which, in certain cases, could also attract the death sentence, albeit one of a different kind: death by hanging carried out according to an altogether different ritual. The conclusions reached by Michel Foucault do not bear generalisation, even those which concern the crime of treason which sometimes led to other outcomes, such as the grant of a royal pardon. So it would prove to be, in a case well known to Peter Lewis, that, on 8 October 1458, at the *lit de justice* (trial before the king) held at

1] M. Foucault, *Surveiller et punir. Naissance de la prison*, Paris, 1975, pp. 36–72.

Vendôme, Jean Juvénal des Ursins begged Charles VII to show compassion and mercy (*clémence et miséricorde*) to the Duke of Alençon, who secured an assurance from that king that his life would be spared and, ultimately, that he would receive a pardon (*lettre de rémission*) from his successor, Louis XI.[2]

Recourse to narrative sources invites confusion. The chronicles and journals of the late medieval period draw particular attention to the most spectacular and exceptional cases, above all to political crimes. Thus the so-called 'Bourgeois de Paris' (probably a clerk of the chapter of Notre-Dame) describes a hundred or so executions which took place in the capital between 1405 and 1449. While some were for crimes against public morality, most were punishments for political crimes.[3] At the same time, the 'Bourgeois' says nothing about everyday crime, whether thefts or quarrels which led to bloodshed; these merited his attention only when either the location of the crime or its victim was of particular importance.[4] The chronicler is interested in a wide variety of events, and we must not allow ourselves to be misled by his choice.

Such preliminary thoughts allow us to understand that, in the Middle Ages, the death sentence is properly judged when it can be associated with the power of the state. Political crimes, when heavily punished, leave a deep impression. Yet, should the use of the death penalty, and the manner and frequency in which it was applied, necessarily be associated with the development of the powers of the state, whose growth recent research has shown to have taken place between the thirteenth and the fifteenth centuries? Is the power of the state to be related to the degree of coercion it exercises?

Rare Cases of the Death Penalty at the *Parlement* of Paris

An initial consideration of the problem should enable us to specify how often the death penalty was applied within the kingdom of France at the end of the Middle Ages. We may begin by considering the theoretical position, as it was revealed in the *coutumiers* which, as is well known, were heavily dependent upon Roman law. An examination of those clauses relating to criminal cases reveals that the death penalty was prescribed for many crimes. In the *Coutumes de Beauvaisis* (Customary of the Beauvaisis), composed late in the thirteenth century, Philippe de Beaumanoir would recall that 'there are several crimes

2] *Ecrits politiques de Jean Juvénal des Ursins*, ed. P. S. Lewis, 3 vols, SHF, Paris, 1978–92, Vol. II, pp. 407–23 ('Exhortation faicte au roy'). See the *lettre de rémission* accorded to the Duke of Alençon on 11 October 1461 (AN, JJ 198, no. 36). For the whole episode, the reader is referred to G. Du Fresne de Beaucourt, *Histoire de Charles VII*, 6 vols, Paris, 1881–91, Vol. VI, pp. 179–98.

3] *Journal d'un bourgeois de Paris, 1405–1449*, ed. A. Tuetey, Paris, 1881.

4] I refer the reader to my discussion of this matter in C. Gauvard, *'De grace especial'. Crime, Etat et Société en France à la fin du moyen âge*, 2 vols, Paris, 1991, Vol. I, pp. 17–57.

which must be punished by one kind of death sentence or another'; he then set out the various penalties according to the types of crime to which they related. Murder, treason, homicide and rape demand that the guilty party shall be drawn and hanged; arson and theft that he be simply hanged; heresy and sodomy that he be burned; while the forger of money was to be boiled before being hanged. Beaumanoir also referred to suicides and to cases of poisoning, without being specific about the penalty.[5] Such information, with variations, would also be set out in fourteenth-century *coutumiers*, in particular by Jean Boutillier and Jacques d'Ableiges.[6]

Students of law and criminality have readily assumed that the reality followed close on the heels of theory, and they have drawn the all-too-hasty conclusion that every kind of crime referred to above was punished according to the penalties set out in the *coutumiers*. It was long thought that the accused was, as in our day, confronted by the law. This is true yet misleading: true, in that counsel and judges could have recourse to the letter of the law to help them develop their arguments and form their judgements;[7] misleading, because other factors influence the relationship between the judge, the accused and society. All share the aim of maintaining the values upon which society is based: honour, and its corollary, vengeance, as well as other factors which may influence a judgement.[8] In delivering his verdict, a judge must take account of the respect due to the injured party; but he cannot ignore the threat which the accused constitutes if the verdict does not win acceptance. Thus the judgement may reflect less than it should the objective criteria upon which it is based, and more a consideration of the possible threat of vengeance. Under what conditions, then, may a judgement acceptable to all parties be made? What makes any particular decision or sentence appropriate? The gap between ideal and reality is a wide one. Certainly, theory provides one set of references, namely the law; it allows for exemplary justice to be meted out; and it links human justice to the divine. Yet it says nothing of daily practice which may help to rectify the harm caused by a crime, enabling men to continue to co-exist in society. The advances made by inquisitorial procedures never succeeded in closing this gap, making the task of analysing justice in the late Middle Ages a particularly difficult one.

5] Philippe de Beaumanoir, *Coutumes de Beauvaisis*, ed. A. Salmon, 2 vols, rev. edn, Paris, 1970, Vol. I, ch. XXX, pp. 428–33.

6] Jean Boutillier, *Le Grand Coutumier et Practique du droit civil et canon observé en France ... cy devant imprimé soubz le nom de la Somme rural*, ed. L. Charondas Le Caron, Paris, 1621; Jacques d'Ableiges, *Le Grand Coutumier de France*, ed. F. Laboulaye and R. Dareste, Paris, 1868.

7] See the notes made by Jean Le Coq at the end of the fifteenth century in which the author, *avocat du roi* at the *Parlement* of Paris, cites many references to Roman law (M. Boulet, *Questiones Johannis Galli*, Paris, 1944).

8] On the difference between theory and practice, see C. Gauvard, 'Le Jugement entre norme et pratique: le cas de la France du nord à la fin du moyen âge', in *Norm und Praxis im Alltag des Mittelalters und des Frühen Neuzeit*, ed. G. Jaritz, Vienna, 1997, pp. 27–38.

The subject of public opinion and its impact upon the evolution of ideas regarding the death penalty and its application remains to be considered. Faced with the barbarity of the rituals associated with executions and other related practices (for example, leaving bodies to rot for several years on the gibbet), some historians, following the theories of Norbert Elias, have sought to use psychology to explain such acts. Thus Peter Spierenburg, following Philippe Aries, describes the different reactions of men from the Ancien Régime in the face of death, in particular the deaths of criminals. What appeared to be indifference on their part came to change in the course of the seventeenth century, a period which, it is argued, witnessed a marked development of attitudes.[9] Yet, was it indifference? Or should we recognise that medieval people agreed with an exemplary death sentence because they felt that some crimes, though directed against an individual, were detrimental to the collective honour of a group which had to be avenged at all costs? We should ask, therefore, how successfully justice could bring healing to an order violated by a serious crime, a task which, if not fulfilled by the judicial institutions, might be carried out instead through an unauthorised act of vengeance or a lynching.

The study of crime in medieval France, in particular within the framework of the royal courts of which the *Parlement* was the foremost, allows us to answer a variety of questions, in particular how the state's growth was related to the development of coercion. The arguments and penalties discussed before the criminal court of the *Parlement*, which began to extend its authority from the beginning of the fourteenth century, suggest several approaches which we will now consider.

First, however, a word of warning. It should be noted that many of the cases judged in the *Parlement* were being heard in the first instance, while others came on appeal from a lower jurisdiction. In both instances, the cases decided in this great Parisian institution primarily concerned members of the nobility who, in criminal cases, constituted about one-third of the plaintiffs. In both kinds of case, too, inquisitorial procedures assigned a role of great influence to the *procureur du roi*, or royal attorney. This officer became the defender of the king's rights and of public justice. His pleadings were thus made in the name of society and of the public interest, which reflected the influence of Roman law according to which 'interest rei publicae ne maleficia remaneant impunita' ('he had an interest lest any crime should remain unpunished'). Among these must be the major crimes which, rightly, merited death. By virtue of both its function and its judicial mission, as much as by the sociological profile of the cases which it heard, the *Parlement* acted as a regulator between the king, the noble elites and the rest of society. How was this done? The reality did not necessarily correspond

9] P. Spierenburg, *The Spectacle of Suffering. Executions and the Evolution of Repression: From a Pre-Industrial Metropolis to the European Experience*, Cambridge, 1984.

to the theories expressed by the judges. In practice, many crimes which met the descriptions set out in the *coutumiers* were not punished with the imposition of the death sentence. Between 1387 and 1400, for example, only four men, involved in almost 200 criminal cases heard before the *Parlement criminel*, were condemned to death. Of these, two were involved in a private war in the north of the kingdom, and one of them, Baudrain du Hamel, although a noble, would finally be drawn and hanged.[10] In order to avoid the same fate, the family of his partner in crime, Robert de Vertaing, arranged for him to be drowned at night. As for the other two cases, the nature of the crimes was not formally set out. In the middle years of the fifteenth century, too, just at the time when François Villon, the fifteenth-century poet, thief and convicted murderer, was himself describing executions by hanging which leave such an impression upon the reader, few people, in reality, were being sentenced to die. No unambiguous death sentence was pronounced by the *Parlement* between 1443 and 1448. In one case alone is it likely that the order was given to execute the guilty man: Haquinet de Rosieres, from Tournai, who was said to have attempted to kill, or had arranged the murder of, Colart Le Fevre, and had refused to give sureties as the city authorities demanded of him. This was a serious case, it was claimed in court, for the victim had already lost four fingers and the use of an arm and foot, while having to go around wearing a *hauberjon*, a short coat of mail, to protect himself. In this instance, it was argued, the desire to kill was supported by the recidivist character of the accused, his association with groups of hired and armed men (*bateurs à loyer*), and his refusal to give sureties, all elements which, if combined, undermined public order. The *procureur du roi* could only conclude that the presence of such men caused 'perturbacion de la chose publique'; given the 'orreur' of the matter, he demanded 'grant punicion', for even in so notable a town as Tournai people did not feel safe; the accused merited the sentence of death by virtue of the *pena talionis*, or retaliation, a sentence certainly greater than that which would be imposed upon mere 'insidiateurs et agresseurs de chemins' ('tricksters and assailants of the road').[11]

In other cases, the *Parlement* simply referred the sentencing back to the court from which the criminal had appealed. It was rare for an appeal to be lodged after a sentence had been handed down by an inferior jurisdiction. In theory, this procedure was forbidden even before the royal *ordonnance* of 1454. Appeals from those being tortured were also rare. For the most part they were against interim judgements, a practice which had led to delays and abuses, and which the

10] See the registers in AN, X2a 12 and X2a 13 which contain pleadings and judgements. For Baudrain du Hamel, see X2a 12, fols 180v (1393) and X2a 13, fols 22–23v (1393).
11] '... il y a perturbacion de la chose publique par bateurs a loyer et a appetit d'autruy, en quoy chiet grant punicion veu l'orreur d'iceulx, et mesmement en ville notable alias ne seroit personne qui feust asseur, et y chiet *pena talionis et capital* et plus grant que contre insidiateurs et agresseurs de chemins' (AN, X2a 24, fol. 16v [1444]).

ordonnance of 1454 had sought in vain to check.[12]

Generally speaking, the death penalty was urged by the *procureur du roi*, or was sought by an injured party, in a fictional process of reparation in which the severity of the penalties demanded was gradually reduced. It was usually invoked in a procedure which would begin with demands for the death sentence, only for these to be replaced by demands for penalties involving merely civil rights or financial penalties. In 1447, in the case of false witness committed by Henri Filloix (who had been paid to commit the crime) and which led to the death sentence being imposed upon Loyset Le Petit (a sentence which was actually carried out), the initial demand of the *procureur du roi* for a death sentence was soon reduced to that of the pillory, then to an *amende honorable* (a ritual of shame during which the guilty person very publicly sought a pardon for his crime) and a term of imprisonment, and finally to branding on the forehead and the piercing of the accused's tongue.[13] This succession of penalties was intended to offer a way of restoring honour to the victim, for which the courtroom served as a kind of judicial battleground where spoken words were the weapons used. In this case, we shall never know which of the proposed penalties was finally applied.

A year later, a veritable cascade of punishments, each less severe than the last, was sought in a case involving Henri Bruinant:

> … Barbin pour le procureur du roi apres ce qu'il a eu recité le contenu es informacion faictes en ceste partie et aussi les confessions dudit de Bruinant, a requit et conclut que ledit Henry Bruinant, pour les faulsetez, inducцions, seduccions, decepcions et perviremens par lui faiz en ceste partie, soit puny corporellement, c'est assavoir soit pendu et estranglé et tous ses biens confisquez, ou au moins qu'il soit condemné a faire amende honorable au procureur du roy et a Amiens, en chemise tenans une torche de cire ardant en sa main en disant que faulsement et mauvaisement il a commis lesdites faulsetez, excez et delitz et en crie mercy au roy et a justice, et soit pilorisé par trois samediz es hales de Paris, et batu au cul de la charete et aussi es villes d'Amiens, de Bethune et de la Bruniere, et fletry au front d'une fleur de litz, et aussi requiert que la sentence donnee par le bailli d'Amiens sortisse son effect et que les resolucions et accords qui depuis s'en sont ensuiz soient declarez nulz et de nulle valeur, et aussi soit condemné pour amende proufitable en la somme de Vc livres parisis a prendre sur ses biens avant toute confiscacion et soit banni de ce royaume a tousiours.

12] On this matter, see the comments of Alfred Soman for the modern period (A. Soman, 'La Justice criminelle, vitrine de la monarchie française', *BEC*, Vol. CLIII, 1995, pp. 291–304).
13] AN, X2a 24, fol. 207 (1447).

> Barbin, for the *procureur du roi*, having set out both the content of the enquiry into the case and the confession made by the said Bruinant, demanded and concluded that for all the false statements and deceptions uttered by him in this case, the said Bruinant should be corporally punished, that is to say that he be hanged and strangled, and all his goods confiscated, or that, dressed in a shift and holding a lighted wax candle, he should confess that he had been falsely and wickedly guilty of committing the said crimes and should make an *amende honorable* both to the *procureur du roi* [in Paris] and in Amiens, and that he should beg mercy of the king and of justice, and that he be pilloried on three Saturdays in the market in Paris, and whipped at the back of a cart both there and in the towns of Amiens, Béthune and Bruniere, before being branded on the forehead with the sign of the fleur de lis; he also demanded that the sentence imposed by the *bailli* of Amiens should be applied, and that the compromises made since [by the parties] should be cancelled and nullified; and that the accused be fined the sum of 500 *livres parisis* to be seized from his property before any confiscation, and that he be banished in perpetuity from the kingdom.[14]

The final part of the demand put forward by the *procureur* concerned what were intended to be the firm restrictions on the private compromises which the parties appear to have already made. This shows how, even in the mid-fifteenth century, ways could be found of circumventing royal justice by means of privately negotiated agreements (even in criminal cases), in spite of reforming *ordonnances* which had already been in effect for about a century.[15] It also shows how anxious the *Parlement* was to have the law on the matter applied, so that the king's justice should retain its monopoly, particularly in criminal matters. But we should not be deceived. On the one hand, that monopoly was far from secured; on the other, the judges themselves could encourage the negotiation of such private compromises, even in criminal cases, as attested to by the series of *accords* accepted by the Court in the late Middle Ages.[16] It would be wrong to think that the Court had little interest in *accords* made between the parties, and that it preferred coercion to conciliation. On the contrary, the judgements handed down by the *Parlement*, few of which imposed the death sentence even in the gravest of cases, strongly suggest that the Court preferred a conciliatory view of royal justice to prevail. One may even believe that trials were, above all, a way of bringing conflicts to a peaceful conclusion and, as a result, of preventing a spirit of vengeance from taking control. That is why *Parlement* used the *amende honorable* to bring criminal cases to a conclusion. This way of proceeding

14] Ibid., fol. 220 (1448).
15] See, in particular, the *ordonnance* dated 3 March 1357 (*Ordonnances*, Vol. III, p. 128).
16] See the registers in AN, *série* X1c. On these, see Gauvard, '*De grace especial*', Vol. I, pp. 17–26.

favoured by the Court was a salutary method of resolving crises, for it ensured the vital restoration of the injured party's honour, while obliging the parties to accept a judicial decision taken in the name of public order.[17]

One may ask how the death sentence would be generally accepted at a time when acts of vengeance were still common, and royal justice, due to a shortage of personnel, lacked the means of applying a policy of coercion. The imposition of the death sentence did not always lead to the ending of a conflict. Indeed, it might help to fuel a greater desire for vengeance and, in so doing, could result in a vendetta arising from the execution of the guilty person. In the minds of the judges, an execution did not prolong vengeance, but it is important to understand that a certain ambiguity was bound to persist. This is best seen in the language of the *coutumiers*, for example that of Philippe de Beaumanoir, in which a death sentence assumes the name of vengeance. It may be seen, too, in the importance given by the judges in the *Parlement* to the law on retaliation when they consider the possibility of imposing the death sentence. We have already seen the *procureur du roi* use that law in the middle years of the fifteenth century to justify a demand for the ultimate penalty. In fact, the argument was frequently used.[18] The violent murder of a man might lead to a corresponding death, for example by hanging; other penalties, too, resembled the crimes which they expiated. It was as if the Court had accepted the motivation of vengeance – an eye for an eye – and had transformed it into a principle of justice. Thus, particularly in the case of the worst crimes, the demand might be made for the ultimate penalty as an act of vengeance (*ad penam talionis*), all the more so, as one case suggests, since it could not be applied in civil cases or when the accused was not indicted on a criminal charge.[19] In such cases, the principle was applied as appropriate. So, it is clear that he who had abused an office must surrender that office; the forger of documents must lose his right hand, while the blasphemer must have his tongue pierced.[20] In such circumstances, the death sentence becomes difficult to apply. Nothing suggests that its use could satisfy the desire for vengeance. Numerous examples of disturbances at the place of execution, or of the bodies of those regarded as having been unjustly hanged being taken down, demonstrate opposition to royal orders. Members of the Court did not hesitate to express their view that such demonstrations against judicial decisions were *crimes detestables*, even *capitaux*; yet little attention was paid to them. Judges, therefore, had to struggle against the aggrieved party, against those who might riot in favour of a condemned person, indeed even against the king's

17] C. Gauvard, 'L'Honneur du roi: peines et rituels judiciaires au Parlement de Paris à la fin du moyen âge', in *Les Rites de la Justice: gestes et rituels judiciaires dans l'Occident médiéval*, ed. C. Gauvard and R. Jacob, Paris, 2000, pp. 93–123.
18] Cited n. 11, above.
19] AN, X2a 12, fols. 401–401v (1399).
20] These penalties were still being called for in the fifteenth century (AN, X2a 24, fols 56v, 80v, 207 [1445, 1447]).

support for a man sentenced to die. In March 1406, three men who had tried to prevent an execution from taking place were arrested and brought before the *Parlement*. They were said to have argued about a verbal stay of execution granted to them by the king and to have created a disturbance at the gallows, the execution only taking place thanks to the determined attitude of the executioner who would not be deflected from his task.[21] Addressing the Court, the *procureur du roi* began by making two assertions concerning the king's powers in the matter of justice: 'that all who act against past royal ordinances in the matter of justice shall be severely punished', while 'he who prevents an execution commits a crime of the highest order'. The criminals, he added, should not have obeyed the verbal order for release obtained from the king (surely asking too much of them!) since 'they knew that it was forbidden to petition the king to hinder his own justice; nor should they have been in ignorance of the fact, for others had tried to do the same before, and they should have warned the king that his order was against his honour, and that it should not be put into effect'. In spite of the high principles expressed, the three were simply cautioned and released, only to be lost to history.[22]

In cases involving the death sentence, the judges of the *Parlement* remained very circumspect for a number of reasons. As we have seen, the Court preferred conciliation to compulsion at any price, for the judges always feared that the imposition of the death penalty might lead to violent reaction. The Court had neither the wish nor the ability to rule on cases arising out of local courts from which it received appeals, as the death sentences pronounced in these courts were not always justified. Counsel made frequent reference to the element of hatred which local justice can conceal. Justice is always influenced by hidden pressures to be found in any society made up of divergent and often powerful interests. In practice, the *Parlement* rarely allowed itself to become involved in the details of such conflicts. Rather, its task was to enquire whether the death penalty had been applied by those with a full understanding of the case, and whether it had been carried out in a proper fashion. Summing up this approach, the *procureur du roi* was to state in 1449 that 'quant on traicte de la mort d'aucuns, l'en doit proceder bien meurement et s'enquerir de la verité du cas' ('when one is concerned with the death of individuals, one must proceed with care, and seek out the truth of the matter').[23] In brief, the death penalty was used more frequently as part of an argument than it was in reality. Did the judges, one may ask, have the means of arriving at the truth which, alone, could justify the imposition of the supreme penalty?

21] AN, X2a 14, fol. 310 (1406).
22] AN, X2a 25, fol. 11 (1449).
23] Ibid.

The Dissuasive Effect of the Death Sentence: Capital Crimes and Royal Cases

The death penalty was an argument constantly associated with its deterrent effect and, in this respect, the view of the judges and lawyers of the *Parlement* of Paris did not differ from that of the political theorists, theologians or other members of the legal fraternity at the end of the Middle Ages.[24] Their ideas were based mainly on two currents of thought. One, philosophical, was inspired by Seneca who, in a context of reform, had shown that the harsher a punishment, the greater was the effect on other people.[25] This idea would be prominent in the writings of Christine de Pizan and Nicolas de Clamanges; it may also be found in the works of Jean Gerson.[26] The other current came from Roman law, as expressed in both the Code and the Digest.[27] This would be the point of view adopted by medieval jurists who based the repression of criminality on two factors, one distributive, the other dissuasive, that is to say that the punishment must fit the crime, while at the same time acting as a deterrent to future trouble-makers.[28] In the minds of Philippe de Beaumanoir and his successors, the deterrent factor was clearly linked to the procedure of *inquisitio*, which allowed a judge to initiate an action *ex officio*.[29] It is likely that these two currents, philosophical and juridical, merged towards the end of the Middle Ages. The *procureur du roi* made many statements reflecting their influence before the *Parlement*, under the pretext that crimes involving bloodshed were occurring all over the kingdom, and should be stopped. In one case, it is the grant of a royal pardon which is criticised, since a crime involving wounding and the bearing of forbidden arms should have merited the death penalty. In another, it was a homicide followed by resistance to the execution of a royal warrant and abuse of office which, it was claimed, merited the ultimate penalty, so that it would 'constitue exemple a tous autres veu que teles resistances pululent aujourduy plus que jamais' ('serve as an example to others, since such resistance is more

24] C. Gauvard, 'Les Humanistes et la justice sous le règne de Charles VI', in *Pratiques de la culture écrite en France au XVe siècle*, ed. M. Ornato and N. Pons, Louvain-la-Neuve, 1995, pp. 217–44.
25] Seneca, *De ira*, Vol. III, ch. 19.
26] Gauvard, 'Les Humanistes et la justice', p. 230.
27] 'Ut unius poena metus possit esse multorum' (*Code*, 9, 27, 1); 'Ut exemplo aliis ad deterrenda maleficia sit' (*Digest*, 16, 3, 31).
28] J.-M. Carbasse, 'La Peine en droit français', in *La Peine: Europe avant le XVIIIe siècle (Recueils de la Société Jean Bodin)*, Brussels, 1991, Vol. II, pp. 157–72; idem, '*Ne homines interficiantur*. Quelques remarques sur la sanction médiévale de l'homicide', in *Auctoritates Xenia R. C. Van Caenegem oblata*, ed. S. Dauchy, J. Monballyu and A. Wijffels, Brussels, 1997, pp. 165–85.
29] 'Bonne chose est que l'en queure au devant des maufeteurs et qu'il soient si radement puni et justicié selonc leur mesfès que, pour la doute de la justice, li autres en prengnent essample si qu'il se gardent de mesfere' (Beaumanoir, *Coutumes de Beauvaisis*, Vol. I, ch. XXX, p. 446).

common today than ever before').[30] Every punishment, and that of death in particular, was seen as a way of conveying a moral message which could act as a dissuasive one as well.

What was the political context in which these exemplary punishments might be applied? Contrary to what has long been thought, the element of exemplarity in any penalty was not a last resort, a sign of weakness in the system of royal justice. The available evidence suggests something much more complicated for, if the judges sitting in the *Parlement* were intent upon maintaining at least the possibility of applying exemplary punishments, the manner of resolving judicial conflicts was also heavily dependent on the other face of justice, that which was seen as conciliatory, even liberating. Private compromises between parties were always encouraged, even by members of the Court who might lend an expert hand in arbitration. As for pardons, these were the subject of many a letter issued by the royal chancellery. In this sense, recourse to an exemplary death penalty allowed for the development of both the royal pardon and of acts of conciliation, thus giving the judiciary its two facets.[31] At the same time, the social fabric was preserved. It was never the aim of the death penalty to destroy this; rather, it was to mend the effects of any crime against it. Even if truth itself were unattainable, did this mean that the death penalty could not be applied if there existed any serious element of doubt in the minds of the judges, which had to be in step with public opinion? For the ritual surrounding an execution existed as a reminder that the crowd was an active participant in the event. In spite of developments in the inquisitorial procedure which gave them the right to initiate action *ex officio*, the judges neither wished nor were able to make any decision about a possible death sentence which was not open to challenge by the people. By virtue of its presence at all executions, it was the crowd which decided on last-minute reprieves. It was the crowd which was present to oversee the effectiveness of the ritual surrounding an execution, and to give its approval to the verdict delivered in court. The judges in the *Parlement* paid close attention to the reaction of the crowd. In cases when capital sentences were opposed, counsel did not fail to point out that the crowd had not been heard; and vice versa, if such a sentence needed justification, it was said that it had the approval of the crowd which shouted 'Death, death'.[32] Early in the fifteenth century, the *avocat*, Pierre de

30] AN, X2a 24, fol. 154 (1447); X2a 49, fol. 30v (1483).

31] C. Gauvard, 'Grâce et exécution capitale, les deux visages de la justice royale française à la fin du moyen âge', *BEC*, Vol. CLIII, 1995, pp. 275–90.

32] See the evidence regarding Epernay, where 'il soit accoustumé que quant aucun malfaiteur doit estre executé pour ses desmerites, l'en le mene de plain jour a la justice et doit confesser son malefice a la pierre etc, et au gibet aussi, oyant le peuple ...' (AN, X2a 10, fol. 158 [1383]); while in other examples 'le peuple crioit qu'il n'eschapast qu'il ne morust et pour ce fu a ce condempnez et executez' (X2a 14, fol. 302v [1406]); 'et trouverent bien mil personnes qui crierent que on amenoit point le prisonnier et coururent sus audit prevost et a la justice' (AN, X2a 14, fol. 317 [1406]).

Marigny, summed up the viewpoint of the *Parlement* when, in relation to a case heard at Saint-Quentin, he claimed that the people must be present at an execution as 'la coustume est que les gens y vont pour conforter la justice et pour exemple' ('it is customary that people attend to support justice and to provide an example').[33] It is through this double participation, at once active and passive, that the subjects of the King of France could both accept and obey their country's penal laws.

Let us recall, however, that, being exemplary, such cases were rare. On the whole, reference to the death sentence was part of a lawyer's professional language. Trials themselves helped to classify crimes into major categories, to define the very worst among them, which tended to become *cas royaux* involving the crown. In the absence of clear categories, and in the light of the discretionary powers of judges and the lack of legislative pointers in criminal matters, both the classification of crimes and the penalties which they might attract were far from consistent. To seek a remedy in the *coutumiers* would be unproductive. In this respect, the discussions held in the courts were of the greatest importance, in so far as one of the judges' functions was to categorise crimes according to their perceived seriousness, and, in so doing, to help create a jurisprudence for the future.

Certain crimes were thus termed *capitaux* or *énormes*, the implication being that they would attract the death penalty which would be carried out. Judges came to link the enormity of a crime more and more consistently to the ultimate penalty for, as the *procureur du roi* at Montpellier explained in 1406, 'quand une personne est condempnee pour un crime enorme et qui est contre chose publique, il doit estre executé' ('when a person is condemned for a crime regarded as "enorme" and which is against the public interest, then he should be executed').[34] In the same way, in the mid-fifteenth century, the action taken by Guillaume de Flavy against Pierre de Rieux, which led to the latter's execution in 1441, was regarded as treason, granted that the victim was Marshal of France. As the *procureur du roi* argued, there should be *punicion capital* in this case, since the accusations of carrying arms, having a private prison and abusing jurisdiction were regarded as 'tres grans crimes' ('very great crimes').[35] The step from 'capital' to 'irremissible' crimes was a short one. Opposition to royal pardons, particularly in the fifteenth century, allows us to draw up a list of crimes regarded as *capitaux*. In practice, it corresponds with those set out in the *ordonnance*, dated 3 March 1357, which is referred to in the pleadings as 'les ordonnances faites par le roi Jehan' ('the ordinances issued by King John').[36] The list covers deliberate and wilful killing, the abduction and rape of virgins and married

33] Ibid., fol. 317v (1406).
34] AN, X2a 14, fol. 270v (1405).
35] AN, X2a 24, fol. 41 (1444).
36] AN, X2a 35, fol. 151v (1468).

women, the burning of houses, and sacrilege.[37] During the fifteenth century, the list would become longer, with the addition of the crimes of treason and sorcery.

May one go further still and conclude that the definition of capital and irremissible crimes led to the development of what historians, following Ernest Perrot, call *cas royaux*?[38] A positive answer to this important question would show that royal justice had assumed the more or less exclusive judgement of major criminal cases, as well as the imposition of the death penalty associated with them. In this matter, the policy of the judges sitting in the *Parlement* does not seem very clear. By contrast, that followed at the *Châtelet*, particularly under the government of the Marmousets, and then at the time when Guillaume de Tignonville was *prévôt* of Paris (1401–08), appears clear enough. At the court of the *prévôté*, it was sufficient to have been a threat to public safety on the highway to be considered worthy of execution. The examples drawn up by Aleaume Cachemarée, clerk of the criminal court, for the years 1389–92, and cases involving the status of clerk heard at the beginning of the following century, are significant, for they show the *prévôté* of Paris tracking down 'publici larrones, insidiatores itinerum' ('public robbers and ensnarers of highways').[39] In the *Parlement*, however, the *procureur du roi* did not systematically link the activities of these major criminals to the death penalty. In defining the *cas royaux*, the court preferred to establish the gravity of a crime by judging its effects upon society. It is the word *esclandre*, with its sense of scandalous or public notoriety or effect, which is used, as in the case when the *procureur du roi* claimed that 'l'esclandre est grant auquel est necessité de pourvoir par la Court, et pour ce requiert qu'elle y pourvoye en telle maniere que l'esclandre cesse et qu'elle permette aux juges de corriger et pugnir ainsi que le cas le requiert' ('the effect is widely felt, so that the Court must provide [a remedy], and he therefore demands that it should act in such a way that the said effects should cease, so that the judges may both correct and punish as circumstances require').[40] There exist, therefore, certain offences, such as breaking the king's peace, which define a particular action having public repercussions; these are public crimes, such as the one 'dont Paris et tout le royaume ont esté fort scandalisé et aussi l'a esté le roy' ('by which Paris and the entire kingdom have been deeply shocked, as has been the king').[41] Here, again, we find traces of the influence of public opinion. In order to extend its authority over the public domain, the *Parlement* did not use the threat of the death sentence. Rather, it simply defined privileged places, such

37] See n. 15, above.
38] E. Perrot, *Les Cas royaux. Origine et développement de la théorie aux XIIIe et XIVe siècles*, Paris, 1910; new edn, Geneva, 1975.
39] Gauvard, 'Les Humanistes et la justice', p. 242. On criminals tried at the Châtelet and called *larrons*, *forts larrons* or *larrons publics*, see *Registre criminel du Châtelet de Paris du 6 septembre 1389 au 18 mai 1392*, ed. H. Duplès-Agier, 2 vols, Paris, 1861–64, passim.
40] AN, X2a 35, fol. 231 (1470).
41] Ibid., fol. 157v (1469).

as the public highway, and privileged cases. These crimes, thus defined, could be punished with death; yet it was not the penalty imposed which transformed them into 'public' cases. The typology of such crimes was created in a different way, as is shown by the case of theft, regarded as a highly criminal activity in the late Middle Ages. In this case, the crime and its circumstances (location, time, issues and persons involved) interacted to encourage the forces of repression, particularly when it was a case of the accused having committed 'plusieurs larrecins, roberies, sacrileges, crocheteries, et piperies, lesquels crimes pour la plupart sont publiques' ('several larcenies and robberies, as well as sacrileges, petty thefts and frauds, most of which crimes are public').[42]

In the mind of the *Parlement*, the death penalty could thus become a means of developing its judicial authority. But here we must be careful. It was not to be a keystone in the creation of that authority. Although heading the list of penalties, as the tradition inherited from Roman law demanded, the imposition of the death penalty was little used by the highest court in the land. It remained an option available to lesser jurisdictions; the task of the *Parlement* was to ensure that it was properly used.

Incorrigibility and Justification of the Death Penalty

There remain the small number of cases for which the death penalty was mandatory. In most cases it involved persons who had passed themselves off as clerks, over whom the ecclesiastical courts were claiming jurisdiction. The context was, therefore, one of a conflict between rival jurisdictions, which also reflected the bad name of certain clerks in the France of the late Middle Ages. It was for these that the notion of incorrigibility was put in place. Robert Genestal dated its origins to the end of the fifteenth century.[43] It is true that, at that time, the idea was widely accepted, as is shown by the evidence of the trial, held at Fontenay-le-Comte in 1484, in which the judge had to justify his imposition of the death penalty upon a thief. The condemned man had previously been expelled from the town, but had continued his nefarious activities; he was said to have belonged to a group called the 'bons enfants' of La Rochelle. The judge claimed that he would willingly have spared him 's'il eust appareu qu'il eust esté corrigible' ('if he had appeared corrigible').[44] In another case, a man was said to have been justly condemned to death since, 'obstiné en sa mauvaise volonté' ('obstinate in his determination to do ill'), he had not repented of his crimes which, it was assumed, he was ready to commit again.[45] At that time, the concept

42] Ibid.
43] R. Genestal, *Le Privilegium fori en France du décret de Gratien à la fin du Moyen Age*, 2 vols, Paris, 1921.
44] AN, X2a 49, fols 143–143v (1484).
45] Ibid., fol. 16 (1483).

was already so firmly established that it was beginning to be applied to lay people.

In fact, the origins and application of the doctrine of incorrigibility appeared well before the end of the fifteenth century: Genestal's timescale should be put back by at least a century. Incorrigibility in a criminal was used in the *Parlement* as early as the late fourteenth century; it is likely that the period of rule by the Marmousets, and the judicial reforms sought by Guillaume de Tignonville in the *prévôté* of Paris, were largely responsible for this definition taken up in the pleadings made before the *Parlement*. Thus when Baudrain du Hamel, who was fated to end his life at the end of a rope, first appeared before the Court on charges of waging private war, he was condemned to such penalties as giving help to pious foundations, paying fines and purchasing annuities (*rentes*) for his victims. It was only when he resumed some of his worst activities that the Court came to regard him as an incorrigible criminal, and finally condemned him to drawing and hanging.[46]

What were the origins of this notion of incorrigibility? They are very closely linked to those of recidivism, but should not automatically be associated with them. To be regarded as incorrigible, a man must be a recidivist, but not all recidivists are incorrigible. The registers of the *Parlement* show that about a quarter of those criminals who appeared before it were recidivists, while those regarded as incorrigible were, in fact, rare. The difference between the two concepts, a subtle one, none the less gave judges a measure of freedom to increase repression according to the circumstances of the case or, in particular, according to the 'profile' of the accused.[47]

From a juridical point of view, incorrigibility depended less on civil than on canon law. The term, originally mainly applied to clerks, was to be found in Gratian's *Decretum* (1140), and would be developed in canonical writings from the twelfth century onwards. Gratian's idea was that those who had succumbed to sin, or who appeared incorrigible, should be separated from the Church. He went on to say that clerks adjudged incorrigible should not be pardoned.[48]

Gratian's thoughts on this matter formed part of a long clerical tradition owing its origins to the widely read works of Gregory the Great, Bede and Isidore of Seville.[49] The idea, if not the word 'incorrigibilis' itself, had appeared in the *Rule* of St Benedict, and would be used in later monastic rules, for instance

46] AN, X2a 13, fol. 143 (1396). See also n. 10, above.

47] On the discretionary powers of judges, see B. Schnapper, 'Les Peines arbitraires du XIIe au XVIIIe siècle (Doctrines savantes et usages français)', *Revue d'histoire du droit*, Vol. XLI, 1973, pp. 237–77; ibid., Vol. XLII, 1974, pp. 81–112.

48] '... a peccatis aut incorrigibiles apparuerint, ab ecclesia separentur ... incorrigibilis dampnationis sententia relaxari non potest' (*Decretum*, C. 24. 3. 14 [T], 994, 49; C. 24. 2. 5 [R], 986, 8).

49] According to the *Corpus Christianorum*, there are numerous references under 'incorrigibilis' and 'incorrigibiliter' in the *Moralia in Job* of Gregory the Great.

those of the Cistercians and the orders of canons regular which date from the twelfth century.[50] The origin of the notion, then, was monastic rather than secular. The problem raised by these statutes was a double one, moral and juridical. It was a matter of defining at what moment an individual became involved in a sin or crime from which there was no return; and was it the nature of the offence or the repetition of offences, or even the two interacting, which proved irreversibility? The responses varied, but in general the recidivist was allowed to return three times to his wrong-doing, and the crimes, if they are detailed, follow the list of irremissible acts (sins against nature, aggravated theft, homicide, arson, conspiracy, etc.). From a juridical standpoint, it was a matter of defining clearly the rules to be followed in cases of incorrigibility: the fate of the offender depended upon justice, normally that of the monastery, administered by the abbot or prior, who must be responsible for fixing a sentence, in theory excommunication or expulsion. It was for these reasons that incorrigibility was incorporated into the monastic rules.

Then, from the twelfth century, the notion spread from the monasteries to all parts of the Church, so that in 1198, Innocent III could resume the situation in these words:

> Si qui vero in purgatione defecerint vel ad sinodum venire contempserint, ad proximam ecclesiam secunde sinodi vocantur pro contumacia corrigendi. Qui si forte non venerint vel incorrigibiles ibi apparuerint, ad terciam ecclesiam tercie sinodi legitime citabuntur et, si incorrigibiles adhuc extiterint, pro contumacia sua anathematis sententia ferientur.

> Those who have not done penance or have refused to come before a synod shall be called for purposes of purging this refusal to the venue of the next synod. If, by chance, they do not appear or appear incorrigible, they shall rightly be summoned to the church of the third synod and, if they still appear incorrigible, sentences of anathema shall be imposed for their contumacy.[51]

We may note that the term *incorrigibilis* was to pass into common use in the ecclesiastical world just at the moment when inquisitorial procedure, whereby the struggle against heresy was developed, was put in place. At the same time, the idea would spread through synodal statutes to be applied to all the faithful who had committed crimes, such as adultery,[52] normally judged by the Church. By

50] *Benedicti Regula*, ed. R. Hanslik, in *Corpus Scriptorum Ecclesiasticorum Latinorum*, Vol. LXXV, Vienna, 1960, pp. 85–86.

51] *Die Register Innocenz III*, ed. O. Hageneder and A. Haidacher, 2 vols, Graz and Cologne, 1964; Rome and Vienna, 1979, Vol. I, p. 630, no. 420 (13 November 1198). The clerk defrocked for a crime faced a succession of ecclesiatical censures, and no longer remained subject to church tribunals after his solemn excommunication, which made him subject to the secular arm.

52] Take, for instance, the following example from Rouen (1238–44): 'frequenter contra

the thirteenth century, the notion of incorrigibility had travelled far beyond the monastic setting which had given rise to it.

To these categories, clearly influenced by canon law, were to be added certain philosophical considerations. Let us consider two examples. In the first, dated 1460, it was argued that Jacotin Le Clerc, accused of breaking into the house of the widow of Pierre Michel under cover of darkness, should not be handed over to the bishop's official, 'de tous temps a esté noyseux, natif de Picardie et a esté banni de Tournay et a fait pluseurs noises en ceste ville au cymetiere Saint Jehan ... est ruffian et pour ceste raison de pluseurs cas a esté pluseurs fois emprisonné ... est incorrigible, banny de Tournay et de ceste ville, goliart et a coustume des sa jeunesse en mal' ('for he has long been a regular trouble-maker, a native of Picardy who has been expelled from Tournai after having caused several disturbances in the cemetery of St John in that town ... a scoundrel who has been put in prison several times for the same offences, an "incorrigible", banished from Tournai and from this city, a ne'er-do-good accustomed since his youth to doing wrong').[53] Four years earlier, the *procureur du roi* had reported of another miscreant who 'est incorrigible, par deux ou trois foiz a esté rendu a l'eglise et neantmoins est recheu, mais il a esté banny et lui a esté defendu soubx peine d'estre jetté en la riviere de non plus revenir a Paris' ('is incorrigible and has been handed over to the Church two or three times, but has none the less reverted to his old ways, and has been banished and forbidden, under pain of being thrown into the river, from ever returning to Paris').[54] Let us leave aside the strategy which aimed at preventing as many clerks as possible from recognising the jurisdiction of the official's court by making them forfeit their privileges as clergy. This policy was surely intended to counter ecclesiastical justice which did not condemn to death and founded its judgements on the idea of purgation and remissibility.

In defining the incorrigible, the reasons proposed by lay judges were basically of three kinds; a life given to crime since youth; a life given over to repeated wrong-doing; and the sort of crime committed, in particular, crimes which brought dishonour to the victims, notably sexual crimes and those involving bloodshed or theft. The categories follow stereotypes which were to evolve during the Middle Ages, and which reflect the desperate struggle against vagabondage, the illegal carrying of weapons, and sexual perversions.[55] Persistence in

---

adulteros, incestuosos, usurarios notorios clament et predicent sacerdotes; et si incorrigibiles videantur seu inveniantur, denuncient eos nobis' (*Statuts synodaux français du XIIIe siècle*, ed O. Pontal, 2 vols, Paris, 1971, 1983, Vol. II, p. 132 ('Les statuts de 1230 à 1260').

53] AN, X2a 28, fol. 320 (1460).

54] Ibid., fol. 56v (1456).

55] On the stereotype of bad reputation, see A. Porteau-Bitker and A. Talazac-Laurent, 'La Renommée dans le droit pénal laïque du XIIIe au XVe siècle', in *La Renommée*, ed. C. Gauvard, *Médiévales*, Vol. XXIV, 1993, pp. 67–80.

wrong-doing came together with consideration of recidivism, but with a moral connotation. He who practised this kind of relapse eventually surrendered to sin, 'in profundum malorum'.[56] It was to admit that the practice of crime had become a habit (*habitus*) in the sense of the word given by Aquinas. The basis of the notion was theological.[57] To this 'habit' might be added predispositions visible since a man's youth. The question then became: was there a predisposition towards wrong-doing? Following Aristotle's *Rhetoric* and *Nicomachean Ethics*, Aquinas showed that society must be held together; but he excluded from it brutes and saints, a-social since birth. As for criminals reputed to be incorrigible, they were descended from the category of brutes, so that in this matter theology and law came together. The need to pursue a criminal inquest upon a man's reputation (*fama*) meant interrogating his past as far back as his childhood. The judges came to learn about 'les enfances mauvaises' ('the wicked infancies') of the man who 'onques ne fit bien mais tousjours depuis et des son enfance s'est appliqué a mal faire, a jouer aux dez, a la paume, suir les tavernes et les fillettes diffamees, pieça se rendi carme dont laissa l'abit et devint chevaucheur et homme d'armes et vagabond' ('has never done good but who, ever since his childhood, has sought to do ill, to play at dice and at "paume", has frequented taverns and girls of bad repute, may have become a Carmelite only to give up the habit to become a thief, a man of violence, a vagabond').[58] The man is then lost to society which no longer has any scruple about excluding him. One understands better the heroic efforts of criminals who, under torture at the *Châtelet*, tried to show that they had enjoyed a normal childhood, living peacefully and quietly with their parents. Can one go so far as to speak of men predestined to wrong-doing? Numerous examples (*exempla*) used by preachers underline the influence of education, and how the father is to blame for not having restrained his son's tendencies to delinquency.[59] Education could also influence the role of heredity, increase self-control and train persons in the exercise of free will. By contrast, the guilty man may appear as a gangrenous member which society must cut away, in so far as he may give a bad example to young children and pervert the future of the social body.[60] For those hardened

56] AN, X2a 28, fol. 359v (1461).
57] *Summa theologica*, Ia IIae qu. 77, 81, 93.
58] AN, X2a 14, fol. 10 (1401); X2a 17, fol. 236v (1416).
59] See the *exemplum* of the son who, on the scaffold itself, bites the nose of his father who has come to embrace him, for not having prevented him from turning to crime (Eloi d'Amerval, *Le Livre de la deablerie*, ed. R. Deschaux and B. Charrier, Geneva, 1991, pp. 567–68, vv. 15008–15056).
60] See, for instance, the case against Sevestre de Bailleul, at La Rochelle, who has encouraged children 'a jouer aux dex et autres jeux, et a ce dient plus de XXX, fait espier quant les peres et meres sont dehors pour entrer aux hostelz pour illec jouer, fait aler lesdits enfans sur les murs de la ville et au port afin de jouer plus secretement, induit lesdits enfans quant ont joué et perdu leur argent a desrober peres et meres' ('to play at

by crime who have no attachments in the world, the death penalty is thus fully justified.

We should recall that we are concerned with a very small number of people. The *Parlement* is not so much the place where the death sentence is justified as the one where norms are defined and where society's various groups are classified. The death sentence is not to be excluded from that process. None the less, it is a sentence only rarely applied, because those who are judged in the Court are often nobles, office holders, men of respectable position in society. The death penalty is handed down largely to those whom society has chosen to reject without real risk of reprisal: thieves, vagabonds, men carrying arms. These men stand at bay: they have less and less chance of being saved by the Church which, in the view of secular courts, takes a lax view of the law. In effect, they have become victims of a criminal justice, which makes their fate a political issue. The winner is royal lay justice which has taken over the death penalty. This does not mean that the application of that penalty is more rigorously applied, nor that its use is being developed. There are other ways, indeed many other ways, of dealing with crimes, including capital crimes. It is all a question of men and their priorities which express themselves in particular fashions, while the exercise of the king's justice remains full of contradictions which more or less paralyse it. It was not simply the right of the *Parlement* to exercise the death penalty, but also its right to speak about it, which led to the growth of the judicial power of the King of France. What was at issue was not simply the need to restore peace between parties, as had always been the case. It was not even to make judgements which would then be carried out. Developments were now in a period of transition, when it was more important to be able to discuss cases in order to preserve intact the reputations (and honour) of the victims which, although those of individuals, were seen more and more as reflecting the very reputation (and honour) of the king himself.

---

dice and other games, as more than 30 persons claim, or has children on the look-out to see whether their parents are out in order to enter their houses to play therein, or get the said children on the town walls or down at the port to play there more out of sight, or persuade children who have gambled and lost their money to steal from their fathers and mothers') (AN, X2a 32, fols 50v–51 [1461]).

12

Membra disjecta of the Breton *Chambre des Comptes* in the Late Middle Ages: Treasures Revisited and Rediscovered

MICHAEL JONES

The dramatic story of how Héracle-Olivier-Jean-Baptiste de Blocquel de Croix, Baron de Wismes and his friend, Arthur Le Moyne de la Borderie, later the outstanding nineteenth-century historian of Brittany, discovered and rescued a small part of the archives of the former Breton *Chambre des Comptes* in 1857 was told two years later in a fascinating article, 'Le Trésor de la rue des Caves à Nantes'.[1] While walking past an old house, de Wismes recalled, 'j'aperçus deux ou trois individus accroupis près d'un puits situé dans l'angle de la cour de cette maison et occupés à laver des piles de vieux parchemins' ('I saw two or three individuals squatting near a well by the corner of this house, all busily engaged in washing piles of old parchment'). Overcome with curiosity, he entered the court, to be met by a man from Alsace, who showed him three rooms full of drying parchments. Recognising that many were medieval, de Wismes struck a bargain, offering to buy documents at two francs a pound. The deal completed, he carried home several kilos, and then immediately wrote to his friend La Borderie about his find, offering to share future spoils with him. A few days later, together they returned to repeat the procedure:

> Qu'est-ce donc, en effet, cette feuille que je tiens entre les mains? Ne sont-ce point les comptes de quelque belle campagne du grand connétable, notre duc Arthur de Richemont? Et vous, La Borderie, quelle attention soutenue! quels regards flamboyants! que fixez-vous donc ainsi? Mais vraiement, votre admiration ne m'étonne pas, je reconnais la signature de notre grande duchesse Anne. C'est un état de dépense de sa maison qu'elle a voulu approuver elle-même. Du reste, il n'est presque pas un de nos ducs, dont nous ne retrouvons ici une partie des comptes pendant le cours des XIVe et XVe siècles ...[2]

1] Le baron de Wismes, 'Le Trésor de la rue des Caves à Nantes', *Revue de Bretagne et de Vendée*, Vol. V, 1859, pp. 152–61 and 311–35. His most important work was *L'Anjou historique, archéologique et pittoresque*, 55 livraisons (1854–62), re-edited by A. Sarrazin (no place, 1982).
2] de Wismes, 'Le Trésor', pp. 152 and 155–56. See C. Joret, 'Notice sur la vie et les travaux de M. de la Borderie', *BEC*, Vol. LXIII, 1902, pp. 177–219, and J.-Y. Guiomar, *Le Bretonisme. Les historiens bretons au XIXe siècle*, Mayenne, 1987, passim, for the giant figure of La Borderie.

> What is this sheet which I am holding in my hands? Aren't they the accounts of some fine campaign of the great constable, our duke, Arthur de Richemont? And you, La Borderie, what unremitting attention, what intense looks, what are you looking at in this way? Decidedly, your admiration does not surprise me; I recognise the signature of our beloved Duchess, Anne. It is a statement of household expenses. Moreover, there is hardly a single one of our dukes of the fourteenth and fifteenth centuries of whose accounts we don't find here at least a part …

Seeing a notice reading 'les frères G…t, relieurs-archivistes',[3] the two friends questioned the Alsatian further on what he was doing and how the documents had come into his hands. It transpired that he was the leader of a small itinerant band which, as it made its way around the country, had been offering to bind the *Bulletin des Lois* and other official publications that every commune regularly received, before asking whether there were any other archives which required attention. They had made a surprisingly good living: many *maires*, embarrassed by the relentlessly accumulating mass of the *Bulletins* and copies of the *Moniteur*, and having made little provision for their preservation, proved only too eager to seize the chance to clean up their archives and restore municipal pride with newly bound volumes. Thus, following a tradition that can easily be traced back into the Middle Ages, but one which had above all flourished from the first days of the Republic, these enterprising *relieurs-archivistes* had used many allegedly redundant documents to furnish material for the covers of registers of births, deaths and marriages and anything else which required binding; hence the washing and reprocessing of parchment in the rue des Caves that had first attracted de Wismes' attention.

In this instance, it soon became clear that the parchments concerned were originally from the former Breton *Chambre des Comptes*. This sat for the last time on 30 June 1791. Its records, chiefly relating to the administration of the royal (previously ducal) demesne in the province, had then been deliberately dispersed as a result of *ordonnances* issued in 1792 for the destruction of 'useless papers' (interpreted as accounts more than thirty years old) and the subsequent appointment by the *Directoire* of a *Commission de Triage* to decide on the fate of documents produced under the Ancien Regime. Initially some were burnt, but it was then realised they could be sold or recycled in other ways, and a clandestine market for old parchment developed. In February 1793, for instance, Citizens Couy, Moreau, Menant, Neveu, Barras and Grasset acquired a lot of former Breton *Chambre des Comptes* records for 3478 *l.* 4*s.* 9*d.*[4] But when, later in that

3] de Wismes, 'Le Trésor', p. 156; later, the anonymity of the brothers is disguised as 'R…t' (p. 335).

4] Ibid., p. 160; cf. H. de Berranger, *Guide des Archives de la Loire-Atlantique*, 2 vols, Nantes, 1962–64, Vol. I, pp. 20–27 for a brief survey of the *Chambre* and its records. The most recent authoritative discussion of its history is J. Kerhervé, *L'État breton aux*

year, in addition to the condemned Ancien Regime governmental records, there were new orders to destroy 'titres féodaux et nobiliaires' ('feudal and noble titles'), the commission had its hands so full that more radical measures were required: it was at this point that large quantities of records were despatched to the state departments responsible for maritime affairs and war, where parchment was used in arsenals as wadding for artillery or for 'autres usages' ('other purposes').

Finally, between July 1795 and October 1796, the *Commission de Triage* at Nantes systematically examined what still survived not only from the *Chambre des Comptes* but also from the archives of the *États de Bretagne*, ecclesiastical houses and seigneurial families, in all some 3000 *liasses* in addition to those already found in the *Chambre*.[5] Of these, 1900 were condemned, leading to the destruction of the papers of many leading noble families of the Nantais, the records of abbeys such as La Blanche-Couronne, and those of all the major mendicant houses of the diocese of Nantes. Of 470 *liasses* relating to the *États*, only 26 were saved; from the *Chambre des Comptes*, 959 *liasses* were suppressed and only 125 saved, perhaps a total loss of some four-fifths of its records, and no less than 13 000 lbs of parchment was sent to the navy and army. Only by chance was the aptly named *Trésor des Chartes des ducs de Bretagne* saved, since the doorway leading to the cupboards (*armoires*), which contained the still-surviving wooden boxes (*cassettes*) made for the main ducal archives in the reign of Anne of Brittany (1488–1514), was fortuitously hidden behind barrels of coins.[6] Thus this invaluable *fonds* for the history of the medieval duchy was preserved long enough for its value to be recognised and acquired for the *département* of Loire-Inférieure in November 1795. Then, by a law of 5 Brumaire An V (26 October 1796), all papers and titles acquired by the Republic were to be gathered together in the *chef-lieu* of each *département*, the birth-certificate of the *archives départementales*.[7]

In the case of Loire-Inférieure (since 1957 Loire-Atlantique), this has happily meant the preservation of the majority of the records which the *Commission de Triage* allowed to survive, including those of the defunct *Chambre des Comptes*.

14e et 15e siècles. Les ducs, l'argent et les hommes, 2 vols, Paris, 1987, Vol. I, pp. 341–405; see also Kerhervé, 'Les Présidents de la Chambre des Comptes de Bretagne au XVe siècle', in *La France des principautés. Les Chambres des Comptes en France aux XIVe et XVe siècles*, ed. P. Contamine and O. Mattéoni, 2 vols, Paris, 1996–97, Vol. I, pp. 165–204, with a documentary appendix in Vol. II, pp. 127–79.

5] de Wismes, 'Le Trésor', pp. 320–22 for this and following details.

6] On my first visit to Nantes in 1964, documents were still delivered in the *Salle de travail* in these fine oak boxes. The famous inventory of the ducal archives completed by René de Bourgneuf in 1579 (of which many later copies survive) classified documents in the form *Arm[oire] A, Cass[ette] B. no. 1*, and these references, often added again when the surviving documents were re-inventoried in the ninteenth century, still retain value for purposes of identification.

7] de Wismes, 'Le Trésor', p. 324; de Berranger, *Guide des Archives*, Vol. I, pp. 74–79 for the 248 *liasses* of the *Trésor des Chartes*, now Arch. Dép. Loire-Atlantique, E 1–E 248.

Thanks to the *Inventaires sommaires* of *Série B*, compiled by three successive archivists, most of this surviving *fonds* is readily accessible.[8] It will concern us only marginally; what is in question here is the fate of some records 'liberated' at the Revolution and rediscovered later, such as those in the rue des Caves, and their own subsequent fate, since as the activities of the brothers G...t in the mid-nineteenth century showed, even where medieval records had survived the depredations of the Revolutionary period, their survival to our own day was not necessarily guaranteed.

Indeed, to take the case of the *trésor* of the rue des Caves, although de Wismes and La Borderie obtained some important records, the brothers G...t and their unsold stock of parchments disappeared as mysteriously as they had come before the two *savants* were able to recover all they wanted.[9] Moreover, the present whereabouts of some of these recovered records remains obscure. Noting in 1962 that La Borderie's share was by then in public ownership in the *archives départementales d'Ille-et-Vilaine* at Rennes, Henri de Berranger also bleakly commented, 'On ignore ce que de Wismes fit de la sienne' ('It isn't known what de Wismes did with his').[10] Fortunately, as will shortly become apparent, though my own intermittent contacts with the current baron de Wismes, which began in 1964, have not provided any further clues on the present location of the records obtained by his predecessor, some of them at least have recently been relocated.[11]

It has been necessary to dwell at some length on the fate of these medieval Breton financial records in order to account for the different ways, beginning with the discoveries of de Wismes and La Borderie, that some have been recovered, so that it has been possible to reconstitute, in part at least, some lost riches of this former archive. The way in which the diaspora occurred also helps explain why so many of those documents which have been recovered are now in a poor physical state of preservation and, often, exceedingly fragmentary, single folios from accounts which originally ran to a hundred pages and more.[12] For

8] L. Maître, E. Gabory and S. Canal, *Inventaire sommaire des Archives départementales antérieures à 1790. Loire-Inférieure. Tome premier, Archives civiles. Série B: Chambre des Comptes de Bretagne*, 3 vols, Nantes, 1902–45, repr. 1991. Kerhervé (*L'État breton*, Vol. I, pp. 410–11) lists the main surviving medieval ducal domainal accounts of which some 1700 still survived at Nantes in 1679.

9] de Wismes, 'Le Trésor', p. 335.

10] de Berranger, *Guide des Archives*, Vol. I, p. 22 n. 2; for La Borderie's share, see below.

11] In 1964, le baron Armel de Wismes showed me a chest full of documents in the *appartement* which his family has occupied at Nantes since 1844. On a later visit, he allowed me to handle some, including those used in his *Aussi vivaient les Français des Croisades à la Troisième République* (Paris, 1962; 2nd edn, Le Poiré-sur-Vie, 1988). But I did not recognise any as coming from the rue des Caves, none of which now appear to be in his possession; nor has he been able to shed further light on when the family may have disposed of them. For the rediscovery of some of them, see below, p. 216.

12] For example, a mere snippet from fol. 57 of a ducal wardrober's account *c.* 1472, or fols 89, 92, 100, 105, 112 and 115 from the accounts of Auffroy Guinot, treasurer and

while one may hope for substantial individual finds, it seems clear that the rediscovery of long series of financial records, which existed in the *Chambre des Comptes* in the eighteenth century from around forty domainal receipts of the dukes of Brittany and a comparable number of receipts for *fouages* and other taxes, is now extremely unlikely.[13] Nor, to reveal the scale of Breton losses, has a single account of the main financial officer, the treasurer and receiver-general, survived in its entirety, so that Breton dukes will always cut poor figures in this respect in comparison with their princely peers, for example, in fifteenth-century Anjou or Burgundy, for whom financial evidence is almost overwhelmingly plentiful. Modern historians of medieval Brittany have to reconcile themselves to living on scraps. Nevertheless, as Jean Kerhervé's remarkable study, *L'État breton aux 14e et 15e siècles. Les ducs, l'argent et les hommes*, showed, even the most unpromising and bitty material (including mournful lists of now-lost accounts) can be made to yield fascinating and significant evidence.[14] A careful survey of the late medieval *membra disjecta* now known (many of them, both because of inaccessibility and poor physical state, still little exploited) should provide a considerable increment to knowledge; they certainly deserve to be better appreciated. Before surveying their content in more detail, however, a brief account of how some documents dispersed at the Revolution have reappeared is in order.

As already noted, the process had begun in the mid-nineteenth century. Mystery still surrounds how the documents came to be in the rue des Caves; had they been placed there at the Revolution and simply forgotten, or had they been brought there by the *relieurs-archivistes* themselves from locations elsewhere in

---

receiver-general, 1430–36 (Arch. Dép. Loire-Atlantique, B, Chambre des Comptes, Parchemins non classés, which, following Kerhervé [*L'État breton*, Vol. II, p. 966] will be referred to as B, reliures).

13] Arch. Dép. Loire-Atlantique, B 4295–4297, provide inventories of the domainal, *fouage* and ports and harbours accounts surviving in the *Chambre* in 1679; B 12844 lists the records transferred when the archives of the *Chambre* were moved to the convent of the Franciscans at Nantes in 1760. For some tantalisingly brief extracts made in the seventeenth century from late fourteenth- and fifteenth-century accounts of the receivers of Quimperlé and Carnoët, see P. Le Duc, *Histoire de l'abbaye de Sainte-Croix de Quimperlé*, ed. R.-F. Le Men, Quimperlé, 1863, pp. 623–35, and BNF, ms. fr. 11531. For similar extracts for Quimper, Cap-Caval and Cap-Sizun, see Arch. Dép. Finistère, A 84. Recently the *apurement* (final auditing) of a *fouage* account for the diocese of Nantes (1445–46) has come to light (Arch. Dép. Loire-Atlantique, 2E 1349; printed in Kerhervé, 'L'Impôt direct dans l'évêché de Nantes au milieu du XVe siècle, d'après un compte inédit', *Bretagnes. Art, négoce et société de l'Antiquité à nos jours. Mélanges offerts au professeur Jean Tanguy*, Brest, 1996, pp. 193–214), together with a fuller *fouage* account for the diocese of St-Brieuc, 1490 (BNF, ms. fr. 8325).

14] Cf. Kerhervé, *L'État breton*, Vol. II, pp. 963–66, discussing his sources at Nantes. Some indication of losses from the *Chambre* is given by the fact that before 1789, inventories list 57 accounts of ducal *argentiers*, 10 for *trésoriers de l'épargne*, 28 for *garde-robiers*, no fewer than 320 for the *trésoriers des guerres*, and 211 'very old' ones (de Berranger, *Guide des Archives*, Vol. I, p. 23).

Nantes or neighbouring communes? We simply do not know. But of the documents then discovered, we can be certain of the subsequent history of only the share which fell to La Borderie. An avid (but, alas, not always over-scrupulous) collector of medieval records, his share was added to an eventually enormous private collection. Among La Borderie's own papers, there are transcripts or notes on a considerable proportion of these financial records from the rue des Caves, showing that he continued to work on them intermittently for the rest of his life.[15] On his death in 1901, his widow agreed to transfer both the original documents and all his working papers to the Archives départementales d'Ille-et-Vilaine. There they constitute the impressive *Fonds de La Borderie.*[16] Though a detailed catalogue of the material specifically from the former *Chambre des Comptes* has not been attempted, the documents have been exploited more or less constantly since their rediscovery; La Borderie himself edited a few, and other choice pieces have been published by later scholars.[17]

It was in 1908 that the *archives municipales* at Nantes acquired from the *mairies* of Nantes, Chantenay and Doulon some miscellaneous bundles of covers used for civil registers in the Revolutionary period, which on closer inspection also proved to include much material from the former *Chambre des Comptes.* This led to a further search among registers already in the archives which revealed some additional pieces, that were subsequently listed in a very thorough *Inventaire sommaire*.[18] Two *liasses*, in particular, contain remnants from the *Chambre des Comptes*, dating from between 1390 and 1696, the majority of pieces from before 1550.[19] At the same time, aware of the potentially important early records that might be found in similar later bindings, the staff of the *archives départementales* at Nantes had been inspecting some of its holdings, and gradually accumulated some 50 *liasses* of fragmentary material, principally

15] Cf. Arch. Dép. Ille-et-Vilaine, 1 F 624–630, 653–658.

16] H. Bourde de la Rogerie and H.-F. Buffet, *Répertoire numérique de la série F*, Rennes, 1949, pp. 10–46.

17] Arch. Dép. Ille-et-Vilaine, 1 F 1111–1120; for example, A. de la Borderie, 'Inventaire des meubles et bijoux de Marguerite de Bretagne, première femme du duc de Bretagne, François II (29 sept. 1469)', *Bulletin de la société archéologique de Nantes*, 1864, pp. 45–60, the original of which is in Arch. Dép. Ille-et-Vilaine, 1 F 1118 (formerly *Trésor des Chartes, Arm. R, cass. C no. 25)*, and a copy in 1 F 657; idem, *Choix des documents inédits sur le règne de la duchesse Anne en Bretagne*, Rennes, 1902, pp. 106–07, original now Arch. Dép. Ille-et-Vilaine, 1 F 1118; B.-A. Pocquet du Haut-Jussé, 'Le plus ancien rôle des comptes du duché, 1262', *M[émoires de la] s[ociété d']h[istoire et d']a[rchéologie de] B[retagne] (MSHAB)*, Vol. XXVI, 1946, pp. 49–68, original now Arch. Dép. Loire-Atlantique, 3 J 194 (fragment found at the *mairie* of La Marne); idem, 'L'Hôtel de Jean IV, Fragment du compte des dépenses (*c.* 1365–70)', *Bulletin de la société archéologique du département d'Ille-et-Vilaine*, Vol. LIX, 1953, pp. 66–77, original now Arch. Dép. Ille-et-Vilaine, 1 F 1111 (though to be re-dated to *c.* 1390 – Kerhervé, *L'État breton*, Vol. I, p. 244 n. 3).

18] *Inventaire sommaire des Archives Communales, Ville de Nantes (antérieures à 1790)*, Vol. III, *GG (suite), HH, II et Supplément*, ed. R. Blanchard, Nantes, 1919, p. viii.

19] Nantes, Arch. Mun., II 120 and II 121 (cf. *Inventaire sommaire*, pp. 292–93). The first contains some 38 items, dated between 1390 and 1493.

derived from *Chambre des Comptes* records. Dating for the most part from the sixteenth to the eighteenth century, they also include some fragments from as far back as the thirteenth.[20] Unfortunately, no detailed inventory has yet been made of this material, which is accessible only with special permission, though it has been used by some modern scholars, most notably by Pocquet du Haut-Jussé, de Berranger and Kerhervé.[21]

Given that much material from the *Chambre des Comptes* was despatched to the navy at the time of the Revolution, it was perhaps not surprising that Mlle Geneviève Beauchesne came across a further small cache of material in the *Archives de la Marine* at Rochefort in the early 1950s.[22] Among the documents which she found, some sheets came from accounts rendered by Raoullet de la Lande, receiver of St-Aubin-du-Cormier for the years 1432–34,[23] while other

20] Y. Renaudin, 'Les Domaines des ducs de Bretagne. Leur administration du XIIe au XVe siècle', École des Chartes, dissertation, Paris, 1957 (copy at Arch. Dép. Loire-Atlantique), Vol. II, pp. 278–411 contains a transcription of the most important of these new fragments, part of a general account for 1263–67 (original in 3 J 194), as well as from the accounts of the executors of John II in 1305 (for which see also Arch. Dép. Loire-Atlantique, E 20, nos 4–16, and E 21–23 passim, edited in A. de la Borderie, *Nouveau recueil d'actes inédits des ducs et princes de Bretagne (XIIIe et XIVe siècles)*, Rennes, 1902, pp. 108–56, 166–89). A fragment of an account for a *fouage* in 1481 from a binding found in the *mairie* of La Trinité-Porhoët is now Arch. Dép. Loire-Atlantique, 1 J 142; *inter alia* it mentions expenses for keeping Jasper, Earl of Pembroke in custody.

21] H. de Berranger, 'Fragments de comptes de la maison ducale de Bretagne, XVe et XVIe siècles', Comité des travaux historiques et scientifiques, *Bulletin philologique et historique*, années 1951–52, pp. 89–94; Kerhervé, *L'État breton*, passim. When I compiled my *Recueil des actes de Jean IV, duc de Bretagne* (2 vols, Paris 1980–83), I was allowed access to some of the unclassified material; however, in the summer of 1998, I was able to see another seven (unnumbered) boxes, which now contain some of the material I had previously seen some twenty years earlier, together with many documents I had not examined before. These have yielded considerable new evidence for a *Supplément au Recueil des actes de Jean IV* (forthcoming). Kerhervé describes some of their main contents: '4 liasses – 1 pour les règnes antérieurs à François II, 1 pour François II, 2 pour Anne – contenant au total plusieurs centaines de pièces, parfois mal «classées», apportent des renseignements non négligeables en dépit de leur état. On y trouve des fragments de comptes de la Trésorerie Générale (1393–94, 1447–8, 1458, 1467), de l'Argenterie (1425, 1438), de la Garde-Robe (1445–7, 1455), de la Provision générale (1430–34), de l'Argenterie de la duchesse (1463–64) et de celle de Richemont (1454–6), des trésoreries de la duchesse (1406–7, 1443–46) et de la comtesse de Montfort (1451), de la recette générale de la maison d'Étampes (1446–48), des recettes ordinaires de Saint-Aubin (1404–5), Goëlo (1424–5), des ports et havres et des brefs (1433–40) etc...; pour le règne de François II, nombreuses décharges de la Garde-Robe et de la trésorerie générale' (*L'État breton*, Vol. II, p. 966).

22] G. Beauchesne, 'Notes sur des documents du XVe siècle provenant de la Chambre des Comptes de Bretagne', *MSHAB*, Vol. XXXIII, 1953, pp. 73–89. These are now Archives Historiques de la Marine, Rochefort, 8 S 1–11.

23] Arch. hist. de la Marine, Rochefort, 8 S 2. I am grateful to M. Marc Fardet, Conservateur en chef, for providing me with a detailed list of the contents of this *liasse*, and a photocopy of Mlle Beauchesne's transcription of La Lande's accounts of which some 20 folios survive.

fragments of his accounts for 1435 can now be found in the *Fonds de La Borderie* at Rennes.[24] Mlle Beauchesne later found documents of similar provenance at Vannes, which had probably also arrived there originally as a consignment for use by the naval authorities.[25]

Another major find has recently been made, which in part resolves the question of what happened to le baron de Wismes' share of the *trésor* of the rue des Caves. For among a magnificent legacy of books and manuscripts left by Dr Louis Lebreton (d. 1991) to the Abbaye Saint-Guénolé at Landévennec, which for the most part concern the history and culture of Brittany,[26] there can be found fragments of over 200 accounts and associated documents ranging in date from 1380 to 1616, of which approximately two-thirds concern the province's history down to the death of Queen Anne (1514).[27] Some of these fragments bear similar modern pencil annotations to those found on pieces in the *Fonds de La Borderie* at Rennes, while others can be demonstrated to have once been part of the de Wismes collection at Nantes since they were used from this source by René Blanchard, when compiling his *Lettres et mandements de Jean V*, thus suggesting a common provenance in the rue des Caves for many documents now in the *Fonds Lebreton*.[28] However, other medieval Breton documents and associated material at Landévennec have a different provenance, having been acquired by Dr Lebreton from other private nineteenth- or twentieth-century collections or at public sales, usually at a date unknown.[29] It has proved impossible so far to determine when the de Wismes collection of Breton material was dispersed, nor when Dr Lebreton acquired his share of it and whether, in doing so, he acquired all the documents that Héracle de Wismes had recuperated.[30] If the scale of de

24] Arch. Dép. Ille-et-Vilaine, 1 F 1113 (edited in A. de la Borderie, 'Recueil des documents relatifs aux monuments de l'architecture militaire du Moyen Age en Bretagne', *Association Bretonne, Bulletin archéologique*, sér. 3, Vol. V, 1886, no. XIX (reprinted in de la Borderie, *L'architecture militaire du Moyen Age en Bretagne*, ed. R. Sanquer, Rennes, 1991, pp. 118–22); also Arch. Dép. Loire-Atlantique, B, reliures (1435).

25] Arch. Dép. Morbihan, J 624, 'Fragment de compte de la recette d'Auray-Quiberon, 1474–77'.

26] See M. Simon, 'Le Docteur Louis Lebreton', *Chronique de Landévennec*, no. 68, October 1991, pp. 149–51 for an appreciation of this Breton 'Sir Thomas Phillipps'.

27] Listed in M. Jones, *Catalogue sommaire des archives du Fonds Lebreton, Abbaye Saint-Guénolé, Landévennec*, Nottingham, 1998, Appendice 1, 'Liasses 4A–B, Bretagne: Comptes et mandements ducaux et royaux, 14e–17e s.'

28] R. Blanchard, *Lettres et mandements de Jean V, duc de Bretagne*, 5 vols, Nantes, 1889–95, nos 2102–06, citing the '2e compte de Guinot' then in the 'Coll. le Baron de Wismes', now Abbaye Saint-Guénolé, Landévennec, Fonds Lebreton, *liasse* 4A no. 55; other original fragments from these accounts can be found in *liasse* 4A nos 56–58 and 60, and Arch. Dép. Loire-Atlantique, B, reliures. See also below, p. 218 and n. 36.

29] Landévennec, Fonds Lebreton, *liasse* 4A no. 23, letters of John V, 19 February 1413, for his chamberlain, Pierre Eder, were in the 'Archives du château de Callac', and no. 46, letters of John V in favour of Guillaume de St-Gille, 14 December 1425, were in the Archives of M. Guy Ropartz of Lanloup, when seen and published by Blanchard, *Lettres de Jean V*, nos 2656 and 2672.

30] See above, n. 11.

Wismes' acquisitions is not exaggerated in his 1859 article, it is more than probable that Lebreton did not, and that there still exist in other private collections, awaiting identification, more of the documents that were found in 1857. It is certainly the case that modern bindings have not yet rendered up all their late medieval Breton treasures. Furthermore, effective access to ultra-violet lamps would significantly increase what information can be recovered from often very mutilated fragments.[31] An essential *desideratum* for advancing knowledge of these records is a thorough inventory of what has so far been discovered, since it is clear, as in the case of Raoullet de la Lande's accounts, that original sheets from the same or closely connected accounts (or later transcripts) currently survive in several different archives.[32]

Viewing these dispersed records as an entity, how do they illustrate the history of late medieval Brittany? Obviously they provide, in the first instance, additional evidence for the development of ducal financial practices and institutions and for personnel from the second half of the thirteenth century onwards. The earliest fragments, for instance, add to what was known from records published in the eighteenth century from now lost accounts for the ducal demesne when the future *Chambre des Comptes* was still at a very embryonic stage in the reigns of Dukes John I (1237–86) and John II (1286–1305).[33] There is then a gap until the early years of the reign of John IV (1364–99), for whom a more considerable volume of financial records survives than has generally been appreciated. Among these, there are not only demesne records, but also some sadly mutilated household accounts, as well as some furnished by his influential English treasurer, Thomas Melbourne.[34] For the reign of John V (1399–1442) there is a wide and (comparatively speaking) voluminous body of material, again combining demesne evidence and household accounts, but also the most extensive

31] Landévennec, Fonds Lebreton, *liasse* 110, the boards of a volume of accounts for 1786–88 for the lordship of Villemoisan (Morbihan), are covered with parchment derived from accounts of a receiver of ?Châteaubriant (Loire-Atlantique) for 1514–15, listing payments made to the foresters of Teillay for wood purchased for the repair of ?Teillay castle.

32] The cover from the volume of accounts of Jean Brocart, receiver of St-Renan (Finistère) for 1401–02 is in Arch. Dép. Loire-Atlantique, B, reliures, while some sheets of these accounts are in Landévennec, Fonds Lebreton, *liasse* 4A nos 12, 13 and 15; fragments of the accounts of Jean Beauboais, receiver at Hennebont (Morbihan) of a *fouage* levied in the diocese of Vannes in 1412–13 can be found in *liasse* 4A no. 22 and Arch. Dép. Ille-et-Vilaine, 1 F 1113; fragments for the seigneuries of Assérac and Ranrouët (Loire-Atlantique) for the years 1430–37 may be found in Arch. Dép. Ille-et-Vilaine, 1 F 1113, Landévennec, Fonds Lebreton, *liasse* 4A nos 64, 65, 67 and 68, and Arch. Dép. Loire-Atlantique, B, reliures, etc.

33] See Pocquet du Haut-Jussé, 'Le plus ancien rôle' (above, n. 17), and Renaudin, 'Les Domaines' (above, n. 20).

34] Arch. Dép. Ille-et-Vilaine, 1 F 1111, provides the most significant number, but Landévennec and Nantes also contribute some important material (some of it inadvertently boxed with material for the reign of Duchess/Queen Anne).

surviving fragments of accounts of any treasurer and receiver-general of Brittany, the leading ducal financial officer. These concern the administration of Auffroy Guinot, treasurer from 1430–36, for whom, in addition to some original folios of his accounts for 1432–34, now at Landévennec and Nantes,[35] can be added extracts made in the early eighteenth century, by or for the Maurist historians of the province, Dom Lobineau and Dom Morice, who published lengthy extracts.[36] The most extensive of such notes and transcripts are found in Bibliothèque Nationale de France, ms. fr. 11542.[37] Yet further additional extracts, including some still unedited material, can also be found in former Phillipps MS 18465.[38] From all of this, it is clear that less than a fifth of the surviving fragments of Guinot's accounts are currently easily accessible to scholars.[39]

In addition to material relating to all the fifteenth-century dukes, their households and estates, surviving accounts reveal something about the affairs of ducal cadets, most notably François, comte de Montfort (the future Francis I, 1442–50), and his uncles, Richard, comte d'Étampes (d. 1439)[40] and Arthur de Richemont, constable of France, who also ruled briefly as Arthur III (1457–58). The finances of various duchesses (regnant or dowager), most obviously and extensively of Anne herself (1488–1514), are also illuminated by numerous fragments; there is even some very mutilated evidence about the dower lands in

35] See above, nn. 12 and 28.

36] Dom G.-A. Lobineau, *Histoire de Bretagne*, 2 vols, Paris, 1707, Vol. II, cols 1016–21, 1033–37; Dom H. Morice, *Mémoires pour servir de preuves à l'histoire ecclésiastique et civile de Bretagne*, 3 vols, Paris, 1742–46, Vol. II, cols 1231–36 and 1259–63; see also (for a further fragment of Guinot's accounts, from BNF, ms. nouv. acq. fr. 21689, fols 48–55) B.-A. Pocquet du Haut-Jussé, 'Le Comptes du duché de Bretagne en 1435–1436', *BEC*, Vol. LXXVII, 1916, pp. 88–110.

37] In the hand of Dom Lobineau; a nineteenth-century transcript may be found in Arch. Dép. Ille-et-Vilaine, 1 F 629.

38] In the possession of the author, again in the hand of Dom Lobineau; cf. *Bibliotheca Phillippica*, new series, 9th part, (Sotheby's) Sale of 25 and 26 June 1973, lot 1943. This MS is briefly described in H. Omont, 'Manuscrits relatifs à l'histoire de France conservés dans la bibliothèque de Sir Thomas Phillipps à Cheltenham', *BEC*, Vol. L, 1888, p. 81, when it contained 335 pages; it now consists of only 104 sheets. Apart from the extracts from Guinot's accounts (pp. 49–79), the most important contents are extracts from the various accounts of Jean Mauléon, *trésorier de l'épargne*, for 1414–22 (pp. 81–131) and 1434–42 (pp. 39–43) and of Jean d'Ust, *trésorier et receveur-général*, 1436–37 (pp. 45–47), of which Lobineau (Vol. II, cols 964–70, 1037–39) and Morice (Vol. II, cols 1103–09, 1269–71, 1298–99) published only extracts.

39] La Borderie, who collated the published and unpublished extracts from BNF, ms. fr. 11542, numbering individual entries separately, counted 383 items of which only 73 were published by Lobineau and Morice (Arch. Dép. Ille-et-Vilaine, 1 F 629); collation with MS Phillipps 18465 shows a similar discrepancy between published and unpublished items.

40] See Landévennec, Fonds Lebreton, *liasse* 4A nos 43 and 49 (fragments of accounts of Jean de Henleix, his *trésorier*, 1423–30), and 84 (*apurement* of accounts of Henleix as receiver-general of the late Count of Étampes, 16 February 1444); for Richemont, see below, n. 43.

Brittany of Jeanne de Navarre (d. 1437), widow of John IV, and mother of John V, who married, secondly, Henry IV of England.[41] Some evidence survives, too, for the finances of the dowager countess of Étampes, mother of the future Francis II, who in her declining years displayed a strong interest in gardening.[42]

Of the documents concerning Arthur de Richemont, perhaps the most informative are various *décharges* given to his treasurer which provide valuable information on his itinerary, his diplomatic and military activities, household consumption and even cultural interests.[43] The same is to a large extent true of documents relating to the reign of Francis II (1458–88), in which, in addition to the usual demesne and *fouage* accounts, the most revealing and precise evidence comes from a series of *décharges* for payments made by his confidential secretary, François Avignon.[44] For Avignon's predecessor as *commis* of the 'mises extraordinaires' (extraordinary levies), Guillaume Moulnier, there also survives an extremely rare file for medieval Brittany of some 85 subsidiary documents, chiefly warrants and quittances, which were presented in justification by his executors, when summoned to conclude his accounts in the *Chambre des Comptes* after 1490.[45] Commonplace as such documents must once have been, no other similar original cache has been discovered up to the present. Together, all this material demonstrates a wide range of governmental activity, especially of a diplomatic kind which by its very nature was secretive, though also throwing light on military and judicial affairs, as well as providing much evidence on membership of the ducal household and exercise of patronage. The

41] Landévennec, Fonds Lebreton, *liasse* 4A nos 25 and 26, fragments of the accounts of Regnaud Galivier, receiver at Nantes for Queen Jeanne, 1412–13, and Arch. Dép. Ille-et-Vilaine, 1 F 1113 for another fragment of the same account.

42] Landévennec, Fonds Lebreton, *liasse* 4A nos 86, 87 and 91 (accounts of the receiver of Châteaumur, dép. Vendée, 1444–48), no. 99 (accounts for various objects delivered by the countess to the *trésor* of the late François I, *c.* 1450), no. 110 (accounts for her gardens, 1458).

43] Cf. Landévennec, Fonds Lebreton, *liasse* 4A nos 66 (fragments of the accounts of Michel Baudon, receiver of Parthenay for Richemont, 1436) and 103 (fragments of the accounts of his *argentier*, February 1453). Other important fragments unknown to E. Cosneau (*Le Connétable de Richemont*, Paris, 1886) survive at Rennes and Nantes, only partially exploited by J. Kerhervé, 'Une existence en perpétuel mouvement. Arthur de Richemont, connétable de France et duc de Bretagne (1393–1458)', *Viajeros, peregrinos, mercaderes en el Occidente medieval, XVIII semana de estudios medievales, Estella '91*, Estella, 1995, pp. 69–114.

44] Cf. Landévennec, Fonds Lebreton, *liasse* 4A nos 123, 125, 127 and 129; cf. also no. 116, another *décharge* for 1467, while others survive in Arch. Dép. Ille-et-Vilaine, 1 F 1117 and Arch. Dép. Loire-Atlantique, B, reliures. In 1467, François II gave Avignon 1000 *l.* on his marriage (Arch. Dép. Loire-Atlantique, B 5 fol. 80v); he was ennobled on 24 January 1476 (ibid., B 125/5). Certainly a ducal secretary by 1476, for most of his career he was *clerc et commis* of the treasurer, Pierre Landais, charged with paying the *mises extraordinaires*; extracts from his otherwise lost fourth account were made by the Abbé Legrand in the eighteenth century (BNF, ms. fr. 6982, fols 326–27).

45] Arch. Dép. Loire-Atlantique, B, reliures, mostly relating to payments in 1473–74 and providing a wealth of evidence, especially for diplomatic and military activity.

duke's family and spiritual life is also evidenced.[46] The same is true for the documents that concern Duchess (later Queen) Anne. Again some informative *décharges* for the critical period 1488–91 survive which have not been exploited,[47] while, for her period as queen, there is a predominance of records relating to the finances of Anne's household, above all to her lavish purchase of clothing, jewellery and other material possessions, and for the payment of household servants.[48]

In fact, it is probably true to say that frustratingly cryptic, horribly incomplete and fearfully messy as many of these documents are,[49] there are few areas of ducal activity between the latter half of the fourteenth century and the beginning of the sixteenth that are not illustrated in these *membra disjecta*. Peter Lewis has on occasion been concerned with the minutiae of administrative procedure as in his analysis of a pension list of Louis XI; he has also worked on records from the *Trésor des Chartes des ducs de Bretagne*, most notably in 'Of Breton *Alliances* and Other Matters', and he would surely have used any records at Nantes for his incisive study of the 'Breton Estates' had they survived the *Commission de Triage*![50] I hope he will forgive the inadequacies of this brief survey in a volume that is a tribute for what all those interested in late medieval French history owe him. It will already have served a purpose if it alerts others to the golden nuggets that may still be mined from the *trésors* of the rue des Caves and those other remnants of the former Breton *Chambre des Comptes* archives that have come to light in recent times but which are still under-appreciated.[51]

46] For example, the many expenses incurred sending chaplains to pray at various shrines (many outside Brittany) for the health of Duchess Marguerite (d. 1469) during her last illness, donations for the repair of various churches and chapels, the acquisition of an organ, etc.

47] Notably, Landévennec, Fonds Lebreton, *liasse* 4B, nos 132–36.

48] Ibid., nos 139–43, 145–52; Arch. Dép. Ille-et-Vilaine, 1 F 1118–1120; Arch. Dép. Loire-Atlantique, B, reliures.

49] Cf. Blanchard's remarks on 'le déchiffrement souvent pénible de ces débris desparates, tachés, mutilés, pâlis ...' (*Inventaire sommaire ... Ville de Nantes*, Vol. III, p. viii).

50] P. S. Lewis, 'Of Breton *Alliances* and other matters', in *War, Literature and Politics in the Late Middle Ages: Essays in Honour of G. W. Coopland*, ed. C. T. Allmand, Liverpool, 1976, pp. 122–43, repr. in *Essays in Later Medieval French History*, London, 1985, pp. 69–90; 'Les Pensionnaires de Louis XI', in *La France de la fin du XVe siècle. Renouveau et apogée*, ed. B. Chevalier and P. Contamine, Paris 1985, pp. 167–81; published as 'The Pensioners of Louis XI', in *Essays in Later Medieval French History*, pp. 91–104; and 'Breton Estates', in ibid., pp. 127–38.

51] I am particularly grateful to le Père Marc Simon, librarian, and to the whole monastic community at Landévennec for making it possible for me to work on the Fonds Lebreton, and to the British Academy and the University of Nottingham for financial aid. Thanks are also especially due to Mme Chantal Reydellet, Conservateur, Arch. Dép. Ille-et-Vilaine and to Mme Vivienne Miguet, Directrice, and M. Jean-François Carhaës, Conservateur, Arch. Dép. Loire-Atlantique for easing access to some of the material cited here, and for other help.

Glossary

alliance	contract for service
amiral	admiral
archives départementales	archives of a [modern] *département*
bailli	royal officer in charge of a *bailliage*
bailliage	royal administrative district (in northern and central France)
ban	[feudal] military levy
Bulletin des Lois	official journal recording new legislation
Chambre des Comptes	chamber of accounts/ royal finance office
chanson de geste	poem of heroic and often legendary deeds
Châtelet	court of the *vicomté* and *prévôté* of Paris
chef-lieu	chief town [of a *département*]
commis	lieutenant/deputy
commissaire	[royal] representative appointed for special purpose
connétable	constable
corps d'état	state institution
Cour amoureuse	group, under Charles VI, devoted to poetry written in the courtly spirit
coutumier	customary
département	large administrative unit in modern France
Directoire	regime governing France, 1793-99
écu	coin; monetary value
Echiquier	*Exchequer [highest court in Normandy]*
écuyer d'écurie	squire of the stable
élection	fiscal administrative unit
entrée royale	formal royal entry into a town
familia regis	royal household
fief rente	annuity granted for homage or service
fonds	collection [in a library/archive]
fouage	form of [hearth] tax

généraux des finances	senior financial officers
grand conseil	great council
grand sénéchal	high seneschal
homme d'armes	[mounted] man-at-arms
inventaire sommaire	summary catalogue
jongleur	juggler/entertainer
lèse-majesté	treason
lettre de retenue	indenture, contract
liasse	bundle, file
mairie	town hall
maître d'hôtel	master of the household
maître des requêtes	master of requests
noblesse seconde	secondary nobility
notaire et secrétaire	notary and secretary
Parlement	supreme court of France
Parlement criminel	part of the *Parlement* hearing criminal cases
pas d'armes	formal, partly theatrical defence of a passage by a group against all comers
pastourelle	song concerning a lord and a shepherdess
pena talionis	retaliation/revenge
petite noblesse	minor nobility
recette générale	receipt of the kingdom
sénéchaussée	seneschalcy, royal administrative district (mainly in the south of France)
taille	a form of tax
trésorier	treasurer
verderie	forest area under the jurisdiction of a *verdier*
verdier	guardian of the forests
vicomté	administrative unit, part of a *bailliage*

Index

Aaron 28
Ableiges, Jacques d' 192
Grand Coutumier de France 192n
Abrégé des chroniques de France: *see* Fribois
Acciaiouli, Donato 83
affinities 178, 183, 189
Agincourt, Battle of (1415) 39, 53, 102, 138, 164n
Albergati, Cardinal 84
Albigensian heresy 138
Alençon,
Charles d' 139
chronicle 141, 143
duke of, process against 89, 139, 191
genealogy of 131, 139
house of 138–40, 142–43, 176
Jean I 138
Jean II 138–40, 191
Jean VI 143
negotiations at (1418) 85
païs of 140: *see also* genealogies
Alexander romance cycle 3, 10
King 10
alliances 178
Allières, Jean d' 182n
ambassadors xiii, 8, 51–53, 115
Amboise 115n
Amer, Pierre 74
Amiens 104, 195–96
bailli 195–96
Ancien Régime 193, 210
Anglo-Norman, use of 8
Anjou 98, 213
Charles, count of Maine 89, 133–34
court of 40
Duke of 32
house of 62, 176
Louis of 40
Louis II, King of Jerusalem and Sicily 40
Marie of 40
Yolande of, Queen of Jerusalem and Sicily 40, 44
Annales school 175
Anthon, Battle of (1430) 136
Antwerp 147
appeals 194
Aquinas, St Thomas, on crime 207
Aquitaine 32, 86, 96, 132
Eleanor of 96
Prince of: *see* Edward, Black Prince
Aragon 130
arbitration 199: *see also* conciliation
archives xv, 11, 74–75, 82n, 84, 86, 88
Breton 210–11
Foix 130
searches in 74, 85
Ardenne, abbey of 81
Arian Goths 132
Ariespeil, Michaus, copyist 11
Aristotle
Nicomachean Ethics 207
Rhetoric 207
Arles 149
Armagnac
Bernard, Count of 138n
Count of 137–38
party 40, 50, 55, 176
army, role of 101, 103
Arnaldi, Guillaume 150
Arques, captaincy of 187

Arras 57, 61, 63, 81, 148n
Congress/Treaty of (1435) 68–69, 77, 79, 81, 152, 160–61, 167
Treaty of (1482) 78, 91
Artevelde, Philip van 27–28, 30
Arthur, King 97
Arthurian literature 3, 9
Artois 152, 172, 180
Estates of 155n
Robert d' 5, 19
Assérac 217n
Astesan, Antonio 83
Aston, Andrew 86
Aubigny 42
Aubrecicourt 15
Nicolas d' 7
Aubuisson, Antoine d', seigneur de Monteil 187
Augustine, St 76, 80
De civitate Dei 76, 80
influence of 122
Aumale, Count of 47–48
Austria, Duke of 74
Avesne, family 2: *see also* Blois
Avignon 39, 53
François 219
Avranchin, nobles from 180
Aydie, Odet d' 178, 185

Bacheler, Jacques 157
Bailleul, Sevestre d' 207n
Baisy, Guy de 132
ban 180
Basin, Thomas, chronicler 108, 116, 119, 187
Basle, Council of (1431–49) 87
bastard feudalism 177
Bâtard de Bouillon, Le 4
Bath and Wells, Bishop of: *see* Bekynton
Baudon, Michel 219n
Bavaria 64
Albrecht of 13, 30
Jacqueline of, Countess of Hainault 152
Louis of, Emperor 2
William of 13
Bayonne 165
Béarn xiv, 24, 30, 130–31, 137–38: *see also* Foix
Beaumanoir, Philippe de 173, 191, 197, 199
Coutumes de Beauvaisis 191
Beaumont, Jean de 4, 6–7, 11, 14, 18–19
castle at 19
Lord of 5, 9
patronage of 4
Beauneveu, André, sculptor 18
Beauvais, see of 81
Beauvaisis 131
Bede 204
Bedford, John, Duke of 55, 93n, 97–98, 152
Bekynton, Thomas, diplomatic papers of 77, 85–86
bendes 186
Benedict, St, *Rule* of 204
Berkhamsted 13–14
Bernis, Michel du, chronicler xiv, 130, 137–38, 140n
Berranger, H. de 212
Berry, John, Duke of 30, 82–83, 154
his daughter, Marie 30
Berry Herald 89
Recouvrement de la Normandie 89
Béthune 195–96
Beverhoutsveld, battle of (1382) 27
Bible 112
Bien Public, war of 89, 91 176, 185, 187
Black Prince: *see* Edward
Blaisy, Jean de 82
Blois 30
county of 29
Gui de Châtillon, Count of 6, 18, 22, 29
Regret Guillaume 12
Jeanne de 18
Louis I, Count of 18
Blondel, Robert 56, 59, 62–69
De Complanctu bonorum Gallicorum 62, 65–67
La Complaincte des bons François 62
Boethius
De consolatione philosophiae 51
Bohemia, kings of 74
Ladislas of 74
Bologna, university doctors 76
Bonin, Pierre 182n
Bordeaux
Archbishop of 84
reconquest by the French 167
sénéchaussées of 78n

Bordelais 165, 170
Bouchain 15
Boulogne 77
Boulonnais 152
Bourbon 139
  Charles: *see* Clermont
  ducal library 130
  genealogies 139
  house of 138, 142
  Jean I 138
  Jeanne, Duchess of 89n
  Louis II 139–40
  Louis, bastard of 185
  païs of 141
  procureur of: *see* Chauveau
  register of ducal rights 141
Bourbonnais 139
Bourges 42, 52
  Gallican church council (1438) 129
  'kingdom' of 127
Bourgneuf, René de 211n
Boutillier, Jean 192
  Grand Coutumier 192
Bouvet, Honoré 81, 87, 112
  Apparicion maistre Jehan de Meun 81
  L'Arbre des Batailles 87, 112
Brabant
  duchy of 2
  Jeanne de 30
  John IV, Duke of 152n, 163n
  Wenceslas of 29–30
Brennus 97
Brétigny, treaty of (1360) 13, 18, 75–76, 78, 85–86
Brézé
  affinity 183
  Louis de 184
  Pierre de, *Grand Sénéchal* of Normandy 178–79, 183–84
  ordonnance company 183
Brittany xiv, 126, 128, 132, 149, 180
  Anne, Duchess of, Queen of France 209, 211, 215n, 216, 217n, 218, 220
  Arthur III, Duke of: *see* Richemont
  Chambre des Comptes xvi, 209–11, 213–15, 217, 219–20
  diplomacy with 79
  dukes of, 78, 140–41, 185
  Etats of 211
  former kingdom of 132
  Francis I, Duke of 218–19
  Francis II, Duke of 74, 185, 215n, 219
  Jeanne de Navarre, Duchess of 219
  John, I, Duke of 217
  John II, Duke of 215n, 217
  John IV, Duke of 217, 219
  John V, Duke of 44–45, 217, 219
  Marguerite, Duchess of 220n
  Montfort family 126
  'national sentiment' in 126
  païs 126
  treasurer of 212n, 215n, 218: *see also* Guinot
  Trésor des Chartes des ducs 211, 220
Broons, Olivier de 179, 185
Bruges 4n, 23, 27–28, 147, 148n
  population 145
Bruinant, Henri 195
Brully, Raoul de 180
Brutus 97
Budé
  Dreux 74
  Jean 73, 89n
Bueil, Jean de, admiral 181, 184–85
Bulletin des Lois 210
'Burgundianism' 176, 186
Burgundians 39–40, 42, 136, 186
Burgundian 'state' 166
Burgundy xiv, 106, 126, 147, 213
  Antony, 'le grand bâtard' 133–34, 151
  Catherine of 40
  court of 47, 130, 150–51, 153–54, 164
  ducal council 150
  dukes of xii, 32, 79, 81, 121n, 129, 132, 139–40, 148–51, 160, 168: *see also* Charles; John; Philip
  house of 39–40, 176
  kingdom of 132, 134, 136
  Margaret of 58n
  Mary of 113
  Michelle of 46: *see also* France/ 'centre'

Cabaret d'Orreville, Jean dit, chronicler 130, 139–40
  Chronique du bon duc Loys de Bourbon 130, 140
Cabochian revolt (1413) 64
Cabourg 20
Cachemarée, Aleaume 202

Caen 41
Caesar, Julius 118
Cagny, Perceval de, chronicler 130, 131n, 139–40, 142–43
Cairo 120
Calais
  negotiations near (1439) 82, 85
  siege of 20
Cambe, Bertrand de le 170
Cambrai 30, 74
  text of Froissart 33
canons regular, rule of 204
Capetian domains 127
capital punishment: *see* death penalty; penalties
Carcassonne 46
Carolingians 126, 132
Carthagenian invasions 162
Carvin, Jehan 170
cas royaux 201–02
Castiglione, Branda da, Cardinal 184
Castois dou jouene gentil homme 10
Cato, Angelo, royal physician 112
Cato, Marcus 99
Caux
  bailliage 187
  pays de 178–79
Caxton, William 102n, 105
Chabannes, Antoine de 178
Chamber, 109
Chambre des Comptes 71, 73–76, 79, 88, 177, 186: *see also* Brittany
  memorials of 74
Champagne 34
Chandos, Sir John 18, 98
Chandos Herald 18
  Life of the Black Prince 18
chansons de geste 4
Chantenay, *mairie* 214
Charenton 44–45
Charlemagne, Emperor 83, 136, 169
Charles, King of Navarre 75, 81
Charles IV, Emperor 74
Charles IV, King of France 19, 168
Charles V, King of France 74, 87, 111, 112n, 141, 168, 186
  intellectual legacy 87
  ordinance of 1374 59
  patron of translators 80
Charles VI, King of France xii, 29–30, 37, 40–41, 48, 50, 54–55, 58, 69, 83, 85, 138, 154, 161, 173
Charles VII, King of France 41, 50–52, 54, 69, 73–79, 81, 83, 118, 121, 126–27, 129–30, 132, 134–35, 137–38, 140, 143, 147, 152–53, 156–57, 159, 160n, 161–62, 163n, 164, 165n, 167n, 169–73, 181, 183–84, 186, 188–89, 191
  coronation 52
  le Bienservi 189
Charles VIII, King of France 115n, 120
Charles 'the Dauphin', lieutenant-general/regent of France xii, 37, 39–42, 44, 47–48, 50, 54–56, 59–61, 67
Charles de France 89n, 91, 113, 161
Charles the Bald 132
Charles the Bold, Duke of Burgundy 79, 113, 150–51, 161, 164n
Chartier, Alain xii, xiii, 37–53, 56, 63, 67–68, 70, 96n, 102–03
  Ad detestacionem belli gallici et suasionem pacis 50
  Ad universitatem parisiensem 48
  De puella 52
  Dialogus familiaris amici et sodalis 50
  Lay de Paix 51
  Livre de l'Esperance 51
  Livre des Quatre Dames 39n, 53
  Quadrilogue Invectif xii, xiii, 37, 41n, 48–51, 53, 96n, 102
  Salve, rex 52
  See also polemical treatises; propaganda
Chartier, Jean, chronicler 54
  Chronique de Saint-Denis 54
Chartres, Regnault de, archbishop 78
Chastel,
  Raoul Tainguy du, scribe 35
  Tanguy du 48
Chastellain, Georges, chronicler 116
Chateaumorand, Jean de, sire de Poligni 130–31, 141–42
Châtelet, court 202, 207
Châtillon, Louis de 30
Chaucer, Geoffrey 2, 13, 17–18
  Canterbury Tales 18: *see also* Roet
Chauveau, Huguenin 140
Cherbourg 187
Chevalier au cygne 4
Chinon 78

chivalric displays 9
chivalric orders 178: *see also* Bourbon; Garter; Golden Fleece
chivalry 1, 9–10, 25, 27, 104, 137, 139n: *see also* 'noblesse'
Cholet, Jean 180
Choletière, seigneurs de la 180
chroniclers: *see* Basin; Bernis; Cabaret D'Orreville; Cagny; Chartier, Jean; Chastellain; Esquerrier; Froissart; Le Bel; Nangis; Pintoin; Thomassin; Walsingham
chronicles: *see Grandes chroniques*; Joinville; Saint-Denis; Savoy; Valenciennes
Chronique de Flandre 33–34
Chronique de la traison et mort de Richart II 89
Chronique du bon duc Loys de Bourbon: *see* Cabaret
Cicero 98–99
  De Officiis 89n
  De Rhetorica 98n
Cistercians, rule of 204
Clamanges, Nicolas de 54, 199
  Epistola exhortatoria ad iusticiam et alias virtutes 54
  See also polemical treatises
Clermont, county/duchy
  Charles, Count of, Duke of Bourbon 130, 138–39, 141–42
  Robert of 139
Clientage xv, 175–77, 179, 181–82, 184, 186, 189: *see also* patronage
Clovis, King 132, 136
Coictier, Jacques, royal physician 110
Col, Gontier 43
Colins, minstrel 6
Commentaries, humanist 87
Comminges, Mathieu, Count of 137–38
Commynes, Philippe de xiii, 106–23, 158, 161n
  Mémoires 106–10, 112–13, 115–22
  on kingship xiii-xiv, 106–23
Condé, Baudouin de, poet 16
  Jean de, poet 3–4, 9–10
Condé-sur-l'Escaut, tournament at (1327) 9
Conflans, Treaty of (1465) 160
Constance, Council of (1414–18) 64
Corbeil 44
Côtentin, *baillis* of 180
Cour amoureuse 17, 154
Courre, Jacques 157
Courtrai 148n, 163n
courts, eccclesiastical 203, 206: *see also* Châtelet; Paris/ prévôté; Parlement
Cousinot II, Guillaume 72, 79, 91
  Pour ce que plusieurs 69, 72–73, 76, 88–89, 91
coutumiers 191–92, 194, 197, 201 *see also* Beaumanoir
Couvin, Watriquet de 6
Couvran, Geoffroi de 179, 185
Crécy, Battle of (1346) 6
Crespin
  Jacquet de 164n
  Jean de 164n
crimes
  abduction 201, 206n
  abuse of jurisdiction 201
  abuse of office 197, 199
  adultery 205
  against nature 205
  against public morality 191
  arson 192, 202, 205
  attacks on public highway 202
  blasphemy, 197
  bloodshed, 191, 206
  breaking the king's peace 202
  capitaux/énormes 201–02, 208
  carrying weapons 172n, 199, 201, 206, 208
  categories of 201
  coining 172n, 192
  conspiracy 205
  false witness 195
  forgery 197
  fraud 203
  heresy 192
  homicide 190, 192, 199, 205
  incest 206n
  'irremissibles' 201–02
  murder 192, 194, 197, 201
  opposing royal ordinances 198
  oppposing royal pardons 201
  poisoning 192
  political 190–91
  private prison 201
  private war 194, 204
  quarrels 191

rape 192, 201
sacrilege 202–03
sexual 192, 206
sorcery 202
suicide 192
theft 190–92, 203, 205–06, 208
usury 206n
vagabondage 206–08
wounding 199
Custos processuum 84

Dame France 38–39
Dampierre, family of 2
Darius, King of Persia 81
Dauphin
Charles 47, 59–61, 67
Jean 83
Louis II 129–30, 134–36: *see also* Louis, dauphin
Dauphiné 129–30, 135–37, 142
genealogies of 134
païs 134, 136
part of the Empire 135–36
people of 45, 136
sovereign of 135
succession in 135
Dauvet, Jean 160
Dax, siege of 137
death penalty xv, 190–91, 193–200, 202–03, 208
Débats et appointements 55, 89
decayed feudalism 177
Decius, Publius 100
Denmark 111
Deuxième cycle de la croisade 4
dice, playing of 207
Dieudonné de Hongrie 3
Dijon 160
diplomatic dossiers xiii, 72–79, 81–82, 88–89
Mémoire abrégé grossement (1390) 75
Extractum ab originali libro antiquo cronicarum Sancti Severini Burdegalensis 85
diplomatic proceedings 7–8, 73–75
Dit des .III. mestiers d'armes 10
Dordrecht 147
Doriole, Pierre 156
Dormans
Guillaume, royal advocate 90
Jean, Cardinal and Chancellor of France 90
Douai 15, 160
double-monarchy (England and France) 54, 57, 77
Doudin, Enguerran 158
Dunois, Jean, Count of 178, 179n, 181, 189

East Anglia, decorative art from 11
Eawy 181
Edmund Ironside 97
Edward II, King of England 7, 10, 81n
Edward III, King of England 2, 5, 7–8, 11–13, 18–19, 32, 75, 77, 86, 98
claim to France 85
Edward IV, King of England 76, 84, 85n, 86, 94, 99, 104, 113–14, 161
described by Commynes 113–14
Edward, the Black Prince 7, 13–14, 32, 84, 98
Enseignements written for 8
Prince of Aquitaine 13
Egyptians 28
Eltham, royal residence at 13
Empire
Carolingian 126, 132
Freistädte of 147
Holy Roman 84, 136
England
ancient enemy of France 41, 50, 55
court of xi, 1, 9, 12–13, 17, 20
Parliament 96n, 105
polemic against 64
succession in: *see* Fortescue
See also East Anglia; Edward II; Edward III; Edward IV; Henry I; Henry III; Henry IV; Henry V; Henry VI; Henry VIII; Isabella; John; Katherine; Philippa; Richard I; Richard II; William I
English xii, 64, 133, 140, 143, 152, 164n
claims to France 76, 79, 82, 85–86, 94–97, 102–03, 127
nation xiii, 93, 95
settlers in France 93, 95, 98
view of the French 94–96, 98, 100
entrées royales 116, 156
Epernay 200n
Epinal 163n, 165

Epinay-Montauban, house of 133–34
Escaut, river 151, 155
Esquerrier, Arnaud 130n, 138
  Chroniques des comtes de Foix 130n, 138
Este 116
Estinnes 19
Estouteville 185
  Bricquebec d' 180
  Guillaume d', archbishop 184
  Jean d': *see* Torcy
  Louis d' 178–80
  Moyon d' 180
Etampes
  Pierre d' 74
  Richard d' 218
Evreux: *see* Floques
executions 190–91, 197–98
  crowd at 197, 200–01
  opposition to 197–98
  rituals 193–94, 198, 200

Fastolf, Sir John 92n, 93, 100, 103–04
  owner of *De re militari* 103
Faucigny 135n
fidelités 177–78
fief-rente 177–78
Fiennes, Robert de 7
Filloix, Henri 195
Flanders 128, 132, 148, 163, 168
  count of 160
  county of 2, 81
  Estates 150
  French negotiations with 74
  Robert of 9
Flavy, Guillaume de 201
fleur de lis 107, 115
fleurs de lys 173
  branding 195–96
Flocques, Robert de 179–80
Florence 83
Foix 130, 132
  archives of 130
  chronicle of the house of xiv, 130: *see also* Bernis
  Eleanora of Navarre, Countess of 130, 137–38
  Gaston IV Fébus, Count of 130, 137
  house of 130, 137–38
  Jean I, Count of 138n
  Roger Bernard II, Count of Foix 137
Fontenay-le-Comte, trial at (1484) 203
Formigny, Battle of (1450) 95
Fornovo, Battle of (1495) 106, 120
Fortescue, Sir John xiii, 83, 85, 92, 94, 105
  De laudibus legum Anglie 92
  De titulo Edwardi comitis Marchiae 83
  Defensio juris domus Lancastriae 83
  Governance of England, The 92
  Replicacion ageinste the clayme and title of the Duc of Yorke for the crownes of England and France 85n
Fou, Jean du 187
Fougères 75, 79, 140
France 12, 48–51, 127, 180
  admirals 182, 185
  admiralty of 183, 185
  army of 139
  bonnes villes 90, 145, 147, 154, 156, 159, 162, 173–74
  'centre' xiv-xv, 124–25, 127–30, 136, 142–43, 147, 149, 154–57, 159, 161–62, 165, 169–73
  chancellery of 41, 46, 48, 76, 87–89, 200
  chancellor: *see* Dormans
  constable (*connétable*) of 43, 183
  crown of 87, 131, 135, 139, 164n
  estates of 38, 48
  Estates General 90, 118, 142–43
  généraux des finances 182n
  Grand conseil 90
  Grand Sénéchal 182–83
  king as emperor in 135–36, 172
  marshal of 201
  Merovingian kings 162n
  national identity 128
  'periphery' xiv-xv, 125–27, 130, 136, 143, 147, 155–59, 162, 167, 170–73
  provincial governors 181–83
  royal succession xii, 56–60, 63, 69
  sénéchaux 182
  Table de Marbre 185
  Trésorier: *see* Budé
  See also *Chambre des Comptes*; Charles IV; Charles V; Charles VI; Charles VII; Charles VIII; Clovis; Isabeau; Jean II; Katherine; Louis IX; Louis XI; Philip [II]-Augustus; Philip VI
Frankish kingdom 132
Fresne, Bertrand du 179n

Fribois, Noel de xiv, 72–73, 76, 80, 129, 131–34, 143
Abrégé des Chroniques de France 72–73, 80, 89, 129, 131–33
Mirouer Historial Abregié de France 72–73, 89, 129, 131–33
other chronicle 129
Froissart, Jean xi, 1–2, 11, 13–36, 141n
as a poet xi, 14–15, 24, 30
Joli Buisson de Jonece 14–15
Méliador 17
Chroniques 14–16, 19, 22–25, 27, 30–31, 121
manuscripts cited 19, 23, 27, 30–35
First Book 19, 21, 24–25, 27, 29, 33–35
Second Book xi, 21–25, 27, 29–36
Third Book 21, 24–25, 29, 31
Fourth Book 21, 25, 27, 29, 31
Middle Dutch translation 33
Société de l'Histoire de France edn 31–34
social ideals of 22–23
Voyage en Béarn 24: *see also* Blois, Gui de Châtillon, count of; Brabant
frontiers xv, 130, 132, 147, 151, 163n, 165, 167, 190

Gaguin, Robert 119
Ganelon 64
Garter, Order of 98
Gascony xiv, 85, 97, 137, 170
appeals 90
Gaston IV, Count of Foix 137–38
Gaunt, John of, Duke of Lancaster 82, 178
Genealogie des rois de France verite est que 73: *see also* Alençon; Bourbon; Montreuil
genealogies xiv
of the house of Alençon 139
of the house of Bourbon 139
royal 73–74, 83, 86, 89
Genêts 180
Geneva 156
Gerson, Jean 52, 56, 64–68, 70, 199
Deploratio 65–66
Vivat rex 52
works 59
Gesta Henrici Quinti 84, 86
Ghent 23, 147–48, 166–67, 170
haut-bailli 153
militia of 27–28
politics in 23
rebels 21
war 27–28, 167, 169–70
White Hoods in 23
Gien 140
Gilles, Nicole 73
Gloucester
Humfrey, Duke of 86, 152
Thomas, Duke of 82
Gobinet, Jean 164n
Golden Fleece, Order, chancellors of 150
Gouy
Arnoud de 153
family 153
Goyon, Main 180
Grand Maître des Eaux et Forêts: *see* Harcourt
Grandes chroniques de France 106, 109, 125–27
Granville, siege of (1466) 180
Gratian
Decretum (1140) 59, 204
Graville
Louis Malet de 185
Malet de 185
Great Schism 33, 150n
Gregory the Great, Pope 204
Moralia in Job 204n
Grenier, Pasquier, tapestry maker 148
Grenoble 129n
parlement of 130
Grosmont, Henry of 8, 104
Livre des Seyntez Medicines 8
Gruuthuse, Louis de Bruges, lord of 89n
Guebienfay, Hutin de 181
Guelders 121n
Adolf of 121
Duchy 2
Guerre Folle (1480s) 176
Guicciardini, Francesco 106
Storia d'Italia 106
Guiers 135n
Guise, house of 184
Guyenne 55, 78n, 84–85, 97, 132, 137
Duke of 88
English claim to 79

Hainault 3, 5–7, 15, 20, 22, 147, 152, 164n, 180
- bourgeoisie of 6, 8–9
- county 2
- court of xi, 1–4, 6, 9–11, 13, 17
- Elizabeth of 18
- historiographical tradition in 5–6
- literary circle 12
- literature of 2–6
- Margaret of 2, 13
- men-at-arms from 7
- nobility of 8, 15
- relations with England 7–8, 10–20: *see also* Bavaria, Jacqueline; Beaumont; Chandos; Jean II; Jean le Bel; minstrels; Philippa; William I; William II

Hamel, Baudrain du 194, 204
Hannibal 105
Harcourt, Guillaume d', Count of Tancarville 184
Harfleur 100
Haucourt
- Jean de 181
- Lancelot de 181

Hayes, Guillaume des 179n
Hemricourt, Jacques de 6
Henry I, King of England 97
Henry III, King of England 96
Henry IV, King of England 62, 139, 219
- treaty with French princes (1412) 140

Henry V, King of England xii, 38–39, 48, 50, 54, 57–58, 63, 67, 83–86, 98
- French opinion on him 54–55
- regent of France 54

Henry VI, King of England 69, 76–78, 81, 83–85, 88, 94, 161n
Henry VIII, King of England 161
Hermanville, Charles de 181
Herod, King 66
historiography
- Breton 126
- Foix 137–38
- French 124–44, 175–78
- political use made of 50, 55–56, 81, 83, 92, 95–97, 125
- seigneurial 126–27: *see also* Hainault

Hoccleve, Thomas 85
Holland, county 2, 152
Honfleur 179
honour 192, 195, 197–98, 208
- collective sense of 193

Howardrie, de la, family 153
humanism in France 87
Humbert II, Count of Vienne 134
Hundred Years War 6–7, 70, 82, 84, 127, 178
Hungary, kings of 74

Ile de France 181
Ille-et-Vilaine
- *Archives départementales* (Rennes) 212, 214
- *Fonds de La Borderie* 214, 216

incorrigibility 203–07: *see also* recidivism
indentures 177–78
Innocent III, and incorrigibility 205
Ireland 97
- English claim to 86
- John
  - *Vraie cronicque dEscoce* 76

Isabeau, Queen of France 41, 54, 57–58, 160
Isabella, Queen of England 7, 10, 19
Isidore of Seville 204
Israel, people of 28
Italians 116, 120
Italy
- humanists 87, 122
- princes 116

James I, King of Scots 52
Jean II, King of France 13, 75, 141, 201
Jeanne d'Arc 52, 140, 163
Jersey 17
Jerusalem 40, 62
John 'the Fearless', Duke of Burgundy 39–40, 42, 44–48, 55, 59, 61–63, 66–69, 71, 82, 139, 154, 156n, 159n, 160n
John II, Count of Hainault 2
John, King of Bohemia 9
John, King of England 101
Joinville, sire de 108–09, 115, 120
- *La vie de St Louis* 108

jousts 9–10
judges
- factors influencing their judgements 192

Judith 27
- daughter of Charles the Bald 132

justice xvi
  Royal 208
  royal ordinances on (1357, 1454) 194–95, 196n, 201

Katherine of France, Queen of England 42, 48, 58, 80
Keeper of the Privy Seal: *see* Bekynton
Kemp, John, Archbishop 78
kingship xiii, 106–23
  demythologisation 118
  emblems 111
  Holy Ampulla 115
  hunting 119
  ideals of 52, 54–55, 92–93, 118, 132–34, 191
  legitimacy 116–18
  majesty 117
  'natures' of 110
  relations with nobility 125
  rituals 121–22
  symbolism 115, 119
  thaumaturgic 115
  'travails' of 108, 112–14
  'virtues' 118

La belle Hélène de Constantinople 3
La Blanche-Couronne, abbey 211
La Borderie, A. Le M. de, historian 209, 212, 214
La Rochelle 185, 207n
  'les bons enfants de' 203
La Trinité-Porhoet 215n
Lancaster, house of 55: *see also* Fortescue; Grosmont; Vale
Landais, Pierre 219n
Lande, Raoullet de la 215
Landes, *sénéchaussée* of 78
Landévennec 216, 218
Langres, governorship of 187
Languedoc 138n, 156, 187
Lannoy, Jean de 153
Latini, Brunetto
  Livre du Trésor 11
Laval, Louis de, seigneur de Châtillon 187
law
  canon 132, 204, 206: *see also* Gratian
  political use made of law 56–57, 59, 76, 87
  Roman (civil, *Code, Digest*) 191, 192n, 193, 199, 203–04
Le Bègue, Jean 73–74
Le Bel, Jean, chronicler 5–6, 8, 11, 18–19, 22
Le Bis, Etienne 180
Le Blanc, Louis 72, 74
  Pour vraye congnoissance avoir 72–73, 88
Le Clerc, Jacotin 206
Le Coq, Jean, *avocat* 192n
Le Daim, Olivier 158
Le Fevre
  Colart 194
  Jean (*Songe du Vergier*) 76
Le Maire
  Michel 148
  Olivier 163n
  Raoul 150
Le Petit
  Loyset 195
  Raoul
    Dit de Fauvain 11
Le Picart, Jacques 73
Le Plessis, castle 111
Le Sénéchal, Robinet 181
Legnano, John de 76, 87
  Tractatus de bello 87
lettre de retenue 177–78
Leulingham, negotiations at 75
Li Muisis, Gilles 12
liber recordorum 84, 86
Liège 5, 164n
Ligne, Michel de 7
Lille 160, 166, 173
Lincoln, bishop of 8
Lion de Bourges 3
Livius, Titus, da Forli 86
Livre des homages 84
Livy
  History of Rome 162
Lobineau, Dom Gui-Alexis, Maurist historian 218
Loire, River 39, 54, 127, 156
Loire-Inférieure/Atlantique 211
  Archives départementales (Nantes) 214, 215n
London
  people of 25
  Treaty of (1474) 161

Longueville, county of 178, 189
Lorris, Guillaume de 8
Louis, dauphin of France (Louis XI) 52, 136–37, 142, 171, 184
See also Dauphiné; dauphin Louis II
Louis IX, Saint, King of France 96, 111, 114, 120, 137, 139
Louis XI, King of France xiv, 73–74, 77, 79, 81, 83–84, 89, 91, 104, 111, 113–17, 129, 134, 147, 152–54, 157–58, 160–61, 163n, 167, 176, 179, 182, 186–88, 191, 220
death of 108, 110–12, 114–15, 120–21
personality 113, 116, 119
physicians: *see* Cato; Coictier
Louis de Guyenne, dauphin (d.1415) 80
Low Countries 2, 5, 8, 21–23, 146n, 167, 171
Loy Salicque premiere loy des François, La: *see* Cousinot, *Pour ce que plusieurs*
Luxembourg, Jean de 166n
lynching 193
Lyndwood, William 87
Lyon 41–42, 45, 129, 155–56
people of 43

Machaut, Guillaume de 13
Machiavelli, Niccolo 123
Mâcon, county of 79
Madrid, treaty of (1526) 91
Maignelais, Antoinette de 185
Maine, county of 55, 98
maintenance 179, 188
Male
Louis of 27
Margaret of 160
Margaret of Scotland 52
Marigny, Pierre de, *avocat* 202
Marmousets 176n, 202, 204
Marseille 149
Mauléon, Jean 218n
Mauni 15
Mauny, Sir Walter de 15
Melbourne, Thomas, treasurer of Brittany 217
Melun, Jean de 153
Memoire abregée grossement 75: *see also* diplomatic dossiers
Meriadec, Hervé de 154
Merovingians 126
Meulan 181n
Meun, Jean de 8: *see also* Bouvet
Meyronnes, François de
De civitate Dei 76
Mézières, Philippe de 81
Songe du vieil pèlerin 81
Michel, Pierre, widow of 206
Migli, Ambrogio dei 44
Milan 83
ambassadors 115
Duke of 52: *see also* Visconti
Latin history of 83
Millau 165
minstrels 11, 16: *see also* Colins; Condé; Mote, Jean de le
Mirouer Historial Abregié de France 72–73, 76, 80, 129, 131–32, 134, 143: *see also* Fribois
Moncade 17
Moniteur, Le 210
Mons, Bibliothèque centrale de l'Université, ms 240/359 31
Mons, feast at (1310) 9
Montaigu, Gérard II de 74–75, 80
Montauban, Jean de 184–85
Montenay, Jean de 185
Montereau-fault-Yonne 45–47, 53, 55, 59, 67, 69, 71, 156n
Montferrand, David de, archbishop 84
Montivilliers 181n
Montlhéry, Battle of (1464) 180
Montpellier 75
procureur du roi at 201
Montreuil, Jean de 43, 72–73, 75–77, 80, 82–83, 85, 87
A toute la chevalerie 80, 88
Genealogie des rois de France, Verite est que 73, 88
Regali ex progenie 72–73, 80, 83, 89n
Résumé du Traité contre les Anglais 73, 77, 88
Traité contre les Anglais 72–73, 77, 83, 88
Mont-Saint-Michel 179–80
Morice, Dom P.-H., Maurist historian 218
Mortagne 160
Moses 28
Mote, Jean de le, minstrel 11–12, 16
Regret Guillaume 12

Motte, Isabelle de la 12n
Moucident, sire de 33, 35
Moulins, ducal library at 130
Moulnier, Guillaume 219
Murol, Guillaume de 177
Murimuth, Adam, chronicler 85
Murten, Battle of (1476) 164n
musters 180, 182n

Nancy 136
Nangis, Guillaume de, Latin chronicle of 83
Nantes 209, 212, 213n, 218
  Archives municipales 214
  diocese of 211, 213n
  Franciscan convent at 213n
  mairie 214
Naples, Angevin succession to 87
national loyalties 63
Navailles, sire de 47
Nebuchadnezzar 27
Nemesis 29
Nero 66
Neuss 151
Nimrod 119
nobility 125, 131, 176–78, 185
  Breton 176, 185
  Burgundian 176
  cases concerning heard in the *Parlement* 193
'noblesse' 95, 97–99, 103–04
Normandy xv, 22, 55, 96–97, 101, 132, 181, 183–84, 187, 189
  Echiquier 181, 185
  English claim to 79, 86
  English conquest (1417–) 64, 102
  English occupation 128
  French reconquest (1449–) 95–96, 143, 165, 180, 184
  French rights to 77
  Grand Sénéchal: *see* Brézé
  Lower 55n, 184–85
  offices 184, 187
  status debated (1468) 91
  Upper 55n
notaires et secrétaires du roi 73–74: *see also* Le Blanc; Chevalier; Fribois; Montreuil; Rinel

offices 178–79
Old Testament, cited
  figures: *see* Aaron; Egyptians; Israel, people of; Judith; Moses; Saul
Olivier, Richard, Bishop of Coutances 171
Orange, Louis de Chalon, Prince of 136
orateurs 37
Orchies 160
Ordonnance companies 179–81, 183
oriflamme 107
Orléanist (party): *see* Armagnac
Orléans
  Charles, Duke of 83, 161n, 167
  ducal secretary: *see* Astesan
  dukes of 129
  Estates General (1439) 90
  house of 39, 140, 176
  Louis, Duke of 39, 47, 62–63, 66, 139, 161, 176n, 178
  siege of 52
  university of 129
Orthez 24
Oudenaarde 160n, 164
Oxford, university of 93

pacifism 5
pardons 190, 199
  'lettres de rémission' 191
Paris 41, 46, 53, 64–67, 74, 127, 129, 154, 156–57, 173, 180, 195–96
  'Bourgeois de' 191
  city of 22
  Estates (1421) 159
  massacre in (1418) 39, 42–44, 63–65, 73
  Notre Dame 38, 64, 191
  Prévôt 202
  Prévôté, court of 202, 204
  support for Burgundy 55
  treaty of
    (1259) 96
    (1355) 135
  university of 46, 64, 67–68, 77
Parisians 44, 47
Parlement of Paris xv, 71, 90, 136, 152, 172, 186, 193–204, 208
  accords (conciliation) 195, 198
  criminel (criminal court) 193–94
  procureur du roi 193–95, 197–99, 201–02, 206: *see also* Cambrai; Dauvet; Grenoble; Poitiers; Rouen

Parthenay 219n
pas d'armes 9
Paston Letters 93
patronage xi, xv, 1, 4–6, 22, 29, 175–77, 180, 183, 189, 219: *see also* clientage
Pavia, Charterhouse 117
Peacock, Feast of (1330) 10
pena talionis 194, 197
penalties
 amende honorable 195–96
 anathema 205
 banishment 172n, 195–96
 beheading 190
 boiling 192
 branding 195–96
 burning 192
 censure 205n
 confiscation 195–96
 defrocking 205n
 drawing and hanging 192, 194, 204
 drowning 194
 excommunication 205
 exemplary 192
 expulsion 203, 205
 fines 195–96, 204
 flaying alive 190
 hanging 190, 192, 195–97
 helping pious foundations 204
 imprisonment 195
 loss of right hand 197
 piercing of the tongue 195, 197
 pillory 195–96
 'punicion capital' 201
 purchasing annuities 204
 quartering 190
 strangulation 195–96
 surrender of office 197
 torture 194
 whipping 195–96: *see also* death penalty; lynching; punishment
pensioners 178–79, 220
pensions 177–79, 187
Perche, county 55
Persia 81
Petelia 162
Petit, Etienne 188n
Petit, Jean 64
Petrarch, Francesco 12
Pevrel, Jean 179
Pharamond, King 172n
Pharaoh, of Egypt 28
Philip [II]-Augustus 95, 125
Philip IV, le Bel, King of France 190
Philip VI, King of France 2, 75, 77, 139, 168
Philip the Bold, Duke of Burgundy 30, 153–54, 160
Philip the Good, Duke of Burgundy 46, 48, 52, 54–55, 57–58, 61–63, 66, 69, 79, 81, 126, 149, 151–54, 160, 166, 170n
Philippa of Hainault, Queen of England 7, 11–13, 20
 her support of Froissart 1, 13–18, 20, 22
Picardy 172, 180
 criminal from 206
 translation into dialect of 11, 18
Picquigny, treaty of (1475) 104
Pigache, Jean 180
Pintoin, Michel, chronicler of Saint-Denis 129, 131
Pippinids 126
Pius II, Pope 83
Pizan, Christine de 70, 112n, 199
Plessis, Le, castle 111
Poitiers
 Battle of (1356) 13
 Parlement of 57, 59, 69, 156
Poitiers, Diane de 184
Poitou 32
polemical treatises xii-xiii, 71–80, 83–84, 86–88, 92: *see also* propaganda
Pongnant, Pierre 187
Pons, Michel de, *procureur général* 78, 91
Ponthieu, Count of: *see* Charles 'the Dauphin'
Pontoise 47
 Siege of (1441) 153
Popes: *see* Gregory; Innocent III; Pius II
Pot
 Philippe 118
 Regnier 48
Pouilly-le-Fort 46–47
Praguerie (1440) 139, 176
Premierfait, Laurent de 43
Presles, Raoul de 80
 translation of *De civitate Dei* 80
Propaganda 42, 45–51, 56–66, 70, 83, 117: *see also* polemical treatises

Proust, Marcel 20
Provence 149
public good ('res publica': 'bien public') 92–93, 95, 98–104, 136, 193–94, 201–02: *see also* 'noblesse'
public opinion xii, xvi, 56, 193, 202
public order 194, 197
public service 53
punishment, as deterrent, 199
exemplary 199–201
Punic wars 162
Purgatory 115
Pyrenees 132, 138

Quest of the Holy Grail romance cycle 10

Rabelais, François 10
Ranrouet 217n
rebellion 21, 57, 61, 64–66, 89n
rebels 42–43, 61, 97, 132
recidivism 204–05: *see also* incorrigibility
Recouvrement de la Normandie: *see* Berry Herald
Recueil des traités de la France 74, 80
Regali ex progenie: *see* Montreuil
regalian right 74
Reims, coronation at (1429) 52, 115
Rély, Jean de 118
repentence of crime 203
Réponse d'un bon et loyal François 57, 59–60, 71, 80
Résumé du Traité contre les Anglais 79n: *see also* Montreuil
retinues 179
Richard I, King of England 95, 97
Richard II, King of England 25, 32, 62
funeral of 25–27
Richemont, Arthur de (Arthur III of Brittany) 183, 209, 215n, 218–19
Rieux, Pierre de, Marshal of France 201
Rinel, Jean de 77, 88
Robert (Bruce), King of Scots 7
Duke of Normandy 97
Robinet, translator of Blondel 62–64
Rochefort, *Archives de la Marine* 215
Guillaume de 118
Roet, Philippa Paon de 17
Roland 64
Roman de Brut 26
Roman de la Rose 8
Roman de Perceforest 3, 9–10
Romans 39, 97, 104
Rome 52, 104, 134
History 50, 94, 96, 102–03
wars with Carthage 101, 105
women defend the Capitol 103
Rosières, Haquinet de 194
Rosnivinen, Guillaume de 185
Rouen 67, 184, 205n
Archbishop: *see* Estouteville
Echiquier at 185
garrison 182
Parlement of 184
Rouergue 165
rule 'by the grace of God' 132, 134, 137–38, 140

St-Aubin-du-Cormier 215
Saint-Denis, abbey 106, 107n 125
chronicles 106, 125, 129: *see also* Fribois; Pintoin
Saint-Genois
Agnes de 153
Simon de 153, 160n
St-Gille, Guillaume de 216n
Saint-Guénolé, abbey, Landévennec 216
Saint-Landelin, monks of 3
St Luke, cited 28
St-Malo 149
Saint Mard, Jean de 181
Saint-Martin, abbey 166
Saint-Maur, peace of 44–45
Saint-Nicholas, abbey 166
Saint-Omer 76, 148
Guillaume de 7
St Quentin, 161, 201
St Paul, cited 28
Salic Law 86, 91, 127
Saliceto, Richard 76
Saul, King 120
Savonarola, Girolamo 120
Savoy 135
chronicle of 131n: *see also* Cabaret
count of 135
Scépaux, René de 182n
Scotland 84–85, 97
campaign in (1327) 7, 11
court of 52
customs of 10–11
French embassy to (1428) 51–52

Vraie cronicque d'Escoce 76, 77n, 89
See also James I; Robert (Bruce)
Sebourc, Baudouin de 4
Seine, river 156
Seneca the Younger
De Ira 199
Sforza, Francesco 117
Shakespeare, William 26
Sicily, kingdom of 40
Sigismund, Emperor, King of the Romans 52, 83, 136
Silly, Berthin de 180
Simon, Pierre 182n
Sluys 30
soldiers 1
training of 101
Sollier, Jehan du 170
Somme
towns 160
Songe du Vergier 59, 87, 112n
sovereignty, ideas of 135, 186
state 176
powers of coercion 191, 193
Stavoren, Battle of (1345) 5
Surienne, François de 75
Sweden 111

Tancarville: *see* Harcourt
taxes 167
in Brittany 213, 219
in Tournai 167–68
Terrevermeille, Jean de 56, 61–62, 66–69
Tractatus contra rebelles suorum regum 59, 61
Thomassin, Mathieu xiv, 129, 134–37, 141–42, 144
Breviaire des anciens droiz... du dauphiné 134
'Registre delphinal' 130, 135
Tielt 158
Tignonville, Guillaume, *prévôt* of Paris 202, 204
Torcy: *see* Estouteville, Jean
Toulouse, Alphonse of Poitiers, Count of 137
Touraine, Louis of 29
Tournai 41–42, 145–74
arms 173
bishops 149–50
bishopric 149
cathedral chapter 149–50, 162n, 166
cemetery of St John 206
chronicle tradition 147
civic militia 172
consaux 146, 150, 151n, 152, 155–56, 158–59, 160n, 161, 164n, 166n, 167–69, 170n, 171–73
criminal from 194, 206
crossbowmen 153, 162n, 168
deacons (*doiens*) 153, 169–70
'democratic revolution' (1423) 153, 163
economic position 147–49, 151, 165
élus 161
English claim to 161
fears of alienation 161–62
frontier city xv, 147, 151, 165
governor 158
grande procession 149
Great Schism in 150n
guilds 153, 159, 160n, 161, 163n, 169–70
mint 152, 172
origin legends 162n
privileges 171n, 173
processions 162
regional position 147–48
relations with Burgundy 149–54, 160–61, 164
representatives in Paris 156–59, 172
royal envoys in 163n
royal visits to (1382, 1464) 156, 162
stone 148
taxes 167–68
victory commemorations 164–65: *see also* Li Muisis
Tournaisis 151
Tournai-Tournaisis, *bailliage* 153, 155, 157, 160, 163n, 166, 172
tournaments 9–10
Tours
Estates General (1468) 90, (1484) 118
truce (1444) 95
Tractatus contra rebelles suorum regum: *see* Terrevermeille
Traité contre les Anglais 72–73, 77, 83, 88: *see also* Montreuil
treason 12, 42, 57, 61–64, 132, 140–41, 190, 192, 201–02
'lèse majesté' 58, 61, 171, 172n, 190
Trémaugon, Evrart de 76, 81, 90

Somnium viridarii 76, 81, 90
Songe du Vergier 59, 76
Trésor des Chartes 73, 74n, 79
Garde du: *see* Montaigu
inventory of 74
Tristan de Nanteuil 3
Trojans 97
Troy 62
Troyes 46, 58
treaty of (1420) xii, 48, 50, 53–55, 57, 59, 62–63, 69, 71, 76–77, 80–81, 85–86, 159
tyrannicide 64

Ubaldis, Baldus de 132
Ursins, Guillaume Juvénal des 72
Ursins, Jacques Juvénal des 158
Ursins, Jean Juvénal des 68, 72, 76, 79, 81, 83, 89–91, 191
Audite celi 69, 72, 76, 81, 89
Tres crestien, tres hault, tres puissant roy 72, 76, 79, 83, 89

Vale, John
Book 85n
Valenciennes 2–4, 8, 10–11, 14–15, 148n
chronicles 6
church of Saint-Géry 11
court 3
puys at 6: *see also* Beauneveu; Peacock, feast of
Valerius-Maximus 112
Valois
Charles of 139
Jeanne de 2
monarchy xii, 75, 84, 86, 127
Vegetius, Flavius Renatus 101, 103n
De re militari 103
Venality 179n, 186
Vendôme, *lit de justice* at (1458) 139, 190
vengeance 192, 196–97: see *also pena talionis*
Venice 52
vernacular translations xii, 80: *see also* Charles V; Presles; Robinet
Verneuil, Battle of (1424) 136, 138–40
Vertaing, Robert de 194
Vienne, archbishop of 135
Villain, Marc 164
Villebresme 45n
Villefranche 165
Villeneuve 165
Villeneuve-Saint-Georges 41
Villon, François 194
Visconti 116
Giangaleazzo, Duke of Milan 117
Vitri, Philippe de 12
Voeux du Héron xii, 5

Wales, English claim to 86, 97
Walsingham, Thomas, chronicler 86
Ypodigma Neustrie 86
Warwick, Richard Nevill, Earl of 117
William I, Count of Hainault 2–4, 7, 9–13, 16, 19
William I, King of England, Duke of Normandy (Guillaume le Bastard) 96–97, 132, 143
William II, Count of Hainault 5, 9, 13
Winchelsea, naval battle (1350) 17
Wismes, H.-O.-J.-B. de B. de Croix, Baron de 209–210, 212, 216
Wittelsbach, family 13
Worcester, William of xiii, 92–105
Boke of Noblesse xiii, 86, 92, 94, 98–104
date of composition 94, 104
use of history 92, 95–99, 101–02, 104
Itineraria 93, 103

Zeeland, county 2